# Break All the Borders

D1607745

# Break All the Borders

*Separatism and the Reshaping of the Middle East*

ARIEL I. AHRAM

**WOODROW WILSON
CENTER BOOK**

OXFORD
UNIVERSITY PRESS

## OXFORD
UNIVERSITY PRESS

Oxford University Press is a department of the University of Oxford.
It furthers the University's objective of excellence in research, scholarship,
and education by publishing worldwide. Oxford is a registered trade mark of
Oxford University Press in the UK and certain other countries.

Published in the United States of America by Oxford University Press
198 Madison Avenue, New York, NY 10016, United States of America.

© Oxford University Press 2019

Library of Congress Cataloging-in-Publication Data
Names: Ahram, Ariel I. (Ariel Ira), 1979- author.
Title: Break all the borders: separatism and the reshaping of the Middle East/Ariel I. Ahram.
Description: New York, NY, United States of America: Oxford University Press, 2019.
Identifiers: LCCN 2018030695 | ISBN 9780190917371 (hardcover) |
ISBN 9780190917388 (pb : alk. paper)
Subjects: LCSH: Arab countries—History—Autonomy and independence movements. |
Separatist movements. | Arab countries—History—21st century. |
Arab countries—History—20th century.
Classification: LCC DS39.3 .A36 2019 | DDC 909/.0974927082—dc23
LC record available at https://lccn.loc.gov/2018030695

3 5 7 9 8 6 4 2

Paperback printed by Sheridan Books, Inc., United States of America
Hardback printed by Bridgeport National Bindery, Inc., United States of America

We visited some two thousand places, many of which were almost unknown, many of which proved unacceptable.... The imaginary universe is a place of astonishing richness and diversity: here are worlds created to satisfy an urgent desire for perfection.
　　　　　　　　—Alberto Manguel, *The Dictionary of Imaginary Places*

CONTENTS

*Acknowledgments*   ix
*Abbreviations*   xi

Introduction   1
1. The Rise and Decline of Arab Statehood, 1919 to 2011   19
2. 2011: Revolutions in Arab Sovereignty   43
3. Cyrenaica   69
4. Southern Yemen   95
5. Kurdistan   121
6. The Islamic State   161
Conclusion: The Ends of Separatism in the Arab World   199

*Notes*   207
*Index*   261

# ACKNOWLEDGMENTS

In the course of researching and writing this book, I have incurred considerable debts personal and professional. Hopefully, my talented coauthors—Ellen Lust, Barak Mendelsohn, Rudra Sil, Patrick Köllner, Mara Revkin, Harris Mylonas, and John Gledhill—rubbed off on me. Writing a book this broad in scope required consultation with country experts, many of whom indulged me with their time and insights far beyond what I could have reasonably asked. Fred Wehrey, Osama Abu Buera, and Lisa Anderson were kind enough to share their insights on Libya. Nadwa al-Dawsari, Ian Hartshorn, April L. Alley, and Stacey Yadav answered innumerable questions about Yemen. Amatzia Baram, Steve Heydemann, Kevin Mazur, Ranj Alaaldin, Avi Rubin, Daniel Neep, Harith al-Qarawee, and David Patel deepened my education on Syria and Iraq. Ranj Alaaldin and Pishtiwan Jalal gave me a crash course on Kurdish politics. Any mistakes are mine, not theirs. I also wish to thank Sam Parker, Miki Fabry, Marc Lynch, Amaney Jamal, Jonathan Wyrtzen, Elizabeth Thompson, Mahdi el Rabab, Ryan Saylor, Arnaud Kurze, Mohammed Tabaar, Dina Khoury, Benjamin Smith, Amy Myers Jaffe, and Charles Tripp for their conversation and encouragement. Charles King, Gabe Rubin, and Sara Goodman provided me kind and thoughtful advice about how to structure the manuscript. I particularly thank Rachel Templer for helping to make this manuscript readable. Thanks also to David McBride and Oxford University Press for taking a chance on difficult material.

Different versions of this paper benefited from presentation at the Weiser Center for Emerging Democracies at Michigan, the Program on Governance and Local Development at Yale, the Bobst Center for Peace and Justice at Princeton, the Program in International Relations at New York University, and the American University in Cairo. Thanks to Marc Lynch and Lauren Baker at the Project on Middle East Political Science (POMEPS) for providing opportunities and venues to discuss these topics. I was fortunate to spend nine months as a fellow at the Woodrow Wilson International Center for Scholars, one of the most fruitful endeavors of my professional life. I thank Henri Barkey, Rob Litwak, Chris Davenport, Marina Ottaway, David Ottaway, and the Wilson Center library staff, as well as my research assistants, Adena Moulton, Adnan Hussein, Chelsea Burris, and Taha Poonwala.

I have the good fortune to work with excellent students and colleagues at Virginia Tech's School of Public and International Affairs in Alexandria. I thank Greg Kruczek, Nahom Kasay, Giselle Datz, Joel Peters, David Orden, Patrick Roberts, Anne Khademian, Tim Luke, and Gerard Toal. Special thanks are due to Bruce Pencek and the university library. I gratefully thank the Institute for Society, Culture and Environment at Virginia Tech and the Carnegie Corporation of New York for funding the book's research and writing.

Due to the insanity of traffic in Washington, DC, much of the final composition took place in the friendly confines of Ohr Kodesh Congregation. I thank Jerry Kiewe and his staff for allowing me to treat the synagogue as a second office.

Finally, this book would be impossible without the love of a wonderful family. My mother, Judi Ahram, continues to be a voice of encouragement for me. Though it pains me to admit this as a writer, my wife, Marni, means more to me than I can put into words. Leonie, my eldest daughter, kindly offered her version of cover art for this project. I regretfully declined. My youngest daughter, Tillie (Matilda), has been waiting her entire life for me to finish a book that would mention her by name. I thank her for her patience.

# ABBREVIATIONS

ADM     Assyrian Democratic Movement
ASMB    Abu Salim Martyrs Brigade
AQAP    Al-Qaeda in the Arabian Peninsula
AQI     Al-Qaeda in Mesopotamia/Iraq
CDF     Cyrenaica Defense Forces
CPB     Cyrenaica Political Bureau
CTC     Cyrenaica Transitional Council
CUP     Committee of Union and Progress
DFNS    Democratic Federation of Northern Syria
DPA     Declaration of Principles and Accord (Yemen)
DRY     Democratic Republic of Yemen
FLOSY   Front for the Liberation of the Occupied South Yemen
FoS     Friends of Syria
FoY     Friends of Yemen
FSA     Free Syrian Army
GCC     Gulf Cooperation Council
GNA     Government of National Accord (Libya)
GNC     General National Congress (Libya)
GPC     General People's Congress (Yemen)
HNC     Hadramawt National Council
HoR     House of Representatives (Libya)
IKF     Iraqi Kurdistan Front
INC     Iraqi National Congress
IS      Islamic State (ad-Dawla al-Islamiyya)
JAN     Jabhat al-Nusra
JRTN    Jaysh Rijal Tariqat Naqshbandi (Army of the Men of the Naqshbandi
        Order)
KDP     Kurdish Democratic Party (Iraq)

KNC Kurdish National Council (Syria)
KRG Kurdish Regional Government (Iraq)
KRI Kurdish Region of Iraq
KRM Kurdish Republic of Mahabad
LCC Local Coordinating Committees (Syria)
LCG Libya Contact Group
LIFG Libyan Islamic Fighting Group
LNA Libyan National Army
MENA Middle East and North Africa
NCC National Coordination Council (Syria)
NDB National Defense Battalion
NDC National Dialogue Conference (Yemen)
NFZ No-fly Zone
NLF National Liberation Front (Yemen)
OLOS Organization for the Liberation of the Occupied South Yemen
PDRY People's Democratic Republic of Yemen
PFG Petroleum Facilities Guard (Libya)
PKK Kurdistan Workers' Party
PLO Palestine Liberation Organization
PMU Popular Mobilization Units (Iraq)
PRSY People's Republic of South Yemen
PUK Patriotic Union of Kurdistan
PYD Democratic Union Party (Syria)
SAL South Arabian League
SCIRI Supreme Council for Islamic Revolution in Iraq
SDF Syrian Democratic Forces
SM Southern Movement
SNC Syrian National Council
SOC National Coalition for Syrian Revolution and Opposition Forces
SPKI Socialist Party of Kurdistan in Iraq
STC Southern Transitional Council (Yemen)
TNC Transitional National Council (Libya)
UN United Nations
UNSCR UN Security Council Resolution
YPG People's Protection Unit
YSP Yemen Socialist Party

# Break All the Borders

# Introduction

## #Sykespicotover

Strolling amid the rubble of an abandoned military post somewhere along the Syrian-Iraqi boundary, Abu Sufiyya had reason to boast. "This is the so-called border of Sykes-Picot," he said, referring to the secret 1916 agreement to divide the Ottoman Empire into English, French, and Russian spheres of influence. "*Hamdullah* [praise God], we don't recognize it and we will never recognize it. This is not the first border we will break. God willing [*inshallah*], we will break all the borders."[1] Where Iraq and Syria's red, green, and black tricolors had flown side by side like fraternal twins for nearly nine decades, now the black flag of the Islamic State (IS) stood alone, emblazoned in austere calligraphy: *No God but God*.

The summer of 2014 was the apogee for IS. Working from its stronghold in eastern Syria and western Iraq, IS's forces stormed Nineveh Province and seized Iraq's second-largest city, Mosul. This put IS in control of an archipelago of dust-bitten towns and riparian cities, dams, oil depots, and desert trade routes spanning some 12,000 square miles ($31,000 \text{ km}^2$). In place of the Syrian and Iraqi governments, IS announced itself as a caliphate, the direct successor to the Prophet Muhammad's medieval Arabian state. The colonially implanted state system, IS propagandists opined, divided and weakened the unitary Muslim people. They had allowed Western powers to dominate them and permitted infidels, atheists, and religiously deviant Shi'is to rule. Within the new caliphate, though, orthodox "Muslims are honored, infidels disgraced." IS called on Muslims worldwide to join them in revolt, either by emigrating or building IS colonies in other countries.[2] IS propagandists flooded social media with images of bulldozers demolishing border crossings and ripping apart fences. They even introduced a catchy hashtag: *#sykespicotover*.[3]

IS was hardly the only group intent on breaking borders in the Middle East and North Africa (MENA).[4] Abutting IS-controlled territory, Kurdish leaders seized upon the opportunities of civil war and state failure to gain unprecedented levels of autonomy in Syria and Iraq. Massoud Barzani, president of the Kurdish Regional Government in Iraq, told a newspaper in 2015 that forced division cannot last indefinitely. Instead of the Sykes-Picot border, the new border is drawn in blood.... A new Iraq must be formulated. The former Iraq has failed.... Look at what is happening in Yemen and look at what is happening in Syria. Other countries have tribal and regional problems, such as Libya. The decades-old equations of World War I were shaken with violence.[5]

At the bottom of the Arabian Peninsula, members of the Southern Movement (*al-Hirak al-Janubi*) in Yemen seized the opportunity of civil war to claim a new state, tied to the memory of the once-independent South Yemen. Concurrently, in eastern Libya a federalist movement demanded autonomy, if not outright self-governance, for the once-independent Cyrenaica (*Barqa*).

These uprisings represent the latest in a century of strife in the Arab world. As soon as regional states were conceived, there were calls to abort them. The systems of rule and political boundaries that appeared in the Arab world seemed incongruent with popular identities and aspirations. As a result, for the last century Arab states have endured a maelstrom of wars, revolutions, coups, and insurrections.[6] Much of the blame for the region's malformed states, as IS propagandists demonstrate, is laid at the feet of two men—François Georges-Picot and Sir Mark Sykes. Picot trained as a lawyer and joined the French diplomatic corps, serving as consul general in Beirut. Sykes, heir to a Yorkshire baronetcy, dropped out of Cambridge, wrote books, fought in the Boer War, and served in Parliament. Working under Lord Kitchener during the Great War, Sykes took a hand in Britain's Near Eastern policies. Picot and Sykes met several times in 1915 and 1916 to discuss the disposition of the Ottoman domains once the war ended. The document that would forever be associated with their names was signed in St. Petersburg in February 1916 in consultation with the Russian Foreign Ministry, which had its own designs on the Caucasus and Black Sea region. The agreement was supposed to be secret. It only came to light because the Bolsheviks, eager to embarrass the Allies, released the classified diplomatic correspondence in November 1917. As memorialized in a thousand-word memo and a finely hued watercolor map, they agreed to French control over southern Anatolia and the northern Levant, where they had a long-standing relationship with the Maronite Christian community around Mount Lebanon. Britain would hold sway over the southern linkages between Baghdad and the Persian Gulf through to the port of Haifa.

A century later, Sykes-Picot is discussed as MENA's original sin, the root of its malformed states and malignant politics. Yet this is a bad historical caricature. For one thing, Sykes and Picot discussed not states but rather zones of colonial control. These colonial footprints were significant, but rarely conclusive, in determining the course of state formation. This jaundiced view also slights the agency of indigenous actors who authored their own drives to statehood and tried simultaneously to take advantage of and resist colonial encroachment.[7] Additionally, this view overlooks the role of new norms of self-determination and popular sovereignty in inspiring and substantiating statehood. These ideas, propounded by Woodrow Wilson at the end of World War I, became core principles of international society. International institutions like the League of Nations, Wilson's brainchild, and the United Nations, articulated these norms as they orchestrated the transition from colonialism to independence. The emergence and endurance of Arab states, therefore, were part and parcel of the crystallization of mid-century liberal internationalism.

Still, the Ottomans used the leaked documents to embarrass Arab rebels like Emir Faisal bin Hussein al-Hashemi, who had cast their lot with the infidel British instead of fellow Muslims. Arab leaders were outraged at what they saw as Britain's double-dealing, realizing that the agreement undercut promises to support an Arab kingdom.[8] The agreement blocked the possibilities of establishing states based on regions' presumed organic unity, under the aegis of either Arab nationalism or pan-Islam. Discussing the impact of Sykes-Picot during a private meeting with Saddam Hussein in 1988, Iraq's foreign minister commented derisively (and largely erroneously) that "Lebanon, which is the size of an Arab county, became a state. . . . Qatar, which is a small, tiny municipality, is now spoken of as one with history, culture, and literature of its own. It is like someone comes and talks about the inhabitants of Mahmoodiya [a small Iraqi city] . . . the history, literature, and culture of Mahmoodiya!"[9] In a 1998 epistle, Osama bin Laden used similar terms, calling Iraq, Saudi Arabia, Egypt, and Sudan "paper mini-states."[10] On the eve of the 2003 Iraq war, he directly blamed the Sykes-Picot Agreement for bringing about the "the dissection of the Islamic world into fragments" and pronounced the American-led campaign against Iraq "a new Sykes-Picot agreement" aimed at the "destroying and looting of our beloved Prophet's *umma* [people]."[11] As his country descended into civil war in 2012, Syrian president Bashar al-Assad said, "What is taking place in Syria is part of what has been planned for the region for tens of years, as the dream of partition is still haunting the grandchildren of Sykes–Picot."[12]

The Sykes-Picot Agreement takes on a subtly different meaning in Western discourse. Whereas the Arab nationalists and pan-Islamists faulted the agreement for creating states that were too small, the Western pundits saw these states as too large. Colonialists clumsily lumped too many fractious primordial ethnosectarian communities together. In the Western imagination, breaking the Sykes-Picot border would yield not a single coherent mega-state but a plethora of more compact states, their borders fitted to individual ethno-sectarian communities. Instead of a single Gulliver, they anticipated a multitude of Lilliputians. In early 2008, an *Atlantic* magazine cover showed a regional map featuring potential states like the Islamic Holy State of the Hijaz, the Alawite Republic, and distinct Sunni and Shi'i states in Mesopotamia. The accompanying article asked: "How many states will there one day be between the Mediterranean and the Euphrates River? Three? Four? Five? Six?"[13] Seasoned journalist Robin Wright speculated that Libya, Syria, Iraq, Saudi Arabia, and Yemen could readily splinter into fourteen states.[14] Yaroslav Trofimov, another veteran observer of the region, asked, "Where exactly would you draw the lines? And at what cost?"[15]

This book is about the separatist movements that have tried to change states at a fundamental, territorial level since the 2011 Arab uprisings. "Separatism" is a sterile term for movements that are typically politically dynamic and incendiary. Within the Arab world, incumbent regimes sometimes denigrate their enemies as "separatists" (*infasilun*). Few groups refer to themselves that way, however, preferring instead "freedom fighters" or "movements of national liberation." I use "separatist" to mean those groups taking unilateral steps to break away from an existing state and attain some form of self-governance over territory. Secession is the fullest form of separatism. Secessionists seek to quit a parent state and establish a fully independent sovereign entity. But separatism also encompasses extra-legal movements demanding control over legislation, resources, and the means of coercion in a territory. Separatists defy the central government, typically when the state is too weak to resist. While such groups stop short of calling for independence, they displace state sovereignty in function, if not in form.[16]

The central puzzle is why these conflicts erupted and how separatist movements used the opportunity of state weakness to assert or expand territorial control. Arab politics is often stereotyped as a contest of ancient clans, tribes, and sects masquerading under the banner of modern states and political parties. "Sykes-Picot" is a metaphor gesturing to that fundamental mismatch between deep primordial identities and contemporary political institutions.[17] But why do separatists appear, expand, or entrench in certain conditions and not in others? Given the presumed ubiquity of sub-state identities, the region should be rife with separatist rebellions seeking to break every border. Yet most of the rebels involved in the 2011 uprisings sought to overthrow individual rulers and regimes and did not contest the territorial integrity of the state. Why and how do some rebel actors seek territorial separation while others seek to control the entire state?

The book argues that the legacies of early- and mid-twentieth-century state building in the MENA region are key factors in both fostering and constraining separatist conflicts. Separatism, therefore, does not spell descent into ethno-sectarian pandemonium, or resurgence of primordial identities, of either the macro or micro variety. On the contrary, separatists resurrect prior state-building efforts that drew inspiration from what Erez Manela calls the "Wilsonian moment" and the norms of self-determination.[18] Although many of these efforts failed to attain statehood, they laid the foundation for future separatist struggles. The legacy of these "conquered" or "missing" states worked through two distinct but often interlinked mechanisms. First, at the domestic or internal level, the memories of conquered states provided an institutional focal point for mobilizations against existing political regimes. Failures were not forgotten. On the contrary, they left faint but indelible imprints and could be recalled and reimagined in collective and institutional memory. Separatists used these memories to galvanize and mobilize domestic constituencies. Second, at the international or external level, prior statehood provided separatists a platform from which to address the international community and appeal for its material and moral support. The fact that existing states were built on the graves of discarded ones suggested that the current constellation of states was contingent and dispensable. The international community, therefore, was more amenable to arguments about eventually—and perhaps inevitably—replacing dysfunctional states, opening up the possibilities for a new Wilsonian moment to arise. With each step toward regional disarray, the prospects for separatism came tantalizingly closer. As with any self-fulfilling prophecy, the more the overturning of Sykes-Picot and the demise of existing states was contemplated, the more realistic such outcomes became.[19] But what would come next?

This question is of great policy significance, as the people inside and outside the region struggle with instability in MENA. This book shows that disintegration did not affect every state equally and did not lead to hysterical fragmentation. Separatism only took root in certain kinds of states at specific moments of crisis. The ultimate fate of separatists, though, depended as much on their own actions as on external involvement in their conflicts. The United States, Iran, Saudi Arabia, Russia, and other actors quickly inducted separatist movements as proxies in their larger campaigns for regional hegemony.[20] While this strategy was sometimes successful in the short term, however, its overall impact on stability was dire. Separatists believed that by assisting great powers and abiding by international norms, they would "earn" sovereignty and recognition.[21] So far, however, none of these groups have been rewarded with statehood. The quest to rectify the mistakes of the first Wilsonian moment therefore continues.

Moving forward, regional order will require a reorientation of the entire regional system, including its integration with the larger international society. As Raymond Hinnebusch put it, "While Middle East states help make their own regional international society, they do so in *conditions not of their own making*."[22] Outside actors play a critical role in establishing—or violating—standards of conduct conducive to peace. Stability can only arrive through redefining the formulae by which sovereignty is granted and how states themselves are organized. Without such a redefinition, statehood itself may be doomed, replaced by other political models.

## Separatism, Sovereignty, and the Making and Unmaking of States

Making and unmaking states involves a double transformation. On one hand, states maintain and enforce order. In a lecture delivered during Germany's post–World War I turmoil, Max Weber defined the state as a political entity that successfully claims "the *monopoly of the legitimate use of physical force* within a given territory."[23] States are first and foremost providers of security. The weakening or collapse of the state necessarily involves a breakdown of this monopoly. In such anarchic conditions, people are forced either to submit to or to invent new institutions to provide for security. Separatists are among the actors trying to build new institutions that can assert physical domination over territories in lieu of the state.

Yet, as Weber himself understood, the legitimacy of a state's claim to dominance depends on its accordance with the norms, identity, and culture of its population. Historically, rulers have legitimated their rule in myriad ways. But in the modern era, by far the most prominent and potent has been through nationalism. The long-running debate between primordialists and constructivists as to the origins and nature of national identity has now reached an uneasy truce. Some nations may be more ancient than others, but all nations emerge in relation to the power of state institutions.[24] In the post-colonial world especially, state institutions are key propagators and promoters of particular notions of national identity, at once emphasizing and synthesizing the organic connection between ruler and ruled. Moreover, elites often use these institutions to shape citizens' self-perception and images of community. Absent institutions, state or otherwise, identities are so protean as to be endlessly shifting. State encouragement of national identity formation facilitates collective action and assures political acquiescence. [25] When states dissolve, therefore, it is not just a brute Leviathan that is lost; it is also a focal point of communal identity. In such instability, separatists act as political entrepreneurs, seeking to promote new notions of identity as alternatives to the state's official version of nationalism while building new organs of political control.

The topic of separatism rests astride multiple disciplinary, theoretical, and analytical seams.[26] Comparative politics and comparative sociology tend to favor an inside-out approach, looking at separatist conflicts as the product of domestic or internal political cleavages and tensions. International relations tends to favor an outside-in approach, looking at separatist pressures as a response to incentives and opportunities provided by the international community. Both of these approaches are nomothetic in orientation, seeking to develop and test broad generic theories about the origins of separatism and its impact in as a wide a population of cases as possible. A third approach, associated with comparative historical analysis and historical institutionalism, is less interested in generalization than in attending to unique and historically contingent features of individual cases. If separatism is about the political disintegration of state institutions, then its course is deeply constrained by particular historical experiences of political incorporation. Separatism is thus the analytical mirror image of state formation.

*Inside-Out Approaches.* For a long time the primary thinking about separatism was that it amounted to an internal challenger to statehood. Weber's equation of statehood with the monopoly of force has long stood as maximal ideal-type, not a reality. Some states come closer to achieving it than others.[27] Moreover, states rarely get to impose their notions of national identity without a fight. Ethnic conflict, disputes about communal identity, and disagreement about the distribution of power among groups spur people to resist that state. But grievances alone are not sufficient to cause rebellion. Rebellions are dangerous and their rewards uncertain. Any effort at rebellion must overcome the prohibitive inertia of the collective action problem, in which some people sacrifice but all reap rewards.[28]

Instrumentalist analyses focus on factors that lower the cost and increase the gain from rebellion. James Fearon and David Laitin, among many others, stress the ecological and geographical determinants of rebellion. Mountains, jungles, and other difficult-to-patrol terrains offer rebels succor and bases for operation. Where and when states are weak, rebels advance.[29] Access to natural resources, like diamonds, oil, or other kinds of loot, provide crucial incentives to rebel foot soldiers and leaders alike, raising the benefits of rebellion.[30] When they have the opportunity, rebels build more robust infrastructure of governance, including police forces, courts, schools, and welfare programs, in effect supplanting the dysfunctional state and becoming proto-states.[31]

Separatism is a distinct form of rebellion and has specific etiological characteristics. Rather than overturn a specific regime, separatists want to break a state's hold over particular territories. Separatist leaders make strategic choices about how and when they claim specific territories, as Harris Mylonas and Nadav Shelef discuss.[32] They are engaged in a particular kind of demographic and physical engineering. They try to ensure that their group constitutes a majority (or at least plurality) within its claimed territory.[33] The availability of oil or other natural resources in that territory is also important. Access to rent-generating facilities can help rebels overcome collective action problems in recruitment.[34] Moreover, the presence of natural resources in what is considered a group's historical homeland can become grist for grievances. While the central government hordes resources, it denies residents opportunities for political and economic advancement.[35] Beyond fighting the titular state, as Kathleen Cunningham and others argue, separatists also contend with other rival rebel organizations. Building cohesion around the cause of separatism, either by defeating or agglomerating other armed groups, is a key for success.[36] For this reason, separatist rebels are typically the most eager to set up parallel state institutions that can monopolize coercive control.[37]

*Outside-In Approaches.* International relations scholarship has only recently engaged with the topic of separatism. This line of inquiry has yielded important insights about how separatists respond to the constraints and incentives provided by the global balance of power and the norms and practices surrounding sovereignty. Sovereignty and statehood are adductive. Sovereignty, according to K. J. Holsti, "helps create states; it helps maintain their integrity when under threat from within or without; and it helps guarantee their continuation and prevents their death."[38] At a minimum, separatists pose a challenge to a state's domestic or empirical sovereignty, the ability to exercise de facto control on the ground. Full-blown secessionists challenge the state's juridical (de jure) sovereignty, its standing as a member of the society of states, as well. From this outside-in perspective, then, the international community's support or opposition to separatism is crucial.[39] Outside states determine their orientation toward separatists based on their material interests and their normative commitments.[40] Reyko Huang and Bridget Coggins show how separatists, in turn, appeal to the international community on both geostrategic and moral grounds.[41] Military and economic aid helps separatists effect their own de facto sovereignty. Diplomatic support, up to and including formal recognition of sovereignty and independence, provides crucial juridical support. Incumbent states, for their part, try their best to deny rebels such material and moral resources.[42]

For much of the twentieth century, global norms of sovereignty formed an important bulwark against separatism. Robert Jackson argues that the international community's emphasis on de jure sovereignty effectively made territories inviolable and borders immutable. Cold War geopolitics reinforced this general deterrent toward separatism. Efforts to break the borders of one state might spill over to others, creating a slippery slope for state dismemberment and general disorder.[43] Pierre Englebert, straddling the comparative-international relations divide, argues that international recognition provided regimes a crucial symbolic resource to regimes and dampened the hopes of any group that might seek separation.[44] Since the end of the Cold War, though, this obstacle appears to have lessened. New norms of humanitarian intervention seem to dovetail with claims for self-determination by oppressed minorities.[45] The geopolitical alignment no longer precludes external actors from backing separatists, as the United States did in Kosovo and Russia in South Ossetia.

*Longitudinal Approaches.* Drawn from the tradition of comparative historical analysis, longitudinal approaches to separatism move away from general theory and toward more specific explanations grounded in particular times and places.[46] In their seminal studies of the drivers of state formation in Europe, Charles Tilly, Hendrik Spruyt, and Thomas Ertman each emphasize distinct path-dependent dynamics. Early movers had unique advantages in a highly competitive landscape. Polities that managed to achieve military, economic, and bureaucratic competence were able to survive to take their place in the modern international system. The continual need to assert themselves militarily, fiscally, and administratively became self-reinforcing, leading to ever more robust states. Polities that couldn't compete effectively, like the Duchy of Burgundy or the Kingdom of Aragon, were dismembered, absorbed, and typically forgotten.[47] These dynamics do not translate directly to the developing world, but the vocabulary of path dependence suggests ways to approach separatism as a temporally and historically variant but bounded phenomenon.[48]

In particular, the breakup of the USSR and Yugoslavia prompted a consideration of the historical processes of segmentation and sedimentation within states affected by the trajectories of separatism. The USSR, as Yuri Slezkine put it, was not a unitary state but a communal apartment, a series of stratified autonomous republics and regions.[49] Ostensibly, the ethno-federalist arrangement was supposed to mollify demands for self-determination while fostering cohesion under state socialism. In reality, these territorially segmented units became the perches for separatism when the central state faltered. When the USSR buckled, those groups already enjoying control over autonomous institutions had the best chance to seek independence.[50] There was an additional external support to such transition from segmentation to separatism. The international community generally abhorred altering international borders. By retaining the pre-existing territorial demarcation, though, separatist movements were able to show they posed less of a threat to global order. Moreover, parent states were likely to accept secession by higher-order administrative units in order to forestall the more disruptive departure of lower-level ones.[51]

In addition to contemporaneous segmentation, processes of sedimentation within state institutions also proved to have a significant impact on separatism. Michael Hechter shows how losing autonomy or statehood is a major motivator for ethnic resentment and grievances. Rebellion becomes more likely when the strength of the central governing authority wanes and the original bargain between center and periphery no longer holds.[52] Examining the wave of separatist and secessionist bids that emerged in the 1990s and 2000s, numerous cross-national statistical studies found that those groups making separatist and secessionist bids in the 1990s and 2000s and had engaged in failed rebellions and resistance in the late nineteenth century and earlier in the twentieth.[53] The pock-marked ethno-federalist structure of the USSR was not a product of overarching design but an improvised attempt to incorporate ethnic groups that had long resisted Russian domination. When the Romanov empire crumbled in 1917, many of these groups tried to launch their own independent states. The Soviets offered autonomy in the hopes of appeasing the earliest and most potent potential resisters. As the Soviets reconsolidated power, though, they were less accommodating. They used violence to suppress opposition and unilaterally revoked or diluted previous autonomy provisions.[54] Just like ethno-territorial segmentation, the sedimented history of failed state building can have path-dependent effects. The experience of having once enjoyed self-governance granted groups the institutional structures necessary to undertake rebellion; the revocation of that autonomy gave them motivation to break away. Such experiences counteract the integrative efforts of state building and provide a catalyst to separation.

Still, the mechanism behind what Philip Roeder calls the "conquered state syndrome," the propensity of separatism to arise among groups that had lost autonomy, remains obscure.[55] Rebel groups can take a multitude of forms and make a variety of claims about identity. Why would separatists seek to resurrect old, seemingly defunct, notions of political community instead of creating new—and potentially more attractive and suasive—ones? How does an extinct political order have enduring power to shape the future?[56]

This book offers two interrelated answers. First, the memories of bygone institutions are seldom lost, even though states do their best to supplant them with new notions of belonging. Thus, once initiated, identities themselves have a propensity for endurance. They can remain entrenched socially and culturally even after their initial impetus has dissolved. Elites and activists instrumentally try to refurbish and retain the memory of these past political institutions as a way to oppose or resist existing state power. As Allan Hoben and Robert Hefner put it, these institutions and identities are "taught and learned, often quite deliberately . . . [and] provide the social categories of discourse that define who is likely to be good and to be trusted, and who is bad and should be hated and feared."[57] When the central state's authority dissipates, this prior statehood is a natural or default focal point around which to organize collective actions, similar in many ways to the ready-made platform of ethno-federal segmentation. Parliaments and other institutions can be used to govern this recently regained homeland. Flags, anthems, and banners already exist to represent it. Militias can be raised to defend it. All of this helps separatists to accumulate power in conditions where the state is no longer effective and there are multiple groups vying for territorial control.[58]

Second, making claims to reinstate prior lost states also has important ramifications for separatists' engagement abroad. Separatist movements face an uphill battle given the international community's general tendency to preserve existing territorial boundaries. But by claiming to reinstate a political entity that had already existed in modern history and had standing in the international community, they hope to give themselves a head start. They signal their understanding of the rules of the international system and their right to belong in international society. The existence of prior statehood can also help in delimiting borders and territory of a future state, further mitigating potential disturbance to the global order. This ultimately increases the chance of gaining external support, up to and including de jure recognition of sovereignty.

## Separatism and MENA's "Missing" States

There has been a great deal of attention to ethnic cleavages and conflicts that divide MENA states, but relatively little to the potentialities of separatism. In the 1970s, leading scholars like Michael Hudson and Iliya Harik wrote about the "horizontal" challenge to Arab states and the difficulty of bringing disparate communities under a single, coherent national identity. Yet they presumed that some form of vertical agglomeration was a foregone conclusion. Harik, following Clifford Geertz's influential theory of "integrative revolutions," expected a conglomerate national identity to arise, such as in Lebanon's confessional system. Hudson foresaw an eventual Gulliverian turn toward pan-Arab regional integration. In both scenarios, political conflict focused on controlling the center, not carving out territories at the periphery.[59] Arab states generally did not follow the Soviet example of building segmented ethno-federalist territorial structures to accommodate disparate communities' demands for self-rule.[60]

More recent studies of Arab politics emphasize the durability and persistence of states and tend to ignore separatism altogether. Taking an inside-out approach, Sean Yom, Rolf Schwarz, and Thierry Gongora focus on how the political economy of Arab states created its own centripetal power. The arrival of massive oil rents short-circuited the process of state development. With no need to extract taxes or resources from their own population, Arab states did not build durable institutions and national identities. Instead, states took on a kind of armed mediocrity, using rents to bribe their populations into acquiescence or to build ruthless security services to beat down dissent.[61] Viewing the region from the outside in, Ian Lustick, Keith Krause, and Boaz Atzili argue that norms of territorial integrity linked to juridical sovereignty and practices of external intervention effectively kept relatively weak and illegitimate Arab states intact. Though they do not deal directly with separatism's horizontal challenges per se, they agree that ideational and geopolitical factors made changing borders impossible.[62] Both the outside-in geopolitical and inside-out political economy approaches point ultimately in the same direction: a collection of states getting a free ride on the rules of sovereignty granted by the international community. They are prone to violence but incapable of—and possibly even disinterested in—asserting effective control over the breadth of their allotted territories or building the penetrating infrastructural power that binds citizens to the state. To use Nazih Ayubi's terms, Arab states are simultaneously fierce and weak.[63] They are also, though, enduring and immutable.

The uprisings of 2011 demonstrated just how sclerotic many Arab states had become. The overthrow of Ben Ali, Mubarak, Saleh, and Qaddafi undermined common assumptions about the adaptability and durability of Arab authoritarianism.[64] Deeper than changes at the regime level, the uprisings also raised questions about the durability of states themselves. Barely a year after the 2011 Arab uprisings, Marc Lynch predicted "a powerful change in the basic stuff of the region's politics. . . . New rules and norms will emerge to govern regional interactions."[65] With civil wars and insurgencies roiling the region, scholars like Mehran Kamrava, Louise Fawcett, Lorenzo Kamel, and Ibrahim Fraihat discuss the possible fragmentation of incumbent Arab states.[66] Still, there has been scant attention to the separatist movements that sought to supplant them, how they emerged, and what they wanted to achieve.[67]

By taking the current regional constellation for granted, all of these studies overlook one of the key insights of the historical, longitudinal approach— namely, the importance of failed state-building efforts and consideration of the region's "missing states." David S. Patel notes that since 1914 at least sixty now-defunct polities once operated across the region.[68] The number gets even larger when you look to the late nineteenth century.[69] As was the case for Burgundy, Aragon, or the other vanished kingdoms of Europe, most of these have been consigned to historical footnotes.[70] But their exclusion is a form of selection bias, examining only cases in which the outcome of interest (i.e., statehood) has already occurred.[71] This yields a blinkered and teleological understanding of how MENA states endured and how they might change.

Including missing or conquered states into the analysis brings back this important element of open-endedness and contingency in the political changes. Every separatist conflict after 2011 emerged in states where there had been missing, dead, or conquered states. Libya was built over the defunct Tripolitanian Republic (d. 1923) and agglomerated the Emirate of Cyrenaica in 1951. The Yemen Arab Republic supersedes the People's Democratic Republic of Yemen (d. 1990) in the south, as well as prior iterations of the Aden settlement and various sultanates that collapsed in 1967. Iraq overtook the failed Kingdom of Kurdistan (d. 1924). Modern Syria incorporated various French-created mini-republics and autonomous zones from the 1920s and 1930s, such as the Jabal Druze State, the Alawite State, and the Hasakah/Jazira autonomous area. Yet only states that endured significant upheaval during the 2011 uprisings saw the separatist conflicts erupt. The book therefore argues that opportunities of buckling central state power during the revolution was a proximate cause that enabled separatist actors to mobilize around the more distant historical legacy of dead statehood.

Separatism did not emerge absent destabilization at the center, even when dead states existed, such as the case of Morocco and the Rif Republic. Conversely, states that did not have the same history of incorporation and sedimentation, like Tunisia, Egypt, or Bahrain, experienced revolutionary upheaval but not separatism. Moreover, the legacy of dead states is even more important than ethno-sectarian cleavages. Ethno-sectarian tensions in Syria and Iraq were long-standing, if not always clearly salient. But the separatist movement in Libya shared language, ethnicity, and religions with its antagonists. In Yemen, the grave sectarian gap between northern Shi'is and southern Sunnis is relatively novel and even contrived. It does not map on the division between separatists in the south and other political actors.[72]

The coming chapters try to tell the story of conquered and missing states as if they were real and viable, in a sense resuscitating them intellectually the way that separatists tried to do politically. The chapters will probe the mechanisms connecting the conquered states to contemporary separatist movements, how these movements engaged the international community, and how they mobilized their own populations to make the claim for self-rule, often by trying to harden political divisions into ethnic cleavages. Although these movements looked back to history to buttress their legitimacy, their efforts were not indicative of deeply rooted essential characteristics. Though leaders tried to "ethnicize" their status and claims for autonomy, it is difficult to assert that South Yemen, Cyrenaica, or even the Kurds have a long, unbroken history of self-rule dating to antiquity. IS was an idiosyncratic outlier in this, as in many things. Yet it was is not as exceptional as it would appear. Separatist movements tended to focus on the period of the early to mid-twentieth century, when their forefathers asserted standing in the international arena but were eventually orphaned by the Wilsonian moment.

## Methodology

In exploring the connections between separatism and conquered states, this book looks to big structures and large-scale historical processes. It utilizes an "encompassing comparison," viewing separatist movements in Iraq, Syria, Libya, and Yemen as discrete but interrelated manifestations of larger system-level operations and changes.[73] Complementing the encompassing comparison are "incorporating comparisons," in which the emergence of the units themselves became historically variant and contingent.[74] Thus, extinct polities like the Kingdom of Kurdistan, the Emirate of Cyrenaica, and the sultanates of Hadramawt take on new importance as imagined alternatives to Iraq, Syria, Libya, or Yemen.

Admittedly, this is an exercise in methodological acrobatics. While it tends toward the historical and longitudinal approach of comparative historical analysis, it also draws insights from the inside-out and outside-in perspectives. Unlike conventional most-similar and most-different inductive designs, encompassing and incorporating comparisons do not presume that units are independent, homogenous, or fixed. On the contrary, they seek out the connections between ostensibly separate experiences and try to place them on firm historical grounding through process tracing. The aim is not to generalize, at least not too far. Rather, it is to draw an inductive conceptual map that explains the similarities and differences among MENA states and separatist movements by reference to their respective position within an evolving global system.[75] For this reason, it is less important to pursue variance in the dependent variable than to trace the complex, long-duration, and potentially multifarious causal pathways that lead to a shared outcome.[76]

As is common in comparative historical analyses, I have relied largely on secondary sources published variously about Libya, Yemen, Iraq, and Syria, especially for periods before the 2000s.[77] I have tried to be attentive to issues of historiography within each country. Most importantly, I have tried not to succumb to the bias of methodological nationalism, the tendency to see states as historically, territorially, and ontologically fixed entities, and rather consider the processes that went into their emergence—and potentially their undoing.[78] When possible, I have relied on archival and primary sources. The dire security conditions in each of these countries prevented me from conducting intensive field research. I have had to rely on newspapers and blogs published both in the region and without to get data on more contemporaneous events. Fortunately, many of the rebel groups are quite verbose and eager for an audience in the Western world. I have also conducted interviews with some of the protagonists in these conflicts. For reasons of safety, reliability, and transparency I have chosen to keep my conversations with figures in these groups as deep background and rely only on publicly available sources.

## Plan of the Book

Part I of the book examines the historical evolution of the international system and MENA's integration into it. Chapter 1 details how Arab states came of age in the midst of a global transformation of sovereignty, self-determination, and statehood following World War I. The coupling of Wilsonian liberal norms with changes in the global balance of power afforded some local actors pronounced advantages in attaining and building statehood. For others, though, the new rules of the international system obstructed the pursuit of sovereignty. Struggles in the Arab world, accordingly, became more about vertical or centripetal tendencies and less about separatism.

Chapter 2 discusses the breakdown of the normative and practical consensus surrounding sovereign statehood and the possibilities of a new Wilsonian moment in MENA. The 2011 Arab uprisings represented a continuation of a global crisis that led to the proliferation of civil wars, state failures, and state births. None of the initial uprisings were bent on separatism. But the outside intervention gave separatists new ways to challenge the legitimacy and capacity of existing states and make claims for self-determination.

Part II takes on individual cases of separatists, viewing regional order from the ground up. Chapter 3 examines the separatist conflict in Cyrenaica, eastern Libya. With the central government effectively moribund, federalists sought to take over ports and oil facilities in the east. Federalists in Libya made direct reference to the Emirate of Cyrenaica and demand the restitution of autonomies enjoyed prior to the Qaddafi era. Libyan federalists faced opposition not only from the central government, which deemed federalists' seizure of power illegal, but also from Islamist factions in many eastern cities. Federalist forces fought against these groups and gained control over oil resources. The federalists, therefore, appealed to the international community for support on the basis of their potential to stabilize a country in disarray.

Chapter 4 looks at the Southern Movement (SM) in Yemen. Like separatists in Libya, the SM took advantage of the ouster of a dictatorship and the crumbling of an already weak central government. The Yemen civil war, which erupted as Houthi forces from the north stormed Sana'a, gave the SM a new opportunity to take control in the south. SM claimed the once-independent South Yemen as its direct forebear. There was disagreement within SM about whether to seek outright secession or accept federalist devolution. Various factions within SM vied for control over Yemen's oil deposits and ports. SM tried to win international support but ultimately became a pawn in the battle between larger regional powers.

Chapter 5 focuses on the Kurds, the region's largest stateless minority group. This chapter compares and contrasts the efforts by the Kurdish Regional Government in Iraq, which gained autonomy in 1991, and Rojava, the Kurdish entity that appeared during Syria's civil war. Both maintained liminal positions within their parent state, at once pledging their loyalty to the state while at the same time maximizing their autonomy from any central control. They articulated their demands for separatism by pointing to the denial of Kurdish self-determination at the end of World War I and engaged international society for support. Both, however, saw their hopes dashed as geopolitics turned against them.

Chapter 6 is about IS. IS stood somewhat as the outlier among these other separatist movements. It adamantly rejected the sovereignty of all existing states and asserted that its own independence represented the re-creation of the medieval Islamic caliphate. In so doing, IS disrupted not just Syria and Iraq but the entire structure of the international system. Still, much like other separatists, IS also used the vocabulary of self-determination derived from the Wilsonian moment to denounce the existing regional order and offer its own alternative. It similarly sought to establish undisputed physical control over territories left unguarded by Syria and Iraq, creating parallel state institutions that tried to supplant the nominal sovereign. Its doom, too, came from the actions of the international community.

The conclusion takes a step back to examine the ultimate ends of separatism. The struggle to struggle to realize the revolutionary potential of the Wilsonian moment in the Arab world remains unfulfilled. It is up to the international community to form a new consensus about sovereignty, statehood, and the rights of peoples to self-determination. Without such a consensus, the states in the Arab world are likely to continue crumbling, leaving an even more chaotic outcome than the prospects of allowing separatists to adjust borders and build new states.

# PART I

# 1

# The Rise and Decline of Arab Statehood, 1919 to 2011

Palestine, June 10, 1919

*The USS* Luce *arrived in Jaffa harbor bearing the evangelists of a new age. The party was led by two men of very different backgrounds. Henry Churchill King, an ordained minister and experienced missionary, was the president of Oberlin College in Ohio. He had spent the Great War as director of the religious works at the Paris YMCA. Charles Crane, heir of a Chicago toilet manufacturer, was a college dropout, world traveler, and Democratic Party power broker. They had set out from Paris a month earlier, journeying by rail across a still battle-scarred Europe, sailing from Costanza to Istanbul, and then cruising through the Dardanelles and Aegean and into the Mediterranean. Along with the Baedeker-recommended matches, candles, candies, chocolates, tinned meats, powdered coffee, alcohol, shoe nails, toilet paper, and mosquito netting, the Americans carried copies of Woodrow Wilson's Fourteen Points like a new gospel.*[1]

*Wilson himself was in Paris overseeing the most ambitious gambit in American foreign policy history. Wilson envisioned a new world order based on "mutual guarantees of political independence and territorial integrity to all states." A new international organization, formed on a covenant of peace, would provide the framework for global security. The idea of self-determination was central to this vision. "People and provinces," Wilson said, "must not be bartered about from sovereignty to sovereignty as if they were chattels. . . . National aspirations must be respected; people may now be dominated and governed only by their own consent. Self-determination is not a mere phrase. It is an imperative principle of actions."*[2]

*The promise of self-determination turned Wilson into a global celebrity. Crowds cheered him throughout Europe. Prominent anti-colonial activists stalked the antechambers and lobbies hoping for an audience with him. In the negotiating halls, though, many presumed Wilson a fool. Britain, France, and Italy had no desire to see self-determination applied to their imperial holdings, even if they saw its utility in weakening the Habsburg, Ottoman, and German Empires. Robert Lansing, his own secretary of state, wrote that the idea of self-determination was "simply loaded with dynamite. It will raise hopes which can never be realized." He expanded:*

> What effect will it have on the Irish, the Indians, the Egyptians, and the nationalists among the Boers? Will it not breed discontent, disorder, and rebellion? Will not the Mohammedans of Syria and Palestine and possibly Morocco and Tripoli rely on it?[3]

*Outside the negotiating halls, Soviet propagandists equated self-determination with secession. Vladimir Lenin called on colonized peoples to unite in global revolution.[4]*

*Wilson confessed that he knew little of the ethnic mosaic of Europe or the far-flung imperial domains. Forever a southern racist, he believed that certain ethnic groups were unfit for self-rule.[5] For Wilson, self-determination had to be pursued responsibly, under the supervision of the international community so as not to jeopardize global peace.[6] Detailed questions regarding the implementation of self-determination should be left to the peacemakers of the League of Nations.[7] The League would oversee plebiscites and popular elections and set new borders. Collectively, the League would guarantee the integrity of recognized states, helping them to sustain their borders and govern their territories.[8]*

*As Lansing had predicted, the peoples of the Ottoman Empire were particularly receptive to Wilson's message. The empire held a precarious position within the global system, beset internally by demands for communal autonomy, if not secession, and picked apart by the European powers.[9] Wilsonianism provided a new moral vocabulary for resistance, often far beyond what Wilson himself had anticipated. Egypt, nominally under Ottoman suzerainty but really under British imperial control, was in open insurrection through 1918 as Sa'd Zaghlul and the nationalists demanded permission to lead a delegation (wafd) to Paris. He aimed to make the case to the assembled world leaders that Egypt could and should be free. A leading opposition figure was arrested allegedly carrying copies of the Fourteen Points.[10] Algerian and Tunisian activists were blocked from making the journey to Paris, so they sent telegrams and letters entreating American support to end French colonialism. German newspapers, eager to highlight the Allies' foibles, published letters from Tunisian exiles denouncing French rule.[11] Word came in November 1918 of revolt in the Italian protectorates of Libya. Rebel leaders of the Tripolitanian Republic telegraphed and dispatched envoys from Misrata, their self-proclaimed capital, to Paris and Rome in hopes of gaining recognition.[12]*

*Throughout the course of the war, France and Britain sought to exploit the Ottoman nationalities problem. In 1916 T. E. Lawrence made contact with Arab guerrillas under the command of Faisal bin Hussein al-Hashemi. Faisal's family were direct descendants of the prophet Muhammad and hereditary protectors of Mecca and Medina. His father was the Ottoman's vassal in the Hejaz but came to chafe under the government's centralizing inclinations. With his father's backing, Faisal supported the British war effort on the promise of British backing for an Arab state. When British troops took Damascus in October 1918, Faisal followed on their heels. The British dispatched a car to pick up him at the city gates. Acutely attuned to symbolism, Faisal instead entered the city on horseback.*[13] *He told supporters that the favors and recognition offered by the Allies were "only figurative; we get nothing except what we take with our own hands."*[14] *Faisal promised an Arab constitutional government enjoying "complete independence" (al-istiqlal at-tamm).*[15]

*In fact, Faisal knew that Syria's independence depended on British forbearance. He assured British officials of his acceptance of their status as occupying authority and sailed to Paris when the peace talks commenced. He got the opportunity for a formal audience with the Allied leadership on February 6, 1919. The meeting marked the debut of Arabs on the stage of modern international politics. Though he was raised among the cosmopolitan imperial elite of Istanbul, Faisal donned the robe and head-dress of a traditional Arab sheikh. He spoke in formal Arabic about the Arab people's status as both ancient and civilized, ready for and worthy of sovereignty. He urged the Allies to abide by their wartime promises and provide for an independent and undivided Arab Syria. Responding to questions from Lloyd George, Faisal stressed the Arab involvement in the war effort.*[16]

*Yet there were others in Paris that claimed a stake in Wilson's project. Britain pledged its support for a Jewish national home in Palestine in the Balfour Declaration of November 1917. The Zionists, too, had contributed to the Allied cause, although the prevailing prejudice that Jews controlled the levers of global finance probably led to an overestimation of their impact.*[17] *They had the ear of the Wilson administration and were well represented in Paris. Zionists insisted on their right to build a state through immigration and land acquisition in Palestine. Lebanese Christians also harbored aspirations for statehood. Mount Lebanon had been a semi-autonomous, Christian-ruled enclave within the Ottoman domains since 1861. Christians saw themselves as a cultural bridge to France and as victims of Ottoman Muslim repression. Picot himself tried to rally Christians, Druze, Shi'is, and other minorities to oppose Faisal. With French encouragement and the support of the Maronite patriarch, leading Christians had dispatched their own delegations to Versailles to assert their right to an independent Lebanon.*[18] *Seasoned Ottoman diplomats became spokesmen for the Armenian and Kurdish national causes, each offering his own vision of states to be carved into Anatolia and the Levant.*[19] *Finally, of course, there was the delicate Anglo-French relationship itself. Neither party would sacrifice their concord for the good of quibbling petty nations.*

*In dispatching King, Crane, and the others, Wilson's approach to this nationalist thicket was the opposite of the backroom dealings typified by the Sykes-Picot Agreement or Lawrence's adventures among the Hejazi Bedouin. The Americans set out to ask the people themselves what form of government they wanted. Yet their* travails underscored the difficulties of translating Wilsonian ideals into reality.[20] Over six weeks the commissioners zigzagged to Jerusalem, Ramallah, Nablus, Damascus, Beirut, Tripoli, Homs, Aleppo, and Adana before finally returning to Istanbul by boat. Seeking out the few suitable hotels in the Ottoman backwaters, they met with over four hundred delegations. Almost all of these consisted of local notables, tribal grandees, and dignitaries vetted by the US State Department. Part pollsters and part admen, the commissioners set out to capture the sentiment of the entire population of Syria by subdividing and categorizing its interlocutors by ethnicity, religion, gender, region, and social standing. They met with Sunnis and Shi'is, Jews and Christians, Arabs, Turks, and Kurds. Interviews were conducted according to a standardized script. Every audience, telegram, and postcard the commission received was filed and tabulated. Each meeting was treated as a microcosm of public opinion.[21] Faisal impressed the commission. He propounded on how American idealism, as opposed to the self-interested and conniving European powers, would open the door for Arab statehood. Crane telegraphed the president enthused over the apparent liberality of the self-styled king.[22] King noted the circulation of leaflets in the city's bazaar supporting total independence and unity for the Arabs.[23] Indeed, since the inauguration of the peace conference in Paris and especially with the commissioners' arrival, Faisal's backers had trumpeted the new language of self-determination in newspapers and flyers.[24] Syrians, they argued, were no less developed than "Bulgarians, Serbians, Greeks, and Romans [Romanians] at the beginning of their independence."[25] They had no need for internationally mandated trusteeship.

The members of the commission were enthralled by the strong pro-American sentiments they encountered in Syria. "The people of Syria and Palestine [have] come to trust America…," Crane wrote in his diary. "Everywhere our mission went we got that note. Even the Bedouin of the desert said, 'We want America to come here and do for us what she has been doing for the Filipinos.'"[26] Over three-quarters of respondents, the commission concluded, favored absolute independence for the whole of Syria. Zionism, on the other hand, was a dead letter. Jewish immigration would infringe on the rights of Syria's Arab majority and stoke animosity. Calls for a separate Lebanon were similarly disregarded. An American mandate for the entirety of Asia Minor was the only way to assure Syrians of the unified, sovereign state they deserved.

Despite pretenses to impartiality, though, the commission proved wanting both scientifically and politically. Its final report seemed unaware of the political maneuvers going on within Syria. The pro-independence sermons, pamphlets, and placards the commissioners encountered represented, in the historian James Gelvin's term, a "large Potemkin village."[27] The notables who met the commissioners were disengaged from the masses they claimed to represent. There was no way to judge the depth of Faisal's support among the peasantry. The commissioners were equally obtuse about international politics surrounding the region. Britain and France were not disposed to cede control over territories, and the United States had no appetite to take on a massive overseas occupation.

*William Yale, the most junior member of the party, dissented from his colleagues. Yale was, by his own admission, unchurched. A graduate of Yale University's engineering school, he had worked in the oil industry in North America and then Syria. He learned Arabic and was recruited as a special US intelligence agent in Jerusalem and Cairo. Most importantly, Yale was a technician, interested in practical solutions to political problems.[28] He was initially skeptical of the idea of self-rule for any of the Ottoman subjects. He admired Faisal but was dismissive of his Arab kingdom. Syrian Muslims, he averred, were "illiterate, uncivilized, ignorant, and semi-savage," lacking in "national spirit," and unable to govern themselves.[29] Any state conferred on the bases of Arab nationalist claims was bound to be dysfunctional. Over the course of the summer, though, Yale changed his views on the state-building efforts of the Lebanon Christians and the Jewish Zionists. These, he concluded, were cohesive nations, with the requisite human and economic capital. Given a chance by the international community, they might actually build states, govern territory responsibly, and become strategic allies of the West. Yale identified in concrete terms a central dilemma of Wilson's program, exactly what made his ideas so explosive: if the international community took the lead in conferring sovereignty and effectively created states on the basis of self-determination, then what would become of sovereignty's internal components, the functional ability to rule? The crucial question, then, was not to whom states should be granted, but who could actually make states work.*

## Self-Determination and the Origins of Arab Statehood

History has not been kind to the King-Crane Commission, nor to Wilson in general when it comes to the Middle East and North Africa. Most historians depict their venture as either cynical or naïve. In any case, Wilson appears as a false messiah.[30] He promised liberation and peace yet helped deliver the region into strife and subjugation. Though Wilson did not realize the full implications, Wilsonian ideals became a moral soapbox in the struggle to escape imperial subjugation. As Erez Manela describes, Wilsonianism

> encouraged, indeed required, that groups who wish to rule themselves appeal to the doctrine of national self-determination and re-imagine themselves as nascent nation-states as keys to claiming legitimate places within the expanding and reconfiguring space of international society.[31]

The advent of Wilsonianism marked the beginning of the end of the European imperial project. By the midpoint of the twentieth century, empires in Asia and Africa would give way to newly sovereign states. The commitment to international law and organization and the emphasis on self-determination would be embedded in the covenant of the League of Nations and the charter of the United Nations and become foundations of a new world order.[32]

The realignment of global power, the rise of the USSR, and the exhaustion of imperial powers provided an opportunity to alter the foundations of sovereignty. Wilsonianism offered a normative framework for the new era, specifying how statehood could be attained and by whom. No longer would claims to sovereignty be based solely on the possession of empirical control, as Lansing had once defined it in a scholarly paper.[33] Rather, sovereignty could be conferred by the international community itself acting in furtherance of self-determination and world peace. Leaders within the region grasped this essential fact perhaps better than Wilson himself. They invoked the Wilsonian vocabulary in making the case for statehood. If the international community was the gatekeeper, then the Wilsonian creed was the shibboleth, necessary (but insufficient) for entry to international society.

The immediate aftermath of the Wilsonian moment in the Middle East and North Africa was unquestionably bleak. The US State Department shelved the commission report, and Wilson suffered an incapacitating stroke before ever reading it.[34] The US Senate refused to ratify the League of Nations treaty, hobbling the institution that was intended to serve as the guarantor of the new liberal international order. In September Britain and France agreed to split Syria into separate zones roughly according to the terms of the Sykes-Picot negotiation. The League had no choice but to ratify this split, issuing mandates for French control in Syria and Lebanon and for British control in Palestine, Transjordan, and Iraq at the San Remo Conference in April 1920.

The Syrian National Congress tried to preempt the colonial carve-up by declaring the formation of the Arab Kingdom of Syria with Faisal as king. Their declaration of independence again reminded the Allies of their obligation to the Arabs and appealed to the

> noble principles laid down by President Wilson, that recognized the liberty of the peoples, great and small, and their independence upon a footing of equal rights, that disapprove the policy of conquest and of colonization, that abrogate the secret treaties which affect the rights of the peoples, and that give the liberated nations the right to their own lot.[35]

The Congress rejected the idea of a foreign mandate for Syria and the partition of Palestine, although it was willing to accept Lebanon provided it was "free from all foreign influence." Egged on by his own supporters, Faisal reluctantly challenged French control. Arab forces were defeated at Maysalun, west of Damascus, in July. Faisal fled, first for the tribal hinterland of Dara'a, then doubling back for British-held Palestine.[36] With the Arab nationalist thwarted, the French focused on their long-standing allies in the Christian communities in Syria. Lebanon was gerrymandered into a razor-thin Christian-majority state. The rest of their mandatory territories were subdivided into ethno-sectarian mini-states. In the 1930s, Syria was reconstituted from Sunni-dominated state-lets in Damascus and Aleppo, the Alawite State in Latakia, and the Jabal Druze State. French troops were called upon repeatedly through the 1920s and 1930s to put down rebellions and insurrections.[37]

Britain faced similar challenges in its mandatory charges. In Mesopotamia, a massive uprising began in the Sunni heartland west of Baghdad and spread to the Shi'i tribes of the south in 1920. With its garrison badly overstretched, the British turned to "air policing"—a euphemism for punitive aerial bombard-ment.[38] Faisal was granted the throne of the newly created Kingdom of Iraq. He had never before visited Baghdad or the other eastern provinces of the Ottoman Empire. Already, Iraq seemed fractured along ethno-sectarian lines. A clumsily staged plebiscite confirmed Faisal as the people's choice for king. Disappointed Arab nationalists deemed Faisal a traitor for his willingness to work with the British.[39] In Palestine, British efforts to placate Arab and Jewish nationalists left both sides disaffected and led to a spiral of intercommunal violence and heavy-handed counterinsurgent responses. Britain's and France's need for conciliation with the resurgent Turkish Republic superseded the vague promise of Armenian and Kurdish states. Zaghlul eventually did reach Paris, but only after the United States acceded to the British protectorate for Egypt. Crestfallen, Zaghlul cabled the president personally:

> The Egyptian people hailed you more than any other people as the Chief of a new doctrine which was to have assured peace and prosperity to the world. This era which your principles promised would indeed have given satisfaction to all, to the great as well as the small, the strong as well as the feeble, and the powerful as well as the oppressed. For having had faith in your principles ... [Egyptians] see themselves today suffering under the barbarous treatment of [sic] the part of the British authorities.[40]

The onslaught continued in the Maghreb. Britain, France, and Italy insisted that their colonial possessions be left out of discussions at the peace accords and off-limits to the League's scrutiny. French control in Algeria, Morocco, and Tunisia went on unimpeded by outside oversight. Italy, its colonial forces badly depleted in Libya, at first seemed to concede to rebels' demands and Wilsonianism's moral weight. It offered elected legislatures and citizenship rights for Tripolitania and Cyrenaica. As the Libyan leadership succumbed to infighting, though, Italy's policy shifted from prevarication to retaliation. Italy moved to crush the short-lived Tripolitanian Republic and had regained control of most of western Libya by 1922. Cyrenaica remained in open rebellion in the early 1930s, as Italy constructed networks of blockhouses and barbed wire fences to corral civilians into concentration camps.[41]

Despite these dire initial outcomes, looking at the Wilsonian moment through more expansive lenses shows significant shifts in the ways regional actors articulated political claims. Leaders of sects, ethnic groups, and even tribes adopted Wilsonian norms and rhetoric in appealing to the international community and challenging the legitimacy of colonial rule. Resistance was hardly novel. Every European penetration in the region had engendered protests. Most of this was sporadic and diffuse, such as brigandage, riots, or strikes.[42] Some adopted the language of jihad, as in the Wahhabi movements in Arabia, the Mahdi Uprising in Sudan, and the Abd al-Qadir revolt in Algeria.[43] Yet very few were oriented toward gaining independent statehood.[44] The Urabi revolt in Egypt (1879–82), often seen as a proto-nationalist assertion against British domination and the Turco-Egyptian elite, was still fundamentally about restoring Ottoman rule, not Egyptian independence.[45]

Wilsonianism provided a language to address the international community and make a positive claim to sovereignty through self-determination. The refusal of the international community, specifically, the League, to respond to these claims in the 1920s and 1930s did not dampen enthusiasm for the principles.[46] In fact, it made them even more important sources of leverage to colonized peoples. The failed effort to reform colonial governments and provide equality of citizenship for colonial subjects in Morocco, Algeria, and Tunisia left self-determination as the only option.[47] In 1921, with Italian forces still mopping up in Tripolitania, the Republic of the Rif issued a "declaration of state and proclamation to all nations" addressed to the ambassadors of Europe and America. This remote, mountainous, Berber-speaking region of Morocco had a long history of resisting central authority. The republic, though, was something new. Led by Mohammed (Muhend) ibn Abd al-Karim al-Khattabi, a low-level government functionary in the Spanish protectorate zone, the republic issued its own currency and banned blood feuds in the name of public order. Its declaration repudiated the Franco-Spanish division of Morocco as null and void. Equally importantly, it declared the Rif to be free from the sultan's control as well.[48] Though the declaration did not mention Wilson or the League, its authors clearly understood the spirit of the times and justified theirs as a struggle for national liberation:

> The Riff has always led an independent life and has possessed since the 10th of June, 1920 a modern Republic Government, with which Spain has treated as equal to equal.... The Riff notifies solemnly to all Powers

that it intends to preserve its political independence absolutely and that she will continue to fight for official recognition as persevering as necessity demands. But on the other hand, to see her great riches rationally exploited, she wants to institute the rule of the open door to all industrial and commercial foreigners. . . . The Riff wishes to live in good friendship with all nations—small or great. . . . She asks all countries to establish Consular and Diplomatic Services at Ajdir, Capital of the Riff.[49]

Spain and France took drastic measures to defeat the Rif. In 1924 Spain began dropping mustard gas on Rif villages and towns, reasoning that since "rebellion" did not constitute "state," it was not covered in the new protocols banning the use of poison gas.[50] Elsewhere in North Africa, Tunisian activists continued quoting the League's covenant to back their claims against French domination. Palestinian Arabs cited the Fourteen Points repeatedly in their protests against the British mandatory rule.[51] Kurds saw their bid for self-determination cast aside yet still tried to press their case before the League. Statehood was refused, but the League did insist on provisions for Kurdish minority rights in the mandate for Iraq.[52] Far less probable missives went to Geneva: from Sunni tribes in the Asir seeking to avoid falling under the domination of Imam Yahya of Yemen in 1925;[53] from Assyrian Christian refugees wishing to evade submitting to Iraqi authority in 1932; and from the largely Armenian merchant community of Qamishli hoping to detach the Jazira region from Arab-dominated Syria in 1936–37.[54] These petitions seldom swayed their intended audiences, and most ended with brutal repression. Yet the ubiquity and novelty of this type of claim demonstrated just how readily state-aspirants across the region grasped Wilsonian norms.

More than just a normative language, the Wilsonian moment also implanted an institutional framework in which statehood was forged. Though begrudged by Arab nationalists, the League's mandates provided the platform upon which leaders like Faisal or Hatem al-Atassi in Syria were able to build states, demand political emancipation, and attain sovereignty. Contrary to the wishes of the mandatory powers themselves (and what Lansing considered good sense), the League insisted that mandate countries could not be treated merely as imperial appendages. Rather, Article 22 of the League covenant specified that the mandates were held in "sacred trust." It was the task of the international community to help mandatory countries to "stand alone."[55] This placed a positive obligation on the international community to make good on self-determination. Mandatory leaders operated on a different plane than other imperial subjects.[56] Rather than simply being clients to an imperial patron, Faisal and Atassi were representatives of provisional states. They could base their claims on international norms and, through the League, seek an audience with the international community at large.[57]

Relying on the international community and adopting such an extraverted understanding of sovereignty meant that the achievement of independent statehood always came with strings attached. Iraq was the first Arab state to join the League, but only after negotiating a treaty assuring Britain access to military bases in 1932. In public, the British assured the League that Iraq was ready to stand on its own. In private, they doubted that Iraqis could run their own affairs and anticipated Iraq would remain informally within Britain's sphere of influence.[58] Not coincidentally, it was Iraq that first invited Egypt, another British client, to apply for admission to the League in 1937.[59] France used the Anglo-Iraqi treaty as a model in its negotiation for Syrian emancipation. The Syrian nationalists jumped at this offer in 1936, but the French parliament reneged.

The tension between de jure and de facto dimensions of sovereignty is nowhere more apparent than in the case of Saudi Arabia's halfhearted introduction to international society. Saudi Arabia had fashioned its statehood the old-fashioned way—by defeating its neighbors and taking their land. Indeed, Ibn Saud was notoriously averse to demarcating linear boundaries on his expanding domain. He was ambivalent about the League. Yet, in conquering and absorbing the Hashemite Kingdom of the Hejaz in 1925, Saudi Arabia became a candidate for membership. Ibn Saud's British counselors debated whether League membership might aid Saudi claims to Aqaba or otherwise destabilize British clients like Transjordan or Yemen. They worried, too, that Saudi Arabia would not be able to uphold the standards of conduct of the League, such as suppression of the slave trade. In the end, the British decided to let the idea drop. The Saudi kingdom was too strong, independent, and potentially disruptive to have its sovereign standing confirmed.[60]

The Second World War further weakened Europe's colonial grip in the region, renewed the moral suasiveness of self-determination, and reinforced the linkages between external recognition and the attainment of sovereignty.[61] Syrian and Lebanese leaders effectively bartered their support to the Allies in return for recognition and independence. Syrian leaders remained ambivalent about the mandate but resoundingly cited the Atlantic Charter in order to block reassertion of French control.[62] Moroccan nationalists capitalized on a promise to support independence allegedly given by Franklin Roosevelt to Sultan Mohammad in 1943. Like the hopes invested in Wilson, the "Roosevelt Myth" helped to inspire and legitimate Morocco's struggle against French rule.[63]

At the war's end, six Arab states—Egypt, Iraq, Lebanon, Syria, and Saudi Arabia—would be among the founding members of the United Nations.[64] The UN served as an institutional platform encouraging, authorizing, and ultimately demanding the transfer of sovereignty to new states. It played a particularly prominent role in North Africa, which had been off-limits to the League.[65] Libya, Morocco, and Tunisia were ushered into the UN in the mid-1950s. The exceptional and belated example of Algeria's decolonization in 1962 underscores the rule. Unlike its neighbors, Algeria could claim credit for its own liberation through its own massive war of independence. Yet again, the crucial struggle was not on the battlefield but in the global arena. By enlisting the United States, the UN, and the power of Third World nations, Algerian nationalists won independence without winning control over any significant colonial territory.[66]

## Within the Orbit of the State

While external recognition granted states international legal personality, it did not address the question of internal functionality and domestic capacity. Just as Yale had anticipated in 1919, the international community's effort to create states anew papered over gaps between the juridical and legal aspects of sovereignty and domestic components of ruling. Nine months after Iraq gained independence, King Faisal noted in his diary that "there is still—and I say this with a heart full of sorrow—no Iraqi people but unimaginable masses of human beings, devoid of any patriotic idea."[67] Faisal had always had reservations about Iraq. While in Paris in 1919, he wrote a memo describing Iraq (and the Jazira in eastern Syria) as a semi-primitive region inhospitable to democracy. Any government would have to be "buttressed" by a foreign power. Only then could "educational processes . . . advance the tribes to the moral level of the towns."[68] As king of Iraq, Faisal put aside the costumes of Bedouin nobility and assumed suits and military-style tunics befitting a modernizing ruler. Even after a decade under mandatory rule, though, the king bemoaned the continued absence of effective state institutions that might "train, educate, and refine" Iraqis. At its root, this was a problem of coercion, or lack thereof. By Faisal's estimate, the people had "more than 100,000 rifles whereas the government possess[es] only 15,000."[69] Iraq's challenges were acute, but hardly unique in the region. Egypt and Tunisia enjoyed more august historical lineages and continuity but nonetheless found themselves ill prepared for independence. Their entire administrative apparatuses, after all, had been designed to facilitate colonial penetration.

States across the region began the difficult process of establishing new pacts between ruler and ruled. Although the content of the social contract varied by regime, its basic form was similar region-wide. Rulers demanded political acquiescence from their citizens. Citizens, in return, expected economic benefits and social protections from rulers. These pacts necessitated dramatic expansions in the state's infrastructural and coercive capacity. States launched massive campaigns on health, education, and housing in the 1950s and 1960s. Land reform and redistribution took on new urgency. With the help of Western engineers and technicians, electrical grids, irrigation systems, and paved roads winnowed into the countryside. At the same time, military budgets exploded. Repression of tribal revolts and rural uprisings became commonplace. Agents of the *mukhabarat*, the dreaded secret police, multiplied.[70] The Soviet and Western blocs competed to supply advanced military hardware and technologies to their clients. The acceleration of coups further intertwined the functions of provision and repression. In offering jobs, education, welfare, and other resources, states became indispensable to many of their citizens. The added element of coercion—the forcible demand for compliance—made this into an offer that few could refuse.

These "authoritarian bargains" conferred a centripetal power upon the state.[71] Sami Zubaida describes how the Iraqi state established its own "facticity" and compelled citizens to imagine their destinies "within its orbit."[72] The same could be said of states throughout the region. The results were starkest among the nomadic population, whose peripatetic lifestyle seemed the bane of state builders. A member of the Rwala tribe, whose traditional migratory routes crossed Saudi Arabia, Jordan, and Syria, reflected how

> the *khiwa* [tribal tax] was fairer. You agreed to pay first, and you got protection in return. If they didn't protect you, then you didn't pay them next time or you got your money back. If you didn't like the contract, you went elsewhere. But with the state taxes, there's no option; if you don't pay, your water and electricity are cut off. And with state borders and nationality, there's nowhere to move to.[73]

Peasants joined compulsory agricultural cooperatives. Industrial laborers and white-collar workers were absorbed into the burgeoning public sector. Conscription, mandatory schooling, and tax collection touched nearly everyone. Beyond the physical was the symbolic and cultural insinuation of state hegemony. Citizens lived their lives according to the state's calendar, its festivals and commemorations.[74] They were ensconced in its emblems of banal nationalism and its cults of personality. Images of the dear leader adorned currency and appeared in storefronts and car windows and on billboards.[75]

Opposition forces accommodated the increasing girth of the state. The Free Officers and Ba'th Party cadres that took power in the 1950s and 1960s around the region touted plans for territorial agglomeration and unification, rectifying colonial-inscribed borders and ridding the region of neocolonial influences. As rulers, though, they were largely content to pursue pan-Arabism in one country. Though they publicly declared devotion to a greater Arab nation, they acted out of concern for regime endurance and state stability.[76] Moreover, they were more than willing to take military and economic aid from the anti-imperialist and imperialist camps alike.[77] In countries with deep ethno-sectarian cleavages, politics became about demands for accommodation and inclusion in the national bargain, not separation. Berbers in the Maghreb, Kurds in Iraq, Christian and animists in southern Sudan, and Shi'is in Bahrain, Iraq, and Lebanon began to see their fate as inextricable from the states they were trying to contest.[78]

But while the combination of inducements and intimidation increased states' resilience, the social contract itself proved tenuous. They were prohibitively expensive. Onetime cereal exporters like Iraq, Egypt, and Syria began importing food to keep up with massive subsidization of basic commodities.[79] Moreover, administrative bloat, mismanagement, and venality siphoned off these benefits.[80] The turn to neo-liberal economic policies in the late 1970s further strained the provisioning of social welfare. Regimes narrowed their bases of support, selectively co-opting favored constituents and relying on repression to keep the rest in line.

Citizens responded in the familiar modes of mostly hidden or passive protest. They malingered on the job. They toiled in the informal economy and black market. They ate subsidized bread while squatting on state-owned land. They quietly mocked and stealthily graffitied their disaffection.[81] Opposition organizations clung to the limns of legality, with little hope to challenge the state's coercive power. Groups like the Muslim Brotherhood in Egypt and Jordan did not win over supporters by propounding the esoteric points of pan-Islamic unity. They worked within the confines of existing states. They ran candidates in patently rigged elections. They operated clinics, schools, and mutual aid societies. They offered food and shelter to those left out of the shrinking authoritarian bargain. They presented a moral paragon contraposed to the state's corruption and inefficiency. They exploited the quotidian shortcomings between public expectations and public performance of the state.[82]

Yet when and where a state failed, there were chances to escape its inextricable gravity. These occasioned what Charles Tilly calls "multiple sovereignty," when several armed groups vied for political and military supremacy.[83] Slivers of captured (i.e., liberated) territory became effectively states-within-states, rivals to the authority of the national government. Weak states also became cockpits for regional and global competition. Egypt and Saudi Arabia, aligned with the USSR and United States and locked in battle for regional dominance in the 1960s, supported differing sides during the civil war in North Yemen. Iranian forces backed Kurdish rebels in Iraq. Iranian and British troops served to support the Sultanate of Oman in the Dhofar War. Israeli and Syrian troops faced off during the brief Jordanian civil war, when Palestinian and Hashemite forces were in open combat during September 1970.

Lebanon stood out as the region's perennially failing state. To Arab nationalists, Lebanon was an egregious colonial artifact, its borders deliberately construed to thwart unification. The country's precarious ethno-sectarian balance precluded effective central state building. Instead, political factions operated as rival oligarchic networks, mediating the provision of public goods, including security. Private armed retinues, such as the Maronite Phalange and the Shi'i Amal and Hezbollah, overshadowed the national army.[84] Outside actors treated these militias as proxies.[85] But even as militias undermined Lebanon's de facto sovereignty, its de jure standing remained. Lebanon was the "final homeland," even for those who had long been marginalized from the seats of power.[86]

The Palestinian position in this context was exceptional but also illustrative. Beginning in the 1960s and accelerating through the civil war of 1975, Palestinian factions established control over refugee camps in southern Lebanon and around Beirut. They built the very infrastructure that Lebanon denied them.[87] With support from the UN Relief and Works Agency, the Palestine Liberation Organization (PLO) supplied water and electricity within the camps. It ran schools, factories, and hospitals. It conscripted, taxed, and meted out justice.[88] More than a state-within-a-state, the Palestinian leaders saw these so-called Fatah-lands as remote way stations on the road to recovering the lost homeland.

Regardless of the strengths Palestinians accrued on the ground, they could never challenge Israel's military might. Armed struggle complemented diplomatic strategy and the pursuit of de jure standing. By gaining recognition from international society, they hoped to achieve by diplomacy what they could not gain by force.[89] The Arab League designated the PLO as the sole legitimate representative of the Palestinian people, and the Cairo Accords of 1969 provided a legal basis for Palestinian control over Lebanese territory.[90] In 1974 PLO chairman Yasser Arafat reached the threshold of international society, speaking to the UN General Assembly. Arafat grouped the Palestinian cause among the struggles for "freedom and self-determination." Appealing specifically for American assistance, he spoke of Woodrow Wilson, "whose doctrine of Fourteen Points remains subscribed to and venerated by our people."[91]

Yet Arafat's invocation of Wilson came as the valence of Wilsonianism in the international arena was shifting. Self-determination had provided a normative blueprint for dismantling European empires, but now the leaders of "new" states realized that the norms that facilitated their birth could also spell their dismemberment. Both the old empires and new post-colonial states now saw reasons to alter the rules of the game of sovereignty and restrict the application of self-determination. They preserved Wilsonianism's juridical components, specifically its territorial integrity and non-aggression, as necessary to preserving peace. Both agreed, however, that self-determination could not be used to justify further secession or irredentism.[92]

Arab states were among the earliest to adjust to—and even to ingest—these new rules. One by one national leaders abandoned the ambition for pan-Arab unification and instead joined ranks in a common Westphalian front. They implicitly adopted the doctrine of *uti posseditis* ("that which you possess"), which had first emerged following the Latin American wars of independence in the nineteenth century. The borders of new states would coincide with prior colonial divisions.[93] When Saddam Hussein ordered Iraqi forces into Kuwait in August 1990, he was reasserting a territorial claim that dated back to the 1930s. Iraq intended to "return the part and branch, Kuwait, to the whole and origin, Iraq," canceling an unjust colonial partition.[94] Kuwait would be annexed as Iraq's nineteenth province. Saddam even made the case that the invasion was as a triumph of Wilsonian principles. The people of Kuwait had risen up against the corrupt Sabah monarchy and invited Iraqi forces to effectuate unification based on self-determination.

The international community, though, reaffirmed a commitment to preserving borders. The United States and USSR worked together in the UN Security Council to condemn Iraqi aggression and assemble a military response. The Arab League concurred. Some two dozen countries dispatched nearly a million troops. Three weeks of aerial bombardment and a hundred-hour ground war drove the Iraqi army entirely from Kuwaiti soil. There was no choice but to accept the boundaries that the colonial powers had demarcated and the international community had ratified. Once recognized, states received assurances from the international community as a whole that their sovereignty would be protected and their boundaries unscathed. The Arab League, founded in 1945, espoused unity while serving as an institutional ballast for individual member states.[95] In deference to Arab fraternity, states would not war directly on each other, but neither would they readily cede their independence to the other. Rivalries became an intrinsic part of the regional system, but their enactments were constrained by these normative principles. Interference and incursion into the affairs of neighboring states was common. Invasion, on the other hand, was rare; annexation, impermissible.[96]

At the moment of independence, few states in MENA had achieved the centralization over the use of force commensurate with domestic sovereignty. The process of building up internal capacities—pulling people into the state's orbit—was inextricable from the circulation of material and normative power within the much wider global system. A flood of foreign aid and armaments helped underwrite the authoritarian bargain. Regional states offered programs of social protection and redistribution in hopes of winning the allegiance of their citizens. And when inducement didn't work, intimidation was always at the ready. But while states took on ever larger proportions in the lives of their citizens, state failures became more apparent and consequential. Weak and frail states were paradoxically exposed and protected by the global system.[97] On one hand, a state like Lebanon was clearly unable to assert itself against the Palestinians or other

militias, much less against Syria and Israel. It was, consequently, always suscep-
tible to meddling. On the other hand, the territorial integrity and ultimate survival of the state were assured. What saved Lebanon—and doomed the
Palestinians—was not merely the Syrian invasion of 1975 or the Israeli invasion
of 1982 but a global concert orchestrated between Washington and Moscow
that favored Lebanon's juridical sovereignty over the claims of a new state-
aspirant to self-determination. The dismemberment of states was too dangerous
to allow. The same could be said of Kuwait's salvation by the international community, despite its obvious military shortcomings. Conversely, the few de facto
states that managed to endure, such as the Sahrawi Arab Democratic Republic,
did so not by virtue of innate strengths but by dint of foreign protections.[98] The
end result rendered juridical sovereignty immutable, regardless of the ability to
rule. Once recognized, no states were eliminated. The regional system endured,
and individual states prevailed.

## The Global Nation-State Crisis and the Arab World

If the repulsion of Iraq's invasion of Kuwait was the high water mark for the mid-
century international system, then an undercurrent was rapidly forming. Just as
the allies were ready to declare victory, retreating Iraqi soldiers in the south
turned their weapons against the regime. Shi'i militiamen, some of whom had
spent years in exile in Iran, entered the holy cities of Najaf and Karbala bearing
the banners for Islamic revolution. Kurdish insurgents took over cities and towns
in the north. Though US propaganda had encouraged Iraqis to rise up, the
United States and its regional allies were not willing step into the morass of Iraq's
internal affairs. Such a move, President George H. W. Bush and his advisors said,
would surpass the original mandate to liberate Iraq as specified by the UN.[99] UN
Security Council Resolution 686 accepted Saddam's offer of a ceasefire and explicitly affirmed "the commitment of all Member States to the independence,
sovereignty, and territorial integrity of Iraq."[100] As coalition forces stood down,
Saddam mustered his forces and moved on the rebels. Basra, the largest southern
city, fell on March 9; Karbala and Najaf, the following week. The Kurdish zone
was encircled and besieged. A humanitarian disaster ensued, captured live on
fledgling satellite news stations like CNN. Tens of thousands of Iraqis took flight
through the marshes to the Iranian frontier or to the mountains abutting Turkey.
Many observers feared a reprise of the genocidal campaigns of the 1980s, when
Saddam killed tens of thousands of Kurds through a campaign of village evacuation, shelling, and poison gas attacks (abuses the international community had ignored at the time of occurrence).[101] The United States tried to assuage the concerns
and stem the refugee outflow. On April 4, 1991, the UN Security Council passed
Resolution 688. The resolution began by ritually reaffirming the commitment to

"sovereignty, territorial integrity and political independence of Iraq and of all States in the area." But its actual content cut in a different direction. It specifically condemned and demanded cessation of Iraq's repression of the Kurds and other civilians. It further instructed the Iraqi government to allow international humanitarian organizations immediate access to Iraqi territory.[102]

Britain and the United States cited Resolution 688 and the need to protect humanitarian operations to justify the establishment of no-fly zones (NFZs) in both northern and southern Iraq. Iraqi officials presciently complained that neither the NFZs nor the safe havens squared with any meaningful interpretation of territorial integrity or sovereignty. Kurdish nationalist groups consolidated their control and launched a regional government that operated completely outside of Baghdad's control. The United States also pushed economic sanctions and inspections to prevent Iraq from rebuilding its military, particularly its arsenals of chemical, biological, or nuclear weapons. Every portion of Iraqi soil was exposed to scrutiny through ground inspections and aerial surveillance.[103]

Iraq's fate was part of a global shift in the priorities and privileges the international community afforded to sovereign states. Saddam gestured toward this epochal change in announcing the ceasefire:

> The stage that preceded the great day of the call of 2 August 1990 [the invasion of Kuwait] had its own standards, including dealing with what is familiar and inherited during the bad times, whether on the level of relations between ruler and the ruled, or between the leader and the people he leads. The relations between the foreigners among the ranks of infidelity and oppression and among the region's states and the world had their own standards, effects, and privileges.... The conflict was exacerbated by the vacuum that was created by the weakness of one of the two poles that used to represent the two opposite lines in the world. After 2 August 1990, however, new concepts and standards were created.[104]

But what were those concepts? And who set and upheld those standards?

Just like the demise of the Habsburg, Romanov, Ottoman, British, and French Empires, the implosion of the Soviet Empire in the 1980s touched off a new round of state creation and opened the international system to new entrants. Philip Roeder describes this as a global "nation-state crisis," a critical juncture when the chance to change the configuration of statehood became eminently possible.[105] Over the course of the next two decades, established states died or disintegrated; new states rose from the wreckage. Wilson's concept of self-determination became revolutionary once more.[106]

Fearing a slippery slope toward global fragmentation, the United States generally favored reform over revolution. "Freedom is not the same as independence,"

President Bush said in an August 1991 speech in Kiev, then capital of the Soviet Socialist Republic of Ukraine. "Americans will not support those who seek independence in order to replace a far-off tyranny with a local despotism. They will not aid those who promote a suicidal nationalism based upon ethnic hatred."[107]

But suicidal—or rather, homicidal—nationalism is what they got. The ethno-federalist structures of the USSR and Yugoslavia, with their overlay of autonomous strata upon substrata, were supposed to prevent ethnic untangling. Reformists believed that political and economic liberalization would ease ethnic tensions. Yet these efforts, as Juan Linz and Alfred Stepan put it, repeatedly stumbled into the problem of "stateness." Whatever the inspiration of central government reformers, from the periphery these policy changes appeared simply as an abdication of authority. Political and economic liberalization, therefore, offered opportunities for corruption and state capture. Stalwarts of the local elite converted to become ethnic entrepreneurs, espousing different notions of national identity, citizenship, and state boundaries. Raising the banner of self-determination, they mobilized constituents by claiming to resurrect identities that the central authorities suppressed and usurped.[108] Efforts to make identities concord with territorial boundaries often led to violence, such as among the Armenian activists in Nagorno-Karabakh in the late 1980s. The year 1990 marked the beginning of a "parade of sovereignty," as leaders of different sub-national units demanded greater political prerogatives and often alterations to territorial borders. Once Russia and the other Soviet Socialist Republics unilaterally declared independence, there was nothing to hold back the onslaught. Separatist conflicts broke out in Azerbaijan, Georgia, and Tajikistan and within Russia itself. Moldova and Yugoslavia followed a similar course into failure and the emergence of multiple contenders for sovereignty.

Gradually and begrudgingly, the United States came to accept that secession might be the only way to mitigate the destabilizing impact of civil wars.[109] Some policy makers even embraced the Wilsonian mantle, championing once again the US role as the liberator of people.[110] New claimants came forward as the prospects for statehood grew stronger. But just as in 1919 or 1945, it was impossible to accommodate every claimant to statehood or to ensure congruence between national identity and state boundaries.[111] The international community repurposed the principle of *uti posseditis*, trying to hold together pre-existing administrative structures as the borders for new states. Those groups that already held titular control in the ethno-federal structure of the USSR and Yugoslavia had the best chance of gaining international recognition.[112] This, however, only reinforced the disjuncture between national identity and territorial boundaries. Moreover, in many cases there was a glaring gap between empirical control and legal entitlement. The newest states tended to be the most fragile, prone to internecine

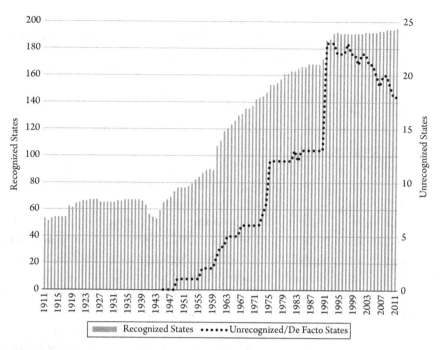

*Figure 1.1* Recognized and Unrecognized States in the International System, 1911–2011

Source: Data on recognized states in the international system come from Griffiths, Ryan D. "Between Dissolution and Blood: How Administrative Lines and Categories Shape Secessionist Outcomes." *International Organization* 69.3 (2015): 731–751. Data on unrecognized/de facto states come from Florea, Adrian. "De Facto States in International Politics (1945–2011): A New Data Set." *International Interactions* 40.5 (2014): 788–811.

violence and dependent on the international community.[113] Bosnia, East Timor, and Kosovo gained international recognition only to become wards of the international community. South Sudan succumbed to civil war only a few months after gaining independence.

The emergence of de facto or unrecognized states, shown in figure 1.1, paralleled the entry of newly recognized de jure states into the international system. De facto states carved out footholds where parent states proved incapable of exerting physical control, such as in Iraqi Kurdistan, Transnistria, Nagorno-Karabkh, and the Karen uplands. They provided security, public welfare systems, and schools. The claim to fulfill the aspirations for autonomy that the international community formally refused. Like their parents, these de facto states were also reliant on foreign patronage. Despite accruing physical control over territories and population, and often seeming to fulfill aspirations for self-determination, the international community formally refused to recognized de facto states, making them outsiders to the society of states.[114]

The countenance of secession, de facto statehood, and the apparent fragility of many of the newly recognized states underscored the doubts surrounding their sovereignty. Europe had begun its experiment with a borderless, single-currency union, making sovereignty itself appear obsolete.[115] New technologies, from the global financial flows to satellite and internet-based media, effaced the idea of territorial boundaries, one of sovereignty's essential components. Moreover, these technologies granted a wider range of state and non-state actors sway in setting regional agendas.

Emergent discourses of humanitarian intervention further undercut the certainty surrounding sovereignty. The conferral of sovereignty had always depended to a certain extent on the comportment of the state with basic standards of civilization. After states were admitted to the international system, they enjoyed near-impunity in the conduct of their internal affairs, including gross violations of human rights. During the Cold War, superpower rivalries stymied most efforts to mobilize interventions against human rights abuses. Yet now there were new possibilities to take action. Discussions about intervention began in the 1990s in the aftermath of the wars in Iraq, the Balkans, and Rwanda. By the early 2000s they had crystallized into a full-blown doctrine asserting the international community's "responsibility to protect" (R2P). Acting through the UN or other regional body, the international community could collectively decide to revoke a state's sovereignty and intervene directly when a state failed to uphold basic human rights.[116] The rise of R2P correlated with a more expansive role for international peacekeeping. Peacekeeping became a new form of trusteeship in which the international community collectively took responsibility for sovereignty with the aim of eventually building a stronger and better state. Paradoxically, humanitarian interventions were meant to save sovereign states from themselves.[117]

Iraq was not dismembered on the altar of Wilsonian principles, but the knife was always looming. The George H. W. Bush and Bill Clinton administrations continued to try to find ways to oust Saddam but retain Iraq's sovereignty and territorial integrity. The fractious Iraqi opposition parties realized the opportunity raised by the US war against Saddam but struggled to form a common front. Shi'i opposition groups like the Da'wa Party and the Supreme Council for Islamic Revolution in Iraq (SCIRI) were closely tied to Iran and thus wary of the United States (and vice versa). Kurdish parties seemed bent on independence. After the disaster of the 1991 uprising, exiled opposition leaders began more concerted planning about Iraq's future. A meeting in October 1992 in Salahuddin, part of the liberated zone in the north, yielded a new opposition pact. Kurdish factions pledged to respect Iraq's territorial integrity. The Arab opposition guaranteed Kurdish autonomy through a federal system. The Salahuddin Conference also solidified the role of the Iraqi National Congress (INC) as the opposition's

umbrella organization.[118] Ahmed Chalabi, the INC chairman, personally embodied what the Americans wished for in an Iraqi leader. Hailing from a prominent Shi'i family, Chalabi studied mathematics in the UK and the US and then
went into finance. He was an adept operator in Washington and London, despite
a reputation for shady business dealings. The United States funneled millions to
the INC, helping to set up military training centers in the Kurdish autonomous
region and build an intelligence network inside Iraq. The INC described itself as
"a responsible and credible authority with a base in Iraqi soil to provide humanitarian relief for the Iraqi people . . . and to enlist the support of the international
community."[119] Even after Saddam's troops stormed the INC strongholds in
1994, Chalabi maintained himself as the leader of a provisional government. All
that he needed was for the United States to strike the blow that would usher him
to power.[120]

In resisting Washington, Saddam sought to position himself as the next
leader of a global anti-imperialist movement. He provoked confrontations with
Washington over perceived violations of Iraqi state sovereignty, measures he
claimed returned Iraq to the status of colonial trusteeship. Resolution 688, Iraqi
officials pointed out, never authorized the use of force. The NFZs, therefore,
contravened international law. Iraqi antiaircraft batteries periodically harassed
American and British air patrols.[121] When the United States agreed to loosen
the embargo, Baghdad petitioned to replace international aid administrators
in the Kurdish zones with Iraqi government officials. As one Iraqi diplomat
opined in 1996:

> The Americans and British have already said that they will refuse on the
> distribution issue, but it's not going to be too easy for them to show too
> much obstinacy because all of the U.N. resolutions have emphasized
> the importance of maintaining the integrity and sovereignty of Iraq.[122]

No issue highlighted the unsettled relationship between sovereignty and intervention in Iraq as much as international sanctions. The sanctions throttled Iraq's
main revenue source by placing international oversight over oil sales and restricted purchase of any potential "dual use" items like fertilizers and pesticides.
Wartime damage to roads, bridges, power plants, and water treatment facilities
went unrepaired. Health workers, teachers, and other civil servants saw their
wages slashed or go unpaid. Medicine and food became scarce. Malnutrition
and infectious disease spiked. Infant mortality more than doubled. The United
States attributed the tragedy to Saddam's misallocation of government revenue,
spending more on palaces and presidential guards than on public welfare.
Subject to the same sanctions, the Kurdish region had witnessed a developmental
renaissance. Nevertheless, many observers in the Arab world as well international

relief agencies questioned how a self-described humanitarian mission could im-miserate millions.[123] Whether intentionally or not, Iraq's state and society were literally wasting away.

Iraq was synecdoche for the 1990s debates about what rights and obligations sovereignty entailed and who was entitled to get them. Multilateral sanctions, NFZs, and peacekeeping missions became preferred means to pressure the re-calcitrant "rogue" states. American and European officials discussed ways of amending and diluting sovereignty to accommodate intervention, secession, and de facto statehood. The more peripheral members of international society clung to the mid-century rules that had sustained them. Many leaders of the de-veloping world doubted the legitimacy of this new interventionism, claiming it trampled on fundamental notions of sovereignty and would demote developing states back into dependency.[124] Algerian president Abdelaziz Bouteflika, speak-ing on behalf of the African Union after NATO's intervention in Kosovo in 1999, deemed sovereignty "our final defense against the rules of an unjust world."[125]

The launch of the global war on terror in 2001 deepened the confusion. American counterterrorism strategy had long stressed the need for strong—or at least well-armed—states in the Arab world. Where states flagged, radicals in-filtrated. The United States funneled aid and arms to regional proxies to help them fill these vacuums of power. Al-Qaeda was the ideal foil in this schema, a genuine transnational operation, an enemy both of Arab despotism and of US global power. Osama bin Laden's epistles on the decadence and depravity of the international community, including its complicity in starvation in Iraq, pushed against both Arab despotism and American global power.[126]

In invading Afghanistan in 2001 and Iraq in 2003, though, the United States voided even the pretense of juridical sovereignty and committed to rebuilding states from the ground up, insisting that it acted in self-defense and for the pres-ervation of peace. It imagined that a rehabilitated and realigned Iraq and Afghanistan would take their places as a picket in the alliance against global jihad. Pivoting to humanitarian themes, the Bush administration also depicted the invasions as acts of liberation. Territorial integrity was to be preserved and sovereignty restored as soon as possible. This resonated when it came to Afghanistan but was far less persuasive when it came to Iraq. As Tanisha Fazal observed, American actions created "ambiguity as to what kinds of occupation and conquest might be permissible," muddling what had been "bright-line rule" surrounding sovereignty and territorial integrity of existing states.[127]

Occupation, especially in Iraq, brought another uncomfortable reckoning with problems of stateness.[128] Chalabi and the INC had promised that Iraq would be a cakewalk. Iraq (unlike Afghanistan) had been a prosperous, devel-oped state—and could be again. Freed from Saddam, Iraqis would greet the Americans as liberators. The United States aimed to install the newly elevated exile elites and quickly exit. Yet almost all of these initial calculations were mistaken. The pact struck among the exiles in 1992 proved difficult to enforce. Shi'i parties, savoring their demographic supremacy, pushed for centralization and majoritarianism. Kurdish leaders insisted on retaining the right to secession. Arab Sunnis, who had been marginal players in the exilic opposition movement, were also the most suspicious of the American plans.[129]

Even when the United States managed to strong-arm these groups into forming a new federalist constitution, none had the means to govern on the ground. The decision to dissolve the Iraqi army further denuded the Iraqi state of what little coercive capacity it had left. Political parties, tribes, local strongmen, and religious dignitaries maintained armed retinues and personal militias outside state control. Different political factions, some barely disguised organized crime or extortion rackets, entered the void and took over urban quarters and rural hinterlands, providing security where the state was demonstrably absent. In the primarily Sunni areas west and north of Baghdad, violence escalated in a full-blown insurgency. Saddam loyalists, former soldiers, Islamists, and foreign fighters all converged. The most violent of the revanchist groups was al-Qaeda in Mesopotamia (AQI), a so-called local franchise of the global al-Qaeda movement. AQI wanted to turn Iraq into a global theater of strife. More than just targeting US troops, AQI attacked the symbols of the international community itself, such as the bombing of the UN and Red Cross headquarters in Baghdad in 2003. AQI also used car and suicide attacks against Shi'i religious institutions, including the holy shrines of Najaf, Karbala, and Kathimayn, seeking to incite a full-on sectarian war.

The US military presence continued well past the formal transfer of sovereignty in 2004, but the United States could never get ahead of the task of rebuilding the Iraqi state. It progressively deemphasized its efforts to prop up state security services. Instead, it put more troops on the ground and turned to recruiting tribal leaders, arming non-state actors as a kind of proxy counterinsurgent force. It also became more reliant on drones for surveillance and attack, further effacing the idea of discrete sovereign airspace. Meanwhile, policy makers like Senator Joe Biden espoused applying the belated lesson of Bosnia to Iraq, effectuating a "soft partition" of Iraq. By the end of the decade Iraq had transitioned from an occupied to a failed state, its sovereignty denatured to its most superficial form.[130]

While the United States waded through the quagmire of state building, other countries appropriated American discourse to justify their own trespasses. Russia decried the invasion of Iraq and was positively neurotic about anything that impugned its own sovereignty, it used similar rhetoric in its wars with Georgia in 2008 and Ukraine in 2014. These violations of the territorial integrity of neighboring states yielded the Russian-backed de facto states in Abkhazia,

South Ossetia, and Donetsk.[131] Rising powers like Brazil, India, and China also selectively adopted doctrines of intervention that suggested a diminishment or dilution of sovereignty.[132] Within the Middle East, Iran and Saudi Arabia similarly launched interventions that contravened the basic premise of sovereignty, putting further stress on a fragmented regional order.[133] Instead of a cornerstone of order, sovereignty itself was becoming a fount of turmoil.

# 2

# 2011

## Revolutions in Arab Sovereignty

Doha, January 13, 2011

*Landing in Qatar, one of the richest countries on earth, it was easy to imagine that revolution was far away. Thanks to natural gas exports, Qataris received housing, education, and guaranteed lifetime employment from their government, an opulence increasingly displayed to the rest of the world. Tourists thronged to the country's state-of-the-art football stadiums for the Asia Cup tournament. American universities operated campuses alongside the new Qatar Faculty of Islamic Studies and Hamad bin Khalifa University in western Doha. The Arab Museum of Modern Art had opened just a few weeks earlier. Glimmering skyscrapers and bunkerlike shopping centers seemed to sprout overnight. And in the desert scrub loomed the US Central Command headquarters at Al Udeid Air Base, a hulking guarantor of stability.*

*Doha had been a fishing harbor when Sykes, Picot, Faisal, King, Crane, and Yale put forward their vision for the future of the Middle East. While Iraq, Syria, and Egypt staggered into independence, the petty Arab Gulf sultanates remained ensconced under British imperial control. Yet by the end of the century, oil and gas had transformed the region into a fulcrum of international politics. The rulers of each Gulf state took a different path. The Emiratis parlayed oil wealth into banking and business ventures, becoming a global commercial hub. The Saudis, defenders of the Islamic holy cities, trafficked in religion. In Qatar the al-Thani dynasty became impresarios of influential ideas, mavens of soft power.[1]*

*In 1996 Emir Hamad bin Khalifa al-Thani saw an opportunity in the proliferation of satellite dishes and invested in a new media venture called al-Jazeera. With slick production techniques, al-Jazeera stood apart from the staid Arab state news agencies. Its motto—"the view, and the alternative"—emphasized free thinking. News and talk programs broke taboos, allowing viewers a chance to express and hear full-voiced dissent with the existing political order. Arab leaders dismissed al-Jazeera as an organ of Qatari state propaganda. American authorities complained about its airing statements from al-Qaeda. Indeed, al-Qaeda seemed to grow symbiotically with the Arab satellite television industry, becoming a conduit for bin Laden's message.*

*Al-Jazeera came of age after the terrorist attacks of September 11, 2001. Recognizing its role in shaping Arab public opinion, governments tried to bully or flatter al-Jazeera. Some launched their competing channels, like Saudi-owned al-Arabiyya or the American al-Hurra ("the free"). Still, senior US and British officials granted exclusive interviews to the station that they had once accused of being a terrorist mouthpiece.[2] The al-Jazeera logo stood beside Nike and Starbucks among the most recognized brands in the world.[3]*

*Now the news ricocheting from the stratosphere into homes, coffee shops, offices, and mosques from the Atlas Mountains to the Persian Gulf was difficult to believe. In December a young fruit peddler lit himself on fire in front of a provincial government office in Tunisia. The self-immolation had a remarkable galvanizing effect. The Tunisian opposition mobilized massive street protests using nonviolent tactics adopted from the so-called Flower Revolutions of the 2000s in Serbia, Ukraine, and Georgia. President Zine al-Abidine Ben Ali, who had ruled for over two decades and maintained Tunisia as a secular, Western-oriented state, was flummoxed and hesitant. The regime's inner circle appeared to be fractured. Security services refused to fire on demonstrators. Al-Jazeera's coverage provided a live-action script for rebellion. Dictators across the region were nervous, the opposition emboldened.*

*Secretary of State Hillary Clinton arrived in Doha trying to come to grips with these changes. Repression and disaffection were no surprise. Large-scale protests in Egypt and Lebanon in 2005 had seemed to give voice to popular antipathies and lent hope to the possibilities of change. In 2009 the US ambassador in Tunis wrote a detailed memo, later disclosed by WikiLeaks, about the Ben Ali regime's corruption. But the United States had other priorities at play. President Barack Obama and his administration struggled to encourage political opening while still carrying on fighting al-Qaeda, ensuring Israeli security, and blocking Iranian nuclear breakout. American troops were still trying to disentangle from Iraq. How far could client states be pushed to reform without jeopardizing America's geopolitical priorities?[4]*

*On January 11, Secretary Clinton made a brief, unannounced stopover in Yemen. Yemen was a unique concern of the international community. The poorest Arab state, it faced protracted insurgencies among the Houthi Shi'i movement of the far north and the secessionist movement of the south. Pockets of "ungoverned" territories were open to infiltration by al-Qaeda and other radical elements. Yemeni president Ali Abdullah Saleh, like Ben Ali, was regarded as a key asset both to the Western powers and to Saudi Arabia. Indeed, as WikiLeaks had also revealed, Saleh secretly allowed the United States an "open door" to conduct drone strikes in Yemen. But Clinton also knew of the regime's venality and abuses. Twelve months earlier Britain had hosted the inaugural meeting of the Friends of Yemen (FoY) donor group. The United States continued to provide the muscle, training and equipping the Yemeni army and expanding* its semicovert drone program. Britain and other European powers provided the inspiration, diplomatic language, and the vision of a stable, democratic, and sovereign Yemen. Saudi Arabia and the Gulf countries carried most of the financial burden, pledging tens of millions to reconstruction and development.

Yet Saleh and his cronies proved essential but recalcitrant interlocutors. They grew fat on foreign assistance but were reluctant to make substantive reforms. There were rumors about how Saleh fed false information to the Americans in hopes of inducing them to assassinate a political rival through a drone strike. Development moneys inevitably ended up in the coffers of the Saleh family and its cronies. When pushed by a foreign sponsor, Saleh complained about outside meddling and the primacy of Yemen's sovereignty. Before departing Sana'a, Secretary Clinton praised Saleh as a "very strong partner in our counterterrorism effort," but warned that military ties should not outweigh "other priorities."[5]

Meanwhile, in Doha's Ritz-Carlton, the Forum for the Future was already under way. Perched on a peninsula jutting into the Gulf, the hotel featured the kind of gilded, Arabesque style for which Qatar was famous. The Forum was a ritual of diplomatic affirmation. Government officials, business moguls, and civil society figures gave formal speeches and circulated the halls for informal (but typically still choreographed) rendezvous. Now Clinton gave the audience tougher talk:

> We all know this region faces serious challenges, even beyond the conflicts that dominate the headlines of the day. And we have a lot of work to do. This forum was designed to be not just an annual meeting where we talk with and at each other, but a launching pad for some of the institutional changes that will deal with the challenges that we all know are present.[6]

The depletion of oil, scarcity of water, endemic youth unemployment, corruption, and resentment toward a "stagnant political order" threatened to tear down what had been achieved. "In too many places, in too many ways," Clinton said, "the region's foundations are sinking into the sand. . . . If leaders don't offer a positive vision and give young people meaningful ways to contribute, others will fill the vacuum." The following day, television sets in the hotel and around the world flickered with news of Ben Ali fleeing Tunisia.

## Uprising, Intervention, and the Problems of Statehood

Revolutions cut at the ligatures that bind peoples, territories, and governing authorities—the core of sovereign statehood. They create uncertainty, vacuums of power that tempt interventions as revolutionaries and counter-revolutionary

actors alike seek to build external alliances.[7] The revolutions began differently in
different parts of the Arab region, but all pointed to the collapse of the old authoritarian bargain. The region's developmental and state-building leaps of the
1950s and 1960s were far behind it. Decades of misrule had squandered the
gains and goodwill of previous generations. Arab society, as Hillary Clinton described it, was underemployed, young, and angry. Early protests, spontaneous
and often leaderless, voiced quotidian demands for jobs, pay hikes, and respect.
But as satellite television and social media brought news of the Tunisian uprising, opposition activists across the region grew bolder. They converged on a
common strategy to confront the regimes' facile claims to embody national self-
determination and identity. Following the playbook from Belgrade and Kiev,
they occupied key public spaces, urban squares, and intersections.[8] The ubiquitous slogan of protest—"The people demand the downfall of the regime!"—
expressed the revolutionaries' intent to wrest control over symbols of nationalism and citizenship. Yet the specific revolutionary agenda remained circumspect.
Opposition leaders sought to reassure both their own domestic constituency
and the international community, whose members opposition leaders hoped to
induce to intervene on their behalf. Their aim was to unseat autocrats, not to
break apart states.[9]

This guarded optimism, though, quickly gave way. From the Sahel to the
Anatolian foothills, revolution turned to civil war. Platitudes about national
unity seemed more and more implausible. To the international community and
their own people, Arab dictatorships had long posed as bulwarks against anarchy, but when threatened they often did their best to sow chaos. Rival branches
of the security and intelligence services turned on each other. Rulers called in
vigilantes and pro-government militias, fostering a general sense of disorder
while enacting repression. President Hosni Mubarak's dispatch of the camel and
horseback *baltigiyya* (thugs) in Cairo signaled the abdication of even the pretense of a coercive monopoly.[10] The revolutionaries, in contrast, tried to preserve
the structures of the state as embattled dictators were pulling it down upon their
heads. Elite praetorian guards, staffed by the ruler's closest kin, were unlikely to
turn against the regime. But regular army and police officers might defect if they
felt they had more to fear from the ascendant opposition than from the incumbent power.[11] The more rulers depended on the shifting logic of patrimonialism,
the more their political authority crumbled when challenged. This became especially apparent in the least institutionalized, most personalistic regimes, like
Qaddafi's Libya, Assad's Syria, and Saleh's Yemen. Military defections did not
come en masse but in splinters, fragmenting the state's edifice of coercive power
and confusing the question of who had control on the ground.

The problem wasn't just sorting out de facto statehood but also locating a
normative footing from which to claim juridical sovereignty. Rebels scrambled

to plant their flags in slivers of liberated territory. Self-proclaimed provisional governments, what Glen Rangwala calls governments-in-waiting, acted as repositories of the legitimate and authentic popular sovereignty.[12] In a region where extraverted, juridical sovereignty defined statehood, external recognition and the conferral of legal status was a critical and contestable resource. Similar to Thomas Masaryk and Edvard Benes engaging the Allied powers in World War I on behalf of Czechoslovakia and to the Iraqi National Congress in the 1990s, these provisional bodies lobbied the international community to intervene for the sake of humanity and to make good on the promise of self-determination. They sought to position themselves as partners for the international community, responsible interlocutors that could help set dysfunctional states right.[13] European powers and the United States, especially, saw the uprising as a definitive test of their commitment to humanitarian principles like R2P. They set up new multilateral bodies to interact with rebel entities, providing diplomatic, economic, and even military support. Interventions, advocates suggested, could not only alleviate immediate suffering but also restore states to their normal, beneficent functioning.

But this view was hardly universal. As one observer noted, the response to the uprising revealed the

> fading authority and consensus on the world stage. The cold war "spheres of influence" between two powers are long gone. The new world order of American dominance has faded. But no clear leadership or rules have replaced this. New fights between trends of human rights and democracy—and sovereignty—have no rules as of yet.[14]

Russia had geostrategic reasons to object to interventions and had growing diplomatic and military tools to stymie them. Emergent powers like India, South Africa, and China were unconvinced for different reasons. To many, R2P appeared a retread of colonial-era mandates, allowing stronger powers to assume trusteeship over sovereignty while turning populations into wards of the international community.[15] Accordingly, these states sought to limit the application of R2P and to retain as much as possible of the mid-twentieth-century notion of sovereignty that had birthed them.

The first government-in-waiting to emerge, Libya's Transitional National Council (TNC), was a prototype, an example bearing an inordinate impact on the subsequent progress of the revolution and interventions. Like the Iraqi National Congress in the 1990s, the TNC struggled to maintain its relevance on the ground. The TNC had more success engaging and mobilizing support from diasporic networks and the international community. It tried to bootstrap its international imprimatur into domestic power. But the ineptitude of the TNC as Libya's provisional government only deepened the chasm between de facto and de jure power. The Syrian National Council was an even less successful emulator of the TNC. It, too, appealed for international intervention and tried to build support on the ground, yet it elicited a far more hesitant and convoluted response. Nevertheless, the breakdown of order and fracture of authority in Syria mirrored Libya's descent. Finally, in Yemen there was no need even for a self-proclaimed provisional rebel government. Yemen's sovereignty was already so flimsy that the international community's transition to stewardship was but a small step. Yet again, the disjuncture between the empirical and juridical elements of sovereignty became more glaring. In both senses sovereignty was obliterated. Statehood reverted to its colonial origins: contingent, provisional, and ultimately dispensable.[16] Such a vacuum invited new challengers to emerge from within.

## Libya

The TNC appeared at a critical moment early in the Libyan uprising. On February 14 protests began in Benghazi, precipitated by the arrest of a lawyer investigating a decades-old prison massacre. Some security forces fired at the crowds, but many soldiers, typically conscripts, appeared sympathetic to the protesters. Over the following days protests expanded eastward to neighboring Green Mountain regions of Cyrenaica and Tobruk. Some demonstrators threw Molotov cocktails and tried to seize armories. Many military commanders and full units in the east defected. Protests also began in the west in Misrata, Libya's third-largest city and a major commercial center, as well as the Nafusa mountain region and Tripoli. Unlike in the east, military units in the west tended not to defect together but to collapse through mass desertion of conscripts.

Mustafa Muhammad Abd al-Jalil, Muammar el-Qaddafi's former justice minister, led the launch of the TNC after resigning his post in protest on February 21. Abd al-Jalil returned to his home region of the Green Mountains and Benghazi to meet with disaffected diplomats, military officers, tribal leaders, and dissidents. The TNC formally convened in Benghazi on February 27 and established its own military council, comprised of fourteen senior officers, on March 2.[17] Major General Abdul Fateh Younis, a former interior minister who had defected after refusing to launch an attack on Benghazi the previous week, was named head of the military council and commander of the self-styled Libyan National Army (LNA). Several of the leading local revolutionary factions announced their support for the TNC. A committee of activists, lawyers, and academics that had organized the Benghazi protests dissolved in deference to the TNC's position as the leader of the national revolution.[18] Still, internal divisions racked the TNC, and several LNA commanders jockeyed for supremacy.

As the uprising spread, armed groups appeared organically, including militias associated with local revolutionary committees, tribal forces, and armed Islamist groups.[19]

By the end of February, the uprising had stalled. Along with the remainder of the regular armed services, the 32nd Brigade, an elite praetorian guard unit commanded by Qaddafi's son Khamis, went into action. Qaddafi marshaled tribal militias from his home region of Sirte and from Bani Walid clans, a loyalist stronghold in the west, and hired mercenaries from sub-Saharan Africa. Government forces quickly put down the uprising in Tripoli and moved to strike Misrata and Zuwiya. In the east, government troops took the key oil installations of Brega and Ras Lanuf and began marching along the coastal strip toward Benghazi.[20] In a television address on February 21, Qaddafi's eldest son and heir apparent, Saif al-Islam, warned that Libya would not follow the peaceful transition of neighboring Egypt or Tunisia. Rather it would degenerate into tribal warfare and produce "rivers of blood."

> You will emigrate from Libya, because the oil will cease to flow, and the foreign companies will leave Libya tomorrow. The oil companies will leave Libya. The oil ministry will cease to function, and tomorrow, there will be no oil and no money.

Saif blamed "bullies and traitors, who live abroad" for fomenting the unrest. "Prepare yourselves for colonialism, on top of everything else," he said. "Colonialism is coming back. It will return. The Europeans and Americans will return and will enter Libya by force."[21]

The elder Qaddafi picked up these same themes in a televised address two days later. He called the rebels "rats who are getting paid by foreign powers" and warned that the uprising would produce civil war and terrorist infiltration and ultimately lead to foreign occupation:

> Beware that al-Zawahiri [bin Laden's deputy] will come and rule you. Do you want Americans to come and occupy you? Like Afghanistan and Pakistan and Iraq? Our country will become like Afghanistan if that's what you want.[22]

Importantly, Qaddafi's hour-long diatribe meandered into a deeper discourse about Libyan statehood and the nature of its sovereignty. Qaddafi portrayed himself as the personal embodiment of Libya's centuries-long resistance to imperialism. His confrontation with the United States in the 1980s continued the 1920s battle against Italian colonialism. It was this struggle, Qaddafi asserted, that sustained Libya's independence and granted him the right to use force:

If we have to use the force then we'll use it. According to the international law, and according to the Libyan constitution. . . . They don't
want me, they don't want Libya. This is the criminal act. Anybody who
lifts an arm, any Libyan who lifts an arm shall be punished with death
sentence. Those who spy with other countries shall be punished with
death sentence. Anybody who undermines the sovereignty of the state
shall be punished with death.[23]

Such threats reverberated in the international community, confirming Qaddafi's
image as a shambolic and erratic leader. Over forty years in power, he had few
friends abroad, although his image had been somewhat rehabilitated in the mid-
2000s. Already opposition figures were estimating some five hundred people
had died at government hands. Absconding Libyan fighter pilots reported receiving orders to bomb civilians.[24] Regime officials tried to downplay the casualties and blame the rebels for the violence. Al-Jazeera, though, assisted by social
media, tended to highlight, and in some cases exaggerate, the level of state-led
violence. Whatever the veracity of these reports, many in the international community were convinced that a mass atrocity was imminent.[25]

Qatar saw in the Libyan chaos a chance to reshape regional politics. Al-Jazeera
had played a critical role in disseminating information about the protests in
neighboring Tunisia and Egypt to Benghazi, and in bringing news about the
Libyan protests to the world. Serving in the rotating presidency of the Arab
League, Qatar took the lead in drafting resolutions that censured and suspended
Libya from the international body. Instead of waiting for Western governments
to take action, Qatari officials argued that Arab states should respond collectively to a problem of one of their own. The African Union and other global
bodies similarly condemned the regime's brutality. The UN Security Council
took up the case of Libya in an emergency session. President Obama spoke of
the "the universal rights of the Libyan people. That includes the rights of peaceful assembly, free speech, and the ability of the Libyan people to determine their
own destiny."[26] Just days after defending Qaddafi at the Security Council, Libya's
UN ambassador broke ranks and urged international action to defend the Libyan
people from the regime. Libya's diplomatic representatives seemed to be defecting in droves. On February 26, the Security Council unanimously passed
Resolution 1970, imposing an international embargo on weapons sales in Libya,
as well as banning travel and freezing the personal assets of Qaddafi and his
senior officials.[27]

Newly emergent as the face of the popular revolution, the TNC evinced a
vision of the linkages between the international community, the Libyan state,
and its people that differed dramatically from Qaddafi's. In its first proclamation
of March 5, the TNC declared itself the sole legal representative (*mumathl*

*al-shari'ai al-wahid*) and assumed a self-assigned mission "affirming the sovereignty (*tu'akid as-siyada*) of the Libyan people over the entirety of the territory, land, sea, and air."[28] Although the TNC included opposition figures of many stripes, the core leadership was largely liberal, Western oriented, and technocratic. Abd al-Jalil had a reputation as a reformist from his tenure as justice minister. Mahmoud Jibril, prime minister and chair of the TNC executive board, held an American PhD and had been an economic advisor to Qaddafi. The TNC's oil and finance minister, Ali Tarhouni, taught economics at the University of Washington for over twenty years.[29] As if to underscore the connection between the TNC and the international community, the council rejected the use of the green banner that Qaddafi had designed for the Libyan state. Instead, it used the tricolor of the Libyan monarchy, the flag under which Libya had gained independence and entry into international society through direct UN supervision.

The UN actions did not deter Qaddafi's advances. In fact, they may have only spurred him to hasten the assault before outside actors could respond. Tripoli was pacified, the siege of Misrata tightened, and on March 15, Qaddafi's force routed the rebels in Ajdabiya and appeared poised to move on Benghazi. Qaddafi taunted rebels in Benghazi in a radio address. "No mercy," he promised. "We are coming tonight. . . . We will find you in your closets."

The TNC called desperately for a safe haven to protect the uprising, specifically invoking R2P doctrines. An invitation to intervention undercut the mid-century notion of sovereignty that undergirded Libya's statehood.[30] Yet such steps were needed to protect Libyan lives. "We have made the international community aware of its responsibilities concerning the suppression, attacks, and shelling," Abd al-Jalil said. "We think that the Security Council can skip international sovereignty and protect the civilians by all means necessary."[31]

For the international community, the question was not just about Libya's civilians but about the larger principles of humanitarian interventions associated with R2P.[32] Bernard-Henri Lévy, a public intellectual and leading proponent for the 1990s intervention in the Yugoslav civil war, traveled overland from Egypt to Benghazi to meet with Abd al-Jalil at the end of February. Lévy opined that if Qaddafi was allowed to continue his counterattack, there would be "a massacre in Benghazi, a bloodbath." Lévy brokered introductions between the TNC and the government of Nicolas Sarkozy. Embarrassed for having backed the Ben Ali regime in Tunisia, France quickly extended diplomatic recognition to the TNC on March 10.[33]

Qatar, meanwhile, pushed the Arab states to take action. The Arab League passed an even more stringent resolution and petitioned the Security Council to consider an NFZ and civilian safe havens.[34] Although the final vote was unanimous, only eleven of twenty-two member states actually cast votes on the resolution. Many saw the resolution as a departure from the League's long-standing avoidance of interfering in the internal affairs of its members.[35] The resolution "violates the sovereignty, independence and unity of Libyan territory," the Syrian ambassador stated.[36] The Qataris argued, however, that the enormity of Qaddafi's threats outweighed such considerations. Moreover, they reasoned that the Western powers might take action without League approval, a step that would further sideline the Arabs. Ultimately, the wording of the resolution reflected the recurring ambivalence toward sovereignty. On one hand, the resolution clearly called for the use of force against the Libyan state in response to internal suppression. On the other hand, it committed

> to preserve Libyan unity, territorial integrity, political independence as well as civil peace, and to ensure the safety and security of Libyan citizens, the national unity of the Libyan people and their independence and sovereignty over their territory, and to reject all forms of foreign intervention in Libya, and to emphasize that the failure to take necessary actions to end this crisis will lead to foreign intervention in internal Libyan affairs.[37]

The Arab League resolution also called for greater cooperation and communication with the TNC. Qatar joined France as an early champion of the rebels, officially recognizing the TNC at the end of February and pledging $400 million to support the body. It also provided water, heating oil, and other humanitarian relief to rebel-held areas. Jibril effectively relocated his international lobby operations from Benghazi to Doha, increasing his connectivity to the international community.[38]

Despite its caveats and contortions, the Arab League resolution was a catalyst for intervention. The Obama administration had tried initially to keep the TNC at arm's length, doubting its ability to achieve command and control on the ground. Furthermore, it suspected that the revolutionary coalition might be secretly dominated by radical Islamists. Through March Secretary Clinton downplayed the possibility of intervention, despite the urgings of Senator John McCain and others. Yet, she said, the Arab League had "changed the diplomatic landscape" in favor of action.[39] The United States joined Britain and France in a Security Council resolution authorizing military action. China and Russia were willing to defer to the Arab League's call to arms and abstained from the vote. Brazil and India, both non-permanent Security Council members, had their own reservations about intervention but ultimately abstained as well.[40] Resolution 1973, like its Arab League predecessor, offered a convoluted assessment of how Libya's sovereignty and territorial integrity could endure despite external intervention. The resolution stressed that the objective was to bring government and rebel sides to a ceasefire. At the same time, though, it called for "all necessary measures" to protect civilians, "excluding a foreign occupation force of any form on any part of Libyan territory." This explicitly permitted outside actors to impose an NFZ and provide defenses to humanitarian safe havens. It also froze the Libyan central bank and the national oil company, further intruding onto the fiscal anatomy of the Libyan state.

Full-scale intervention started badly. Coordinating among the more than two dozen countries, including most NATO members and Arab states was a logistical and command-and-control nightmare. France started off the campaign by bombing armor and antiaircraft batteries near Benghazi on March 19, but Turkey and other NATO allies refused to abide France's leadership. The United States, which had initially wished to avoid a large-scale military commitment, had to take up the slack. By the end of March NATO assumed operational control over the hodgepodge of naval and air force, but problems of coordination with the rebel forces on the ground remained. On April 4, Younis complained that "NATO has disappointed us [and] has not given us what we need."[41] NATO's delays put Libyan lives at risk. "If NATO wanted to free Misrata, they could have done that a few days ago."[42] What Younis did not say—but was becoming apparent—was that the rebels could not do the job themselves.[43]

The NATO air supremacy, though, did help the rebels to stabilize their lines and make some modest gains. NATO forces, along with the UAE, Jordan, and Qatar, set up training and support programs for rebel troops. Ignoring the UN arms embargo, they also clandestinely funneled weapons to the rebels.[44] Qatar's was by far the most impactful of these training missions. Libyan officials estimated that Qatar provided tens of millions of dollars and some twenty thousand tons of weapons, but only a small fraction of that went to the TNC. The Qataris concentrated their attention on Islamist groups, like the Libyan Islamic Fighting Group and the Rafallah al-Sehati Companies, an Islamist brigade renowned for its expensive equipment and supplies.[45] Rebel mobilization intensified, but in a highly localized fashion, with battalions organizing by town, district, or neighborhood. Though different foreign sponsors tried to help the TNC expand its organizational capacities to incorporate these groups, foreign powers also maintained direct bilateral relationships with different armed factions, effectively bypassing the TNC.[46]

While the military campaign demolished Libya's de facto sovereignty, the international community began to restructure Libya's sovereignty at the juridical level. On March 29 the foreign ministers of some forty-four countries (largely European and Arab), as well as Secretary Clinton, UN Secretary General Ban Ki-moon, and representatives from NATO, the Arab League, and the EU, convened in London to discuss Libya's future. This led to the establishment of the Libya Contact Group (LCG), which met over the next four months in Doha, Rome, Abu Dhabi, and Istanbul. Later renamed Friends of Libya, LCG came to resemble an impromptu international trusteeship. All that it needed was Qaddafi's downfall to implement its plans for reconstruction and rehabilitation. The TNC was not formally seated at the initial conference, but at the first LCG meeting in Doha it was granted a position as the sole "representative of the Libyan people." Qaddafi's representatives were excluded. By the fourth LCG meeting in Istanbul in July, the United States and over thirty other states granted the TNC full recognition as Libya's lawful government.[47]

TNC leveraged its position in the LCG to stake a claim to Libya's sovereign wealth fund, the central bank, the national oil company, and other state assets. Qatar assisted the TNC in marketing Libyan oil, although many foreign buyers refused to purchase oil whose provenance might be challenged. There were rumors that the TNC was willing to trade oil for political considerations.[48] The TNC also pushed to get access to military hardware, despite the embargo. In meetings with the UN envoy in April, Jibril reportedly argued that the ban should exempt rebel-held territories in order to allow the rebels a measure of defense.[49] This assertion on the part of a provisional government with only partial territorial control raised questions about whether Libyan territory should remain unified going forward.

Qaddafi harped on the international community's hypocrisies. He told international envoys that the rebels were to blame for atrocities and for rejecting ceasefire terms. He tried to call in diplomatic favors from other African leaders, some of whom he had paid healthy subventions in oil and money. He even supposedly tried to reach out to Israel.[50] Moreover, Qaddafi representatives accused the LCG of bad faith, claiming to support a ceasefire but really seeking to unseat Qaddafi. Prime Minister Al-Baghdadi al-Mahmoudi claimed that the LCG "enabled a certain group who are seeking to assume powers," rather than adhering to UN principles. Nevertheless, the international community was "betting on a losing horse" by backing the TNC.[51] The following month, al-Mahmoudi declared that NATO's "interference in the Libya issue is considered an interference in Libyan sovereignty."[52]

Few countries sided openly with Qaddafi, but many saw the intervention as an abuse of humanitarian principles and trespass on sovereignty.[53] Russia suffered buyer's remorse almost immediately. Moscow complained that NATO had exceeded the UN mandate in seeking to bring down Qaddafi, not just protect civilians, and griped that the LCG usurped the authority of the Libyan state and of the UN.[54] Eventually, though, both Moscow and Beijing resigned to the TNC's permanence and initiated diplomatic ties with Benghazi.

By the summer, the rebels were finally able to advance under the allied military umbrella, pushing Qaddafi's forces into isolated pockets around Tripoli, Sirte, Bani Walid, and Sabha.[55] Mediation offers by South Africa, France, and Russia went nowhere. The rebels rejected proposals to deploy Turkish troops as peacekeepers under the NATO aegis. The International Criminal Court issued a warrant for Qaddafi's arrest for war crimes.[56] In the midst of this success, though, internecine conflicts within the rebel movement intensified. Younis was assassinated on July 28 in Benghazi, most likely by Islamist factions that considered him a rival and a holdover from the old regime. Indeed, across the country Islamist militias, many of which enjoyed backing from Qatar, became more prominent and assertive. In late August, militias associated with the Islamist factions of Misrata and the Nafusa mountain region stormed Tripoli. Although Qaddafi escaped, the conquest of the capital seemed to mark the ultimate triumph for the revolution. Qatar had a major role in the operation. The Qatari chief of staff later described how Qatari special forces "supervised the rebels' plans because they are civilians and did not have enough military experience. . . . We acted as the link between the rebels and NATO forces."[57]

The ascent of such foreign-backed forces posed a direct challenge to the TNC, the internationally recognized Libyan government. TNC officials criticized foreign powers generally and Qatar specifically for meddling in Libyan affairs. The UAE, Saudi Arabia, and many NATO players, too, were concerned that Qatar was empowering some of the most hard-line and radical Islamist factions in Libya. Still, while Qatar's engagement was the most visible, nearly every actor had picked some horse in the Libyan race.

The TNC's operational oversight and moral authority receded. On October 20, nearly two months after the liberation of Tripoli, allied planes spotted Qaddafi fleeing Sirte with an armed cortege. Allied bombers intercepted Qaddafi's caravan. Rebel fighters from the Misrata battalions attacked from the ground. The TNC initially reported that Qaddafi had died in either the bombing or the ensuing firefight. Cell phone video, though, revealed that Qaddafi had in fact been tortured and executed in the field, a violation of the laws of war that embarrassed the TNC. Jibril, who had announced plans to step down after the liberation of Tripoli, resigned immediately after Qaddafi's assassination. He blamed Qatar, and its support for militias, for hamstringing the TNC. He described a situation of impossible disorder. The TNC had planned to reopen Libya's education system in the autumn but found that various militias had commandeered schools and other public buildings and refused TNC directives to relocate. "I cannot claim to have control over these [military] formations," he said, which "[take] matters into their own hands . . . and violate human rights." The international community was no help, as the UN had still not released the moneys from the central bank to TNC control. As a result, the TNC lacked the weapons or the funds needed to subdue them.[58]

The interaction between the TNC as a provisional government and the international community exacerbated the difficulties of exerting control on the ground. After the capture of Tripoli, TNC finance and oil minister Ali Tarhouni made an unsubtle jab at Qatar: "Anyone who wants to come to our house has to knock on our front door first. I hope this message will be received by all our friends, both our Arab brothers and Western powers."[59] Yet it was the TNC, as much as any other actor, that had left the door ajar. The TNC touted itself as the government of liberated Libya but never even approached a monopoly over the use of force across Libyan territory. It claimed to affirm the sovereignty of the Libyan people over the entirety of Libyan air, land, and sea. Yet its consent to intervention effectively led to the revocation of Libya's sovereignty in favor of an arrangement that resembled international trusteeship through the LCG.[60] For their part, the participants in the LCG suspended their own skepticism in order to justify intervention. The interruption of Libyan sovereignty, they agreed at the outset, was temporary and necessary for the good of the Libyan people. Upon the fall of the Qaddafi regime, the TNC proved incapable of accepting the handoff of power, despite its juridical status. Once the linkage between the state, the people, and the international community broke, Libya could not be reestablished, even as a semi-functional state.

## Syria

In Syria, the Syrian National Council (SNC) and its successor National Coalition for Syrian Revolution and Opposition Forces (*al-itilaf al-watani li'quwa ath-thawra wa al-ma'radha ath-thawra,* SOC), served as a less effective version of a government-in-waiting. The SNC only formed in August 2011, six months after the uprising began with protests in Dara'a. Popular anger erupted over the arrest and apparent torture of local boys for graffitiing anti-regime slogans. Confrontations with security services quickly escalated. Al-Jazeera featured smuggled footage of troops firing at protesters. Local leaders in Banias, Damascus, Hama, Hasakah, Latakia, and Deir Ezzour announced sympathetic "days of rage" demonstrations. The protests snowballed and expanded. Across the country activists formed local coordinating committees (LCCs) to guide and support revolutionary activities. Larger revolutionary councils, which incorporated a number of LCCs in a single municipality or region, formed from this organic base.[61]

From its base in Istanbul, the SNC announced its intention to "overthrow the regime, its symbols, and its head."[62] It took months of meetings between pro-Western liberals, nationalists, Islamists, and a handful of Kurdish and Assyrian Christian representatives to consolidate the SNC. Burhan Ghalioun, a Paris-based sociology professor and long-standing regime gadfly, became the SNC's first president.[63] Yet the unmistakable power behind the SNC was the Muslim Brotherhood. In the early 1980s Brotherhood radicals launched an insurrection against what they deemed the infidel Alawi regime of Hafez al-Assad. Assad responded with massive repression, culminating in the decimation of the Sunni

Arab cities of Hama and Homs in 1982. The Brotherhood never recovered its position inside Syria, but Qatar and Turkey in particular regarded the Brotherhood as the natural representatives of Syria's Sunni Arab majority.[64]

While the SNC depicted itself as inclusive and nonsectarian, there was no way to avoid a distinctly Sunni Arab hue that reinforced the conflict's sectarian framing. Many sectors of Syrian society were visible in the early stages of the protests. As violence intensified, Iraq's civil war hung as an inexorable specter, and concerns grew about ethnosectarian war in Syria. In its rhetoric, the regime downplayed communal difference and elided its reliance on recruiting minority Alawis into the upper military and political echelons. Over the course of decades, the regime had incorporated and co-opted some segments of the Sunni merchant elites. But in putting forward claims that pit the people against the regime, the rebellion heightened the salience of ethno-sectarian cleavages and raised fears of splintering.[65]

The SNC struggled to demonstrate its popular legitimacy and operational control on the ground. Whereas the TNC had been homegrown, the SNC originated and operated mostly outside of Syrian territory. Ostensibly, the SNC general assembly reserved the largest bloc for LCC representatives, but it was unclear how much voice they really had within the SNC. Fewer than half of the LCCs even formally supported the SNC.[66] The divide between the SNC and the National Coordination Council (*haya' at-tanfees al-watani li quwa at-taghayer*, NCC), a coalition of leftist and Kurdish factions based in Damascus, was even sharper. The NCC insisted on negotiation with the regime and continued to operate in Syria as a kind of "loyal opposition."[67] In fact, the Democratic Union Party (PYD), the Syrian offshoot of the Kurdistan Workers' Party (PKK) and major constituent within the NCC, seemed to be working in tacit alliance with Assad. Government troops simply vacated positions in the north and northeast and allowed the PYD to take over control and administration of these primarily Kurdish areas.

The SNC began to call for foreign intervention, even though its early rhetoric rejected any steps that might compromise Syria's sovereignty and unity. This increased the tensions between the SNC and NCC. On September 9, 2011, LCCs associated with the SNC proclaimed a Friday protest demanding "international protection."[68] In October SNC spokesmen called for "international governments and organizations to meet their responsibility to support the Syrian people, protect them and stop the crimes and gross human rights violations committed by the illegitimate current regime." Directly invoking the example of Libya, SNC affiliates increasingly advocated for internationally backed NFZs and safe havens within Syrian territory.[69]

As the rebellion and counter-rebellion became more violent, the SNC came to favor armed resistance. Defecting army officers, almost entirely Sunni Arabs, founded the Free Syrian Army (FSA) in July. Its ranks grew with a steady stream of defections and desertions from the Syrian army. By December the FSA numbered some ten thousand men. Still, the it was disjointed and localized. Its leadership acknowledged SNC authority but bristled at SNC plans to manage military finances and operations.[70] Some rebel units refused to serve under the FSA banner at all. Radical groups like Jabhat al-Nusra (JAN), the Syrian branch of al-Qaeda, and the Islamic State also competed with the FSA for territory, resources, and recruits. There were over a thousand separate active fighting groups in Syria by 2012, with little overarching leadership structure beyond largely informal regional military councils.[71]

But international opinion was turning against intervention by the time the SNC was making its entreaties to the international community. Russia, which had a strong strategic relationship with Assad, would not allow a repeat of the mishap in Libya. China, South Africa, Brazil, and India all came out against intervention. The United States and European powers themselves were less convinced of the efficacy of force and the reliability of the rebel armies. They cautioned Syrian opposition leaders not to count on a large-scale military action.[72] Clinton asked:

> What are we going to arm with and against what? We're not going to bring tanks over the borders of Turkey, Lebanon, and Jordan. We know that [al-Qaeda leader] Zawahiri is supporting the opposition in Syria. Are we supporting al-Qaeda in Syria? . . . If you're a military or if you're secretary of state and you're trying to figure out do you have elements of an opposition that is actually viable, that we don't see.[73]

Even intervention advocates had to explain why Syria would not become "another Iraq."[74]

The situation differed slightly within the Arab sphere, where Qatar continued to hold the vanguard. Al-Jazeera highlighted the atrocities of the Assad regime (sometimes based on questionable evidence). Doha became the largest backer of the FSA, the SNC, and the Brotherhood.[75] Saudi Arabia and the UAE were generally sympathetic to the Syrian opposition, whom they viewed as orthodox Sunnis oppressed by an Iranian-backed Shi'i regime, but remained suspicious of Qatari designs. They funded alternative opposition organizations to counteract Doha's influence. The crosscurrents of government transfers and private fundraising contributed to the fragmentation of opposition groups and relief agencies operating on the ground. But while the Gulf countries engaged in a game of one-upmanship and took increasingly aggressive stands, Algeria and others expressed skepticism about interventionist measures that contradicted the longstanding norms of non-interference.[76] Ultimately, the League did expel Syria and imposed economic sanctions. Qatar later formulated a plan for a joint UN–Arab League peacekeeping mission. Seen through the dark lenses of Iraq's tumult, the entry of these outside powers seemed only to be "weakening the sovereignty of the country and tipping the country further into a sectarian quagmire."[77]

For the SNC, though, this seemed like a risk worth taking. Ghalioun explained the SNC had made important steps by gaining "political recognition" through treating with foreign emissaries but was not yet an "alternative state." "The opposition's insistence on preserving the unity of the country and rejecting any interference that could affect the sovereignty of the country and its independence" had contributed to the Assad regime's improbable durability, he said.[78]

The Assad regime responded to these pressures by posing as the defender of sovereignty while at the same time seeking to inspire fear. In one of his first speeches following the outbreak of the revolution, Assad stressed the importance of the Syrian state and invoked the troubling example of Iraq's "collapse and submission to America." Now Syrians were "at a stage when we can appreciate this stability." The violence, he claimed, was the act of foreigners, criminals, and saboteurs.[79] Regime rallies featured the chant "Assad or we burn the country."[80]

Rather than a definitive rupture, the Syrian state slowly hemorrhaged coercive power. The regime fell back on more explicit ethno-sectarian logic, marshaling support from Alawis and Christians who feared falling under the domination of the Sunni majority. Assad relied more heavily on Iran as well as Lebanese Hezbollah forces for military support. Qassem Soleimani, commander of Iran's expeditionary Quds Force, helped Assad recruit pro-governemnt militias. Officially called the National Defense Battalions but colloquially known as *shabiha* (apparitions), these militias numbered some fifty thousand men and were notoriously brutal toward civilians. Additionally, Iran helped Assad recruit Iraqis and Afghan Shi'is to help battle what they deemed the scourge of Sunni radicalism.[81] Such devolution of violence, as Christopher Phillips notes, further damaged the institution of statehood by eroding the distinction between state and non-state wielders of violence.[82]

As the rebels gained ground, the regime became more adamant about the absolute nature of Syrian sovereignty. In a January 2012 speech Assad declared, "We were focusing on one thing only which is the sovereignty of Syria." He deemed the rebellion an imperialist conspiracy to destroy Syria, similar to what had happened after 1919:

> What is taking place in Syria is part of what has been planned for the region for tens of years, as the dream of partition is still haunting the grandchildren of Sykes-Picot. But today their dream turns into a

nightmare, and if some believe that the time of conflict over Syria is back, then they are mistaken because the conflict today is "against Syria" and not "over Syria" or "on Syria."[83]

Along with the United States and Israel, radical Islamists and the "dishonest" al-Jazeera and Qatar were favorite scapegoats.[84] In June Assad elaborated:

> The masks have fallen and the international role in the Syrian events is now obvious. . . . The first force pushes backward and tries to weaken Syria and violate its sovereignty and perpetrate acts of killing, sabotage, ignorance, backwardness and serve the interests of foreign powers. . . . Our guiding light is always Syria's sovereignty, independent decision, territorial integrity and the dignity of its people.[85]

Indeed, outside interventions impinged on Syria's operations as a sovereign state. US and European embargos on the Syrian national bank and oil companies took a significant fiscal toll, although Russia helped Syria skirt some restrictions. Credit ratings agencies stopped covering Syria's sovereign debt. Hard currency reserves suffered. The Arab League–operated satellite company dropped Syrian state broadcasts.[86]

Following the model set in Libya, the Western powers and their Arab partners set up a donor group, the Friends of Syria (FoS). FoS began in Tunis on February 2012 and met regularly through 2013. There were extensive discussions of R2P and the need to grant the Syrian people means for "self-defense."[87] From the outset of the FoS, the SNC was seated as the representative of the Syrian people. Yet most states refused to grant the SNC full diplomatic recognition as a transitional government. Western powers were alarmed that the moneys earmarked for the opposition were being diverted into the hands of the radicals.[88] Compared to Libya, US secretary of defense Leon Panetta explained, Syria

> [has] triple the problems because there are so many diverse groups that are involved. Whether or not they can find one leader, whether they can find that one effort to try to bring them together in some kind of council—there are efforts to try to make that happen, but frankly they have not been successful.[89]

With no one to serve as trusted interlocutor, the international community was reluctant to push for further intervention. Still, efforts to augment the SNC's oversight of the FSA and LCCs failed. Having lost the confidence of the international community, his fellow exiles, and operatives within Syria itself, Ghalioun resigned.[90] The SNC was finished.[91]

The SOC was born in November 2012 in the same Doha hotel where Clinton had warned of region-wide distress eighteen months earlier. The SOC subsumed the SNC and added more weight to LCC representation, bringing it closer to the ground. Muaz al-Khatib, a former imam of the venerable Umayyad Mosque in Damascus, was elected president of the new body. Unlike the expatriate SNC, Khatib had stayed in Syria through 2012 and suffered arrests and detentions for his support of the rebellion. But Khatib appreciated the necessities of foreign backing. "When we get political recognition," he said, "this will allow the Coalition to act as a government and hence acquire weapons and that will solve our problem."[92] Most Western powers, though, were unwilling to extend full diplomatic recognition to the SOC and stopped short of fully conferring juridical sovereignty.

Ultimately, the SOC succumbed to the same dilemma as the SNC. The Western powers and the anti-Assad Arab coalition would not fully extend support to the SOC until it had demonstrated command of the front lines. But the SOC could not lead the fractious militias and the LCCs without concerted external backing. By the end of 2012 the FSA effectively collapsed, with much of its matériel and fighters absorbed into more radical Islamist fronts. In January 2013, Khatib met with Iranian and Russian officials and announced his intent to hold direct negotiations with the regime. This initiative only sowed further divisions within the opposition and its foreign sponsors, spurring Khatib to resign.[93]

Still, the rebels enjoyed strategic momentum. By 2013 much of Syria's primary agricultural land in the north and northeast had fallen from state control, as had the majority of its few oil wells.[94] The ranks of the Syrian army continued to thin.[95] Assad's increasingly reliance on Iranian military support called into question the volition of the Syrian government. In 2013 the former prime minister Riyad al-Hijab opined that "Syria is occupied by the Iranian regime. The person who runs the country is not Bashar al-Assad but Qassem Soleimani."[96]

Assad avowed his adherence to "the principles and goals of the UN Charter and the international law which all stress on [sic] the sovereignty, independence and territorial integrity of countries and non-interference."[97] Russia became Iran's diplomatic champion, blocking any move toward intervention and adamantly defending Syria's sovereignty. By ritualistically affirming Syria's sovereignty and territory, the international community granted Assad resources for his own defense. Foreign relief agencies were required to partner with state-controlled bodies like the Syrian Arab Red Crescent, allowing the government to throttle the flow of aid to rebel-held territories and funnel money to state-controlled territories in Damascus and on the Mediterranean coast.[98] By July 2015 Assad tacitly admitted surrendering control over portions of Syrian territory.[99] As the government continued to suffer setbacks, he formally requested Russian military assistance. Russian aircraft and ground forces began operations from within Syria in September 2015, launching a devastating assault against the remnants of the FSA as well as JAN and Islamic State strongholds. Launching sixty sorties per day, Russia provided air support that allowed government troops to stem the tide and steadily crush the rebellion.

Though militarily decisive, Russia's presence only deepened the confusions and contradictions surrounding Syria's statehood. Just like the rebels, the Syrian state could not control its own territory without support from external patrons and armed non-state actors like the *shabiha* warlords and the PYD. As in Libya, the result was a practical disregard for the very notion of Syrian statehood. While the UN continued to enunciate Syria's sovereignty, independence, unity, and territorial integrity through 2016, John Kerry, Clinton's successor as secretary of state, opined that "it may be too late to keep it as a whole Syria."[100] Russia, too, seemed to see the obstacles to reunifying the Syrian state. Russian proposals for reconciliation and local ceasefires centered specifically on the idea a radical decentralization of power.[101] The pretenses of Syrian sovereignty rested uncomfortably with the reality of partition.

## Yemen

Secretary Clinton's 2011 Sana'a stopover indicated the unique gravity the world attributed to Yemen well before the uprisings. The protests that began there a few weeks later followed a familiar script. Youth and local activists, often unconnected to the established opposition parties, led the first wave of largely peaceful demonstrations. Regime repression was sporadic but at times severe. Since Yemen was already awash with private weapons, there was little to stop the escalation of violence.[102] Regime loyalists, particularly senior military commanders and tribal leaders, defected. Saleh lurched between efforts to co-opt and intimidate the rebels. He blamed outside instigators for endangering Yemeni sovereignty. He tried to play on his longtime, if not always open, alliance with the West and his crucial role as bulwark against terrorism.[103]

But Saleh's foreign patrons in the FoY were already growing impatient. With the blessing of the UN Security Council, the Gulf Cooperation Council (GCC) took the lead in negotiating Saleh's departure. It offered guarantees of political immunity for the president and his family, warning that if Saleh did not comply, family assets (conveniently housed in the Gulf banks) would be frozen. But the Western powers and the Gulf states all wanted to avoid further political chaos. Senior Yemeni politicians, nearly all onetime Saleh allies, flocked to Riyadh to confer with Saudi officials about the transition. Yet Saleh held out, and violence intensified. In June Saleh was severely wounded and forced to go to Saudi Arabia for treatment, leaving a constitutional and political void in the country. Finally, after added pressure from the GCC, he agreed to resign in favor of his vice president, Abdu Rabbu Mansour Hadi, in February 2012.

The new regime offered greater inclusion to the opposition but remained dominated by Hadi and other holdovers from Saleh's General People's Congress. This arrangement ultimately impugned the credibility of the opposition itself, as they proved unable to make significant change. Moreover, some key opposition groups were excluded, including the Southern Movement (SM) separatists. Still, Hadi claimed—and the international community confirmed—that this was in fact a transitional government. Hadi affirmed Yemen's partnership in the international effort to fight al-Qaeda and pointed to UN backing to legitimate his own position.[104] Members of FoY reciprocated by reciting their own pledges of financial and political support to help stabilize Yemen.

The National Dialogue Conference (*al-mu'atamar al-hiwar al-watani*, NDC), convened in March 2013, was supposed to provide the internal buttressing to Hadi's legitimacy. Modeled on customary modes of conflict resolution, the NDC took place over nine months and involved hundreds of activists, civic leaders, and politicians from across the political spectrum. Again, however, the process's inclusivity was more apparent than real. Hadi handpicked many of the delegates, and the distribution of seats favored figures from the old regime. The longer the NDC wore on, the less hopeful its prospects. One commentator likened the NDC sessions at the deluxe Hotel Mövenpick in Sana'a to "a spectacular wedding where no one wants to get married."[105]

Yet the international community endorsed the NDC as part of the formula for stability and pushed for its continuation even after many members had quit in disgust. The Hadi government, in turn, tried to leverage this external support to bolster its domestic position. Foreign Minister Abu Bakr al-Qirbi (a holdover from the Saleh government) touted that the UN Security Council had determined that the forum had "achieved ninety percent of what has been required of it." Now, he said, there was "a problem about the issue of the form of state, will it be a union or a federation, and what is the number of provinces or regions." Qirbi then pleaded for the international community "to support the armed forces at the logistic and training level, and in providing the resources for the army to undertake its duties."[106] Both normatively and functionally, the Yemeni state was prostrate without international approval and support.

The closed nature of Yemen's transition and the foreign orchestration of Hadi's installation probably helped prevent Yemen from sliding into a full-on civil war at the beginning of the uprising. But as the NDC sputtered and eventually collapsed, the old fissures remained and grew more trenchant.[107] In the south, separatist factions quit participating in the NDC and began setting up their own autonomous control in Aden and Hadramawt. Sensing an opportunity, Saleh reneged on his commitment to relinquish power and aligned his loyalist Republican Guard forces with the Houthi militants in the north. In late 2014 the combined Houthi-Saleh forces stormed Sana'a and began moving southward to Taiz and the outskirts of Aden. Hadi and the other officials beat a hasty retreat, eventually relocating to Riyadh. The international community imposed economic sanctions on Saleh and the Houthis. The self-proclaimed presidential council, a joint body between the Houthis and Saleh loyalists, was ignored internationally. The United States and other global powers still recognized Hadi as the leader of Yemen's government in exile and funneled aid and assistance through it, including control over the Yemeni central bank. But his so-called legitimate government proved to have precious little influence within its own territory.

The joint Saudi-Emirati invasion of Yemen in March 2015 served as an epilogue to the fracturing of sovereignty. Saudi authorities asserted that such measure were necessary "to protect the people of Yemen and its legitimate government from a takeover by the Houthis."[108] They claimed to be responding to the specific request from the Hadi government itself, invoking Article 51 of the UN Charter. But the military campaign evinced little concern for humanitarian hardships.[109] Rather, Saudi Arabia sought to eliminate any Iranian presence along its southwestern border. The UAE focused on using the Yemeni coast to construct a network of bases extending power into the Red Sea and the Gulf of Aden.[110] With American weaponry and diplomatic cover, their blockade and bombing immiserated millions of Yemenis. Yemen faced the largest cholera epidemic since World War II and near-famine conditions.[111] Hadi, whom the Saudis claimed had invited their intervention, became a prisoner in Riyadh's gilded cage.[112]

## Conclusion

The Saudi-Emirate adventure in Yemen marked the definitive transformation of the Arab uprisings and the attendant interventions from tragedy into cruel and bloody farce. The Saudis and Emiratis claimed a mandate under international law, but their actions exhibited a primary concern for geostrategic objectives. Their ostensive humanitarian mission unequivocally worsened humanitarian conditions. Steps taken in the name of preserving Yemen's integrity and sovereignty only further fragmented state authority.

The calamitous ironies, common across the global nation-state crisis from the 1990s into the 2000s, loomed over all of the Arab uprisings. The breakdown was not just of the physical capacity to govern on the ground. MENA had long been accustomed to weak states, like Lebanon, where state authority yielded to a bevy of armed non-state actors. The crisis, though, was also normative and ideational. It undercut assurances of juridical permanence and made states themselves appear superfluous. The international community recited the mantras of sovereignty and territorial integrity but increasingly entertained the possibility of new territorial arrangements and new institutions that might better fit within a changing global order. Just as for Iraq in the 1990s and 2000s, partition loomed large.[113] If intensive foreign intervention was necessary to keep order, then what good were these states anyway? Why should they be preserved?

But while outside actors took up these questions haphazardly and hypothetically, those who lived under failed states faced them with desperate urgency. Most people coped by turning to alternative networks of family, clan, tribe, neighbors, and religion to fill the void. Some found ways to capitalize on the state's enervation, taking up illicit acts like smuggling or extortion. Though technically criminal, these measures, similar to poaching, often implicitly confirmed the absent state's normative power to delineate legality from illegality.

For a handful of actors, though, the combination of normative uncertainty and material exhaustion of existing states provided an opportunity to make direct and positive claims for alternative political association and new sovereignty. These claims could not be judged according to the parochial standards of domestic law. They were supra-legal, legitimated by history and the rights of self-determination that Wilson had promised nearly a century earlier.

# PART II

# 3

# Cyrenaica

Benghazi, June 1, 1949

*This was not the declaration of independence that Mohammed Idris el-Mahdi es-Senussi, guide of the Senussi religious order and emir of Cyrenaica, had in mind. Approaching sixty years old, austere and ascetic, Idris looked the part of an Arab imam-chief, part spiritual guide and part tribal arbitrator. The setting, too, was auspicious. Benghazi was the largest and most important city in Cyrenaica, second only to Tripoli in all of Libya. Idris stood before the Cyrenaican National Congress, an assembly of some 165 notables. Most were tribal leaders, bedouins from the Green Mountains and the Sahelian oases. Their ancestors had sworn allegiance to Idris's grandfather a century ago. The room was draped with the Senussi emblem, the white crescent and black field a reminder of the Senussis' direct descent from the Prophet.*

*But the ties that had once bound the tribes to the emir had frayed over the previous twenty-five years. Idris quit Cyrenaica in 1922 as the Italians began clamping down on what they called their "Fourth Shore." He tried to offer moral and diplomatic support from exile in Egypt but did little to save his people from the onslaught. Tribesmen led by Omar al-Mukhtar waged a hit-and-run guerrilla-style war. The Italians responded with sheer brutality. They built a series of barbed wire enclosures to trap the nomads, denying them pasturages and water, decimating their herds, and starving them into submission. Thousands fell to hunger and exposure. Others retreated through the desert to the Egyptian frontier, "dying of thirst among dead animals and men . . . ragged, emaciated, and friendly."[1] The Italians declared Cyrenaica pacified in 1931 with Mukhtar's capture and hanging. During the Second World War, Idris struck a deal with Great Britain. He would encourage the Arabs to rise against the Italians and form an army to serve alongside the Allied contingent. In return, Britain pledged to prevent the return of Italian colonialism to Cyrenaica. Now, four years after the war's end and at the beginning of what seemed a new era in global affairs, Idris sought to make good on the pledge—and more.*

*The meeting was held at the Manar Palace in Benghazi's modern quarter, an area that had been virtually off-limits to Arabs under Italian rule. The palace was the former residence of Rodolfo Graziani, the Fascist commander who oversaw the counterinsurgency campaign. British military administrators were keen to showcase Idris's taking power in the erstwhile abode of Italian colonialism. Idris, though, was more comfortable in the tribal heartlands than in the city, where commerce and mercantile families, many originating in Tripolitania, predominated. Idris was also aware that the British had their own interests at heart. He did not want to become a fig leaf for their geopolitical ambitions. The inauguration of the United Nations rekindled the hope, first raised at the end of World War I, that Libyans might enjoy self-determination. Yet the UN had failed to come to a resolution about the fate of the Italian colonies, and Rome was vying to regain its empire. Libya was widely deemed underdeveloped, a poor candidate for sovereignty. Cyrenaica in particular lagged behind the richer, more populous Tripolitania to the west. As the British encouraged Idris's return to Libya, he seemed to beg off and malinger, a subtle reminder that Whitehall's end of the bargain had yet to be fulfilled. Yet he also knew that Benghazi and the British were both essential to his own plans.*[2]

*Idris stood before the Congress to tell them that the time for independence was here.*

> I no longer ask you for your patience, but rather I say to you now, we have to declare in this blessed hour on this gleeful day—June 1, 1949 coinciding with the 4th of Shabaan 1368—the complete independence of our homeland [*istiqlal biladuna at-tamm*]. And with the help of Allah and your trust in the authorities of this nation, I will oversee the executive, legislative and judiciary branches [until a national election].[3]

*Idris addressed the British directly, pledging cooperation and alliance and asking "the Government of His Majesty the King of Great Britain to recognize our new political status in order to give us another helping hand to be the first nation to recognize our existence just as it assisted us in liberating our country." Idris next appealed to "brotherly Arab countries and all eminent Islamic nations and every country that values justice and peace to recognize our independence. We assure all of them that our new young nation is not a threat to anyone." Cyrenaica, he said, would be a "tool of world peace." Finally, Idris turned his attention westward to Tripolitania, Cyrenaica's "sister." Tripolitania, he said, should achieve independence soon and, subject to popular approval, unify with Cyrenaica under his leadership.*

*The British chief administrator read a brief statement in formal Arabic. The British would recognize Idris's position as the "freely chosen leader of his people" and head of the government. They also formally recognized the "desire of the Cyrenaicans for self-government" and pledged to take "all steps compatible with their international obligations to promote it." With those words, Cyrenaica reached the cusp of statehood.*

*Still, the clamoring outside the building was impossible to ignore. Cheers erupted at the mention of independence, but the tone turned sour as Idris described the delay in Tripolitania's independence and unification. "United Libya! No independence before unity," shouted the crowd of three thousand. "Down with sham independence!" As*

Idris, his entourage, and the assemblymen left the palace grounds, the demonstrators heckled him. How, they asked, could Cyrenaica pursue independence when Tripolitania remained under colonial control? Idris was startled by the public confrontation. Up until that point, his stage-managed reintroduction to Libya had included only warm receptions.[4] When he toured the Green Mountains, tribesmen waited for days to kiss his hand. Still, the substance of the protest was familiar. At the vanguard was the Omar al-Mukhtar Club, formed during the war by Libyans living in Cairo. By 1945 the club had built a following among the urban youth of Benghazi and Derna, rabble-rousers and firebrands in Idris's estimation. The club articulated a new kind of Arab nationalist, exasperated with rulers like Idris that compromised with imperialist powers. In appropriating the name of the martyred Mukhtar, the club challenged Idris's anti-colonial and nationalist credentials. Putting Cyrenaican independence ahead of Tripolitania would yield a subservient rump state and leave fellow Libyans at the mercy of Italy. Idris, they implied, risked becoming an imperialist stooge.[5] Flustered but un-harmed, Idris urged forbearance to the crowd. Police and bodyguards mustered. Idris fled to his villa on the outskirts of the city, at the edge of the desert he considered his home.

# Introduction

Separatism in Cyrenaica (Barqa), Libya's eastern region, is a largely unantici-
pated outcome of the Arab uprisings. The Libyan state is not the colonially imposed artifice that pundits presuppose all Arab states to be. But neither is it an
autochthonous, deeply embedded political institution. Libya's state formation
was driven by an uneasy collaboration of local elites who resisted imperial subjugation but took advantage of the opportunities presented by outside interventions. Though tribal divisions are clearly relevant, Libya is overwhelmingly
Arabic speaking and Sunni Muslim. Besides the small Berber and African communities, Libya has no obviously stateless minorities and is not deeply divided
in the manner of Iraq or Syria.

The federalist movement in Cyrenaica arose in the midst of a vacuum of
power following the February 2011 revolution. Before the revolution federalism
seemed virtually unheard of, a relic from before Qaddafi took power in 1969. Yet
the collapse of the state in 2011 allowed actors in Cyrenaica to reassert claims to
territorial self-governance. The key actors behind the federalist movement were
the tribes of Cyrenaica's Green Mountains, which had been the backbone of the
defunct Senussi monarchy and the earlier Senussi emirate of Cyrenaica. Like
many other actors, federalist factions fought to command territory and resources, particularly those associated with oil production and export. The movement accumulated the trappings of statehood, including an army, parliament,
and executive authority. Yet the federalist agenda remains undefined. For some,
federalism corrected the hyper-centralized and autocratic administrative legacy
of Qaddafi. For others, it augured a more profound autonomy, returning
Cyrenaica to the kind of self-rule it enjoyed intermittently in the late nineteenth
and early twentieth centuries.

The Cyrenaican federalists competed with Islamists and various nationalist
factions for territory and resources, particularly in the key coastal cities of
Benghazi and Derna. But the battle was also over the symbols of legitimacy and
standing, particularly who had the right to inherit the mantle of Libyan statehood. The federalists' historical claim was tied directly to the Wilsonian
moment after World War I and its reprise after World War II, when the international community affirmed Cyrenaica's right to self-determination. The contemporary federalist movement sought to relive that moment, to reinstate the
idea of a separate Cyrenaica that had formally merged into Libya in 1951, been
abolished with constitutional reforms in 1963, and definitively quashed with
overthrow of the monarchy in 1969.[6] Like their mid-century forerunners, they
appealed to the international community to support their cause on both moral
and instrumental grounds. Whatever its specific political program, the federalist movement added to the symbolic and physical estrangement between

Cyrenaica and Tripoli. Libya become a failed state. It retained de jure status in the international community but lacked de facto power to rule. Cyrenaica, by comparison, became a quasi-state, possessing a measure of coercive, economic, and infrastructural power. Yet it was denied legal recognition either within Libya or by international society. Regardless of whether they wished to remain attached to Libya, the federalists' defiance increased the likelihood of Libya's dismemberment.

## State Formation and Resistance under the Imam-Chief

Historically, Cyrenaica has been distinguished from its western neighbors in Tripolitania (Tarablus) because of its heavy reliance on a desert pastoral economy and nomadic Bedouin society. Nevertheless, there was a circulation of trade and migration between the regions. The arrival of Ottoman troops into the coastal region in 1551 helped solidify the linkages between Cyrenaica, Tripolitania, and the Fezzan. Ottoman rule focused on coastal population centers of Tripolitania.[7] Cyrenaica was more rural and politically isolated, making it more resistant to outside penetration. From 1711 to 1745 the Qaramanli dynasty ruled Tripolitania under nominal Ottoman suzerainty, but the Ottomans later reasserted direct control over the region as Britain and France began pushing farther into Africa. The 1911 Ottoman census reported 576,000 inhabitants in Tripolitania and fewer than 200,000 in Cyrenaica (although this excluded Kufra). Benghazi, the largest city in Cyrenaica, had an estimated population between 17,000 and 19,000, around half the size of Tripoli.[8] Protruding into the Mediterranean between the Libyan Desert and the Gulf of Sirte, the Green Mountains were dominated by Cyrenaica's aristocratic (*saadi*) tribes, who traced their ancestry to Egypt and Arabia and practiced endogamy. Normatively, the aristocratic tribes were superior to the so-called bound or client (*murabiteen*) tribes of Cyrenaica, who claimed descent from indigenous Berber communities. In practice, the aristocratic and client tribes were culturally indistinguishable and openly competed for control over pasturages and trading routes. The powerful Zuwaya tribe, one of the so-called client tribes, ranged all the way to the Kufra oasis. Moreover, tribal ties were flexible and adaptable and did not preclude cooperation and collaboration between individual tribes or between tribes and nontribal peoples.[9] The main coastal cities of Cyrenaica, Benghazi and Derna, traditionally stood apart from tribal pastoralists, having been settled by Andalusian and Tripolitanian merchants in the Middle Ages. Along with Maltese, Italians, Jews, and Greeks, these migrants from across the Muslim Mediterranean dominated coastal commerce. Urban quarters were named after tribes and clans of Misrata and other Tripolitanian locales.

Cyrenaican tribal identity was closely tied to devotion to the Senussi religious order. The Senussis' power rested on interlocking pillars, what Iliya Harik dubs the imam-chief union of religious and temporal power.[10] The Senussis were at once the region's supreme spiritual and religious leaders and authoritative intermediaries in tribal disputes. Muhammed ben Ali al-Senussi, known as the Grand Senussi, fled the French invasion of Algeria in the 1840s. After completing the hajj to Mecca and sojourning in the Hejaz and Egypt, the Grand Senussi established his headquarters in Jaghbub, in the Cyrenaican interior. The Grand Senussi dispatched emissaries to establish *zuwayah* (lodges) in the territories of each tribe. The first Senussi lodge was established in Bayda, high in the Green Mountains, in 1843. The lodges functioned as mosques, primary schools, meeting halls, caravansaries, and residences of the local Senussi delegates. Many lodges had pasturages, orchards, or fields attached to them and received *zakat* (alms) from the local tribes and peasants and extracted taxes on the caravan trade. The Senussis helped funnel trading through the Sahel and the southern oases northward to Benghazi.[11]

The zenith of the Senussi order came under the leadership of Sayyid al-Mahdi al-Senussi (d. 1902), son of the Grand Senussi. Al-Mahdi relocated the headquarters of the order to Kufra, extending his influence into Chad, Egypt, and Sudan. At the same time, areas to the west, like Misrata and Zintan, refused to submit to Senussi hegemony and instead remained loyal to their local Sufi traditions. Al-Mahdi ruled in Cyrenaica in a kind of condominium with Ottoman authority. Through commercial and religious influence, he tried to stem the advance of European power into the Sahel. Both Muhammed bin Abd Allah, the leader of the millenarian Mahdist uprising in Sudan, and Colonel Ahmed Urabi, leader of the revolt in Egypt, appealed for Senussi support. Al-Mahdi demurred in both instances, correctly sensing that these movements were bound for failure and would allow even further European penetration. Working in concert with the Ottomans, al-Mahdi began acquiring modern weapons, adding to the lodge's military functions. By the turn of the twentieth century, the Senussi order operated in Cyrenaica as an amalgamated religious brotherhood, trading company, and embryonic state.[12]

The Italian invasion in 1911 sparked the first concerted expressions of nationalist sentiment in Libya. Though the Ottoman forces quit Libya, they never formally ceded the territory and covertly encouraged Libyans to continue the struggle against European occupation. Sayyid Ahmed al-Sharif al-Senussi, grandson of the Grand Senussi and nephew of al-Mahdi, led the Cyrenaican tribes in a harassing guerrilla campaign. Some of the leading merchant houses of Tripolitania initially welcomed the Italians as an alternative to the Ottomans. Yet Sulayman Baruni, a member of the Ottoman parliament, tried to rally the Berber tribes of the Nafusa Mountains. He was defeated in March 1913. In the southwest, French forces moved into the Fezzan.

Geopolitics began more and more to impinge on the options available to the actors in Libya. When war erupted in Europe, Italy was drawn to side with the Allies in part because of the promise of gaining sovereignty over Ottoman possessions in the Mediterranean. Yet as Italy deployed its forces to Europe, its hold in Libya became even shakier. By late 1914 onetime local collaborators were in open revolt. In April 1915 Ramadan al-Sewehli led Misratan forces that crushed the Italian army at Qasr Bu Hadi. The Ottomans urged Ahmed Sharif to launch a raid against British Egypt, but he instead abdicated in favor of his nephew, Mohammed Idris.

Idris's relationship with the British, particularly his ability to leverage diplomatic status for political power as a voice for the Bedouins, would define the trajectory of state formation in Cyrenaica. Under the 1917 Akrama Agreement, Rome acknowledged Idris's authority in the interior in return for a pledge to respect for Italian sovereignty and control along the coast. Yet the Senussis' aspirations conflicted with those of Sewehli and the Tripolitanian merchant elite. Sewehli's forces repelled Senussi's attempts to extend his political control westward, creating a lasting fissure between east and west.[13]

Italy's colonial holdings were in tatters at the end of the war. In November 1918 Sewehli and Baruni, backed by the Misratan commercial community, declared the formation of the Tripolitanian Republic. Inspired by Wilson's Fourteen Points and the emergent norms of self-determination, the Misratan merchants hoped to win the support of the international community as its members convened at the Versailles peace talks. Italy initially conceded to the rebel demands and Wilsonianism's moral weight. The Italian parliament approved a liberal fundamental law for the colonies, granting both Tripolitania and Cyrenaica elected provisional legislatures as imperial citizens. At the same time, Rome played off the Libyans' rivalries. Within a year the Tripolitanian Republic collapsed into civil war. Berbers and the Warfalla, an Arab tribe centered around Bani Walid, quit the republic and joined the Italian campaign. Sewehli was killed by Warfalla forces in August 1920. Tripolitania was largely subdued by the following year.[14] The Senussis enjoyed a stronger position due to their greater political cohesion and British backing. A 1920 accord granted Idris the title "emir of Cyrenaica" and a stipend from the Italians. He held autonomous administrative rights in the inland oases of Kufra, Jalu, Jaghbub, Awjila, and Ajdabiya.[15] These arrangements, never based on mutual confidence, soured after the Fascist takeover of Italy.

Beginning in 1922, the second war between the Senussis and Italy was even more destructive than the first. The Italian commander Rodolfo Graziani built a network of blockhouses and barbed wire fences to encircle the nomads, pushing them into concentration camps. An estimated one-quarter to one-third of the tribal population perished, mostly due to starvation after the decimation of their herds.[16] At the same time, the relationship between the Senussis and the

Tripolitanian nationalists remained fraught. Still, due to his ties to the British, Senussi alone had any hope of repelling Italian encroachment. The Tripolitanian elite warily acceded to Senussi's leadership, formally requesting that he extend the Senussi emirate to include Tripolitania. In accepting, Senussi openly breached his accord with Italy. In December 1922 he fled to Egypt. Thousands of Cyrenaican tribesmen took a similar route. Libyan exiles and refugees in Damascus, Tunis, Cairo, and Arabia formed Committees for Tripolitanian-Cyrenaican Defense.[17] Idris appointed Omar al-Mukhtar, a Senussi acolyte from a minor tribe, as military commander. Mukhtar set up a unified military council, including representatives from across the tribal confederations. The resistance continued its traditional taxation of the caravan trade. Still, Idris's flight seemed a betrayal of his commitment to the Cyrenaica tribes. Some Senussi order leaders collaborated with the Italian occupation, accepting postings and subsidies. Mukhtar was captured and publicly executed in Benghazi in 1931, becoming a hero of Libyan and Arab-Islamic anti-colonial resistance. His death marked the effective end of guerrilla resistance, as his deputies fled or were captured in the coming months.[18]

The pacification opened up Cyrenaica to renewed Italian settlement and colonization. In Benghazi, the Italians expanded the port, built an airfield, and dug wells. The city center sprouted a two-domed cathedral and its first modern hotel, the Berenice. The population grew to some 50,000, including 16,500 Italians.[19] Outside the city, Rome encouraged Italian peasants to farm in former tribal pasturages and expropriated lands of the Senussi lodges.[20] In 1934 Italy officially unified Tripolitania and Cyrenaica as the colony of Libya.

Just as World War I had sparked the initial drive for self-determination, World War II provided the catalyst for independence. In exile in Cairo, Idris worked with the British to recruit the Cyrenaican tribes into the Libyan Arab Forces to fight against the Italians. Again, Cyrenaica took the brunt of the fighting. Benghazi changed hands five times during the course of the war. Much of the city's modern infrastructure was ruined. Freed of Italian settlers, the pastoral economy recovered somewhat more easily.[21]

Idris pushed the British for assurances about Libya's post-war future and to speed up the transition to self-rule. The British saw in Idris both a potential state builder and a local ally, somewhat overestimating the influence of a man who had spent over two decades in exile.[22] In January 1942 Anthony Eden promised that Cyrenaica would not be subjected to Italian control again. Still, these assurances perturbed the Tripolitanian nationalists, who viewed Idris suspiciously and saw this as a ploy to further colonial occupation through divide-and-rule. Even in Cyrenaica, some younger, nationalist circles associated with the Omar al-Mukhtar Club (later renamed the National Association of Cyrenaica) pressured Idris to refuse a re-division of the territory.[23]

At war's end, Britain, France, the United States, and the USSR all agreed that the Italian Empire had to end, but none had any clear idea what do with Libya. Egypt volunteered to assume a protectorate but was ignored. France had designs on the Fezzan. Maintaining military administration in both Cyrenaica and Tripolitania, the British contemplated assigning Italian trusteeship in the latter. Seeking to forestall a carve-up, on June 1, 1949, Idris stood in Manar Palace, Graziani's former residence in Benghazi, to declare the independence of the Emirate of Cyrenaica. Idris called on Britain to recognize Cyrenaica and appealed for Tripolitania's independence as a step toward unification.[24] Both Idris and the British saw the tribes as keys to political order in Cyrenaica. The Cyrenaican National Congress, first convened in 1947, was dominated by the tribal elite, to the virtual exclusion of representatives from cities and towns. Reversing Ottoman and Italian efforts to quarantine urban affairs from rural tribal influence, the British turned over administration in Benghazi to tribal sheikhs.[25] Facing inexorable strain on its colonial commitments, the British abdicated the military government to the UN oversight. In November the UN General Assembly passed a resolution recommending "that Libya, comprising Cyrenaica, Tripolitania and the Fezzan, shall be constituted as an independent and sovereign state" and instructed the secretary general to assist in forming a national assembly to prepare for independence.[26] The UN sought to broker agreements between the Senussis and the nationalist factions. Tripolitanian leaders begrudgingly acceded to Senussi leadership. Cyrenaican and Fezzani leaders sought to ensure that they would be not be subordinated to the inordinate demographic weight of Tripolitania.[27] The first national assembly of 1951 provided for equal representation of Cyrenaica, Tripolitania, and Fezzan. Half the Cyrenaican delegates represented tribal groups, assuring the preservation of tribal interests and autonomy.[28] The constitution specified Libya as a federal monarchy and King Idris as head of state. On December 24, 1951, King Idris stood again at Manar Palace to proclaim the independence of the Kingdom of Libya.[29]

## Independence and Lost Autonomy

In the first decade of Libyan independence there were constant disputes between the federal and regional governments of Cyrenaica, Tripolitania, and the Fezzan. The constitution granted significant power to these regional governments to handle education, housing, and mineral rights. The staffs of the regional governments combined were some ten times larger than the federal government. As monarch, King Idris rotated his court between Tripoli and Benghazi. He remained the ultimate political arbiter, distributing favors and benefits based on a calculus of kinship and loyalty. He blocked the formation of political parties and undercut the operation of state bureaucracy.[30] Reliant on military support from Britain and the United States, Idris resisted the anti-imperial calls of Nasser and pan-Arabism.

Cyrenaica was considered a royalist stronghold, the darling of Idris's mercurial attentions. The federal senate assured it equal power to the more developed and populous Tripolitania. Tribal leaders from the Green Mountains continued to dominate the provincial legislature and executive committee.[31] The Cyrenaica Defense Forces (CDF), staffed by the major aristocratic tribes, outstripped the Libyan armed forces in men and matériel. Benghazi prospered as the political center of the Cyrenaica province and as the federal cocapital. The national census of 1954 documented some seventy thousand residents in Benghazi, a fourfold increase from the Ottoman era and surpassing even the heyday of Italian colonization.[32] Establishing a new administrative capital in Bayda and universities in Bayda and Jaghbub reinforced the sense of Cyrenaica as a favored territory.[33] The province retained the rights to negotiation with international oil companies on the recently discovered fields, as well as the bulk of the revenue.

The advent of the oil economy pulled the peripatetic tribes further into the orbit of the coastal cities. The Magharba migrated to areas near the Brega oil terminal; the Obaidat staked a claim around the terminals at Tobruk. The Baraasi, Hasa, Dorsa, Abid, and Urfa moved into the environs of Bayda. Many tribes seasonally rotated between city and pasturage. Sheikhs readied their sons for careers away from the tribal homestead in government or military service.[34] Benghazi was the only city capable of absorbing the massive inflows of the new oil economy. Foreign oilmen and consular officials moved into villas in the southern district of Fuwayhat. At the same time, shanty quarters of Sabri sprawled into the desert north of the old city. In the 1920s under a thousand people inhabited the area. By 1962 it had seventeen thousand, accounting for nearly a quarter of Benghazi's population growth. Sabri lacked for public transport, electricity, schools, clean water, and other basic amenities. Most of the housing was traditional tents or rough mud huts.[35] Still, the growth of these areas evinced a kind of optimism. Instead of their traditional tents, tribesmen increasingly aspired to live in cement-walled villas.[36]

Yet urbanization did not necessarily spell the end of tribal affiliations; rather, it brought about their transfiguration. Hadi Bulugma reflects on how the rural migration to Benghazi transposed tribal rivalries into the urban context. Tribal leaders held dual roles as traditional sheikhs and municipal officials. Tribal affiliations were key considerations in business partnerships, voting, and marriage. Feuds and rivalries over control over key urban sites and positions endured, sometimes violently.[37] The situation became even more complicated by migrants from Tripolitania, who seemed to operate as a tribe apart. Tripolitanian wholesalers dominated the food and dry goods sectors of Benghazi.[38]

The oil economy also eroded the ties between the tribes and the monarchy. Oil rents gave the state new capacities for distribution and coercion that surpassed anything the tribes could muster. Always wary of rivals to his authority, Idris sought to centralize control over finance and administration. The Cyrenaica Provincial Legislative Council, dominated by tribal interests, repeatedly moved to block these efforts. Finally, in 1963 Idris definitively overruled these objections, pushing through constitutional reforms that effectively replaced the tripartite federalism with a new system of ten provinces, each headed by an appointed governor. Though tribal notables remained visible in all facets of government, the tribes themselves were no longer an essential power base.[39] The unification of the territories also appeared to be the final element cementing a singular Libyan identity.[40]

But the 1969 Free Officers coup, which toppled the monarchy and brought Muammar el-Qaddafi to power, revealed the rot in Cyrenaica's conservative tribal tradition. The CDF, touted as the king's most loyal defenders, mounted no significant resistance. A handful of royalist politicians tried to set up opposition fronts in exile, but they had little impact inside the country.[41] Qaddafi's system of rule was complex and idiosyncratic. In theory, Libya was a mass republic, with power vested in popular revolutionary committees. The tribes were among the regime's first targets. In April 1970 Qaddafi announced in Bayda that subsidies to tribes and tribal officials were abolished. A new class of revolutionary men and professional bureaucrats took over in their place. The state's core executive functions, including the national oil company, were relocated to Tripoli. The lodges and tribal lands were expropriated, Senussi Islamic University shuttered, and the CDF dissolved.[42] But, paralleling the revolutionary institutions, Qaddafi relied on tribal patronage. Qaddafi may not have harbored any particularly prejudice against the east. Nevertheless, many of the Cyrenaican tribes and figures associated with the old regime perceived his policies as punitive.[43] The construction of the Great Man-Made River, the largest irrigation system in the world, was seen as an attempt to divert the underground aquifers near Kufra and Sarir in the Cyrenaica interior for the benefit of agricultural expansion in coastal Sirte, Qaddafi's tribal homeland.[44]

Cyrenaica did become a center of anti-Qaddafi opposition, but resistance was not overtly regionalist in nature. On the contrary, much of the opposition in the 1980s and 1990s took on a distinctly Islamic outlook. In the early 1980s Qaddafi attacked the Muslim Brotherhood. The regime perceived Cyrenaica, along with Misrata and Tripoli University, as a hotbed of Islamic activism. The mid-1990s witnessed a number of armed clashes between Islamist factions and security forces, particularly in Benghazi and the Green Mountain region.[45] Details about the formation and membership of the underground Islamist opposition are sketchy. One of most significant was the Libyan Islamic Fighting Group (*al-jama'a al-Islamiyya al-muqatila*, LIFG), which recruited heavily from Libyan and Egyptian veterans of the Afghan civil war. Between 1995 and 1998 LIFG launched a string of attacks, including several attempted assassinations of Qaddafi himself. Most of the attacks occurred in Benghazi and the Green Mountains. LIFG portrayed itself as an heir to Omar al-Mukhtar's revolutionary anticolonial legacy.[46] Libyan security services gradually killed or captured most of the LIFG leadership. Using a combination of pressure and selective inducements, Libyan authorities convinced the LIFG to renounce violence in the late 1990s.[47]

To counteract the Islamists' influence, Qaddafi sought to revive and enlist tribal sheikhs. Redubbed "popular social leaders," sheikhs became liaisons with the popular revolutionary committees that formed the backbone of the security state. By 1995 he began issuing certificates of honor to selected sheikhs, granting them a kind of corporal power and creating a sense of collective responsibility and governance for the tribal unit.[48] This allowed many of the Cyrenaican tribes that had fallen out of favor to return to positions in the security services and other government agencies, solidifying a kind of tactical alliance between tribal leaders and the government against Islamists. Amal Obeidi's study of university students in Benghazi from that time period shows how tribal allegiance persisted even among the educational elite. Yet tribalism was still fluid and contingent, coexisting beside commitments to family, Libyan patriotism, and Islam. As Libyans suffered state repression and economic stagnation, tribes offered "sanctity, safety, and support."[49] The turn to tribal customs and institutions was often an instrumental means to solve problems that official state institutions could not.[50]

Just as he had attacked tribal institutions and power centers in the 1970s, Qaddafi targeted symbols that could be appropriated by Islamists. In 2000 he demolished the monument to Omar al-Mukhtar in Benghazi's central square and closed the People's Club (*an-Nadi al-Ahli*) on Omar al-Mukhtar Street (formerly Via Roma), which was regarded as a meeting place for opposition.[51] At the same time, Qaddafi held out significant carrots to the Benghazinos, funding a new medical center and housing complexes and cleaning up the city's putrid central lake. Still, the economic growth had an uneven effect, drawing even more transmigrants from Tripolitania, as well as from Egypt.[52] Egyptian and Cyrenaica were cultural and socially linked. In the early days of the monarchy, Egyptian teachers, judges, and white-collar workers found work in Libya. The oil boom brought Egyptian laborers. The presence of Egyptians, who had been exposed to the Brotherhood's notion of Islamic resistance and rebellion, probably heightened the cultural impact of Islamism in Libya generally and Cyrenaica particularly. Derna, Cyrenaica's intellectual and educational hub, became socially and religiously more conservative.[53] At the same time, though, Misrata was no less affected by Libya's Islamic social turn. Thus, while Islamists capitalized on disaffection among Cyrenaicans, they did not pronounce objections in regionalist terms. Instead, their resistance was articulated as a vertical challenge to the Qaddafi regime, not the territorial structure of the Libyan state.

## Days of Rage: The 2011 Uprising and the Resurrection of Cyrenaica

The uprising of February 2011 induced a re-provincialization of Libyan politics and society, particularly in the re-emergence of Cyrenaica as a political entity. Protests began February 16 in Benghazi, only a few city blocks from the former Manar Palace. Activists were enraged over the arrest of a prominent human rights lawyer who had been investigating abuses at Abu Salim prison. Civic leaders in Derna and the Green Mountains declared "Days of Rage" in solidarity. Security forces initially tried to suppress the protest but fell away as the demonstrations expanded. Witnessing the revolutions in Tunisia and Egypt, Qaddafi apparently anticipated disturbances in the east and began moving additional security personnel there. Yet he coupled this repression with offers of appeasement. Imprisoned Islamic activists were released. There were promises of more economic aid to the east and constitutional reform.[54] The protests spread to the Nafusa Mountains and then Misrata and Tripoli. Qaddafi sought to escape to the loyalist enclave of Sirte but was eventually trapped and killed in October 2011. In areas where the state was suddenly absent, local committees and militias formed to coordinate public security, welfare, and justice. Many crystallized around clan or tribal lines. Others were organized by Islamist factions, especially in urban areas. Although there were common grievances and resentment against the regime, there was little coordination among these factions.[55]

The localization on the ground combined with a revolutionary movement that was distinctly extraverted, oriented toward the international community. Just two weeks into the revolution, senior government defectors in Benghazi formed a transitional body to serve as the face of the revolution. The Transitional National Council (TNC, *al-Majlis al-Watani al-Intiqali*) was dominated by Western-oriented technocrats, both long-standing exiles and more recent defectors. The TNC leadership was acutely aware of the precedent of the post–World War II era, when the UN conferred legitimacy and expertise to help in the transition to sovereignty. Indicatively, the TNC adopted the flag of the Libyan monarchy, with its red, black, and green stripes representing the three original provinces. The ability to engage with the international community was the key. Beginning with France, then Britain, the United States, and other great powers, the TNC gained recognition as "legitimate representative of the Libyan people." This struck at Qaddafi's ability to maneuver in the international system, effectively deeming him a war criminal and impugning his claim to sovereignty. The TNC lobbied for a freeze on Libya's sale of oil, arguing that the revenue belonged to the Libyan people, not Qaddafi's government. The Libya Contact Group ("Friends of Libya") donors began to interface directly with the TNC, creating an alternative fiscal structure to the Libyan state. As Qaddafi's forces began to move on Misrata and a massacre appeared imminent, the TNC successfully called for international humanitarian intervention. NATO air strikes helped the rebels secure their positions in the east and roll back Qaddafi's advances in the west.

Yet the TNC enjoyed only symbolic authority domestically. Many local revolutionary committees verbally assented to the TNC's leadership, but few were willing to place their military might at its disposal. Making matters worse, international actors backed different rebel factions and militias. The TNC was reduced to trying to co-opt or induct the myriad of local forces that had appeared in the wake of the revolution. As a consequence, Libya's sovereignty ruptured, with neither Qaddafi's armies nor the TNC actually able to exert control on the ground.[56]

The first inklings of separatism in Cyrenaica emerged on July 20, 2011, with a meeting of the First Federal Conference for Libyan Victory in Benghazi. The meeting was chaired by Abu Bakr Buera, a professor at Benghazi University. Buera was born in 1942 and graduated from Libya University in economics in 1965. He earned a doctorate in business management in the United States before returning to Libya to become a professor and one of the foremost experts on management in the Arab world. Buera's technocratic, Western-oriented background was thus very similar to the TNC membership's.[57] Additionally, in a country with a median age under thirty, Buera was among the few politicians with memory of the pre-Qaddafi era.[58] The conference committee petitioned the TNC to return to the 1951 constitution and insisted on the re-composition of Libya as the original "three regions" (al-aqalim ath-thalatha).[59] A follow-up conference was held in October in Bayda, the onetime Senussi capital.

The push toward federalism was closely linked to the revival of tribal power in the east. Tribal and kinship-based identities remained trenchant across Libya, despite the progress of urbanization and social modernization. The removal of state forces allowed Arab, Amazigh, and African tribal confederations to assert authority across the country. Cyrenaica's major tribal confederations were larger and more cohesive than those anywhere else.[60] Moreover, while areas like Misrata bore the brunt of the Qaddafi counterattack in the spring of 2011, Cyrenaican tribes had been able to consolidate their control unmolested since the evacuation of security services in February.

The federalist issue stymied the TNC. The eastern tribes had been among the earliest backers of the revolution and the TNC. Yet as the battlefront shifted to the Nafusa Mountains and Misrata and the TNC transferred operations to Tripoli, the weight of easterners became increasingly attenuated. The TNC enlarged to incorporate factions from Misrata, as well as the Muslim Brotherhood and LIFG.[61] The Islamists posed a particular concern to the Cyrenaican tribes. In a general sense, religion seemed to offer an alternative to tribalism as a basis for social cohesion. More particularly, Benghazi and Derna were strongholds of Islamism. Islamist parties recruited largely from younger city dwellers. Some were Tripolitanian "transplants," but others were from Cyrenaica's tribes.[62] The Brotherhood seemed prepared for the transition to electoral politics, but the LIFG splintered. While the main leadership readied for electoral competition, more militant factions broke away. In Derna, LIFG veterans formed the Abu Salim Martyrs Brigade (ASMB). Ansar al-Sharia, another splinter cell operating in Derna and Benghazi, came to be associated with al-Qaeda. Both recruited from veterans of the jihad campaigns of Afghanistan, Iraq, and increasingly Syria.[63]

The assassination of Abdul Fatih Younis, commander of the revolutionary armies, intensified the rivalry between the tribes and the Islamists. The circumstances of his death, along with several of his kin from the Obaidat tribe, in Benghazi on July 28, 2011, remain unclear. The alleged perpetrators escaped prison in Benghazi a few days after their arrest. Younis had served as interior minister under Qaddafi before defecting to the revolutionary cause, and some accused him of being a holdover from the old regime with blood on his hands. Many saw the Islamist factions within the TNC as responsible for his death. The Obaidat began to attack Islamist groups in Tobruk, barricaded the east-west highways, and conducted sit-ins in Benghazi against the TNC. This heightened tensions between the federalist factions and the central government.[64]

As the TNC prepared for elections to the General National Congress (GNC) and the drafting of a new constitution in 2012, friction between the Islamists and the Cyrenaican federalists intensified. The Brotherhood and its associated Justice and Development Party had the most formidable nationwide organizational base. Brotherhood sympathizers sought an electoral system based on country-wide party lists. More secular-oriented and tribal factions favored an individual constituency system that would allow them to demonstrate strength in specific districts.[65] Federalists in the east were doubly concerned that the electoral system would necessarily favor Tripolitania, which alone had some two-thirds of Libya's population. In December 2011 and January 2012 anti-TNC protests erupted in the east. In early January a series of public meetings was held in Benghazi to try to address eastern grievances. Importantly, the Brotherhood, with its own constituencies in Benghazi and Derna, seemed to share these concerns. On January 9 a meeting at the Benghazi University Law Faculty offered the clearest demands for regional autonomy. The TNC offered palliatives, like

designating Benghazi as Libya's "economic capital" and dispersing key administrative functions in the east, but to no avail. On January 20 federalist factions
ransacked the TNC headquarters in Benghazi.[66]

The coastal cities became cultural, economic, and military battlefronts.
Islamists held rallies and parades in Derna and Benghazi intended to demonstrate their strength and impress their version of Islamic law on the population.
Women without hair coverings were harassed, beauty parlors shut down. Shrines
and mosques became loci of conflict. In Libya's traditional piety, shrines were
treated as objects of veneration. Puritanical Salafi Islamists, in contrast, regarded
them as idolatrous. In January 2012 the Sidi Obeid shrine in Benghazi was attacked. In March the tomb of al-Mahdi al-Senussi near Kufra was desecrated.
Particularly in Cyrenaica, where tensions between Islamists and tribal factions
were already high, these attacks emphasized the sectarian dimensions of the conflict, pitting Salafi Islamists against traditionalist Muslims.[67] Islamist militias
began to operate as a kind of mafia. They took control of smuggling activities and
providing protection to hospitals and other key public installations. On March
2, 2012, ASMB fighters in Derna allegedly assassinated Muhammed al-Hasi, a
former Libyan army colonel who had been named chief of internal security in the
city. Within months of the assassination, though, the ASMB had been effectively
deputized as a state-sponsored militia force in the city.

Civil society organizations, more moderate Islamist factions, and especially
the tribes countered the radical sway in the cities. Outside actors, such as the
Muslim Brotherhood and former LIFG members, tried to mediate disputes and
dampen the ardor of the more aggressive Islamists. Local residents, intellectuals,
and academics held anti-Islamist demonstrations. The Shalawiya, al-Hasi's tribe,
temporarily drove the ASMB from Derna. Tribal leaders later agreed to try collectively to prevent youth from joining the radical Islamists. Those who did join
these groups were deemed to have forsaken their tribe, effectively leaving them
outside the traditional system of tribal retribution and blood money.[68]

On March 6, 2012, just four days after the assassination in Derna, some three
thousand notables convened in Benghazi for the Congress of the Inhabitants of
the Cyrenaica Region (*Muatamar as-Sukan Iqlim Barqa*). The Congress unilaterally proclaimed Cyrenaica to be a federal state within Libya and announced the
formation of a Cyrenaica Transitional Council (*Majlis Intiqali Barqawi*, CTC).
Delegates raised the Senussi flag of Cyrenaica, black with the white crescent and
star, and revived the 1949 Barqa national anthem, which made explicit reference
to Idris.[69] Ahmed al-Zubayr al-Senussi, the septuagenarian great-nephew of the
king, was named the figurehead leader of the CTC. Senussi's election had symbolic significance. Beside his dynastic lineage, he was a longtime political prisoner under Qaddafi and a member of the TNC. Descendants of Omar al-
Mukhtar also attended, as did a number of other leading intellectuals and army

officers. The real power behind the CTC, though, was the leaders of the aristocratic Green Mountain tribes, particularly the Awaghir, Obaidat, Hasa, Dirsa,
and Marasha. The CTC repeated the demand that the original 1951 constitution
be the basis for future constitutional revisions. It established a new Army of
Cyrenaica. Still, the exact meaning of federalism remained ambiguous. The conference concluded with a statement affirming Libya "as a unified and sovereign
state," yet the implications of this meeting suggested otherwise.[70]

The March conference alienated many Libyans. The mufti of Libya denounced federalism. Anti-federalist demonstrations erupted in Tripoli. Tunisia
and Egypt both voiced their support for a unified Libya. Some of the strongest
opposition to federalism appeared in the eastern cities, where Islamist factions
clashed with federalist demonstrators. Indicatively, the revolutionary councils of
Benghazi and Derna refused to endorse the CTC. Major youth and civil society
organizations also criticized the federalist movement, which seemed a regres-
sion to anachronistic, tribal values.[71] Beyond the rural-urban divide, though, at
least some of the eastern tribes appeared uninterested in the federalist project.
The aristocratic Baraasi continued to back the TNC. Client tribes like the
Zuwaya did not wish to fall under the domination of the aristocratic confederations. Moreover, the tribes of the oil crescent region from Ajdabiya to Sirte
feared that federalism would essentially substitute domination by Tripoli with
rule from Benghazi. They instead favored the creation of some dozen autonomous provinces (akin to the 1963 administrative boundaries created by King
Idris).[72] In a televised address, TNC president Mustafa Abd al-Jalil (himself a
Baraasi scion) hailed the easterners as "heroes [who] led the struggle in the past
and are leading the struggle now." Still, the federalists' unilateral move
"threaten[ed] national unity." Abd al-Jalil entreated Libyans to "close ranks
around the TNC which enjoys international legitimacy."[73] He ominously added,
"We are not prepared to divide Libya. They should know that there are infiltrators and remnants of Gaddafi's regime trying to exploit them now and we are
ready to deter them, even with force."[74]

In fact, the TNC had no capacity to enforce its writ, regardless of its touted
international legitimacy—and Abd al-Jalil knew it. Behind closed doors he considered calling a vote of no confidence in the interim government of Abd al-
Rahman al-Keib, which seemed unable to deal with the federalist challenge.[75]
The TNC backpedaled to appease federalist demands. First it separated the legislative power of the GNC from the constitutional committee and changed the
formula for the allocation of seats in the GNC. Then it agreed that approval of
the constitution would require a two-thirds vote in the GNC. The CTC rejected
these moves. In April the two-hundred-person Cyrenaica governing council,
ostensibly the regional parliament, convened at Bayda. Finally, the TNC announced the constitutional committee itself would allocate twenty seats each for

Tripolitania, Cyrenaica, and the Fezzan, effectively returning to the formula of 1951.[76]

Despite these concessions, the federalist factions and the CTC seemed badly unprepared for the July 2012 elections. Yet the federalists never put forward a positive formula or clear agenda. Some vowed to boycott them. In the weeks before the vote, federalist groups stormed the electoral commission in Benghazi, spoiled ballot boxes, and tried again to block Libya's main east-west highway. Voters seemed confused about what federalism meant. Many equated federalism with primitive tribalism.[77] Despite the boycott, voters in the east appeared equally enthusiastic for the election as in the rest of the country, with turnout above 60 percent.[78]

Instead of granting the new Libyan government popular legitimacy, the inauguration of GNC deepened the dilemmas of a Libyan state that was internationally recognized but functionally moribund. Islamists in the GNC pushed for a strict lustration law against Qaddafi regime officials, which would have effectively sidelined army officers, diplomats, judges, and tribal leaders who had served in government positions. As the parliamentarians bickered in Tripoli, armed actors across the country gained more power. Various factions within the GNC retained their private or party-based militias. Revolutionary committees and fighters refused to stand down. The international community's efforts to bring former fighters overseas for training and integration into a new national army failed. With no army to join, they simply took their training back to their original militias or started new fighting organizations.[79] Car bombings and assassinations of public officials continued. Attacks on international and diplomatic targets escalated, most infamously against the US consulate in Benghazi on September 11, 2012, likely carried out by Ansar al-Sharia.[80] Sufi shrines, one of the core elements of Cyrenaica's religious practices, came under increasing attack, with the Libyan state appearing unable or unwilling to defend.[81]

Beside the dominance of religious symbols, control over oil had both symbolic and fiscal ramifications. During the initial phases of the uprising in February 2011, one of the sheikhs of the Zuwaya tribe threatened to cut off oil pipelines in his region if Qaddafi's security forces continued to attack protesters. The TNC tried to co-opt revolutionary militias by assigning them to paramilitaries like the Petroleum Facilities Guard (PFG). Yet these forces operated more or less as free agents, without effective oversight from central authorities. Throughout 2012 and 2013 PFG units across the country seized oil fields, pipelines, and other installations in an effort to blackmail the central government or plunder the resources themselves. Ibrahim Jadhran, PFG commander for the oil crescent region, seized the key export hubs of Sidra, Ras Lanuf, Zuwetina, and Brega in July 2013. Born in 1981 and hailing from Ajdabiya and the Magharba tribe, Jadhran and his brothers had been members of LIFG and spent time in the notorious Abu Salim prison. During the 2011 uprising, Jadhran led a revolutionary militia in Ajdabiya. He claimed that commandeering the ports was part of a campaign against a corrupt government that squandered Libya's wealth.

> We halted oil exports after we discovered that it was the only way to stop the Government's exploitation, their stealing of oil revenues to fund their militias.... If that is treason, then it is an honor.... Our initiative is the result of the repeated failures of the state Government in Libya. I hope it will inspire other regions to take the same steps as us.[82]

But Jadhran went further, asserting that the revenue from oil sales rightfully belonged to the Cyrenaica region based on the 1951 constitution. Jadhran described his action as "declar[ing] our independence financially.... We need to be free to create our own administration and to be in charge of our own budgets. Autonomy is the only way to get our proper rights and cast off this oppression."[83] Jadhran announced the formation of a new federalist entity, the Cyrenaica Political Bureau (*Maktab Siyasi Barqa*, CPB). He tapped Abd ar-Rabbo al-Baraasi, an air force officer, to lead this self-styled Cyrenaican government in Bayda. Najib Sulayman al-Hasi was placed in command of the Cyrenaica Defense Forces, a twenty-thousand-man army, presumably subsuming the estimated seventeen thousand PFG units under Jadhran's command in Brega, plus a few thousand more tribal fighters.[84]

Jadhran's emergence illustrated a stark generational gap within the federalist movement. Unlike Abu Bakr Buera or Ahmed al-Zubayr al-Senussi, Jadhran had no experience under the monarchy. He was not part of the old Cyrenaican tribal aristocracy that had championed federalism as the return to a bygone era. His personal experiences were indelibly shaped by the Qaddafi era. While Jadhran militated toward federalism, one of his brothers remained part of LIFG and came to command an Islamist militia in Benghazi. Al-Zubayr al-Senussi, titular head of the CTC, disavowed Jadhran and the CPB. Elders in Jadhran's own Magharba tribe were divided and uncertain about the CPB.[85] Militias in Tobruk cooperated with Jadhran's embargo and closed off the terminals in the east. Still, Tobruk's local leaders preferred to operate as an independent city-state under the umbrella of the Libyan National Forces Alliance rather than the nascent CPB.[86] In November the CPB announced the formation of its own oil company and solicited foreign tenders. It emphasized that it intended only to retain Cyrenaica's share of the revenue and set aside Tripolitania's and the Fezzan's.[87] Both the Libyan government and the international community warned that oil sold by the CPB would be regarded as contraband. Rumors swirled about shady deals with American, Russian, and Israeli buyers. Jadhran hired lobbyists to try to gain favor with the United States and Russia.[88]

The closure of the oil ports cost Libya an estimated $30 billion, precipitating a fiscal and existential crisis of the state. Prime Minister Ali Zeidan threatened to blockade and bomb the ports. He urged citizens to march on Sidra "to reclaim their right to the country's wealth." Other GNC figures considered dispatching their own militias against Jadhran. A military response, though, risked further alienating the east. Instead, GNC leaders tried to turn to the Magharba tribal elders for mediation and offered Jadhran bribes. Ultimately, Zeidan had to beg the international community for help. In March 2014 US naval forces intercepted a North Korean–flagged but likely Emirati-owned tanker carrying 230,000 barrels of crude sailing from Sidra.[89] The UN Security Council unanimously passed a resolution banning the sale of Libyan oil outside government channels and authorizing outside powers to seize suspected smugglers.[90] By June, Jadhran agreed to reopen the ports in exchange for payment of PFG salaries by the Libya Central Bank, annulment of arrest warrants, and a promise to relocate the national oil company headquarters to the Gulf of Sirte.[91] To some, Jadhran and the CPB's gambit illustrated the cynical nature of the federalist movement. Jadhran appeared a political opportunist at best, a criminal extortionist at worst. Yet his claims to the oil wealth in the name of Cyrenaica underscored the hardening of eastern identity. Easterners began to speak of themselves as suffering under the occupation of Tripolitanians. Osama Buera, the son of Abu Bakr, told al-Jazeera that "the inhabitants of Cyrenaica have a unique and common identity. Cyrenaica has always been an independent Emirate. . . . We want political recognition nationally and internationally. This has already begun with support from Russia and certain U.S. politicians."[92] Zeidan lost the prime ministry over the PFG fiasco. The federalist movement demonstrated that it could thwart the central government but not the power of the international community.

## "Even If We Have to Partition the Country": The Second Civil War

Though they increasingly sought to separate their fate from that of the rest of Libya, the federalists had no choice but to treat with many factions from throughout the country, particularly during the Second Libyan Civil War in 2014–15. The conflict began in February 2014 when General Khalifa Haftar demanded the dissolution of the GNC, which had failed to meet allotted deadlines for constitutional revision. Haftar hailed from Ajdabiya and the Farjani tribe, which is centered west of the city and spans across coastal Tripolitania and Cyrenaica. He participated in the 1969 Free Officers coup and was captured while commanding Libyan troops in the war in Chad. Fearing a purge from Qaddafi, Haftar turned to the United States and worked with a CIA-backed anti-Qaddafi cabal.

He returned to Libya with the revolution. Serving as a subordinate to Younis, he repeatedly tried to set up a parallel chain of command in the Libyan National Army (LNA). With the transitional regime in disarray, Haftar began to build alliances across the country. He forged alliances with the Zintan Brigades, a revolutionary militia that opposed the GNC and the Brotherhood in the south. Also in the south, he built ties with the Zuwayas as they fought against African Tebu for control over Kufra. Haftar's self-described Operation Dignity intended to crush the Islamists and to compel the dissolution of the GNC, which he accused of supporting terrorism. Arraying against Haftar was the Libya Dawn alliance, comprising the Misratan merchant elites that backed the rump GNC, the Brotherhood, some Berber leaders, and various local Islamist militias.

The federalists were natural allies of Haftar and the Dignity campaign. They shared the same enemies: the GNC, the Brotherhood, and the Misratans. There was an increasingly nativist sentiment among easterners, emphasizing their "pure" Arab descent (at least those from the aristocratic tribes). It became common to demean Misratans and others as "westerners" (*ghuraba*), as descendants of Turks and Andalusians, and furthermore to stereotype them as fundamentalists. Even those who had resided in Benghazi and other parts of the east for generations were suspect.[93]

Yet in supporting Haftar, the federalist movement allowed its agenda for Cyrenaica's autonomy to be subordinated to Haftar's grander ambitions for transforming Libya. Haftar billed himself as Libya's military savior, defending its unity, defeating the jihadis, and enforcing order. Haftar evinced little sympathy for the federalist program. Moreover, the federalists connected their goals of gaining control over Cyrenaica into a wider campaign extending to Tripoli, the Nafusa Mountains, Kufra, and the Fezzan.

While the international community had united to confront Qaddafi and block Jadhran, it was divided over Haftar's gambit. The United States and European powers declared Haftar a renegade but remained concerned about the power of jihadi factions in the region. Qatar and Turkey supported the Dawn faction. Saudi Arabia, the UAE, and Egypt backed Dignity, forming a regional front against the Muslim Brotherhood and its associates. Egyptian support helped tie Haftar and the federalists together. The nearly concomitant Egyptian and Libyan revolutions in 2011 opened the already porous border to smuggling, human trafficking, and weapons flows. Egypt's military and security officials made early contact with Cyrenaican tribes, providing weapons and support as they fought against Ansar al-Sharia and other jihadi groups. In January 2012 Field Marshal Mohammed Hussein Tantawi, head of the Egyptian Supreme Council of the Armed Forces, visited the TNC in Tripoli. The ouster of President Mohammed Morsi and the suppression of the Egyptian Brotherhood in 2013 made this support more overt. Cairo hosted a series of meetings aimed at reconciliation among

Libyan tribes.[94] The Egyptians tried to place their engagement in Libya as part of a wider international engagement. Libya remained weak and vulnerable to Islamist infiltration. Haftar directly appealed to the new Egyptian strongman, General Abdel Fattah el-Sisi. Sisi described Operation Dignity and the LNA as keys to stability in Libya and deepened Egypt's commitment of money and ma-térial, despite a UN arms embargo.[95]

The parliamentary election of May 2014 opened up opportunities for the separatists at further cost to Libya's unity. The election had scant turnout and rampant violence. Eighteen of the two hundred parliamentary seats in the new House of Representatives (HoR) could not be filled because of boycotts and security problems during the voting. Nevertheless, the United States and the international community accepted the results as legitimate. The National Forces Alliance, which backed Haftar, emerged as the largest parliamentary block. Abu Bakr Buera and fifteen others from the Federalist Union Party won seats. For the first time, the federalist movement had a legislative voice. At the same time, though, they were put in a position requiring negotiation and compromise with those who opposed devolution.[96] The Muslim Brotherhood and the Misratan factions declared the HoR to be tainted. They boycotted the new session and instead reconvened the GNC. By August the Libya Dawn forces had encircled the HoR, forcing 150 of the 200 deputies to flee to Tobruk, under the protection of Haftar's forces and the Egyptian military.

The relocation of the HoR and the government of Prime Minister Abdullah Thinni to the east represented a further boon to the separatist trend and under-scored the multiple claimants to sovereignty within Libya. Thinni and the HoR were the internationally recognized government of Libya, but the GNC in Tripoli and the Libya Dawn militias effectively controlled the capital and key state institutions like the central bank and the national oil company. Now it was Buera's turn to accuse the GNC of "working for the break-up of Libya."[97] The GNC retorted that the HoR government represented a counterrevolutionary push and was laden with Qaddafi regime holdovers. In November the Supreme Court, still operating in Tripoli, issued a ruling nullifying the May 2014 elections. Even those who supported Haftar saw the ruling as undercutting the HoR's legal standing. Defying the Supreme Court would only worsen Libya's divisions. The federalists, though, did not share these compunctions. In fact, deepening divisions worked to their benefit. Abu Bakr Buera stated, "We will not bow to the court's ruling, even if we have to partition the country."[98] Ultimately, the national oil company and central bank were among the few national-level institutions that endured during the HoR-GNC fissure. Local officials oversaw day-to-day operations in the oil fields and tenders in the ports. Relying heavily on oil sale revenues, the central bank continued to pay salaries for government employees (including the PFG) and provide a modest food subsidy across the country.[99]

Yet the federalists backed attempts to launch a new national oil company under HoR control. Salem Jadhran, mayor of Ajdabiya and brother of Ibrahim, told an interviewer that "it is essential that the east be able to access [national oil company] revenues." Some saw this as risking the breakup of the Libyan state. Ultimately, the United States tried to quash the possibility of a separate bank.[100] The HoR moved forward instead to create a separate branch of the national oil company and alternative accounts in the UAE to keep foreign reserves out of Tripoli's hands.[101]

The diplomatic contestation over financial infrastructure paralleled military confrontations over physical infrastructure. In December 2014 Jadhran's PFG faced new assaults from the Libyan Dawn forces in the oil crescent.[102] Haftar launched a multipronged offensive against Islamist militias in Benghazi and Derna. In October 2014 the Youth Shura Council of Derna declared allegiance to the Islamic State and claimed Derna as the seat of the Islamic State in Cyrenaica. The ASMB and other Islamist factions assembled in the Mujahideen Shura Council, aligning with the GNC and Dawn against both Haftar and the IS-affiliated group. In Benghazi, Ansar al-Sharia and other pro-Tripoli Islamist factions ruled the city under the umbrella of the Islamist brigades. Haftar's promise of victory in a matter of months never came true. Haftar's combined aerial, naval, and ground assault pulverized large swaths of the city, creating a humanitarian catastrophe. IS forces in Derna collapsed within a few months, with many of its fighters fleeing to new colonies in the oil crescent region. Still, LNA forces were unable to dislodge the Mujahideen Shura Council. Benghazi was an even larger, and bloodier, prize. By the fall of 2016 Haftar had pushed the Ansar al-Sharia and the other Islamists from most of the city, and by March 2017 was clearing out the last pockets of resistance. Human rights observers accused the LNA and its allies of torture, summary executions, and violations of corpses. An estimated twenty thousand people fled the city for GNC-controlled areas. This reinforced the perception that this was part of an effort to rid Cyrenaica of westerners and recast the federalist struggle into an ethnic conflict.[103]

Beginning in the second half of 2015, the international community began a new initiative for reconciliation and reunification between Tripoli and Tobruk, aiming to create a new Government of National Accord (GNA). Haftar initially seemed to support the reconciliation process but walked away when it became apparent that the GNA would not appoint him commander in chief and might even seek to dismantle the LNA. The prospect of national reconciliation, though, strained the web of alliances surrounding Haftar.[104] Even as he leaned on Jadhran's PFG to combat Libya Dawn in the oil crescent, Haftar had cultivated ties to the Zuwaya, traditional rivals to Jadhran's Magharba tribe.[105] Anticipating a new unity government, Jadhran tried to re-establish political ties to Tripoli and break from Haftar's domination. This put Jadhran's PFG in a two-front battle, to

the west against IS-affiliated militias and to the east against the LNA. The fighting damaged what remained of the region's oil installations. By January 2016
Ajdabiya had become a ghost city, with Jadhran buffeted on both sides and clinging to a handful of neighborhoods and key installations.[106] Ultimately, Jadhran
signed an accord with the GNA and then fled to Tripoli. The PFG collapsed and
the LNA then marched on Sirte, claiming the oil as its spoils.

Jadhran's falling-out with Haftar was part of a wider dispute over control
within Operation Dignity and his relationship with the eastern tribes in general.
In November 2015 Haftar charged Colonel Faraj al-Baraasi, commander of the
LNA's Green Mountain Defense Zone, with insubordination and moved to have
him removed from the field. Haftar's heavy-handed treatment of Baraasi and
the tribal forces incited considerable resistance. Baraasi tribesmen stormed the
Dignity headquarters, and the HoR insisted on Baraasi's reinstatement.[107] Facing
continual harassment, Baraasi and several other commanders associated with
the tribes later quit the LNA.[108] Facing tensions with the tribes, Haftar turned to
anti-Brotherhood Salafi groups.[109] He also redoubled his reliance on Egypt and
especially Russia, which sent military equipment and trainers.

Civilian politicians in the HoR had a different calculation. Some deputies
quit Tobruk after it became clear that they could not effectively represent their
constituents or govern the country. Yet the remaining HoR members followed
Haftar's lead, refusing to endorse the new government. The HoR veto effectively
left the entire GNA structure in legal limbo, although the United States and
European powers insisted that the GNA remained legitimate. Abu Bakr Buera
further sought to make support for the GNA conditional on acceptance of the
federalist formula. If the GNA failed to meet the HoR's demands, Buera vowed,
he would continue efforts to separate Cyrenaica.[110] This reinserted the federalist
issue into the international agenda for Libya.

## Conclusion

At the end of Hisham Matar's novel *In the Country of Men*, a Libyan exile who has
seen his family destroyed by the Qaddafi regime and has been deemed an
"evader" of military service, asks, "Why does our country long for us so savagely?
What could we possibly give her that she hasn't already taken?"[111] Libyans have
been ill served by their state, and, indeed, by the entire apparatus of statehood,
sovereignty, and governance bequeathed to them in the twentieth century.[112] To
many, Libya's modern history appears a continual backsliding, a surrender to the
primordial pull of tribal and ethno-sectarian affiliation. Cast in this light, the uprisings of 2011 and subsequent disarray seem but the latest reversion to pre-
modern forms of social forces.[113]

The collapse of the Libyan state allowed tribes, clans, and armed militias to assert new prerogatives for autonomy and power across the Libyan territory. But Libyans did not make claims on the international community in the name of such primitive and anachronistic social entities. On the contrary, they construed themselves as interim governments, parliaments, political parties, civil society organizations, and movements of national liberation. Their actions derived from the norms and institutions generated from Wilsonianism, when the possibilities for the realignment of statehood became so tantalizing.

Rather than underscore the artificiality of Libya's modern state institutions, these moves emphasized the way modern notions of national rights and self-determination inspire the contemporary struggle for power. In the Nafusa Mountains, Libya's Amazigh population demanded constitutional guarantees of their cultural and political status consonant with ideals of self-determination and their status as indigenous inhabitants.[114] In shantytowns of Kufra, the Tebu similarly adopted the language of national and human rights and reached out to the TNC to try to regularize their status as Libyan citizens and ask the international community to provide peacekeepers to ensure a fair election in 2012.[115] The revolutionary battalions of Misrata drew strength from preexisting kinship ties and built quasi-familial bonds in battle against the regime. Yet their struggle was animated by the memory of Sewehli, the Tripolitanian Republic, and the anti-colonial struggle after World War I.[116] Similarly, Tuaregs in the Fezzan seek a federalist solution to assure their citizenship and integration in Libya.[117] Even the medievalism of the short-lived Islamic State in Derna owed a great deal to the modern intellectual trend of Salafism. Each of these groups, as Matteo Capasso and Igor Cherstich point out, invented ways of belonging in a "new'" Libya.[118] They embedded their current claims within Libya's trajectory from the twentieth century forward.

The case of Cyrenaica is unique in consolidating the functional and symbolic apparatus for an alternative statehood. The federalist movement articulated a distinctive collective identity rooted in the history of Senussi Cyrenaica. Yet it did not seek a restitution of the Senussi lodges or a resumption of the spiritual authority of the order. Though the eastern tribes were clearly the driving force behind federalism, tribalism alone was insufficient for gaining political power. On the contrary. They mobilized tribal relationships to set up modern political structures such as executive committees, legislative bodies, and military organs. They reached out to the international community. They appropriated oil, the key source of economic and political capital, and stand to control much of Libya's water. In short, they began to build a state out of the wreckage of what was once Libya.

The effort to establish a monopoly over the use of force within Cyrenaica was far from certain. The separatist movement was divided by personalities, generational differences, tribal affiliations, and political programs. These differences overlay conflicts over the distribution of oil rents, water, and land rights. The federalist movement also faced rivals within its own aspiring territorial boundaries. The first were the Islamist groups that continue to hold sway in Derna and threaten Benghazi and the oil crescent. These regions were integral to Cyrenaica, but they traditionally thwarted assertions of tribal hegemony from the interior. Like the federalists, the Islamists claimed a mandate derived from the struggle against Italian imperialism and against Qaddafi's tyranny. They offered a vision for an Islamic Libya that is no less rooted in Libyan history and no less modern.[119]

The second major challenger was Haftar. Haftar's relationship with the federalists was always a marriage of convenience. Like his primary international sponsor, Sisi in Egypt, Haftar aimed to defeat the Islamists and re-unify a country marred by internal conflict. Yet Haftar's trajectory is reminiscent of Chiang Kai-shek's fight against the Communist takeover of China. Haftar campaigned to redeem his country from ideological enemies but gradually became more isolated politically and geographically. Both the federalists and Haftar insisted that they were defending a global order from radical Islamic terrorists. Yet the United States and many European powers deemed Haftar as the greater danger to world order. For the separatists, Operation Dignity was a vehicle to help solidify Cyrenaica as a functioning de facto state. But Haftar was also a liability in the effort to gain de jure recognition of Cyrenaica's claims to self-determination and autonomy. As long as the federalists operated under Haftar's shadow, legal endorsement from the international community or the central Libyan government was nearly impossible.

For their part, the federalists in Cyrenaica disavowed any intent to break Libya apart. But under circumstances where the state demonstrably collapsed and outside actors overtly intervened in internal politics, unilateral pushes for devolution naturally led toward secession. If Cyrenaica was deemed essential for global security, then the international community might be more willing to allow its separation. The more squalid and squabbling the rump of Libya appeared, the more valuable—and viable—Cyrenaica became.

# 4

# Southern Yemen

Aden, May 4, 2017

*General Aidarous Zubaidi was no longer governor of Aden and Lahj, at least not officially. President Abdu Rabbu Mansour Hadi had fired Zubaidi a week earlier, upbraiding him as a rebel and foreign agent. But Zubaidi could assume many different personas, appearing variously as a tribal chieftain, statesman, and military officer in murals and placards and in the vast labyrinths of social media. His fighters pasted pictures of their gray-haired, goateed commander to their rifles.[1] Most importantly, Zubaidi was a son of the south (ibn al-janub) and the presumptive leader of the Southern Movement (SM).*

*Zubaidi was born in 1967, the year of South Yemen's independence, and grew up under the People's Democratic Republic of Yemen (PDRY), the only Marxist state in the Arab world. In its first decade, South Yemen took enormous leaps forward in public health and education, economic development, and women's equality. As a junior military officer, Zubaidi had watched the country succumb to bloody internecine conflict and economic stagnation. By 1990 unification with the Yemen Arab Republic, the south's fraternal rival to the north, seemed the only hope. Optimism, though, quickly yielded to disappointment. The regime of President Ali Abdullah Saleh seemed to treat the merger more as a hostile takeover than a union of equals. Tensions were always high and sometimes violent. In April 1994 Zubaidi joined a faction of former southern soldiers and politicians seeking to break away. Northern troops overran them, sacked Aden, and dismantled the remaining political and administrative institutions of the southern republic. Rage against what many labeled the northern occupation (ihtilal) endured into the next decade.*

*In 2011, in the midst of massive nationwide demonstrations, the Southern Movement came to a tactical alliance with Hadi in their common bid to oust Saleh. Hadi himself had defected from the PDRY in 1986 and served as Saleh's vice president and enforcer. He assumed the presidency when Saleh reluctantly stepped down in 2012. The new president's alliance with the SM, though, did little to stem the hemorrhage of state power. In 2012 and 2013 an al-Qaeda affiliated jihadist group seized control over major ports and other cities in the south. In 2014 Houthi militants from the far north and military units loyal to Saleh seized Sana'a and marched southward. The United States and the rest of the international community condemned Saleh, the Houthis, and their Iranian backers. They insisted that Yemen's unity be preserved and that Hadi's was Yemen's only legitimate government. Hadi and his ministers took up accommodations in the plush parlors of Riyadh. Saudi Arabia and the United Arab Emirates mobilized militarily. Hadi had little choice but to grant the separatists government sinecures, turning them into unlikely agents of the central government. The old PDRY flag, with its striking blue chevron, flew openly on government buildings as a rebuke to the pretension of national unity. It was largely SM forces that fought and repelled the Houthi invasion and the al-Qaeda jihadists. SM administrators toiled to keep electricity going in Aden during the blistering summer heat. SM officials worked with international humanitarian agencies to avert a cholera epidemic that scourged the war-torn country.[2] Ignoring directives from Hadi's cabinet, Zubaidi and his allies cultivated direct ties to the UAE, which provided generators, humanitarian aid, and military training and support. Among the wreckage of Yemen, even the fractious SM posed an intolerable challenge to Hadi's precarious authority. On April 27 Hadi announced that Zubaidi and several SM-associated ministers would be discharged for violating Yemen's sovereignty.*

*Zubaidi now took the risky move of trying to call the president's bluff. The central government, Zubaidi wagered, had no ability to enforce its writ in Aden, regardless of its legal standing. Thousands answered the SM's call for multi-day protests at Freedom Square in Aden's Khormaksar district. They carried PDRY flags, and banners, and photos of Zubaidi and exiled PDRY leaders. They chanted slogans born from the anticolonial struggle of the mid-1960s and the more recent protests against northern domination. The location of the protests itself was highly evocative of the anticolonial era and the south's subsequent disappointments. Astride the neck of the Aden isthmus, Khormaksar was not Aden's most historical or scenic quarter. The British had first developed the area to serve as a forward base for the Royal Air Force, intending it as the last reaches of a dwindling overseas empire. The revolution against British colonialism was a crystallizing moment in the south's collective memory. At the same time, the British had helped transform Aden into one of the world's most important ports and installed the first kernels of modern state infrastructure. Khormaksar still contained the city's main hospital, university, and airport and most of its foreign diplomatic missions. Yet the surfeit of vacant buildings and factories and decaying port facilities were reminders of the south's lost glory.[3] Aden was neither a bustling imperial entrepôt nor the capital of a sovereign and progressive state. Instead, a quarter century of Yemeni unity had reduced it to a backwater region of a basket-case country.*

*Zubaidi issued the Aden Historic Declaration in the name of Allah, as in traditional Islamic rhetoric, but also in the name of the people of South Arabia (al-janub al-'arabi), whose suffering and struggle justified their bid for independence. Pointedly, the word "Yemen" was never used. The declaration noted its coincidence with the anniversary of the 1994 civil war, a date marking the definitive end of the south as a political entity, and specified the creation of a new political body, headed by Zubaidi, to begin the transition to statehood. Article 3 declared sanguinely:*

> The millions of Southerners marching reiterate that the South, as a nation and an identity, now and in the future, is for all Southerners by all Southerners. The South after May 4th, 2017, is not like the South before that date, and is based on Southern national partnership and consensus.[4]

*In Article 4, the declaration pivoted toward a global audience. The SM's partnership with Saudi Arabia and the UAE to fight the Houthis and jihadis, it said, were "sealed in blood and continuing sacrifice." The south would uphold commitments to "international law, the United Nations Charter, and the Universal Declaration of Human Rights." Zubaidi hoped to convince the international community that reinstating the independence of the south would benefit not just its own inhabitants but the entire world. Zubaidi and the south had nothing left to do but wait for a reply.*

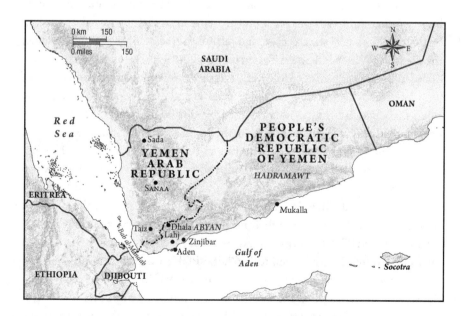

# Introduction

Separatism in southern Yemen did not begin with the 2011 uprising. Indeed, efforts to assert autonomy for the south date back to the civil war of 1994 and appeared again in 2007, with the emergence of the Southern Movement (al-Hirak al-Janubi), a loose coalition of politicians, former military officers, tribal sheikhs, Islamists, and civic leaders. The SM began with peaceful demonstrations. It grew more radical as it faced violent repression from the government of President Ali Abdullah Saleh. Still, the southern issue was not a major driver in the protests of February 2011 or the intra-regime turmoil that brought Saleh down and paralyzed the already feeble Yemeni state. In the south, as in the rest of Yemen, local leaders seized control over critical territory and institutions. Although the Yemeni political elite and outside patrons often tried to insert themselves into these contests, the crucial tasks of providing security, healthcare, education, and other essential services became more localized in the course of revolution and civil war. From 2012 onward, the SM backed the new regime of Abdu Rabbu Mansour Hadi in his struggle against Saleh, but the relationship between the separatists and Hadi's so-called legitimate government remained tentative and fraught. Moreover, internal disagreements about the ultimate goals of resistance hampered the separatists' cohesion and their ability to capitalize on political opportunities.

The demand for separation was at once strange and familiar. Strange, because Yemen is hardly a new state. Centralized rule in southern Arabia extends back at least to the sixteenth century, and arguably further in medieval and pre-Islamic history. What the 1990s merger meant to Yemenis, therefore, varied depending on their region, social stature, class, and relationship to political regime. To some, the merger of North and South Yemen on May 22, 1990, seemed to rectify an artificial colonial imposition. However, as Lisa Wedeen points out, moments of unity in Yemeni history have tended to be brief and exceptional, rather than the rule.[5] The separatist campaign represented an effort to reinstate a political autonomy that had only recently been lost with the liquidation of the South Yemeni state.

More than sour grapes or opportunism motivated the SM to rebel. The separatist raised unresolved questions about the normative formulas and institutional structures that helped to create South and North Yemen and to justify unification in 1990. They also emphasized the cleavages that made the people of southern Arabia different from their neighbors. They drew on alternative political histories and the legacies of lost independence—the sultanates that had been incorporated into South Yemen in 1967, the PDRY that lasted until 1990, and the abortive Democratic Republic of Yemen of 1994. In the midst of civil war, the separatists approached the international community on moral and instrumental grounds. They argued that a revision of territories would accord with the aspirations of the southern Yemeni people and yield peace and stability for the global community.

## Imperial Contestation and Rebel State Building

Geology and topography render Yemen a lattice of microclimates and isolated political communities. The Sarawat Mountains run like a spine parallel to the Red Sea, emerge from the immense tectonic friction between the Arabian and African plates. At elevations above 7,000 feet (2,100 meters), the northern highlands around Sana'a historically provided succor for heterodox Shi'i sects like the Zaydis, devotees of the fifth Imam. The mountains buffet the Tihama, a narrow coastal strip where orthodox Sunnis of the Shafi'i school predominate. Tapering southward and inland, the mountains form a midland plateau around Taiz and a series of basins leading to the Empty Quarter. Pivoting west along the Arabian Sea coast, the Jol peninsula encompasses outcroppings and valleys, such as the natural harbors of Aden and Mukalla and the interior wadis of the Hadramawt region. The monsoon rains feed a significant agricultural surplus and nourish inland oasis cities and trading networks that crisscross the Indian Ocean.[6]

But the line between north and south in Yemen is the result of a geopolitical, not geological, collision. The Ottomans first entered Yemen to block Portuguese from gaining a foothold in the Red Sea. The Zaydi highlanders, though, repeatedly challenged Ottoman rule.[7] By 1629 an alliance of Zaydi highlanders under the Qasimi dynasty and Sunni tribes took Sana'a and Taiz and began pushing toward the Arabian Sea. The Ottoman writ was confined to the Red Sea littoral. The Qasimis built a rudimentary system for taxing trade and agricultural production and established a standing army, incorporating the lowland chieftains as vassals. When the Qasimi house suffered debilitating internal conflict in the early 1700s, these local rulers were able to break away from Sana'a's hegemony.[8] The British landed in Aden in 1839, eying it as a refueling hub in the maritime passage to India. Southern Arabia was ruled by a mishmash of tribal sultans who held the Ottomans and the imamate at arm's length. British forces compelled nine local sultans to submit to treaties guaranteeing Britain's right to use the port. In response, the Ottomans tried to reassert control over the Tihama and Sana'a. Aden's importance increased with the opening of the Suez Canal.[9] The British expanded their defensive perimeter into Hadramawt, backing the Quayti dynasty in unseating the incumbent Kathiris.[10] Competition between the British and the Ottomans in Arabia risked escalating into global conflagration. The British and Ottomans agreed to a rough demarcation, with the British pledging to respect Ottoman suzerainty around Sana'a and Taiz, the Ottomans to defer to British interests around Aden.[11]

The British and the Ottomans both deemed Yemen to be a backwater but responded differently to the challenge of rule. The British concentrated on Aden, which was becoming one of the world's busiest ports. The interior was simply a buffer zone. Adopting the methods of indirect rule used in India, Britain sought to avoid entanglements and expenditures. So long as there were no disturbances of the peace, local rulers had a generally free hand in internal affairs. Interventions against the recalcitrant were swift and severe; collective punishment, the rule. The result was a mosaic of mostly feeble sultanates surviving on British subsidies.[12]

The Ottomans, in contrast, saw the potential to transform primitive, tribal Yemenis into modern citizens. The Ottomans made modest but significant investments in infrastructure and education and worked to win support from the local potentates. Still, Ottoman-Zaydi relations were always fraught. The contest was more political than theological. Zaydi and Sunni religious doctrines were largely congruent. Zaydis and Sunnis intermarried, prayed together, and made common political cause. The Zaydi imam, Muhammad bin Yahya Hamid ad-Din, aimed to regain control of Yemen and possibly even assume the caliphate. Many Sunni tribal leaders were amenable to the imam's political aspirations, though disinterested in his claims to spiritual supremacy.[13] Imam Muhammad alternated between supporting low-level insurrection and cooperating with the Ottomans. His son and successor, Imam Yahya, came to power just after the Anglo-Ottoman line of control in Yemen was conclusively set in 1904. He decried the division of what he saw as the Greater Yemen. Yet Yahya, too, worked adroitly within the Ottoman system. The more the Ottomans diverted troops to defend other parts of the empire, the more power they ceded to the imam. After the Italian invasion of Libya in 1911, the Ottomans vacated the highlands to Zaydi control. Yemen become a joint Ottoman-Zaydi condominium, with Yahya in control from Saadeh to Taiz.[14] During World War I the British tried to woo Yahya with territorial concessions. But Yahya demanded more: all of the Ottoman Yemen territories, Asir, Hadramawt, and most of the inland areas near Aden. In November 1918 the imam entered Sana'a in triumph, receiving the handover of power from the Ottoman governor.

Imam Yahya's domain is often deemed xenophobic and feudal, "Tibet on the Red Sea."[15] But Yahya tried early on to reach out to the international community. A month after taking power in Sana'a, Yahya wrote directly to President Wilson appealing for de jure recognition of Yemen's independence. His missive was never answered.[16] Many actors in eastern Arabia glommed on to the idea of self-determination and the possibilities of international recognition of statehood, including the Hashemites, the Saudis, and the Idrisi dynasty of Asir. The Idrisis incited the Sunni tribes of the Tihama to revolt against the imam, appealing for international trusteeship, if not outright independence. The imam's forces cracked down on the lowland tribes, consolidating his control on the coast.[17]

The peripatetic Charles Crane came to Sana'a in 1926 to discuss mineral rights with Yahya and sought to broker a US-Yemen treaty of friendship. Both initiatives came to naught.[18] Italy, Britain's chief Red Sea rival, was the first to establish diplomatic relations with the Mutawakkilite Kingdom of Yemen.

Yahya ruled his ramshackle kingdom through the exercise of personal power. Economic and social reforms stalled. Peasants were reduced to subsistence-level farming. Yayha pulled together an army of some eighteen thousand to carry out campaigns against tribal leaders. At the same time, he supported tribal rebellions in the British-held south, hoping for territorial adjustment. A 1934 Anglo-Yemeni treaty confirmed the boundary pending a review four decades hence, but this seemed only to suggest a temporary—and thereby flexible—frontier. During World War II, Yahya belatedly broke diplomatic ties with the Axis but still made strategic provocations against Aden, hoping to induce an outside power to intervene against the British.[19] In 1948 Yahya was assassinated by a member of the royal family. His son Ahmed became imam and king. Ahmed took a more conciliatory approach toward the lowland tribes and sought out international development aid, including the US Point Four Program. He remained committed to Greater Yemen and tried to harness the growing intellectual power of the Free Yemeni movement, which favored social reform and Yemeni unification.[20]

By the end of World War II, Britain's position in Aden and the interior stood athwart the global current of decolonization. The UN General Assembly also took up the case of Aden and the protectorate.[21] Influenced by Indonesian and Indian nationalism, the Hadrami merchant community had begun agitating against colonial rule in the 1920s. They criticized the social inequality of the region and the social, economic, political dominance of the hereditary clerical class known as the *saada* (singular: *sayyid*).[22] The rise of Arab nationalism put even more pressure on the British. In 1950 Adeni merchants introduced the classic formula of self-determination as a slogan: "Aden for the Adenese." The South Arabian League (SAL), originally called the League of the Sons of the South, pushed for a handover of power to the sultans. There was increasing discussion of north-south unity. The more militant Arab nationalists and the burgeoning industrial labor movement in Aden demanded the ouster of the British, the sultans, and the imamate.[23]

In 1962 a military clique assassinated Imam Ahmed and then moved on his son and designated successor, Muhammed Badr. On September 26, 1962, the Yemen Arab Republic (YAR) was formed and the imamate abolished. The YAR openly called on its "brothers in the South" to rise against British rule and pursue Yemen's unification. The royalists retreated into the mountain stronghold, where they received aid from Saudi Arabia and Britain and waged an insurgency against the new republic.[24]

Whitehall regarded the military bases at Aden as the prize but saw the sultanates as the key to attaining it. The contrast between the port city and the hinterlands was stark. Aden was a bustling trade hub, with a population around two hundred thousand people. The city had seen dramatic expansion in education, healthcare, industry, and infrastructure. But by the 1950s Aden was no longer a cosmopolitan, imperial entrepôt. Much of its population growth came from migration from the other sultanates and northern Yemen. Aden was thus deeply affected by the currents of Arab nationalism and the Free Yemeni movement.[25]

The protectorate zone lagged in every measure of development and good governance. Of the more than ninety-odd sultans and tribal sheikhs with whom the British had treaty relationships, most were impotent, impecunious, and retrograde. British forces intervened repeatedly in Dhala and Upper Awlaqi, where the petty despots had little control over the tribes in their territory. The Abdali sultanate of Lahj, north of Aden, posed a different kind of problem for the British. The Abdali were poised for leadership in the Western Aden Protectorate and, along with Saudi Arabia, were among the main benefactors of the SAL. They ruled some thirty-nine thousand subjects, had viable agriculture and some of the area's few paved roads. Whitehall estimated that the Abdali took in a respectable £75,000 in annual tax revenue. Yet the Abdalis' political ambitions made the British wary. In 1952 and 1958 colonial authorities conspired to depose Abdali sultans who appeared resistant to British rule. Farther east in Hadramawt, the Quayti sultanate also seemed to be viable. The Quayti territories had irrigated agriculture and the port of Mukalla. The Hadrami émigré community offered access to monetary and human capital. The Quayti built a modern fiscal and administrative system that took in £277,000 annually. The British provided political and military advising. Most importantly, in the 1950s international oil companies identified likely deposits in the region, although these territories were disputed between the Quayti and the lesser Kathiri and Mahra sultans.[26]

The British calculated that by handpicking the political elites, they could negotiate decolonization while preserving imperial interests. In 1962 they announced the creation of the Federation of South Arabia, a confederacy linking the protectorate sultans with Aden. Needing British support, the conservative sultans would check the anti-imperialist sentiments bubbling in Aden. The British touted the federation as a responsible step toward sovereignty, independence, and the fulfillment of self-determination. As a Colonial Office spokesman claimed in London, the federation was "born in response to the will of the people themselves and to common sense."[27]

Yet the federation ultimately satisfied no one. Colonially contrived elections could not offer popular legitimacy. Moreover, the British temporized as to when independence would be granted. Many Adenese nationalists refused to link their political fate to atavistic sultans. Some of the sultans, too, preferred Aden be excluded, fearing that their own polities would be infected by the city's radicalism. The British governor of Aden likened this to bringing together "modern Glasgow, say, and the 18th century highlands."[28] An American diplomat called it a shotgun wedding. The Quayti, Kathiri, and Mahra sultans, still squabbling over untapped oil deposits, remained outside the federation and considered the possibility of Hadramawt's independence.[29]

Popular opposition to the British broadened and intensified. New militant groups, like the National Liberation Front (NLF) and the Organization for the Liberation of the Occupied South (OLOS), launched an insurgency against the British and the sultans who stood to inherit South Arabia. On October 14, 1963, a date that would come to take on a revered place in national memory, a grenade was thrown at British officials at the Aden airport. At the same time, a tribal uprising erupted in the remote Radfan Mountains of Dhala. The British declared a state of emergency. Bombings, assassinations, riots, and tribal rebellions intensified steadily between 1964 and 1967. The British refused to negotiate under fire and blamed the violence on Nasserist and YAR instigation. The UN General Assembly demanded the lifting of the emergency to allow consultation as well as free and fair elections. UN envoys to shuttle between the British, the sultans, and the opposition.

The conflict turned internecine between the NLF, the OLOS, smaller nationalist factions, and the sultans. NLF factions were aligned with the left-wing Movement of Arab Nationalism, reviled in Cairo and Sana'a. The NLF initially agreed to work with the OLOS under the umbrella Front for the Liberation of Occupied South Yemen (FLOSY) but withdrew citing Egyptian interference. After the setback of the June 1967 war, though, Nasser could not maintain the same level of engagement in southern Yemen.

The NLF gained as FLOSY floundered. One by one NLF factions rolled up sultanates and the British military outposts. Junior officers of the federation-designated army defected to the NLF. Hadramawt, despite some of the most glaring socio-economic inequalities, became a laboratory for the NLF's rebel governance. A left-wing clique set out to impose price controls on basic commodities, seized petrol stations, cinemas, and trading houses, redistributed land, and set up a popular militia. In June 1967 NLF insurgents rose in Crater, Aden's key harbor district. Dhala, Lower Yafai, and Audhali fell in June and July, Lahj and Abyan in August. In September the sultans of Kathiri and Quayti fled to Saudi Arabia. The remote sultanate of Mahra and Socotra fell finally in September.[30]

The British saw little option but direct negotiations with the NLF. The NLF had refused to participate in earlier rounds of UN talks, maintaining that Yemen's fate would be decided by force, not diplomacy. But diplomacy was ultimately what settled the matter. Senior NLF leaders finally made the trip to Geneva for the negotiations. The sultans, Britain's designated protégés, were neither consulted nor invited. On November 30, 1967, the NLF delegation flew back to Aden, purposefully avoiding a stop in Egypt, to announce the formation of the People's Republic of South Yemen (PRSY).

## One Half of a Revolution

The year of 1967 was the first time that two independent states existed in southwestern Arabia. Though the YAR-PRSY border overlay the old Anglo-Ottoman frontier, it now took on a different meaning. Instead of demarcating imperial frontiers, the border represented the normative assignment of authority and legality by the international community to sovereign states. Despite the NLF's pretensions to have "won" sovereignty through a military victory, both North and South Yemen had gained entry to international society by making claims of self-determination consonant with Wilsonian principles. The international community confirmed each state's territorial integrity. Nevertheless, the desire for unification of Yemen's two "halves" (*shatrayn*) remained. In both north and south, political leaders exploited the idea of Yemen as single homeland (*watan*).[31] But the notion of Yemen's natural or inevitable conciliation belied the mutual distrust between the two regimes and their divergent political trajectories.

South Yemen faced severe economic and political challenges in its first years. The British cut off aid and closed their military bases, liquidating between fourteen thousand and twenty-five thousand jobs in Aden. Port traffic plummeted with the closure of the Suez Canal from 1967 to 1975, costing significant amounts of revenue and foreign exchange.[32] Anticipating the NLF's quick collapse, tribal sheikhs and sultans continued to challenge the new regime and retake territories they had abandoned in the midst of the revolution. The south also suffered the interference of its northern neighbor. By 1970 the northern civil war had ended with the victory of the right-wing nationalist faction, and the YAR leadership viewed the leftists—and by extension the NLF—as rivals. The YAR continued to back FLOSY and the exiled sultans and tribal leaders from the south. Even with the abolition of the imamate and the defeat of the Zaydi royalists, Sana'a still regarded itself as Yemen's natural political center. The PRSY was a temporary aberration, with less than a third the population of the YAR.[33] The YAR Consultative Council symbolically allocated seats for the yet-absent south.[34] Oman and Saudi Arabia were overtly hostile to South Yemen. The Saudis continued to support SAL raids into Hadramawt, where they also had territorial claims. The Saudi-Yemeni border would remain undefined until a 1992 treaty.[35]

Compounding these challenges was the continuing internecine strife within the NLF. In 1969 a left-wing NLF Marxist faction led by Abdul Fattah Ismail ousted the moderate Qahtan Mohammed ash-Shaabi and declared the formation of the People's Democratic Republic of Yemen. In its first communiqué, the PDRY leaders announced their role as the sole element able to "safeguard the 26 September and 14 October revolutions from conspiracies of the imperialists and reactionaries."[36] The PDRY, then, cast itself as the only revolutionary force in either north or south.[37]

The new PDRY leadership sought to push on with the socio-cultural revolution. The regime nationalized foreign assets and launched new land reform efforts. Peasants denounced their former landlords and expropriated properties in the name of the people. Many tribal chiefs and clerics fled; others were assaulted or killed.[38] The USSR and China helped fund massive increases in social welfare spending, including schooling and public health. There were similar investments in infrastructure. In 1967 South Yemen had a mere 181 miles (470 km) of paved roads, mostly around Aden. By 1983 there were 1,025 miles (1,650 km) of roads, including the backbone Aden-Mukalla highway, and spurs connecting to interior Hadramawt and Taiz in the YAR.[39]

The revolution targeted tribes and tribalism in its drive to remold the culture of the south. The tribes in the south were not as large or coherent as in the grand Bakil and Hashid confederations of the north, but a 1968 decree forbade tribal feuding and banned the bearing of arms, including the traditional curved dagger. Administrative governorates were referred to by number only, an attempt to break associations between tribal and dynastic titles and territories.[40] New laws also curtailed the chewing of *qat,* a common stimulant often blamed for Yemen's social ills. In Aden and western regions consumption was restricted to weekends; in Hadramawt it was banned completely.[41] As for religion, the regime deemed the *saada* landlords of Hadramawt and Yemen's clergy generally as counter-revolutionaries. But they did not go so far as to forbid religion. Instead, PDRY propaganda treated Islam as a kind of liberation theology under state guidance. Equality of the sexes was a key policy agenda. The regime encouraged women's education and employment and promulgated a new secular family law. Still, people were able to carry out customary religious rituals, even as the meaning of the rituals changed. Moreover, it was impossible to shut South Yemen off from the wider regional trend of Islamic revivalism. In the mid-1980s, to the consternation of PDRY officials, some female students at Aden University took the veil, for instance.[42]

The intensity of the PDRY's socio-economic transformation was a result of ideological fervor but also of administrative capacity. As the NLF evolved into the Yemen Socialist Party (YSP), South Yemen became an effective socialist party-state. South Yemen enjoyed a dual endowment: in Aden, the British civil service system, courts, police, and education system continued to operate with relative efficiency.[43] In the former sultanates, the NLF had set up courts, schools, land registries, and party militias as part of the revolutionary counter-state. Advisors from the Soviet bloc, Cuba, Yugoslavia, Albania, and China trained the military, secret police, and party militias. YSP cadres replaced tribal sheikhs and religious leaders as mediators of access to state resources, the source of influence and employment. Just as in colonial times, resistance met with repression.[44]

The YAR and PDRY meddled in each other's internal affairs, but the discourse of unity was dusted off whenever one side seemed to be faltering, often due to bloody intra-regime conflicts. Border skirmishes in 1972 led to a new round of negotiations. The southern army managed to hold its ground over most of the disputed territories. In an Arab League–sponsored peace negotiation, PDRY and YAR officials seemed to concur on the need for eventual unification. Still, the plan yielded little substance.[45]

In January 1986 South Yemen experienced a crisis so severe as to auger the demise of the state. The conflict centered on a long-standing dispute between the so-called left-wing and right-wing YSP factions. Though overtly ideological, these differences overlay regional and clan rivalries within the YSP. The right-wing faction associated with President Ali Nasir Mohammed was backed by the Dathira tribe of Abyan, as well as the Awlaqi and Awdhali tribes. The left-wing factions surrounded elder statesmen Abdul Fattah Ismail and came largely from Lahj, Dhala, and Yafai. On the morning of January 13, Ali Nasir's bodyguards opened fire as the Politburo meeting convened. Over the next twelve days between four thousand and ten thousand people were killed, including Ismail. Ali Nasir fled to Syria. Thousands of YSP officials decamped for the YAR. When the dust settled, Ali al-Beidh and other veterans of the 1967 NLF campaigns in Hadramawt came to dominate the YSP. Yet the depleted party lacked cohesion or an agenda for reform.[46]

With the PDRY limping, the prospects of unification reappeared. The first steps were in jointly developing the recently discovered oil fields in Marib and Shebwa and using Aden's refinery and port, rather than Saudi Arabia's. The balance of power tilted unmistakably northward. YAR president Ali Abdullah Saleh cultivated allies among the southern opposition in exile. Moreover, the PDRY's geopolitical footing was crumbling. Compounding the damage of the 1986 bloodletting, the Soviets were drawing down their economic and ideological support to client states.[47] South Yemen's economy was grinding to a standstill. The treasury verged on insolvency. Farmers refused to sell products at official prices, and Aden faced shortages in foodstuffs and basic commodities.[48]

After a six-month preparatory period, the unification of the YAR and PDRY into the Republic of Yemen came to fruition on May 22, 1990. Saleh and Beidh both stressed the coequality of the YAR and PDRY. They made a point of showing respect for each other's revolutionary heritage. At the proclamation ceremony in Aden, Beidh declared that the new Yemeni state would "become a forum for democracy, equality, and justice" and committed the YSP to "become a guardian force for unity." Saleh spoke of "end[ing] the separation and fragmentation that our people inherited from the era of the imam and imperialism."[49] If May 22 was marked as the birth of the modern Yemeni state, then September 26 and October 14 were equivalent moments of conception. The northern and southern legislatures and cabinets were merged into transitional bodies. Saleh was designated as president, Beidh vice president. As unification proceeded, thousands of councils and dialogue meetings took place across the country to discuss the form it should take.

Still, these symbolic gestures toward unity could not mask the cultural, institutional, and political divide between north and south. Many southerners resented what they saw as the imposition of northern "tribal" and "religious" culture and custom. Some of this was a matter of perception rather than reality. The supposedly "planned" economy of the south was heavily reliant on private capital and often corrupt, while the northern "capitalist" economy involved considerable state planning and intervention (and was no less nepotistic). Still, the rule of law was considered a singular achievement of the PDRY that the unification threatened to upend.[50] Economic liberalization seemed inevitable, but Saleh and his cronies quickly captured the privatization of state assets. There was also a marked imbalance in the way northern institutions agglomerated southern assets. The YAR riyal supplanted the PDRY dinar. Yemenia, the northern airline, absorbed the PDRY's carrier.[51] In response to this corruption, in late 1992 officials in the Aden governorate refused to remit revenues to the central government, instead retaining the funds for local use.[52]

An accompanying political liberalization challenged southern leaders in a different way. Beidh and the YSP counted on winning support from those dissatisfied with the Saleh regime in the north, particularly secularists and leftists.[53] Saleh's General People's Congress (*al-mu'atamar ash-sha'biy al-'amm*, GPC) party, in contrast, operated largely as a conveyance for his political favoritism. Alongside the GPC was the newly established Islah (Congregation of Reform). Islah drew support from the Sunni Islamists, many associated with the Yemeni branch of the Muslim Brotherhood, and from the northern tribal leaders. Islah leadership did not directly challenge Saleh and seemed to cooperate with the GPC electoral campaigns against the YSP. Yemeni Islamists had long dreamt of unseating the socialists in the south. Osama bin Laden, the son of a Hadrami émigré, hoped to organize veterans of the Afghanistan civil war to take on Aden and liberate his ancestral home. In the run-up to unification, Sheikh Abd al-Majid al-Zindani, a leading Sunni cleric in Sana'a and an Islahi ideologue, declared jihad on the "tiny group of pagans within the Communist Party of South

Yemen, who have been influenced by an imported culture and stand disgraced before the Yemeni people."[54]

Political violence escalated as elections approached. Senior YSP leaders, including Beidh's nephew and son, were targets of assassination attempts. Over one hundred YSP officials were killed. The YSP blamed Saleh for permitting (or commissioning) this campaign of terror. Beidh went into hiding, threatening to back out of the unification. In December 1992 a series of bombings struck Aden. Many blamed Tariq al-Fadhli, son of the deposed sultan of Abyan. Fadhli had a unique intersectional role in Yemeni politics as a tribal magnate, an Islamist who had joined the jihad in Afghanistan and befriended bin Laden, and a son of the south who had encouraged Yemenis to attack the "atheistic" YSP. Islah, and Saleh by extension, seemed to be protecting Fadhli.[55]

The election of April 1993 was widely lauded as a milestone of unification. "Something wonderful is happening in Yemen," gushed the New York Times.[56] Voter participation was high, and electoral observers deemed the contest relatively free and fair. The electoral system was designed to ensure the inclusion of all political voices through proportional representation in each district. Still, the YSP suffered a body blow. Of 301 seats, the GPC took 123, Islah 62, and YSP only 57. YSP had won by large margins in the southern districts. But the GPC-and-Islah coordination had blocked the YSP from gaining seats in the midlands or the north. The YSP was thus reduced to a regional party.[57] The rift between Beidh and Saleh deepened. To the YSP leadership, the election demonstrated the need for a federal system. They argued that devolution had been an implicit part of the unity scheme all along.[58] In a television interview in December 1993, Saleh appeared from Sana'a and Beidh from Aden. Beidh began by speaking of the need to build a "bigger and better" Yemeni state, "to avert national divisions" and "resist the logic of annexation." Saleh, though, accused the YSP of reneging only to avoid electoral defeat. The opportunity for federalism, he said, had passed. Such an arrangement "can only be instituted between separate countries, or parts of the same country before their unification."[59] The following day the paramount sheikh of the Hashid tribal confederation and leading Islah parliamentarian echoed this refusal.[60] At a last-ditch meeting in Amman in January 1994 Saleh and Beidh signed the Declaration of Principles and Accord (DPA), offering vague promises to depoliticize the military, limit executive authority, and devolve power to the governorates. Yet, as Fred Halliday noted, the DPA was really a declaration of divorce.[61]

On April 27, 1994, fighting erupted between armored units near Sana'a. While the immediate cause of the conflagration is unclear, pro-Saleh military units immediately moved on the south. Hadi, a former PDRY commander among the 1986 defectors, led the assault. Northern Islamists, including some veterans of the Afghan civil war, and tribal factions also mobilized, eager to settle scores with the YSP. For some, the idea of taking Aden seemed the fulfillment of the vision of Greater Yemen.[62]

The YSP, however, seemed caught off guard. Most of the Politburo still supported unity. It was only on May 21 that Beidh announced the establishment of the Democratic Republic of Yemen (DRY) on Aden radio. Beidh described the DRY as the nucleus for a democratic and united Yemen, incorporating the YSP, FLOSY, SAL, and even some Islamic leadership. The southern armies retreated to defensive positions around Aden and Mukalla, holding out hope for international recognition and humanitarian intervention.[63] Saleh denounced Beidh and the DRY as traitors and secessionists (*infisaliyun*).[64] The United States insisted on Yemen's territorial integrity and retention of the DPA, rebuffing the DRY. The UN Security Council called for a ceasefire and humanitarian relief but offered no support to southern independence. Saudi Arabia and the Gulf states were inclined to weaken Saleh by backing the DRY but ultimately followed the US and UN lead. Saleh's forces captured Aden on July 7. Islamist militias set about to impose Islamic law on the city, seizing spoils, flogging the immodest, and demolishing the venerable Sira brewery. Some seven thousand people died, including a thousand in Aden alone. Beidh and the top southern leadership fled abroad.[65] Yemenis' unity was demonstrated by force, not choice.

## "The Revolution of the Old and the Young"

In the aftermath of the 1994 war Saleh tried to bury the remnants of the PDRY. He cashiered thousands of PDRY military veterans and civil servants. Beidh and the DRY leadership were sentenced in absentia to death.[66] The PDRY's fiscal and accounting system was dismantled. The rump YSP remained with a reconstituted and pliant Politburo. Cultural cleavages between northerners and southerners persisted—and in some ways intensified—with increasing contact between north and south. Northerners were alternatively stereotyped as conniving layabouts or bumpkins. Southerners, in contrast, were citified, miscegenated, and effete. Still, as Wedeen points out, "cross-dressing"—traversing this cultural divide by switching from the traditional white robes of the north to the sarong of the south—was relatively easy and common. There was a regular flow of people and goods between the north and south.[67] The communal *qat*-chew became a truly nationwide phenomenon, a key element in Yemen's civil society. There was also a general resumption of tribal and sultanistic power. Exiled Hadrami aristocrats built ties with the Saleh regime and began investment and building projects. In 1996 the Quayti sheikh returned to Mukalla after nearly thirty years abroad.[68]

Both northern and southern Yemen were also affected by the broad cultural trend toward Islamic politics and piety during the 1980s and 1990s. Throughout the Arab world, the turn to Islam came as a rejection of autocratic politics that had failed to deliver social and economic development. Religious awakening took a wide variety of forms. In its most radical content, it favored violence. In the mid-1990s terrorists, often associated with Yemeni returnees from Afghanistan, began a series of attacks in Aden and Abyan, most famously the bombing of the USS *Cole*.[69]

The legacies of prior statehood gave complaints about corruption and repression in the south specific historical gravity. After 1994 there was nothing to stop Saleh and his cronies from buying up valuable businesses and real estate in the south. Corruption was rampant. Meanwhile, Aden's port languished.[70] While oil rents collected in Sana'a's coffers, little seemed to be reinvested in Shebwa and Hadramawt, where the oil originated. Canadian Occidental, the largest foreign oil company operating in the south, was forced to relocate its headquarters from Aden to Sana'a, where it could be more readily subject to shakedowns. Local tribes that guarded the Hadramawt oil fields were dismissed in favor of troops commanded by Saleh's maternal uncle. In 1995 and 1996 government troops fired on labor protesters in the south. Sporting events featuring northern and southern opponents turned into riots. Southerners blamed northerners for disobeying traffic rules, causing road deaths and adding to a general sense of disorder. A Sana'a university professor and DRY supporter who wrote of the south's "internal colonization" was abducted and tortured by unknown assailants.[71] In some respects, these hardships were not unique to the south. All Yemenis suffered from corruption and repression. Indeed, Yemen had always been among the poorest Arab states, and economic conditions were worsening everywhere. Still, these grievances were easily—and often nostalgically—contrasted with the prior period of southern independence.

Saleh tried to contain southern disaffection by co-opting it. He repeatedly brought up the possibility of implementing the DPA but repeatedly postponed provincial elections. He placed southerners in prominent positions in the GPC party apparatus or as provincial governors, and even prime minister. Hadi became vice president. Still, most of these figures worked under the shadow of Saleh's cabal of tribal leaders and party bosses.[72] In 2001 Vice President Hadi launched a new initiative to extend the GPC patronage network. Islah, too, worked to recruit supporters in the south. The YSP, meanwhile, withered under government harassment.[73]

The efforts to integrate north and south helped to activate and heighten Yemen's sectarian divide. Since the end of the 1962–70 civil war, the traditional Zaydi seat in the far northern region had been marginalized politically and neglected economically. With unification, Sunnis assumed a clear majority in the country, making the exclusion of Zaydis more acute. But the situation became more complicated with the emergence of Salafi and Wahhabi-inspired groups in

Yemen. While traditional Shafi'i-school Sunnis had found a workable modus vivendi with Zaydis, more stringent Salafis and Wahhabis explicitly identified Shi'ism as a sectarian threat. Some took up proselytization among the Zaydis. Others took a more violent approach, launching a string of attacks against Zaydi mosques and other institutions.[74] The combination of oppression and sectarianism spurred a radical sectarian response on the part of Zaydis. Husayn Badr ad-Din al-Houthi, the son of a senior Zaydi cleric, launched a revivalist movement among Zaydi youth. Violence between Houthi supporters, tribal forces, pro-government militias, and state security forces escalated. While denouncing the elitism of the traditional imamate, the Houthi movement focused on reviving and modernizing Yemeni Shi'ism. In 2004 Saleh, himself a Zaydi by confession, launched an all-out campaign against Houthi forces in Saadeh. Playing the sectarian card and vying for US and Saudi support, Saleh depicted the Houthis as Iranian proxies and crypto-imamists. The Houthis, for their part, became increasingly more militant, with Iran providing financial and ideological support.[75]

The emergence of the Southern Movement compounded the problems of an already fragile Yemeni state. In May 2007 an association of retired PDRY military veterans staged demonstrations over their lack of pension benefits. The protests quickly expanded, touching on issues of unemployment, land expropriation, and political disenfranchisement. Some demonstrations drew an estimated hundred thousand people.[76] Movement leaders adopted tactics of peaceful civil disobedience, such as sit-ins, blockades, and demonstrations. They garnered attention on satellite television and social media. On October 13, 2007, government troops fired on protesters in Habilayn, a town in the Radfan Mountains. Coming on the eve of the anniversary of the October 14 revolution and in the same location where the anti-colonial uprising had begun in 1967, the incident reminded southerners of their revolutionary past.[77] At the same time, though, Aden's prosperity under British rule contrasted with its post-unification decline.

Saleh deployed the security services and vigilante squads against the insurrections. SM leaders were arrested, forced underground, assassinated, or driven abroad. The offices of *al-Ayyam*, Aden's oldest independent newspaper and a cultural hub in the city, were attacked and eventually shut down.[78] By 2009 violence engulfed Aden, Dhala, Lahj, and Abyan. Southern militants targeted government buildings and properties associated with the "colonizers" from the north. The south became one of Yemen's bloodiest conflict zones.[79]

The SM grew more radical but also more fractious. Some activists envisioned a devolution of power roughly consistent with the DPA. The key issue was whether the south would be treated as a single federal unit or broken up, potentially allowing Saleh to divide and rule. There were more calls for provincial autonomy and the creation of new super-regions that crossed the original YAR-PDRY border.[80] For others, though, the goal was ending the northern "occupation" and achieving independence. After government troops fired on civilians in Habilyan in April 2009, activists recorded a video decrying the state:

> We are fighting the thieves, the occupiers. Today, we ask, what unity—
> the unity of tanks above our homes? They have started the shooting.
> They have pillaged our land, consumed our wealth. We have no more
> patience for these oppressors, death is preferable.[81]

Activists adopted the PDRY flag and other motifs from the anticolonial era. Exiled southern leaders, including Beidh, Ali Nasir Mohammed, and Abdarrahman al-Jifri, a SAL figure who had been part of the DRY, all tried to claim leadership of the SM.[82] An ode to the SM sung by a popular Aden entertainer declared "people of the south, be ready—this is the revolution of the old and the young."[83]

Southern Islamists and tribal leaders had no fondness for the PDRY but still had reason to back the SM. In 2009 Fadhli broke with Saleh and threw his support to the SM. Building on his experience in Afghanistan, he pushed for a more aggressive military confrontation with the regime. In April 2009 he held a large rally in Zinjibar, along with one of the leaders of the veterans' movement, clad in the garb of a traditional sultan, including dagger and pistol. Fadhli's tribal force engaged in direct combat with government troops in Abyan. In 2010 Fadhli released a YouTube video of himself lofting the US flag over his family compound, a clear appeal for US support.[84] The leaders of al-Qaeda in the Arabian Peninsula (AQAP) saluted the southern uprising, although the central command denounced secession, saying that the goal was to unify Yemen under Islamic rule.[85] Jihadi networks and SM fighters seemed at times to cooperate operationally.[86]

Multiple leadership committees and umbrella organizations emerged in the late 2000s, but none could unify a grassroots and highly localized movement. From exile in Lebanon, Beidh sought to position himself as the south's natural leader, using his access to satellite television to spread word of the SM's disparate activities. Hassan Baoum, another NLF veteran and onetime YSP official, became a leading advocate for non-violent struggle for independence. Baoum was arrested in 1998 for leading protests over police abuses, and he and his family suffered repeated imprisonments. In 2009 Baoum launched a hunger strike from prison.[87]

Saleh tried to exploit the discord within the SM. In 2009 he made new proposals for political devolution, hoping to yoke off the pro-federalist element. At the same time, he accused the SM of betraying the revolutions and endangering the historical achievement of unity. He depicted the SM as a stooge of Saudi Arabia, Iran, the United States, or other foreign powers. To foreign audiences especially, Saleh lumped the SM, Houthis, and AQAP together as part of a global terrorist front and used the threat of terrorism to leverage US support, including strikes against purported terrorists. The international community's support of Saleh was not lost on the separatists. Fadhli followed up his 2010 pro-US video with a new one in which he burned the US, British, and PDRY flags, an ambiguous but certainly defiant gesture.[88] At the same time, Saleh seemed to take a scorched earth approach to the separatist issue. Yemen, he warned,

> won't be divided into two parts, as some might think, but many. . . . People would fight from house to house, and from window to window. . . . They have to learn a lesson from what happened in Iraq and Somalia.[89]

But it was Saleh, as much as anyone, who sowed this sense of anarchy.

## "No Unity, No Federalism"

Though the SM was a potent insurgent force in the early 2010s, the separatists played only an indirect role in the machinations leading to Saleh's removal. Peaceful protests began in Sana'a and Taiz in January 2011, paralleling the demonstrations witnessed in Cairo and Tunis. Saleh's inner circle fractured. Military commanders, tribal and religious leaders, and even GPC mainstays began to distance themselves from the president. International pressure on Saleh mounted. Unlike in Tunisia or Egypt, though, the conflict in Yemen quickly became violent, with armed attacks paralleling the peaceful protests.[90] A rocket attack wounded Saleh, forcing him to seek medical treatment in Saudi Arabia. The Saudis brokered a plan to offer Saleh immunity in return for handing over power to Vice President Hadi. The February 2012 elections were meant as a referendum on the leadership change and a springboard for the transition.

Yet the SM leaders stood aside from the initial protests and distrusted the emergent anti-regime coalition, which featured a mélange of disaffected Islah and the GPC officials, as well as the Houthis. Still, the opportunity could not be ignored. The first "Day of Rage" rallies in Aden on February 2011 coincided with protests in the north. SM leaders tried to focus on common antipathy for the regime, deferring their calls for independence. Protesters attacked police stations and stormed government buildings. Security forces shot and killed at least nine in Aden alone.[91] But as the protests continued, many southerners saw the northern-based opposition as prevaricating and renewed calls for secession.[92] Southerners increasingly described themselves not in the fraternal terms of Yemeni unity but as members of a distinctive South Arabian nation shaped by a unique history. This emphasis on essential cultural cleavages, though, alienated northerners who were inclined to support some southern demands.[93] Baoum called for a boycott of the February elections, arguing that vote legitimized the foreign occupation.[94] The international community lauded the February 2012 voting, just as it had the 1993 unity elections. Running unopposed, Hadi won handily. Yet the south saw significant irregularities, violence, and lower turnout.[95] Hadi tried to appease southern demands, appointing a southerner as prime minister and pledging money for veterans' compensation. The YSP positioned itself as the voice of the south, calling for confidence-building measures such as dealing with the pension issues, releasing political prisoners, reopening al-Ayyam, and issuing an apology for the 1994 war. Still, many in the SM saw this as merely a co-optation stratagem.[96]

Sana'a's decisions were in any case less relevant to the struggle for control on the ground. Local committees and militias, centered on tribes, clans, and political networks, filled the void left by the splintered state security forces. These local forces took control over key infrastructure, such as electrical grids, oil depots, and filling stations, and used this control as leverage over the central government. In the far north Houthi forces pushed out government troops. AQAP established a foothold in Abyan in May 2011. It encouraged locals to administer their own affairs through a front group. overseeing utilities, justice administration, and public safety, and provided compensation to victims of US air strikes. This localized approach won AQAP a measure of public support. In May 2012 tribal forces loosely aligned with President Hadi retook Zinjibar.

At the same time, the SM remained riven by internal disagreements. For some in the east, the SM leadership appeared overly Aden-centric. They offered an alternative vision of a prior statehood rooted in the history of the sultanates. In June 2012 Hadramis approached the British ambassador in Cairo about supporting Hadramawt's secession. Similar calls came from the heir of the sultan of Mahra and Socotra.[97] Hadrami tribal leaders also pushed for greater autonomy and local control. They decried the central government's abuses and failures to provide security. Tribal leaders demanded government troops evacuate and threatened to blockade oil installations. There were some expressions of mutual support between the Hadramawt tribal movement and the SM, but the relationship remained at arm's length.[98]

There was still little progress in rebuilding political order a year into Hadi's presidency. In March 2013 the National Dialogue Conference (NDC) convened under UN auspices. This series of large-scale gatherings was supposed to yield a new framework for stability and inclusion. Although the SM was excluded from the transitional government, the southern issue was a key part of the NDC mandate. The SM had eighty-five delegates and the YSP thirty-six. Still, to many separatists, the NDC was moot. The GPC retained the largest number of NDC seats. Hadi stacked the deck in his favor by handpicking many of the SM delegates from groups known to favor federalism over independence. Moreover, some elements in the SM insisted that South Yemen's status was an international, not domestic, matter; it should be handled in separate negotiations hosted by a third party.[99]

As the NDC began, tens of thousands turned up at protests in Aden, chanting "The decision is ours!" (*al-qarar qararna*). The right to self-determination could not be subject to compromise.[100] Nonetheless, some SM leaders were willing to accept federalism as a transitional measure, provided a binding referendum on independence was held later on. After ten months of deliberations, the NDC concluded with recommendations in favor of federalism but no implementation formula. Hadi forwarded his own "4+2" plan, with four provinces in the north and two in the south (Aden and Hadramawt).[101] Some in the SM, particularly the veterans' association, were receptive to the proposal. Most of the southern leadership, though, rejected it.

The claim to self-determination linked to the south's anticolonial history grew more powerful. New slogans connected the 1967 revolution and the current southern struggle: "No unity, no federalism/ Get lost, get lost, colonialism!"[102] Commemorations of the October 14 revolution in Aden became calls for a referendum on independence.[103] Calls for violent resistance intensified. As Anne-Linda Amira Augustin describes, the ubiquitous pro-independence graffiti in Aden offered the classic themes of self-determination and the promise of independence: "The people want the independence of the south."[104]

The disappointment with the NDC helped pushed Yemen from being a frail state mired in regime transition into outright failure. Events in the north initially overshadowed the disintegration in the south. Rejecting the NDC and taking advantage of the splintering of the state security forces, the Houthis renewed their military assault. Houthi forces, backed by Iran and ex-president Saleh, moved on Sana'a in September 2014 and Taiz in early 2015. In January 2015 Hadi and his ministers fled to Aden and then Riyadh, proclaiming themselves to be Yemen's "legitimate government." The UN coordinator of the NDC resigned to protest the Houthi-Saleh encroachment. The United States backed UN Security Council Resolution 2140, sanctioning travel and imposing financial embargoes against Saleh and the Houthis. Iran openly backed the Houthis. Saudi Arabia and the UAE backed Hadi and launched a campaign of aerial bombardment and blockade against the Houthi-held territory. Expeditionary forces, supported by the United States, deployed to try to roll back the attacks on al-Bayda and Aden. Yet the campaign soon bogged down, producing a humanitarian disaster.[105]

The SM calculus changed with the Houthi advances. The Houthis had once appeared a potential ally in the national arena. Houthis seemed eager to link Yemen's "northern" and "southern issues" and had made electoral alliances with the YSP and backed the NDC's federal proposal.[106] Yet with the Houthis gaining military momentum, the chance for cooperation diminished. The conflict took on a distinctly sectarian hue as a war began between Iranian-backed northern Shi'is bent on subjugating the Sunnis. Outside actors, particularly Saudi Arabia, added to this perception.[107] AQAP became a tacit partner in the anti-Houthi alliance, dispatching its own forces to fight the Shi'i "apostates." The Quayti and Mahra sultans renewed calls for independence, seeking to untether their polities from the Republic of Yemen and the vestigial South Yemen, which they claimed had illegitimately annexed their territory in 1967. The close association between the sultans and Saudi Arabia raised the possibility of a Saudi-Hadrami union.[108] Local resistance committees in the midland and Tihama regions expressed interest in joining the SM's secessionist bid, effectively solidifying a Sunni block that stretched from the midlands to Hadramawt.[109]

An uneasy alliance formed between the separatists and the beleaguered central state. Though still operating in Riyadh, Hadi's government enjoyed international recognition and actively pursued diplomatic and military support from the United States, fellow Arab states, and the UN. Hadi managed to take control over the central bank and relocate its headquarters to Aden.[110]

Despite its de jure sovereignty, though, the Yemeni state lacked command on the ground. The state faced a double bind: from the Houthi-Saleh forces on one hand, and from jihadi groups like AQAP and the Islamic State on the other. To retain a territorial foothold, Hadi had to seek support from those actors exercising physical control on the ground. In much of the south, this meant separatists. Two prominent SM figures, Aidarous Zubaidi and Hani bin Brik, became the de facto rulers of Aden, Lahj, and Dhala. Born in 1967 in Dhala, Zubaidi had been a South Yemen air force officer and fought for the south in the 1994 civil war. He went into exile after 1994, supporting a sporadic guerrilla movement in the south. When the crisis began in 2011, Zubaidi's Popular Resistance militias began attacking pro-Saleh forces in Dhala; in 2015 they helped repel the Houthi invasion of the region. He was appointed as governor of Aden in December 2015 after IS assassinated the prior governor (another veteran rebel from the south).[111] Bin Brik was born in Aden and trained in Saudi Arabia at a Salafi-oriented seminary. Like many other Salafis in Yemen, bin Brik had initially abjured politics. During the chaos of the revolution and civil war, however, he was drawn into campaigning against the Houthis, the Muslim Brotherhood, and Islah. Working in conjunction with the UAE and Saudi Arabia, which shared these enemies, he commended the Security Belt militia, which maintained a cordon around Aden.[112]

Zubaidi and bin Brik swore fealty to the Republic of Yemen, but the PDRY banner flew openly on government buildings in Aden. The SM forces controlled the oil refinery, the airport, and the shipping terminals in the largest city still under the nominal control of Hadi's legitimate government. In the interior, SM forces demanded international companies remit revenue to specially designated accounts for the future southern state.[113] Zubaidi and bin Brik also maintained ties to the UAE, which provided Aden with crucial military support and sought to recruit local tribes into the security forces. With the UAE's backing, southern militias cracked down on suspected terrorists and political opposition.[114] Rumors circulated about northerners fraudulently obtaining local identity papers in order to infiltrate the south. Bin Brik, in particular, was accused of conducting ethnic cleansing of northerners.[115]

The SM also took over broad aspects of municipal governance in and around Aden. Adopting a policy of the past, they tried to restrict the *qat* trade to weekends, only to give up on the measure in the midst of public outcry.[116] The SM leadership also sought to address electricity and fuel shortages. Zubaidi became the key conduit for humanitarian assistance from the U.N. and the UAE. The UAE donated fifty small-scale generators to Aden in summer 2016. Meanwhile, Hadi and his cabinet loitered in plush accommodations in Riyadh.[117]

Hadramawt also gained functional autonomy, but with a different bent. The 4+2 proposal seemed a boon to groups agitating for the region's specific autonomy. The proposed Hadramawt federal region would have just two million people, or about 8 percent of Yemen's total population, but cover 50 percent of the country's landmass. This vast region was a potential powerhouse, with functional ports in Mukalla and Ash Shihr, ample access to water, 80 percent of Yemen's oil fields, and untapped natural gas and gold deposits. Yet with the central government's collapse, these possibilities evaporated. Hadi's government accused rebellious tribes of associating with AQAP. The tribes, in turn, set up roadblocks and embargoed the oil fields, trying to blackmail the government to grant them autonomy.[118] Just a week into the Saudi-UAE campaign, AQAP took control of Mukalla and Ash Shihr. Revisiting lessons from its tenure in Abyan, AQAP worked with local tribes and religious figures to set up the Hadramawt National Council (HNC). AQAP spokesmen claimed that its members were involved in the HNC but as "sons of Hadramawt." Indeed, many of the senior AQAP members hailed from the Hadrami aristocracy. Seizing the Yemeni central bank branch and several commercial banks in Mukalla, AQAP gained an estimated $140 million. Still, HNC general secretary Abdul-Hakeem bin Mahfood, told an interviewer that AQAP helped fund municipal governance of electricity, sanitation, schools, price controls, public safety, and managing the ports. The AQAP-HNC alliance also derived revenue from taxes on cargo shipping and gasoline sales, as well as trying to extort money from cell phone companies for maintaining their networks and from the state oil company.[119] Bin Mahfood depicted the HNC as a bottom-up response to the state's failure to provide safety and security. Nevertheless, he pointed out that Hadi had tacitly approved the HNC. It would dissolve, he said, "when the state returns and resumes its duties from here."[120] Although avoiding calls for secession, the HNC achieved de facto autonomy from state control. Only in April 2016 did Saudi Arabia and the UAE, backed by the United States, belatedly retake Mukalla. Though this was touted as a military triumph, AQAP fighters appeared to escape or melt back into the civilian population, allowing them to retain their close connection to the region's tribal and religious leadership.[121]

The gap between the state's juridical authority and the material power of the separatist movements became glaring as Hadi tried to move against Zubaidi and bin Brik in Aden. Friction between the UAE-backed forces and Hadi's troops intensified, including armed clashes around the port. On April 27, 2017, Hadi dismissed Zubaidi and bin Brik, claiming that they had become agents of a foreign occupation and violated Yemen's sovereignty.[122]

Responding to Hadi's challenge, the SM mobilized a multiday demonstration in Aden, meant to coincide with the anniversary of the 1994 civil war. On May 4 Zubaidi made the Aden Historic Declaration, announcing his intention to lead a Southern Transitional Council (STC) for independence in South Arabia.[123] The preamble of the declaration laid out the justification for independence, pointing to the history of repression, suffering, and resistance in the south, particularly the 1994 war. Article 1 asserted that the establishment of the council and drive for independence derived legal and moral authority from the "will of the people of the South" (al-irada ash-sha'biyya al-janubiyya).[124] With Zubaidi as head and bin Brik as deputy, the STC sought to represent a cross-section of southern politics. Among the eighteen-person STC steering committee were descendants of the pre-PDRY aristocracy, former ministers or governors from the Hadi administration, and professional women. Beidh and other ex-DRY officials announced their support for STC from abroad.[125]

Still, the Aden Declaration failed to generate unanimity. Despite Zubaidi's assertion that the "sons of Hadramawt province" were an integral part of South Arabia's civilization, some Hadramis still preferred to go it alone or become an autonomous federal province rather than unify under the southern cause. Hadramawt, some reasoned, could remain a part of Yemen but continue to operate effectively outside of Hadi's control and with direct ties to Saudi Arabia and its substantial Hadrami diaspora.[126] Baoum questioned how figures who had served Hadi one day could come out for secession the next. He dismissed the Aden Declaration as a foreign conspiracy.[127]

Indeed, the most important determinant of the SM's fate was not its capacity for governance or moral suasion but its ability to win support from the international community and gain juridical recognition. The Aden Declaration began by gesturing toward notions of popular sovereignty and self-determination and concluded on a practical note, describing the strategic partnership between the SM and the Saudi-UAE coalition. It directly addressed the international community, the Arab world, and international organizations to avow a "commitment to international law, the United Nations Charter, and the Universal Declaration of Human Rights." A sovereign south would be an asset for regional security.[128] In late May Zubaidi and bin Brik traveled to Riyadh and Abu Dhabi to make their case for self-determination. The Gulf Cooperation Council categorically rejected secession.[129] Nevertheless, the crucial relationship between the SM and the UAE stayed intact, and the UAE remained entrenched along Yemen's southern coast, including bases in Aden, Mukalla, Socotra, and Perim, a tiny island in the mouth of the Bab al-Mandab. This partnership made it all the easier to accuse the separatists of serving as foreign stooges.[130]

# Conclusion

It is easy to see Yemen as a "typical" Arab state, artificial and overwhelmed by the enduring power of tribal and primordial identities. So much about Yemen's conflict confirms stereotypes about the essential primitivism of Arab politics. Wars seem unending, political order elusive. Even seasoned observers, who wisely avoid such Orientalist tropes, describe a lack of coherent and compelling Yemeni national identity. In hindsight, the unification of north and south was not a reunion of a divided nation or the correction of a nefarious colonial-era scheme but a novel experiment in political cohabitation and nation building. The international community played a key role in preserving this marriage, from the DPA of 1994 to the various UN Security Council resolutions since 2011 that rhetorically affirmed Yemen's territorial integrity.

Such a view, though, still discounts separatism as a contrapuntal political trend and presupposes Yemen's political continuity and endurance. For many in the south, that experiment conclusively failed. The key question was what would replace it. The state of South Yemen represented many things over the past half century, each rooted in Wilsonian ideals of the mid-twentieth century. In proffering the Federation of South Arabia in the mid-1960s, the British and their sultanate allies claimed to respond to indigenous political wishes for independence in a responsible and legitimate manner. For the NLF and its successors in the revolutionary PDRY, political independence was a starting point for further social and economic liberation, fulfilling self-determination in both its Wilsonian and Leninist forms. The short-lived DRY of 1994 claimed to be a democratic, pluralistic, and progressive alternative to northern patrimonialism. The SM tried again to revive the idea of an independent southern state and entreated the international community for support. The collapse of the Yemeni state between 2011 and 2014 made that a possibility seem more realistic.

The challenge of identity was critical. Among the prolific graffiti of post-2011 Aden, Augustin noted the slogan "The South is not the home in which we live, but the home which exists in us."[131] But what was that imagined community? Factions within the SM differed over what the south should be. Some see the SM as reinstating the South Yemeni state within its former borders. For others, the aim is for true federal autonomy, retaining the achievement of unity while blunting the north's demographic predominance. Some envisioned a return to the sultanates, an alternative to the repressive socialist state that actually emerged in South Yemen. In the increasingly sectarian tenure of contemporary conflict with the Houthis, there was also a notion of the south constituting a Sunni orthodox bastion against Iranian-backed Zaydism.[132] Far from being rooted in ancient hatreds, each of these ideas was inspired by Yemen's recent history, extrapolating Yemen's twentieth-century travails into the twenty-first.

To focus on contestations of national identity, though, missed the important role of the state in implanting and demarcating national communities. Thinking and seeing like a Yemeni citizen, as Wedeen puts it, presupposed enactment of and by a Yemeni state. Under Saleh, that state was characterized largely by absences—the lack of democracy, underdevelopment, and farcical rule of law. Making do with meager coercive power and even weaker institutional and administrative capacities, Wedeen argues, Saleh capitalized on ceremonies, rituals, and symbols of statehood, such as the March 22 commemorations of unification, to maintain legitimacy.[133]

The SM inherited its own cultural arsenal as it maneuvered in the shadow of this hollow de jure state. The catastrophe of the 1994 civil war was a focal point of resistance. Other sets of historical memories, such as the memory of British colonial rule, anticolonial uprising, and the agglomeration of South Yemen itself in 1967, drew more ambivalent responses. The uprising of 2011 and the subsequent tilt of the Yemeni state from frailty to failure provided an opportunity for separatists to construct an alternative state structure. Following the script of the mid-century state builders, the SM worked on dual tracks. On one hand, it governed on the ground. It ran the ports, managed electricity and food relief, and sought to control the extraction, refinement, and distribution of oil products. In the midst of chaos, it tried to keep things working. On the other hand, it reached out to the international community for political, economic, military, and moral aid. It sought to make the south not just a good citizen of the global community but an indispensable one. Even though the international community avowed a commitment to uphold Yemen's territorial integrity as mantra, it accommodated the separatists as de facto rulers. These types of gains were hard to revoke and made the separatists essential in any effort to rebuild political order.

# 5

# Kurdistan

*They had been waiting over a generation. After interminable delays, the referendum came in a cascade of ink-tipped fingers. The ballot asked a simple question, repeated in Kurdish, Arabic, Turkish, and Syriac:* Do you want the Kurdistan Region and the Kurdistani areas outside the Region to become an independent state? *Everything in Hawler proclaimed the affirmative. In the midst of the city's hodgepodge of modern and neo-Islamic vernacular apartment buildings and offices, satellite antennas and shopping malls, people donned the costumes of Kurdistan's pastoral past. Men dressed in baggy pants, cummerbunds, and headdresses like mountain shepherds or the military tunic of the Peshmerga, the freedom fighters, "those who face death." Women were resplendent in flowing gowns. The Kurdish flag, a red, white, and green tricolor with the twenty-one-pointed sun disk, was plastered everywhere. Celebratory car horns mixed with verses of the Kurdish national anthem: "Let no one say the Kurds are dead / the Kurds are alive and their flag will never fall!"* [1]

*After World War II a Kurdish separatist movement in northwestern Iran adopted these verses as a national hymn. With Soviet backing, the separatists seized control of the city of Mahabad and declared the formation of a Kurdish republic in 1946. The republic lasted for less than a year. When the Soviets withdrew their support, Iranian forces surrounded and crushed the rebellion. Mahabad became a symbol of Kurdish aspirations for sovereignty.*

*Massoud Barzani, president of the Kurdish Regional Government (KRG) and leader of the Kurdish Democratic Party (KDP), personally embodied the connection to Mahabad. Massoud's father, the legendary Mullah Mustafa Barzani, had led a contingent of Iraqi Kurdish fighters to defend Mahabad and become the republic's military commander. Massoud reminded people that his party was founded at Mahabad and that he himself had been born there, on free Kurdish soil. Massoud talked increasingly about his wish to die in an independent Kurdistan.* [2] *The more Iraq staggered, the bolder Barzani became. Colonially construed states like Iraq and Syria, he said, were malformed, brutal, and ultimately doomed. The Kurds, in contrast, had* proven reliable in the fight against the Islamic State (IS), gaining the goodwill of the international community. World leaders, Barzani told a British newspaper, had concluded that "the era of Sykes-Picot is over. . . . Whether they say it or not, accept it or not, the reality on the ground is that." The Kurds' "compulsory co-existence" within Arab-dominated states was coming to an end.[3] Instead, Barzani prescribed a return to the fundamental premise of Wilsonianism: a plebiscite to decide the fate of nations. "The decision of people," Barzani said, "will be more legal and strong[er] than all other decisions."[4]

The voting was taking place not only in the official and legal boundaries of the Kurdish Region of Iraq. Ballots were also cast in so-called disputed territories—areas that the KRG had long coveted but only captured in 2014 while moving to forestall IS's advances. The most important of these was Kirkuk, which the Kurds likened in importance to Jerusalem. Elation radiated through the region and across the globe. As civil war raged in Syria, Kurds seized control over territories along the Turkish and Iraqi borders, establishing an autonomous entity called Rojava (Western Kurdistan). Rojava's leaders were closely tied to the Kurdistan Workers' Party (Partiya Karkerên Kurdistanê, PKK), a Turkish guerrilla group that had long been antagonists of Barzani and the KDP. The PKK leadership was noticeably divided on the referendum.[5] Nevertheless, residents of the Syrian Kurdish city of Qamishli danced in the

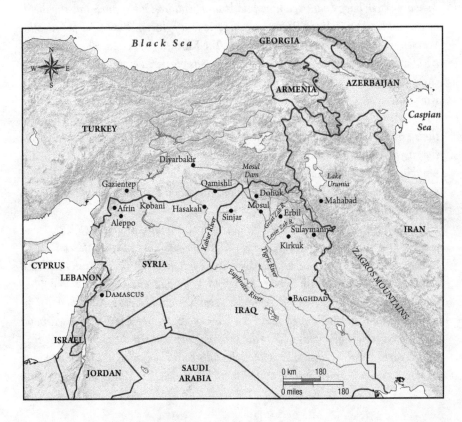

streets in celebration of the referendum.[6] In Iran, public rejoicing turned to rioting in Mahabad and other cities.[7] Overseas voting took place in Europe and the United States.[8] The results, announced later that week, showed over 90 percent approval for secession.

But the euphoria quickly dissipated. The central government in Baghdad moved to cut off the air and ground routes connecting the KRG to the rest of Iraq. Iran and Turkey closed the international border, shutting the pipelines that allowed KRG oil to reach international buyers. The United States deemed the referendum invalid, illegitimate, and unhelpful. The U.N. Security Council expressed concern. In less than a week, the KRG became a beleaguered pariah. The KDP leadership backpedaled, offering to suspend the referendum result, but to no avail. The KRG's tenuous internal solidarity collapsed. Kurdish forces retreated from Kirkuk rather than risk confrontation. At the end of October Barzani announced his resignation. Appearing on television in Peshmerga fatigues and headdress, he blamed the international community for betraying the Kurdish nation again.

# Introduction

Sherif Pasha, head of the Kurdish delegation to the Paris peace talks, submitted his written memorandum six weeks after Faisal's audience, on March 22, 1919. Like Faisal, Sherif was a disaffected member of the Ottoman elite. His father had been foreign minister. Sherif himself was born in Istanbul and had served as ambassador to Sweden. After breaking with the Young Turk government, though, Sherif spent the war in European exile. "In virtue of the Wilsonian principle," he wrote to the Allied leadership, "everything pleads in favor of the Kurds for the creation of a Kurd state, entirely free and independent." He urged an international commission to "trac[e] the frontier line in accordance with the principle of nationality."[9] Citing classical history and contemporary Orientalist ethnographies, Sharif envisioned Kurdistan as a massif encompassing northern Mesopotamia, southern Anatolia, and the Caucusus.[10] The following year the Treaty of Sèvres granted local autonomy to the Kurdish areas of southern Anatolia and prescribed a plebiscite, supervised by the League of Nations, to occur shortly. Beyond what diplomats laid out on paper, there were a number of attempts to seize slivers of land upon which to build a Kurdish state. Though less than what Sherif and others had imagined, this seemed a propitious start to Kurdish self-determination.

Yet by the end of the 1930s the Kurds were effectively orphans of the Wilsonian moment. All of the land where a Kurdish polity might lodge was under the control of other states. Kurds became one of the largest stateless minorities in the world, comprising nearly a fifth of the population in Turkey and

Iraq, a tenth in Syria and Iran, with additional pockets scattered in Lebanon, the USSR, and a growing diaspora. Over the next eight decades, Kurdistan was in nearly continual upheaval. Rebels exploited the difficulty of projecting state power in the rugged highlands. They got training, weapons, and financing from outside powers and from diasporas. They drew strength from tribal connections and solidarity and the discontent of people who saw their native language and lifestyle under assault. But while these factors catalyzed resistance, they often militated against state building. Parochial tribal interests undercut unity. Clashes between traditional tribal magnates and a new breed of urbanized Kurdish elite compounded these tensions. There was no pre-existing administrative structure upon which Kurds could fall back, no province or district that could clearly be counted as Kurdistan. Consequently, it was difficult even to inventory which people and which lands belonged as part of the Kurdish nation. In geopolitical terms, Kurds were pawns, easily sacrificed to the interests of greater powers. The obstacle to Kurdish separatism, as Denise Natali and Akin Ünver argue, was not just an individual state but a system bent on preserving territorial boundaries.[11]

Locked within the framework of national states, Kurdish politics took a scattered trajectory. Kurds faced similar challenges under Iran, Turkey, Syria, and Iraq. They sporadically looked to their ethnic kin across the border for support and inspiration. No one rose to become the champion of a pan-Kurdish agenda, however. Instead, struggles for self-determination became disparate, localized, and constrained by the particular histories of state formation in each country. States often played Kurdish groups off one another, exploiting internecine struggles for supremacy within the Kurdish space to block any attainment of separation.

The global nation-state crisis at the end of the millennium seemed to signal a shift in circumstances. Since its founding in 1991, the KRG in Iraq had touted itself as a regional success story, an island of democracy, stability, and pluralism in a dictatorial sea. In reality, the KRG's political development was brittle and its leadership often thuggish. However, its endurance encouraged other Kurdish activists across the region. Opportunities for rebellion expanded dramatically with the 2011 uprisings.[12] In Syria, state forces abandoned Kurdish areas along the northern and northeastern borders. The Democratic Union Party (Partiya Yekîtiya Demokrat, PYD) used this territory to launch Rojava, a radical experiment in devolved self-rule. The leaders of Rojava claimed to respect Syria's sovereignty but continued to transgress its legal boundaries and operated in self-declared separation. Protests in Iraq upset precarious arrangements for ethno-sectarian power sharing. KRG leadership seized upon the moment of state breakdown to expand territorial control and fiscal powers. Still, these efforts foundered on familiar obstacles: internecine conflict, the difficulty of defining a national agenda in terms of either people or places, hostility from regional states, and the conservative inertia of the global system.

# "A People Apart"

Like the Czechs, Poles, Ukrainians, and other "small peoples" attendant to the settlement of World War I, the Kurds and their claims to future self-determination bore a complicated relationship to the imperial past. In the eyes of the international community, language was a key characteristic defining nationhood. Nationhood, in turn, was a prerequisite of self-determination.[13] Kurdish, a mostly oral language, had multiple dialects, some so removed as to be nearly unintelligible to speakers of the others. Kermanji was spoken in Anatolia, the northern and western portions of Kurdistan. Moving east and southward toward the Zagros Mountains, Sorani Kurdish was predominant.[14] Still, the Kurdish language was clearly dissimilar from Turkish, Arabic, or Iranian, the primary languages of the Ottoman and Iranian Empires. Kurdish-speaking dynasties and potentates had played an important role in Islamic history, most illustriously in the example of Saladin the Great. The Ottomans conquered most of western Kurdistan in the 1500s, sharing the frontier space with the Iranian Empire. Rugged, mountainous terrain and a tradition of autonomous, peripatetic, and well-armed tribes meant that indirect rule was the norm. Kurdish principalities persisted as semi-independent vassals under both imperial suzerainties.[15]

The primary social categories in Kurdistan traditionally involved clan and religion, not language. The Ottomans tended to cultivate relationships with polyglot Sunni Muslim tribal grandees to block Iranian-backed Shi'i infiltration. The Qadiri and the Naqshbandi Sufi orders, influential in the imperial court, linked the elite of Kurdistan to the Sublime Porte. Sufi lodges under hereditary adepts could summon multiple clans together into a kind of supra-tribe and could often link Kurdish, Arabic, and Turkish speakers together.[16] The mountains also provided a haven for Yezidis, Alevis, Shabak, Kakais, and other heterodox sects. Jews, Armenians, and Assyrians spoke their own languages and lived as peasants, artisans, or traders under tribal hegemony.

The Ottomans' nineteenth-century reforms liquidated the dynastic Kurdish emirates, like the Baban in Kirkuk and later Sulaymaniyah, the Soran in Rowandiz, the Bahdinan of Amadiyya and Dohuk, and the Botan in Cizre. At the same time, European powers extended their influence into the region, seeking commercial and political opportunities and claiming to protect local Armenians and other non-Muslim minorities.[17] Following the Russo-Turkish War of 1877, the Congress of Berlin provided specific protections for Christian minorities within the empire. For Kurdish tribal leaders, these were more than humiliations; they were assaults on their traditional local dominance. In 1880 Sheikh Ubaydallah, a Naqshbandi adept from Nehri, invaded northeastern Iran and seized Urumia. Some aspects of Ubaydallah's uprising followed a familiar trajectory of tribal rabble-rousing. Ubaydallah complained that Qajar tax collectors had abused his followers. He attacked rival Kurdish factions that had allied with the shah. But Ubaydallah also adopted a new nationalist vernacular. He wrote to the British consul in Tabriz:

> The Kurdish nation . . . is a people apart. Their religion is different [from that of others] and their laws and customs distinct. . . . The Chiefs and Rulers of Kurdistan, whether Turkish or Persian subjects, and inhabitants of Kurdistan, one and all are united and agreed that matters cannot be carried on in this way with the two governments [Ottoman and Qajar]. . . . We want our affairs to be in our own hands.[18]

Mirroring Armenian nationalist organizations, Ubaydallah courted intellectuals and writers and declared himself the head of a new Kurdish polity. Ultimately, Iranian imperial forces and local tribes moved to suppress the insurrection.

Rolling back the mid-1800s reform, Sultan Abd al-Hamid (r. 1876–1909) built new ties to Kurdish tribal leaders. Abd al-Hamid likely suborned Ubaydallah's tactics as part of a wider effort to block Armenian autonomy. After the rebellion, Ubaydallah retired to a comfortable exile in Istanbul and then the Hejaz. In 1891 the sultan created a light cavalry corps commanded by Kurdish tribal leaders. These forces, known eponymously as Hamidiyya, saw combat on the Russian front. Their greatest impact was in terrorizing, plundering, and massacring Armenians.[19]

Less belligerent expression of Kurdish cultural nationalism also began to percolate. The first Kurdish-language newspaper appeared in Cairo and then in various iterations in Europe at the end of the nineteenth century.[20] A Kurdish mutual aid society formed in Istanbul in 1908 and 1909, with branches in Diyarbakir, Erzurum, Mosul, Van, Muş, and Bitlis. The society promoted schooling in a modernized Kurdish language. There was new interest in folklore and myths, such as finding the Kurdish ancestors in the biblical Medes or the story of Kaveh the Blacksmith, who killed the evil Zahak in the *Shahnameh* epic.[21] Aristocrats of old Kurdish dynasties, particularly the Badr Khan clan, scions of the Botan emirate, were major figures in the Kurdish cultural awakening. Yet there were inherent tensions between the perspectives of Kurds in Istanbul and of the provincial tribal elite. Tribal leaders protested when the Committee of Union and Progress (CUP) deposed Abd al-Hamid. The CUP moved to return plundered Armenian property and dismantle the Hamidiyya. Tribal leaders avowed fealty to the sultan but sought to preserve their local privileges. Kurdish leaders in Istanbul remained firm constitutionalists and disavowed such provincial resistance. Instead, they sought to confirm the Kurds as integral to the empire's cosmopolitan elite. Hewing toward liberalism, they even tried to identify themselves as allies to the Armenians.[22]

The Kurds were probably the last of the empire's Muslim communities to articulate a separate nationalist identity, even after the CUP embraced Turkish nationalism. Only in 1918 was the Society for the Advancement of Kurdistan founded, with an explicitly political (as opposed to cultural) mission. Still, the group splintered due to rivalries between the dynastic families and debates about whether to pursue autonomy within the empire or outright independence.[23]

At war's end, Kurdish leaders had to navigate in a world order in which notions of national self-determination had a new but uncertain currency. Many in the Allied camp regarded the Kurds as fanatical co-conspirators in the Armenian genocide. And indeed, Kurdish tribes were deeply involved in the attacks on Armenian civilians and refugees. Yet these attacks reflected less the agenda of Kurdish nationalism than local grievances, greed, and an anachronistic sense of service to the Islamic empire. Exiles like Sherif made alliances with Armenian leaders in hopes of winning favor from the international community. Sherif also astutely avoided any claims to Iranian territory, focusing on creating a Kurdish successor to the defeated Ottoman Empire.

While exiles ensconced in Europe made fanciful claims, a new nationalist politics emerged within Kurdistan. This new nationalism brought together tribal leaders, who retained independent military means, and urban intellectuals, who could articulate and define a Kurdish national community. The first inkling came in Sulaymaniyah, the former seat of the Baban emirate. With over ten thousand inhabitants, Sulaymaniyah was a substantial provincial city. Through the early twentieth century, it provided a large number of Ottoman officials and officers. The Baban aristocrats (including Sherif Pasha himself) continued to serve in the imperial court. The city was a hub in the turn-of-the-century Kurdish literary revival.[24] In 1918 Mahmud Barzinji, an adept of the Qadiri order and leader of one of the area's most substantial supra-tribes, emerged as the regional paramount. Barzinji had long harbored political ambitions and tried to leverage outside support to bolster his position. He raised troops on behalf of the sultan but quickly came to act as a free agent. Barzinji grasped the importance of both Wilson's and Lenin's versions of anti-imperialism. Largely to counterbalance Turkish and Arab activists, in 1918 Britain named Barzinji governor of an as-yet-undefined South Kurdistan and promoted new Kurdish literary endeavors. Barzinji, however, saw this as a chance to enact the promise of self-determination.

The international environment seemed propitious for this effort. The Sèvres Treaty proclaimed Kurdish national rights as a priority of the international community. At the same time, Mustafa Kemal's repudiation of the treaty and his campaign to oust the Allies from Anatolia tied down British resources. Barzinji tried to extend his reach toward Kirkuk, which had been part of the Baban domains. The British complained that their erstwhile protégé was an active Turkish ally. Iran and France also provided alternative sources of sponsorship.[25]

As Britain tempered its commitment to Barzinji and flirted with rival sheikhs in the area, pretenses of supporting Kurdish statehood evaporated. In 1921 Britain announced plans to attach Sulaymaniyah to the Kingdom of Iraq. Barzinji refused to recognize Iraq's claim to Sulaymaniyah and effectively blocked the referendum that was staged to confirm Faisal's election as monarch.[26] Barzinji responded by declaring the formation of the Kingdom of Kurdistan and adopting the title of shah.

Barzinji's rebel state interwove the traditions of rural tribalism with Sulaymaniyah's urban culture. A tax on tobacco, a key cash crop in Rowandiz, provided revenue to subsidize tribal leaders in the area. In the town, though, Barzinji took on the trappings of modern rule. The kingdom's executive council was divided into several portfolios. Barzinji served as defense minister, his brother as prime minister, and his brother-in-law as interior minister. Finance, justice, and education portfolios went to urban notables, merchants, and landowners (including a local Christian). The kingdom manufactured the banal iconography of national identity, including postage stamps and national flags emblazoned with the serrated solar disk. There was an efflorescence of cultural and literary production. Sorani adopted a standardized Arabo-Persian orthography, a form that would come into use in Iraq and Iran. [27]

The British used inducements and repression to counter Barzinji's encroachments. They recruited Barzinji's traditional tribal rivals as local officials. They brought Assyrian Christians into a separate colonial levy. Probably the most important response, though, was the overawing power of British aerial bombardment.[28] In 1924 the kingdom collapsed and Barzinji fled to Iran. The British lured him back to Iraq with offers of subsidies and sinecures, but these always fell short of the independence Barzinji sought. In his final gambit of 1931, Barzinji claimed to fight to liberate Kurds from alien Arab rule "in the name of the Aryan nation."[29]

Revolt and repression continued sporadically in northern Iraq through the 1930s, but the balance of power tipped decisively in favor of the state. The devastation of what the British called "air policing" continued. Kurdistan remained an underdeveloped periphery within Iraq. Education levels were abysmal, especially in rural areas. Kurdish-language textbooks were in short supply in primary and secondary schools, and there was no university-level training in Kurdish.[30] The state focused on co-opting tribal leaders by allowing them to claim common tribal lands as private property. The advent of the oil economy in Iraq amplified this imbalance. Kurdistan's agricultural sector received comparatively little national investment. The Erbil-to-Baghdad railroad closed down in 1950 due to lack of capital.[31] At the same time, the oil economy also spurred inexorable social transformation. Escaping rural poverty, tribesmen and peasants left the highlands to become wage laborers, often in oil fields surrounding Kirkuk. In the urban environs, mass-based political parties such as the Iraqi Communist Party and Kurdish nationalist factions overrode the pull of tribal identities.[32]

By virtue of becoming a frontier zone, Kurdistan was also uniquely positioned in the illicit market of the regional economy. As soon as international boundaries were imposed, the inhabitants of Kurdistan found ways to thwart and exploit them, often in collusion with the very guards and customs agents who were supposed to ensure the state's exclusive domain. Trafficking in tobacco, meat, wool, weapons, drugs, and oil products soon became a major component of the social and economic life of Kurdistan.[33]

Even amid repression and neglect, the monitoring of the international community granted Kurds a unique status in Iraq. Under pressure from the League of Nations, Britain had first pushed for a constitutional guarantee of Kurdish minority rights. In 1924 the League dispatched an investigatory committee to Mosul Province, which remained in dispute between Turkey and Iraq. The League stipulated Kurdish autonomy and language rights when it awarded the territory to Iraq. It reiterated this point again when it considered Iraq's admission to the League in 1932. Kurdish members of parliament cited the League's concerns when they pressed the Iraqi government to fund Kurdish schools.[34] Just as the leaders of Poland and Romania objected to the "minority treaties,"[35] Iraq's Arab leaders decried this is an affront to Iraqi sovereignty. Yet Iraq's very statehood depended on compliance with the demands of the international community. Consequently, Kurds in Iraq had an opportunity for cultural and political expression that was impossible in most other countries. By law, Kurds in Iraq could receive education, read and publish newspapers, and enter the public sphere using their native language. Even as various Iraqi governments tried to constrain the scope and lessen the depth of this autonomy, they could not ignore it. Iraq affirmed Kurdish nationhood, even if in the breach.[36]

Imperial breakdown and the emergence of new nationalist claimants had a similar impact on northern Kurdistan, areas that eventually fell to Turkey and Syria. During the war against the Allied occupation of Anatolia, Mustafa Kemal appealed to Kurds on the grounds of Islamic solidarity to block the planned Armenian state. After the Treaty of Lausanne and the recognition of the Republic of Turkey in 1923, however, Kemal pivoted toward secular Turkish ethnonationalism. In Ankara's vision, the Kurds were primitives to assimilate or destroy. Ankara conducted large-scale deportation, suppression of Kurdish language and religious practices, and mass killings to reshape the area's demography and culture.[37]

Resistance was immediate but not necessarily nationalistic in bent. In 1924 Sheikh Saïd, a Naqshbandi adept, led a rebellion in Diyarbakir on the Tigris River. Though the movement had backing from the nationalists, its primary goal was the reinstatement of the caliphate and reversion to Islamic law. The Ararat

rebellion (1928–31) was the most overtly nationalist, culminating in the declaration of the self-described Republic of Ararat. Tribal leaders, aggrieved over the
loss of lands and special privileges, spearheaded the Dersim rebellion (1937–
38), probably the single most destructive insurrection. Rebellions faced mounting obstacles. Airplanes, railroads, and other technologies granted states unprecedented power to dominate the highlands. As borders between states congealed,
safe havens became rarer. Neighboring states collaborated with Turkey to contain and degrade the rebellions. Internal factors also hindered resistance.
Allegiance to sects and tribal lineages undercut larger Kurdish national identity.
Heterodox Alevis and Sufi adepts, seen as stalwarts of Sunni orthodoxy, were
mutually distrustful. Some groups opted to ally with the government rather than
work with their long-standing local rivals.[38]

The violence in Turkey had a spillover effect in Syria. Whereas Turkey
denied any inkling of Kurdish national identity, the French mandate authorities were initially eager to cultivate the Kurds as a distinctive minority. The
French wanted to create separate administrations for different communities
that could counterbalance the hegemony of the Sunni Arab majority. Like
Alawis and Druze, Kurds were recruited into the colonial security services.[39]
During the 1920s Alawis and Druze, geographically compact minority groups,
received their own mini-states within the mandate. Some envisioned a comparable arrangement for Kurds in Syria.[40] However, the demographic and geographic dispersal of Kurdish inhabitants made this difficult. There were
long-standing and well-assimilated Kurdish communities in Damascus and
Aleppo. But there were also significant Kurdish enclaves across the still incho-
ate Syria-Turkish border, including in the far northeast around Hasakah and
the Kabur River, at the new railroad post at Kobani, and at Afrin in the mountains north of Aleppo, a region known as Kurd Dagh ("the Kurdish heights").
Rural Kurds tended not to speak Arabic, Syria's sole official language. Many
had only arrived in the French mandate territory as refugees or economic migrants from Anatolia.[41]

Responding to the deteriorating situation in Turkey, Kurdish intellectuals in
mandatory Lebanon and Syria launched a pan-Kurdish liberation movement,
called the Khoybun ("be yourself"). Its leadership drew from the heirs of the
Badr Khan and their tribal retainers. But it also sought to transcend familial leadership and build a fully fledged army of national liberation. Khoybun activists
worked with Armenian nationalists to support the Republic of Ararat in the late
1920s and early 1930s. They lobbied the United States, Britain, France, and Iran
on behalf of the Ararat rebels and tried to mobilize supporters from the Kurdish
and Armenian US diasporas. The Khoybun also launched newspapers and other
publications in the Kermanji dialect. Following in the footsteps of Mustafa
Kemal, they adopted a Romanized orthography.[42]

French officials initially backed the nationalist project but backed away as they realized its cost to their relationship with Syria's Arab nationalist camp and its irritation to Turkey. Although Ankara was the Khoybun's primary antagonist, their main constituency was inside mandatory Syria. In 1928 the Khoybun petitioned the French authorities for the right to teach Kurdish, to form Kurdish military units along the northern border, and to admit and resettle Kurdish refugees from Turkey. France authorities refused, unwilling to antagonize Ankara or the Arab nationalists in Damascus.[43] Kurdish groups in Aleppo and Damascus were restricted. However, some administrators, acting without clear instructions from Paris, began to redirect Kurdish attentions to the far northeast in the Hasakah province (sometimes referred to as the Jazira). Jutting like a duck's bill toward Mosul, the area was distant from Syria's power centers. To solidify its control, colonial officials built a string of blockhouses and garrisons extending from Palmyra into Hasakah. Since the new international boundaries disrupted the ancient caravan routes between Mosul, Diyarbakir, and Aleppo, the French officers launched a new market city at Qamishli and encouraged Kurdish tribes to resettle around there alongside Armenian Christians, many of whom had also fled Anatolia. Kurdish and Armenian became the official administrative languages in the area. The French appointed Kurdish officials and allowed the formation of Kurdish security forces. Rituals, holidays, and a new flag emphasized Kurdish-Christian amity, creating a functional self-rule in far reaches of the mandate territory.[44]

The brief Kurdish autonomy in Hasakah crumbled as France readied for withdrawal. The Arab nationalist government in Damascus rejected constitutional provisions to protect Kurdish language rights, replaced the outgoing French administrators with Arab officials, and encouraged Arabic-speakers to relocate to the northeast. There were violent clashes between the Kurdish tribes and the Armenian dissidents; an anti-Christian pogrom was rumored to be imminent. Ultimately, the French used aerial bombardment to pacify the region.[45]

The outbreak of World War II renewed hopes of rectifying the shortcomings of the Wilsonian moment. Spurred by the Atlantic Charter, diaspora activists envisioned a Kurdish territory that surpassed Sherif's initial vision, extending from the Mediterranean all the way to Iranian Luristan and the Persian Gulf.[46] Nationalist historians fashioned a new national narrative, combining ancient sources with contemporary Orientalist travelogues and League of Nations demographic studies.[47] In 1943 Kurdish intellectuals wrote to the Allied high command describing how a Kurdish state would become a strategic asset. Kurdish exiles gathered in San Francisco for the first United Nations convention but were again refused a seat.[48]

The most impactful efforts still came from the ground up, exploiting zones of crippled state power. The Soviet invasion and occupation of northwestern Iran in 1941 provided such an opportunity. Since 1921 Reza Shah Pahlavi had tried to transform Iran from a polyglot empire into a centralized, Iranian (i.e., Persian) ethno-state. Emulating the Kemalist program, Tehran sought to impose majority Iranian culture on ethno-linguistic minorities and break the power of peripheral tribes. In 1941, however, Britain and the USSR deposed Reza, who was suspected of pro-Axis sympathies. Modifying the Leninist approach to self-determination, Stalin envisioned turning multi-ethnic societies toward socialism, creating reliable client states.[49] Following the model of the autonomous regions within the USSR, the Soviets encouraged minorities like the Kurds (as well as Azeris) to organize for self-rule. Soviet advisors backed the Iranian Communist Party and left-wing nationalists who called for recognition of Kurdish language rights and political autonomy and promoted efforts for social modernization, including women's education and abolition of feudal privileges. Matching the militancy of urbanized Kurds, tribal leaders in the northwest jockeyed to reassert their old dominion in the absence of state authority. Mahabad, a city of some sixteen thousand people south of Lake Urumia, became the hub of an emergent Kurdish movement. The city was outside the formal Soviet zone of control but also removed from Tehran's reach. Qazi Mohammed, the leading figure in the separatist movement, straddled the rural and urban camps. Qazi hailed from a landed family and received a traditional Islamic education. Like many of the old aristocracy, he had transitioned into a role as a civil servant and administrator for the state. His brother served in the Iranian parliament. Qazi was no radical, but he grasped the need for social reform.[50]

The last semblances of state power in Mahabad receded as the war concluded. A Soviet-backed "people's government" emerged in Azerbaijan. With Soviet support, Qazi established the Kurdish Democratic Party (KDP), cementing the alliance between the traditional elite and urban intellectuals. The KDP's Eight Point Declaration quoted directly from the Atlantic Charter and demanded Kurdish self-rule in Iran and unfettered use of Kurdish language. Despite pledging to respect Iranian sovereignty, the KDP intentionally emphasized Mahabad's autonomy and encouraged brethren in Iraq and elsewhere to join the movement. Iran was thus only the first front in the drive for Kurdish liberation. By the end of the year the last Iranian soldiers quit Mahabad, leaving the KDP in complete control.[51]

On January 22, 1946, the central committee of the KDP convened at Mahabad's main square to announce the formation the Kurdish Republic of Mahabad (KRM). Some attendees wore traditional Kurdish turbans or headdresses, others Cossack breeches and felt hats. Qazi initially wore Soviet uniform but was convinced to don a traditional white turban instead. "Kurds are a distinct people, occupy their own land, share a right to self-determination," Qazi stated. "They have a powerful ally in the USSR."[52]

The KRM quickly took on the trappings of a rebel state. Its army numbered an estimated twelve thousand men, mostly raised from the supportive tribes. In the cultural arena, the KRM initiated a new school curriculum, including Kurdish-language instruction. It opened the area's first secondary school for girls. Soviet advisors helped launch new periodicals, like the monthly *Nishtman* (Homeland) and the newspaper *Kurdistan*. The government revised the calendar, replacing Iranian names with Kurdish.[53] But tensions immediately appeared within the KRM ruling elite. The urban intellectuals chaffed at the "feudal" nature of tribal leaders within the KRM. Tribes themselves often harbored animosities and feuds.

The arrival of Mullah Mustafa Barzani, a tribal chieftain from Iraq, further complicated the situation. Mullah Mustafa hailed from the Bahdinan, a mountainous, Kermanji-speaking region on the Zab River between Erbil and Hakkari. His elder brother was a Naqsbandi adept who had led his flock in a number of bizarre religious quests. Mullah Mustafa had taken direct political power over the Barzani flock, instigating a number of rebellions against the British, and been placed in punitive exile in the 1930s. In 1945, though, he launched a new round of attacks before being driven to join with the KDP and the Mahabad group. Barzani's troops were the most seasoned of the KRM's forces. His tribal leadership style clashed with Qazi and antagonized many of the Mahabad locals. Tehran sought to entice tribal leaders away from the KRM with offers of subsidies and protection. Many tribes continued to parlay with Tehran, anticipating the state would eventually catch up with the KRM.[54]

Soviet support was essential for the KRM's survival. The USSR urged the KRM leadership to merge with the Azeri provisional government. Trying to find an alternative to Moscow, Qazi told the American consul in Tabriz that his intention was to achieve home rule, not secession. The United States, however, regarded the KRM as little more than a Soviet puppet state.[55] Iran complained to the U.N. about Soviet violations of its sovereignty. The United States supported Iran diplomatically, economically, and militarily. The Soviets relented, leaving Mahabad at Tehran's mercy. On December 1 Britain, the United States, and the USSR issued a joint declaration affirming Iran's "independence, sovereignty, and territorial integrity."[56] Government troops moved on the KRM in mid-December, capturing Qazi and much of the republican leadership. Early in the morning of March 31, 1947, Qazi, his brother, and his cousin were hanged in Mahabad's central square.[57] The Kurdish émigré press pronounced Qazi a national martyr. Mullah Mustafa fled back into Iraq. Hounded by Iraqi troops at the border, he scuttled to Turkey before arranging safe haven in the USSR. Four of his officers were captured and executed in Baghdad.[58]

The collapse of the KRM and dispersal of the KDP set back the Kurdish struggle for statehood. Kurdish aspirations for self-determination were born from the promise of Wilsonianism. The international community enunciated the need for Kurdish self-rule in the Treaty of Sèvres. Exactly contrary to Wilson's program, however, Kurds were ultimately divided by state borders that they had not chosen. This was not, however, Wilsonianism's failure but the enactment of other parts of the program of liberal internationalism. Kurdish efforts to gain statehood ran up against the guarantees of territorial integrity and border fixity that had also emerged from the Wilsonian premise. The KRM's fate underscored how the international community worked collectively to protect the sovereignty and territorial integrity of its member states. Breaking through these barriers was the enduring challenge for Kurdish separatism.

## The Kurds and the New Authoritarian Social Contract

The mid-century passage from colonial and mandatory rule to full independence in the Middle East ushered in a new era of radicalism. A rising generation of army officers, intellectuals, workers, and technicians rejected the pleadings, supplications, and impositions that had characterized colonial state building. Although they spoke vaguely of anti-imperialism, socialism, nationalism, figures like Gemal Abd al-Nasser in Egypt, Abd al-Karim al-Qassem in Iraq, or the various militant Ba'th Party activists who seized power in Syria and Iraq, had no real animating ideology. They shared, however, an abiding faith in the providential nature of the state, a state that could use technology to jump-start the transition to modernity. This was the heyday of ambitious land reform schemas, agricultural mechanization, large-scale dams, mass schooling, and public health initiatives. At the same time, states had new coercive powers with which to enact their visions of social transformation. The new social contract rested fundamentally on violence. The influx of weapons and moneys during the Cold War gave them new means to compel compliance and punish recalcitrance. Nevertheless, the state's offer was often the best and only option for citizens desperate to escape backwardness.

The social contract had especially hard edges for Kurdish minorities. Comparatively underdeveloped, rural, and tribal, Kurdistan was a region needing remediation. But the introduction of dams, clinics, and schoolhouses there went hand in hand with armed patrols, conscription, and surveillance. Modernization ineluctably entailed state penetration that threatened Kurdish national particularism. Kurdish nationalist leaders responded by clinging to the Wilsonian promise. When available, they used political, military, and diplomatic means to contest the state's hegemony. When state power broke down, Kurdish factions took control over territory and launched new experiments in self-rule. Paralleling the new generation of Arab nationalists, Kurdish leaders became increasingly urbane, literate, and, paradoxically, embedded in the politics of particular states. They were not the aggrieved tribal chieftains of decades past. They came of age not in a borderless imperial backwater but in an era dominated by territorially demarcated, sovereign states. Interstate boundaries thus bracketed the effort to gain Kurdish self-determination both from within and from without. The vision of a Kurdish homeland was segmented even in the minds of its partisans.

The key question in Syria was whether Kurds belonged in the state at all. The experience of the Hasakah autonomy movement raised questions about whether Kurds were an indigenous community. At the outset of independence in 1946, Syrian statehood was still relatively novel and shaky, and the polity was unmistakably divided along ethno-sectarian lines. Most communities within the ethno-sectarian mosaic, though, could fit under some notion of Syria's Arab identity. Not so the Kurds, whose linguistic distinction was the defining communal characteristic. Kurdish demands for autonomy and language rights during the transition to Syria's independence after World War II went unrequited.[59]

Kurds in Syria were both geographically scattered and politically divided. In the mid-1950s veterans of the KRM tried unsuccessfully to implant a wing of the KDP in Syria. Kurdish political parties were banned, and those that tried to operate clandestinely quickly splintered. In contrapose to the KDP's nationalism, leftists saw the solution to the Kurdish problem coming through the end of feudalism. The Syrian Communist Party, led by Khalid Bakdash, a Damascene Kurd who long been a feature in Syrian politics, promised liberation from reactionary forces, Kurdish or Arab.[60]

With the discovery of oil in the far northeast in the mid-1950s, the Syrian government enacted new measures to stifle Kurdish nationalism. They banned the use of the Kurdish language in public and the celebration of Nowruz and other cultural practices.[61] Arab nationalists identified the Kurds as complicit with Israel and a danger to the cohesion of the Syrian state. During the short-lived Syria-Egypt unification from 1958 to 1961, a number of "disloyal" Kurdish officers were removed from the army. In 1962 the left-wing Ba'th government took the most aggressive step to date to curtail Kurdish demography and power.[62] Government officials conducted an extraordinary door-to-door census in the Hasakah province, asking residents to prove their presence in the area prior to 1945. Some 120,000 Kurds were stripped of their Syrian citizenship, deemed foreigners (*ajnabi*) for their ties to Turkey. They had limited rights to own property or access government services like healthcare or schools. Even more severely, 75,000 others were listed as unregistered (*maktum*), further denied even basic documentation or access to government services. [63] Internal security organs began more intensive surveillance in the northeast. The government replaced Kurdish and Turkish toponyms with Arabic and encouraged Arab transmigration to the northeast in order to dilute Kurdish demographic weight in the area.[64] The aim was to deny Kurds any innate communal rights or connection to Syrian territory.

Agricultural initiatives augmented this demographic engineering. Land reform measures expropriated over a million hectares of land in the northeast, much of it from Kurdish tribal leaders. New agricultural collectives further attracted transmigrants. The construction of dams on the Euphrates and Kabur Rivers through the 1970s and expansion of the oil fields spurred the growth of cities like Raqqa and Deir Ezzour. These irrigation plans displaced Kurdish villages, while Arab settlers were granted valuable new lands. By the middle of the 1970s Kurds were effectively barred from the "Arab Belt," a cordon ten to fifteen kilometers deep along Syria's northern and northeastern borders.[65]

Upon coming to power in 1970, Hafez al-Assad dampened the doctrinaire leftist social engineering that had disrupted rural Kurdish life. Tribal leaders, both Kurdish and Arab, resumed control over large agricultural holdings in the northeast and received favored access to government credits for agricultural machinery. Some of the more stringent limitations on Kurdish cultural rights were relaxed. Nevertheless, repression remained a constant. In 1986 police fired at a Nowruz celebration, sparking riots in Damascus and Afrin.[66] Kurdish political parties were illegal but tolerated so long as they maintained a pro-Assad orientation. Those that continued to operate underground were hopelessly divided by personal and ideological squabbles. At the same time, Assad intermittently allowed safe haven to Kurdish groups from Iraq and Turkey, largely as a way to meddle in his neighbors' affairs. Most significantly, he permitted the PKK and its leader, Abdullah Ocalan, to operate from bases in Syria and Lebanon. Ocalan molded the PKK into a highly disciplined insurgent organization, with an almost cultlike devotion to Marxist-Leninist principles of revolutionary emancipation.[67] The presence of these foreign Kurdish groups helped to deflect the nationalist claims of Kurds within Syria. Influenced by the PKK, Syrian Kurds could see their aspirations come through the struggle against Ankara. After Turkey threatened to invade in 1998, Assad agreed to rein in the PKK. By that time, however, the PKK had already cultivated its own base of support within Syria.[68]

Unlike in Syria, the indigenous status of Kurds in Iraq could not be questioned. The League of Nations made guarantees of Kurdish national rights a condition of Iraq gaining statehood, largely in recompense for the failures of the Treaty of Sèvres. The Iraqi government grudgingly conceded the Kurds' right to maintain their language and culture. This, coupled with the Kurds' obvious demographic concentration in the north, meant that there was no way to elide Kurds' belonging in Iraq. Even the vociferously Arab nationalist Ba'th Party acknowledged that the Kurds had the status of a nationality within Iraq.[69] But what did these provisions mean in practice? Would they satisfy Kurdish aspirations for self-determination?

The ascent of Qassem during the 1958 July Revolution in Iraq opened the door to Barzani and the KDP. Of Kurdish descent on his father's side (and Shi'i on his mother's), Qassem described Iraq as a joint Arab-Kurdish polity. Qassem needed backing from Kurdish nationalists and leftists to counter the right-wing Sunni Arab nationalist factions. Barzani returned from his Soviet exile. The revised KDP charter of 1960 set out a distinctly Iraq-centered agenda that downplayed pan-Kurdish unity. It pronounced the party the "democratic vanguard party representing the interests of Kurdish workers, fellahin [peasants], merchants, artisans, and educated elements in Iraq" and committed the KDP to Iraq's "complete national unity . . . [and] combat[ing] separatism and chauvinistic ideas and cosmopolitanism."[70] Barzani and the KDP sought new measures for Kurdish self-rule in the north as well as broader cultural rights.[71] Barzani-aligned Kurdish tribes worked with the Iraqi Communist Party, the most substantial Iraq mass movement at the time, in manning the popular resistance militias that suppressed counterrevolutionary uprisings. These forces were integral to suppressing counterrevolutionary trends. Barzani used the opportunity to settle scores with traditional antagonists, such as the Arab Shammar tribe near Mosul, Turkmen, and the Kurdish Bradost, Herki, and Zibari tribes. But the Barzani-Qassem relationship soon soured. Barzani distrusted the Communists, whom he saw as threatening the power of the tribal magnates and diverting the attention of Kurds from the nationalist struggle. Ever jealous of power, Qassem refused to make good on his promises of Kurdish autonomy.[72]

In 1961 Barzani split with Qassem and fled to the mountains, reconstituting the KDP Peshmerga. The next thirty years of Iraqi Kurdistan would witness the ebb and flow typical of insurgent warfare. The guerrillas established strongholds in the isolated northern highlands and border region, while state forces garrisoned the lowland cities like Kirkuk, Mosul, and Sulaymaniyah. As the guerrillas gained strength and foreign backing, they moved to take the cities. This, however, left them vulnerable to the state's superior armor, artillery, and aircraft. Overextended and outgunned, the rebels eventually retreated up the mountains, beginning the cycle again.[73]

Behind the brute military dimension was a contest for political authority and legitimacy. After the break with Barzani, Qassem turned to Barzani's traditional rivals, such as the Bradost and Zibari tribes. The government granted these tribal leaders, called *mustashar* (consultants), wide latitude. They received arms and stipends to recruit fighters into a new force called National Defense Battalions (NDB). The NDB militias, often referred to by their Kurdish pejorative as *jahsh* (donkey foal), were notoriously ill disciplined. Still, they were a useful in mountainous terrain where regular troops fared poorly.[74] Qassem also launched a new drive to assert administrative control over Kirkuk. Kurds had long maintained that the city represented a prospective capital, highlighting its historical ties to the Baban emirate. However, as well as Kurds, the city itself housed Turkmen, Arabs, Christians, and other minorities. The growth of the oil industry in

Kirkuk's outlying districts drew migrants from across Iraq. Qassem demolished Kurdish villages in the area and launched a new drive to implant Arab settlers there. As part of plans for land reform and redistribution, pasturages held by the Kurdish tribal leaders were turned into new collective farms.[75]

The Kurdish nationalist camp fractured between conservative tribal forces and urban, leftist factions. In the mid-1960s Jalal Talabani, Nuvi Taha, and Ibrahim Ahmed led a left-wing splinter group from the KDP, decrying Barzani's retrograde and feudal leadership. The leading figures of the Kurdish nationalist left were too young to remember the Ottoman imperial past and were often re-moved from the rural lifestyle. They came of age in mandatory Iraq, when Kurdish nationhood was gaining legal substance and recognition, and partici-pated in the transformation of Sorani Kurdish into a full literary language. They had attended high school and universities in Iraq's larger cities, dabbled in Marxism, and gravitated to the KRM's left wing. Barzani, meanwhile, seemed irretrievable from the primitive milieu of the Bahdinan's mountains.[76]

After ousting Qassem in 1963, Iraq's Arab nationalist factions were surpris-ingly amenable to Kurdish demands for self-rule. Both the first Ba'th regime of 1963 and the more military-dominated government of the Arif brothers (1963–68) offered plans for "self-administration" (al-idara al-dhatiyya). Like Qassem's maneuvers, however, these were tactical gestures, meant only to stave off internal challengers. This was especially important for regimes such as these, which drew their base of support from Iraq's Sunni Arab minority and were generally hostile to aspirations from the Shi'i majority to gain control over the state.[77] While the Ba'th paid lip service to Kurdish national aspirations, they asserted that anyone living on Arab soil could be considered an Arab and hoped to eventually assimi-late the Kurds within Iraq.[78]

The Ba'th offered their most far-reaching plan for Kurdish autonomy in a dec-laration of March 1970. The decree established a single northern region with administrative autonomy and recognized Kurds as one of Iraq's two core nation-alities (qawmatayn). The Ba'th agreed to incorporate Kurdish leaders into the cabinet. Baghdad University reinstated its program for teacher training in Kurdish and began publishing texts for Kurdish schools.[79] Saddam Hussein, the declaration's primary author, traveled to Kurdistan a few weeks later to celebrate Nowruz before a crowd of thousands. Barzani countersigned the declaration as president of the KDP and leader of the Kurdish movement. Talabani rejoined the KDP, touting the success of the plan.[80]

But the 1970 declaration proved fatally flawed. There was immediate doubt about the regime's commitment. Autonomy was couched in a framework of Iraqi unity and could be easily revoked. What territories were to be included in the northern region was left unspecified. The government curtailed the scope of Kurdish autonomy by tinkering with internal administrative boundaries. For example, Sinjar, inhabited by Kermanji-speaking Yezidis, was detached from the Dohuk governorate and attached to Nineveh (Mosul). Similarly, district boundaries around Kirkuk were shifted to prevent its incorporation into any Kurdish-ruled areas. Even as they treated with Barzani and the KDP, the Ba'th built ties to his main rivals, namely Talabani and the leftist faction and the pro-Baghdad Kurdish militia groups. [81] This divide-and-rule strategy extended from the elites to the societal level. State officials encouraged Yezidis, Assyrian Christians, and other second-order minorities to self-identify as Arabs in official documents. Separate units of the NDB were organized to accommodate different minority groups within Kurdistan. A new census category for Turkmen was introduced in 1976, reinforcing a cleavage that the regime would exploit to combat the nationalists. [82] The status of the Shi'i (Fayli) Kurdish community, an estimated hundred thousand people, was complicated because the regime maintained that these were of Iranian, not Iraqi, origin. In the mid-1970s tens of thousands of Faylis were deported to Iran. [83]

Barzani also dragged his feet, leading to accusations of bad faith. KDP forces refused to stand down or accept orders from the central government. Violence escalated with assassinations of KDP officials and attacks on government outposts. Barzani insisted that the autonomous area include Kirkuk and called for a new census, with the proviso that only Kirkukis who could prove inhabitance prior to 1957 be included. Even so, Barzani also said that no census result would dissuade him from claiming Kirkuk as part of Kurdistan. [84] Nonetheless Barzani maintained that his vision was commensurate with Iraqi statehood and territorial integrity. "We were seeking self-rule, not separation," he said. "The initial aim of the Kurdish nationalist movement was not separation. Separation was never our slogan." A KDP newspaper, though, pointed out that "self-rule is not a substitute for the Kurdish people's right to self-determination." [85]

After four years of skirmishes and halfhearted negotiations, the Ba'th purged the KDP from the government and moved ahead unilaterally with the autonomy plan. The new autonomous region, called only the "northern region" in Ba'th discourse, proved a sham. [86] The KDP countered with more adamant and expansive demands: a voluntary union of Kurdistan with Iraq, with an officially constituted Kurdish Region retaining broad legislative and executive rights (including over oil), and a proportional share of the national budget. [87] Saddam rejected this flatly, saying, "Kurds don't want self-rule, but a state above the state." [88]

The conflict tilted into full-scale war. Barzani held the initial advantage, as much of the Iraqi army was still tied down in Syria after the October 1973 Arab-Israel war. Barzani, meanwhile, had some forty thousand regular KDP forces, plus sixty thousand tribal militia forces, loyal to him. He also had backing from Iran, Israel, and the United States. Tehran funneled tens of millions of dollars in aid and equipment to the KDP and provided its soldiers with sanctuary, logistics and communications support, and even direct military assistance. By June 1974 KDP fighters were mounting attacks in the lowlands. Confident in the decisive impact of Western backing, Barzani aimed to cut off the flow of oil from Kirkuk and win the war of attrition. [89]

Yet the KDP's strength was more apparent than real. Even before Barzani broke with the Ba'th, Turkey and Syria were alarmed that the KDP might use northern Iraq to back insurrections in their countries and therefore helped the Ba'th quarantine the KDP. In response, Barzani disavowed designs on Turkish or Syrian territory and even offered to help Ankara and Damascus deal with their internal Kurdish issues. Currying favor with Baghdad, left-wing Kurdish factions and the Communists denounced Barzani as a stooge of US imperialism.[90] Saddam, meanwhile, offered to cede territories on the Shatt al-Arab River to Iran if the shah ceased supporting the insurgency. Within weeks of the announcement of the Algiers Accord in March 1975, government forces gained the advantage, dooming the rebellion. Barzani pleaded for Washington's support: "If you will give us arms to march we will fight. Otherwise, we will make peace. We do not want to be massacred."[91] But the United States had already decided that the Kurds were expendable.

Kurdish resistance collapsed in a matter of weeks. Fearing government onslaught, some two hundred thousand refugees took flight to Iran. Iraq established a Kurdish exclusion zone along the border. Over a thousand villages were razed and six hundred thousand people displaced. The Ba'th dispatched Arab transmigrants, including Egyptians and Sudanese, to Kirkuk, diluting Kurdish demographic weight in the city.[92]

Barzani fled to Iran and then the United States, where he died in 1979. The KDP fractured. Talabani established the Patriotic Union of Kurdistan (PUK), an agglomeration of left-wing nationalist factions. Mahmud Osman, one of Barzani's top lieutenants and his personal physician, led another breakaway faction that eventually became the Socialist Party of Kurdistan in Iraq (SPKI). Masoud Barzani and his brother Idris took over the rump KDP. There were a bevy of other smaller leftist and Islamist parties. Bloody turf battles between these factions went on through the end of the decade.[93]

The end of the rebellion gave the state a free hand to refashion the politics, economy, and even ecology of Kurdistan. The regime's core assumption was that Kurds would reject obstructive leaders like Barzani and embrace the Iraqi state once removed from the rural hinterlands and granted opportunity for a modern life. In this view, counterinsurgency and development went hand in hand. Tribalism was already waning in Kurdistan, as it was in all of Iraq, due to massive urban migration. With their villages destroyed, Kurds had no choice but to move into demi-urban towns called *mujama'a* (collectives or congregations). The thirty-thousand-some units of mujama'a dwellings were a lynchpin in the state-led modernization. Within these towns, the state provided water, electricity, roads, markets, health clinics, schools, and labor and women's organizations. On a larger scale, the plan was to transition Kurdistan into a modern economy. Hydroelectric dams on the Diyala, Zab, and Tigris Rivers promised to supply the power for the industrial transformation of the north.[94]

But things did not go as the regime intended. Although the Ba'th claimed to be spending more per capita in Kurdistan than in any other region by the end of the 1970s, corruption, poor planning, and wayward execution marred the resettlement program. The disorienting violence and dislocation led many Kurds to become even more reliant on patrimonial ties of tribe and kinship. By the 1980s, when the government suspended some of its land redistribution policies, tribal chiefs emerged as landlords and commercial magnates.[95] Moreover, although the state had some means to compel Kurds to assimilate into Iraq's majority Arabic culture, such as exiling thousands to southern Iraq, the autonomous region remained intact. The regional parliament still met, even though it was squarely under Saddam's thumb. Schools taught a government-approved curriculum that emphasized Iraqi unity and loyalty to Saddam, but did so in Sorani Kurdish.[96] As Martin van Bruinessen observes, state plans to erode Kurdish identity through mass education and developmentalism actually helped broaden the audience for Kurdish nationalism.[97]

The disastrous cycle of weakening state control, emboldened resistance, and harsh repression was repeated again with the Iran-Iraq War (1980–88). Affairs in Kurdistan seemed well in hand when the war started. The regime leaned on the loyalist NDB and rejuvenated the Sufi orders as an alternative ideological and cultural anchor. The regime allied with the PUK, while the weakened KDP was confined to the far reaches of Bahdinan. As if to underscore its domination, in 1980 the regime abducted and executed hundreds of members of the Barzani clan, including those who had worked with the regime against the KDP.[98]

But as the war wore on and Iraq diverted greater military resources to the front line, the KDP renewed its insurgency in the rear echelons. Although the Islamic Republic had its own Kurdish insurrection to contend with, Tehran backed the KDP as a means to weaken Iraq. The PUK, still trying to salvage something from its alliance with the Ba'th, pressed for concessions on Kirkuk. By 1985, however, Talabani, too, despaired of Saddam's prevarications and aligned with Tehran.[99] Ranging across northern Iraq, guerrillas struck Kirkuk's oil fields and pipelines. The Iraqi military feared attacks on the Dokan and Derbandikhan dams, which could have caused massive flooding downstream.[100] With Tehran's blessing, the KDP, PUK, SPKI, and several of the smaller leftist factions, plus the Assyrian Democratic Movement, formed the Iraqi Kurdistan Front (IKF). The NDB, which was supposed to provide auxiliary support to the military, proved ineffective. Tens of thousands of Iraqi troops were tied down in the north.

The government escalated violence to genocidal proportions. After spending much of the 1970s espousing respect for Kurdish nationalism, Saddam used religious terminology to denigrate and dehumanize the Kurdish opposition, describing them as traitors and *kuffar* (unbelievers, the plural of *kafir*), those deserving of death.[101] Saddam viewed the Kurdish rebellion as an existential threat and authorized more extreme measures, including chemical weapons, in response.[102] In 1987, Saddam appointed his cousin Ali Hassan al-Majid to oversee the campaign in Kurdistan. Majid launched a ruthless series of operations called the Anfal ("spoils of war"). The Anfal represented the culmination of all previous policies of repression and forced relocation. Majid flushed out and destroyed any village suspected of harboring insurgents. Government troops and NDB militias encircled the fleeing residents. Women and children were deported to concentration camps; men were often executed on the spot. As the campaign intensified, the violence became totalizing, expanding from the border zone into the interior, particularly around Kirkuk. Majid refused to exempt NDB commanders and others who had demonstrated their service to the government. The infamous gas attack on Halabja in March 1988 became a key element in the Kurdish collective memory of persecution. An estimated 50,000 to 120,000 people were killed in northern Iraq, 4,500 villages obliterated, and a million people (about a third of the entire Iraqi Kurdish population) displaced. The United States and other Western powers, which had backed Saddam during the war and provided most of Iraq's advanced weaponry, remained silent about his atrocities against his own people.[103]

## Nation-State Crisis and the New Age of Kurdish Rebellion, 1991–2010

The advent of the Kurdish Regional Government in Iraq, just three years after the calamity of the Anfal genocide, stemmed directly from the decimation of the Iraqi state after the 1990–91 Gulf War. Iraq had the most formidable army in the Arab world, but it was no match for the United States and its allies. Iraq's military shattered in the immediate wake of the war, allowing rebel groups like the PUK and KDP to seize territory and begin building a de facto state. Equally important, though, was the shift in the views of the United States and others on territorial integrity and sovereign statehood. By the end of 1991, the international community had begun to question whether these ideas, which had buttressed Iraq's statehood since the 1920s. The KRG's emergence and endurance reflected the abiding ambivalence of the global nation-state crisis. Every subsequent attempt to gain Kurdish self-determination tried to exploit the incongruence between de facto and de jure power and capitalize on the international community's equivocation.

While the United States and its allies readied to confront Saddam in 1990, Iraqi Kurdish leaders were guardedly optimistic that Iraq's near-certain defeat would give them new opportunities for autonomy. Kurdish and other Iraqi opposition figures lobbied Washington, London, and Paris to consider Saddam's removal.[104] Yet President George H. W. Bush knew that the coalition's mandate extended only to defending Kuwait from territorial aggression and worried about destabilizing Iraq. Despite calling on the Iraqi people to "rise up" in February 1991, when the mutinies and insurrections erupted in northern and southern Iraq in March, the United States stood back.

In Kurdistan, the uprising began in Raniya and spread to Dohuk, Erbil, Sulaymaniyah, Zakho, and the fringes of Kirkuk. Armories were looted. Groups tried to settle old scores and feuds. The IKF leaders had little control over the course of events. NDB commanders defected and announced new alliances under the KDP or PUK. After a week, however, the Republican Guard mustered and counterattacked. By mid-March the Kurdish rebels were retreating from Kirkuk and clinging to defensive positions rimming the Syrian, Turkish, and Iranian borders. Similarly, the rebellion in the south stalled. Kurdish and other opposition leaders pleaded for international protection. Keenly aware of how Saddam had dealt with the last insurrection, millions abandoned their homes in fear. Northern Iraq became a melee. Turkish troops crossed the border to attack PKK infiltrators. The PKK aligned with Saddam to fight the KDP, whom they viewed as pro-Ankara.[105] To the dismay of other Iraqi opposition factions, the KDP and PUK moved to cut their losses and entered negotiations with Baghdad again. The arrival of UN Security Council Resolution 688, with its specific condemnation of their repression by Iraq, was a windfall to the Kurds. Britain and the United States cited the resolution and its call to protect humanitarian operations to justify the establishment of no-fly zones (NFZs) in both northern and southern Iraq. The international intervention in Iraq thus opened up a gap in Iraq's de jure and de facto sovereignty, which Kurdish separatists were able to exploit.

Formally established with the election of the Kurdistan National Assembly in May 1992, the KRG was at once audacious and circumspect. The preamble of the KRG constitution offered a historical narrative of Kurdish nationhood that traced the Kurdish "right for self determination . . . recognized for the first time in Woodrow Wilson's Fourteen Points."[106] The preamble became a bill of particulars detailing the disappointments of the Kurdish nation: the nullification of the Treaty of Sèvres, the false assurances of the British and the League of Nations, the violation of Iraq's own constitutional provisions protecting Kurdish rights, and, finally, the Anfal.

Still, the Kurdish leadership refrained from formal secession. Instead, the KRG positioned itself as the delayed enactment of the March 1970 autonomy plan and the logical continuation of the UN's humanitarian mandate. Article 2 of the constitution made an expansive claim for what space Kurdistan entailed. Beyond the territory already under rebel control, roughly comprising the Dohuk, Sulaymaniyah, and Erbil governorates, it also claimed Aqra, Sheikhan, Sinjar, the subdistrict of Zimar in Nineveh, Khaniqin and Mandali in Diyala, the Badra in al-Wasit, and, most importantly, the entirety of the Kirkuk governorate, which would serve as the KRG capital. The KRG arrogated to itself the power to override the central government and to maintain its own security forces. But, as Barzani and other Kurdish leaders would delicately explain, it stayed within the bounds of Iraqi statehood, at least as they defined them.[107]

Iraqi officials predictably differed. They referred to the autonomous Kurdish entity as the "abnormal situation" (al-wad' al-shadhdh), the term Iraqi nationalists had used to roust the British mandate. They claimed the NFZ and the safe havens were a violation of Iraq's territorial integrity and sovereignty.[108] But the Iraqi state was in no position to reimpose physical control in the north. However belatedly and haphazardly, the international community concluded that Saddam's threats to his own citizens were a danger to international peace, allowing them to set aside Iraq's right to for non-interference.

Forswearing secession, at least temporarily, helped mend the rifts between the IKF and other factions of the largely Arab Iraqi opposition. The KDP and PUK were crucial participants in Ahmed Chalabi's Iraqi National Congress (INC). The 1992 Salahuddin Declaration further enunciated Kurdish commitment to stay in Iraq. Kurdish officials touted the KRG as a pro-Western, democratic success story—exactly what the INC promised the rest of Iraq could become.[109]

Yet the KRG's internal politics betrayed tendencies toward banal patrimonialism. The uprising, repression, and the imposition of the economic embargo brutalized a society already scarred by decades of war. During the March 1991 uprising, tribal leaders, many associated with the NDB, used their private military retinues to seize agricultural lands and urban real estate and implanted themselves deeper into the lucrative smuggling market. The KDP and PUK competed to co-opt these petty warlords. The 1992 elections to the regional parliament hastened the ideological denaturing of Iraqi Kurdish politics. Both factions came to operate largely as conveyors of patronage through the emergent neo-tribal system. The KDP's brand of right-wing nationalism and the PUK's progressivism became less distinct. The elections, free and fair by most measures, resulted in a deadlock, an even split of seats between the KDP and PUK (with a handful of seats reserved for the minorities). Barzani's clientelistic network predominated in the north and west, Talabani's in the south and east. The major tribal factions delivered their voters to whichever party offered the best opportunity for patronage. The Bradost, who controlled the territory along the Turkish and Syrian borders, for example, hedged their bets by maintaining ties to the PUK,

KDP, PKK, and Baghdad. The KDP and PUK subsumed smaller political factions, including the once significant Kurdish left.[110]

The PUK and KDP clashed in the mid-1990s over control of the patronage flows. Both linked up with outside actors. After Talabani allied with Iran, Barzani worked with Saddam to storm PUK positions in Erbil and Sulaymaniyah. Seizing on the disorder in the Kurdish Region, Turkey launched another incursion against the PKK's stronghold in Iraqi Kurdistan. Strengthening his alliance with Ankara, Barzani continued to try to contain and push back PKK incursions. Saddam's troops, backed by the KDP, killed hundreds of PUK fighters and liquidated the INC base in Erbil before US air strikes drove him out. Barzani and Talabani reached a modus vivendi in 1998 after mediation by the United States and the small Kurdish Islamist parties. Despite pledges to unify their administration across the KRG territory, the KDP and PUK effectively returned to running separate zones of control.[111]

The anomalous juridical status of the KRG defined the trajectories of economic development. The Kurdish Region of Iraq (KRI), as it would be formally known after 2003, was encircled on all sides. Baghdad imposed an economic blockade and rescinded the salaries of civil servants in rebel-held areas.[112] At the same time, since the autonomous zone was nominally part of Iraq, the UN restricted imports. In the early years of 1991 and 1992, the situation was especially dire. Once the UN-administered Oil-for-Food program came online in 1995, however, the economic situation improved markedly. The KRG was guaranteed 13 percent of Iraq's oil revenue, proportional to the region's population. With these rents, Barzani and Talabani launched into a broad developmental project. These projects were comparable to those of other countries in the region and in some ways a continuation of the Ba'th plans for modernization. There was new spending on public works projects, housing, and education, with the corresponding expansion of the government payroll.[113] With little alternative curriculum, Kurdish schools continued to teach from the Kurdish-language textbooks issued by Baghdad, excising objectionable sections about Saddam or Iraqi nationalism.[114] The rentier nature of the KRG economy reinforced the power of the local power brokers associated with the PUK or KDP instead of the regional government in Erbil.[115]

Though a political hindrance, geography was an important economic asset to the nascent Kurdish state. Although Talabani spoke languorously about Kurdistan becoming a Hong Kong–style free trade area, in fact, the KRI was a smuggler's paradise. Zakho and other border cities saw a boom in construction and real estate. Agricultural products flowed from Kurdistan to the rest of Iraq in semi-clandestine trading routes, averting Saddam's blockade. Oil, construction materials, and other finished goods came north. KRG-based shell companies managed to sell oil smuggled to the international market through Turkey and Iran. All the KRI's neighbors, including Iraq, benefited from its limbo.[116]

As President George W. Bush determined to remove Saddam in the wake of the September 11, 2001 attacks, Kurds became a key part of the opposition coalition supporting the invasion. The INC-affiliated opposition groups lent moral weight to the case for invasion. The gassing of Halabja became a talking point to prove Saddam's criminality. The KDP and PUK stood out as the most proven militarily and the most reliably pro-American. They were also the only groups within the INC to have a demonstrable foothold and following on Iraqi soil. But the Kurdish commitment to Iraq remained contingent. In December 2001 Jalal Talabani reminded audiences at the opening of Kurdtel, a telecommunications firm:

> December 25, 1922 is the day when the right of self-determination of the people of Kurdistan was recognized by the then British and Iraqi government. . . . What comes to mind from this perspective is that Iraqi Kurdistan was attached to Iraq on the basis of a decision by the then League of Nations, which was furthest away from the wishes of the people of Kurdistan, although it was based on the condition that our administrative, cultural and national rights would be protected within the framework of Iraq. . . . We are Iraqis and Kurds of Iraq, but on the understanding that we in Iraq should be an equal partner, have equal rights and have authority within the central government. We should also have a hand and say in establishing the present and future Iraq. That is why our struggle is aimed at setting up a democratic and federalist Iraq.[117]

In the run-up to the 2003 invasion, the US plan for Iraq met skepticism on legal, normative, and pragmatic grounds. The invasion definitively crossed the bright normative line that the 1991 Iraq War had intended to defend. But the INC's support gave the invasion moral and practical plausibility. Reciprocally, by engaging the INC, the United States elevated a mostly exile dissident body into the legitimate voice of the Iraqi people, a government-in-waiting ready to take over upon Saddam's removal.[118]

Rather than deliver a friendly regime, however, the invasion and occupation utterly obliterated the Iraqi state. By dissolving the Iraqi army and dismissing Ba'th Party officials, the United States alienated many Arab Sunnis and drove them into the arms of the insurgency. Due to the presumed Shi'i majority in Iraq, Shi'i Islamist factions like the Supreme Council for Islamic Revolution in Iraq (SCIRI) and the Da'wa Party were the likely victors in any electoral competition. Moreover, SCIRI had its own Iranian-trained Badr Brigade militia. But the exiles faced challenges from the Sunni insurgency and from rival Shi'i factions. Muqtada al-Sadr, a firebrand cleric with grassroots support in Baghdad's poor Shi'i quarters, raised his Mahdi Army to challenge both the United States and

the exiles. Grand Ayatollah Ali al-Sistani, the most revered Shi'i religious authority in Iraq, expressed misgivings about ceding power to U.S.-backed groups.
Anticipating a quick handover and withdrawal, the US occupation force was in-
adequate to maintain order. Deteriorating through the 1990s, the monopoly of
force in Iraq shattered. Iraq descended into a prolonged, brutal, multi-front
civil war.

Most of this turmoil, meanwhile, spared the KRI. The PUK, the KDP, and
several smaller left-wing and Islamist parties formed a unified political front and
became the second-largest bloc in the federal parliament. In the regional parliamentary elections, the first since 1992, the KDP took forty seats and the PUK
thirty-eight (of the hundred openly contested seats). Barzani assumed the KRG
presidency in a grand coalition. Investment and migration continued to flow,
resulting in double-digit rates of growth.[119] As fixtures within US-sponsored interim council and transitional governments, Barzani and Talabani were in prime
position to engineer maximal autonomy.

The drafting of the Iraqi constitution in 2005 was carefully orchestrated to
deliver a power-sharing agreement among the primary actors in the INC coalition,
namely Da'wa, SCIRI, the PUK, and the KDP.[120] The preamble of the constitution acknowledged Saddam's atrocities against the Kurds, effectively incorporating Kurdish nationalism into Iraq's national narrative. Kurdish became one
of Iraq's two official languages. The constitution retroactively normalized the
KRG's anomalous legal status, accepting legislation from the regional parliament
as legally binding. The KRG had the right to maintain its own security force and
was to receive a share of the national budget proportional to its population and
in compensation for the damage of the previous regime.[121] In an important symbolic gesture, Talabani became president and head of state and the bridgehead
between the Kurdish elite and the federal government.

But critical questions remained as to where the KRG's and central government's
respective writs pertained. As soon as Saddam was gone, the PUK and KDP
began to assert control over Kirkuk and other areas that they had claimed under
the 1992 regional constitution. Peshmerga forces set about relocating some hundred thousand Kurds who had been displaced during the Arabization campaigns, evicting Arabs, Turkmen, and others who had taken over purportedly
expropriated property. Sistani and the rest of the Shi'i political establishment
denounced the Kurdish moves. Non-Kurdish residents mobilized self-defense
militias, often with support from figures in the central government. US occupation authorities tried upholding the status quo, rebuffing their previously stal-
wart Kurdish allies. Article 140 in the federal constitution specified that disputes
over territory would be resolved through a local plebiscite by the end of 2007.
UN advisors concluded that voting was impossible given the security climate.
The vote was delayed indefinitely.[122]

Kirkuk became the fault line where the power of the KRG and the federal government collided. Once in power, Iraq's Shi'i leaders were less inclined to honor their prewar commitments to devolution that would blunt their clear demographic weight. Likewise, the Kurdish leaders, realizing their superior military and infrastructural capacity, questioned the wisdom of staying in a decrepit Iraq. Piggybacking on the 2005 parliamentary campaign, Kurdish politicians held an unofficial ballot about independence. The response, unsurprisingly, was almost unanimous support. Pro-independence activists delivered a petition with 1.7 million signatures to the UN headquarters in New York.[123] Kurdish history textbooks, newly issued after the KRG assumed control over the educational curriculum in 2005, downplayed ties to Iraq and Arabs, while stressing loyalty and belonging in a multiethnic, yet still Kurdish-dominated, Kurdistan.[124]

As Diane King put it, the KRI became a "place where the local and global converge[d] in a particularly rich fashion . . . a site of experimentation with the modern."[125] Kurds in Iraq experienced a simultaneous push toward nationalization and globalization. A generation of Kurds had grown up with little knowledge of or affinity for Iraq. English was the essential second language of Kurdistan, not Arabic.[126] The boom in Kurdish media reinforced this tendency, further molding a Kurdish-speaking nation and building connections to Kurdish communities in Turkey, Syria, and Iran.[127] Kosovo's independence in 2008 and Scotland's independence push encouraged the Kurds to think that Iraq's border might change.[128] It was thus easy to imagine a Kurdistan apart from Iraq, at least for Kurds themselves.

But there were more prosaic bonds keeping the KRI within Iraq. Fiscally, the KRG was entitled to 17 percent of Iraq's national budget, no mean sum given Iraq's oil exports. Western portions of the KRI received electricity from the Mosul Dam, while the KRG-controlled Derbandikhan and Dokan dams in the east supplied irrigation for Diyala and points south.[129] Kurdistan-based businesses thrived in the expanded Iraqi market. Two of Iraq's largest telecommunications companies, AsiaCell and Korek (the latter run by Barzani's nephew), were based in the KRI.[130] There were further geo-strategic reasons militating against secession as well. The United States favored federalism but opposed secession. The KRG had strong ties with Ankara, Damascus, and Tehran, but the viability of a small, landlocked, independent Kurdish state was questionable. The Kurds of Iraq had nowhere else to go.

The success of Kurdish nationalists in Iraq emboldened activists in neighboring Syria. Even before the invasion of 2003, there had been an upswing in Kurdish political mobilization stemming from the ascent of Bashar al-Assad to the presidency. After the death of his father in 2000, there seemed a possibility of political and cultural opening. Bashar appeared sympathetic to demands for language rights and willing to regularize the status of ajnabi Kurds. Activists in

Qamishli launched new campaigns to promote Kurdish literacy. Demonstrators used UN Human Rights Day to stage rallies and send petitions to the UN calling attention to restrictions on Kurdish language and the citizenship question. But the promise of opening soon faded, and the regime returned to policies of repression and divide-and-rule.[131]

Still, new political parties tried to distinguish themselves amid the din of Syria's fractious Kurdish groups. The PYD formed in 2003 and 2004 as the Syrian wing of the PKK. PKK operations in Turkey had been severely hurt with the capture and imprisonment of Ocalan in 1999. Several of the PYD founders had emerged from PKK training camps in the Qandil Mountains, a secluded area of Iraqi Kurdistan. Although PYD leaders stressed their independence from the PKK and their focus on Syrian affairs, they retained strong ideological and political ties to their Turkish brethren.[132] One of the reasons for the launch of PYD might have been to block Barzani from extending his sway into Syria. Flush with the success of the KRG's legalization, Barzani positioned himself as a kind of pan-Kurdish champion. He offered to mediate between Turkey and the PKK. Most of the time, however, the PKK regarded Barzani as Ankara's puppet. A second significant group to appear in Syria in the mid-2000s was the Kurdish Future Movement (KFM). Several of the KFM leaders had been involved in the early 2000s with the short-lived Jeladat Badr Khan Cultural Association, named for the founder of the Khoybun. The KFM was part of a growing number of liberal and secular opposition groups in Syria. It sought equality of citizenship for Kurdish Syrians while eschewing claims to self-determination through federalism or secession.[133]

Kurdish disappointment became apparent in March 2004, when rioting and other disturbances rocked Qamishli. The incident began at a soccer match between supporters of the home squad and visiting fans from Deir Ezzour. Qamishli supporters hoisted the KRG and KDP banners; visitors carried banners picturing Saddam and allegedly made joking reference to the Halabja massacre. Taunts turned to brawls, brawls into rioting, which left the local Ba'th Party building aflame and a statue of Hafez toppled. There were at least thirty deaths, and hundreds were arrested. Thousands fled across the border to the KRG.[134]

Kurdish leaders were often estranged from the wider circle of Syrian opposition. In October 2005 leading dissidents penned the Damascus Declaration, calling for reform and peaceful transition from Ba'th authoritarianism. The declaration included a specific call for a "fair solution for the Kurdish issue" and "equality of Kurds with all other Syrian citizens." Although the KDP–Syria and other Kurdish factions signed the declaration, many complained that it failed to acknowledge the Kurds' specific national and cultural rights and historical standing on Syrian soil. [135] Through the 2000s government policies continued to marginalize Kurds, especially in the northeast, where new investment in the oil sector seemed to bypass Kurdish villages.[136] The Kurds' position within the Syrian state remained unassured at exactly the time when their status in Iraq was becoming politically and legally firmer.

## Uprising, War, and Kurdish State Building, 2011–2017

The wave of protests that enveloped the Middle East in 2011 reverberated through Kurdistan. Activists and nationalist leaders in Syria, Iraq, Iran, and Turkey saw the opportunity to assert new claims for autonomy from state power.[137] But the way they pursued separatism—how they organized their institutions, competed with state and non-state rivals, and engaged with the international community—reflected the distinct historical experience within each state. Even in a period when states were failing, efforts to work across state boundaries proved difficult. The rise of the Islamic State in Iraq and Syria simultaneously impinged upon and propelled the progress of Kurdish separatism in both states. By literally demolishing the Iraqi-Syrian border, IS made Iraq and Syria into a single unified vortex of struggle. IS was a menace not just for individual states but for the international order as a whole.[138] But responding to this threat required a massive collective action that included not just Damascus and Baghdad but also the United States, Turkey, European powers, Russia, Iran, and the Gulf states, among others. The emergence of this global coalition brought new opportunities and constraints to Kurdish separatists in Syria and Iraq.

Early in the Syrian uprising, Bashar offered plans to end restrictions on Kurdish property rights and to grant citizenship to as many as four hundred thousand ajnabi Kurds (although it left the position of the unregistered maktum unresolved).[139] The Kurdish opposition responded disjointedly. Mishal Tammo of the KFM attended some of the first opposition meetings in Istanbul and joined the executive committee of the Syrian National Council (SNC), the main US-backed opposition body. He was assassinated in Qamishli in October 2011, however, depriving the SNC of its most significant Kurdish voice. Nearly a dozen other Kurdish factions, including the KDP–Syria, formed a separate umbrella organization, the Kurdish National Council (KNC). The KNC sought national and collective rights for Kurds based on international norms of self-determination and demanded a rollback of the Arabization campaign in the north and northeast. Influenced intellectually and politically by Barzani and the KRG model, the KNC sought to topple Bashar and transform Syria into a federal entity. In this vein, even the name of the Syrian Arab Republic was problematic. Many on the largely Sunni Arab SNC rejected these demands as a prelude to secession. Standing apart from the SNC, KNC activists lobbied the United

States for separate military and financial allocations comparable to those of the Free Syrian Army (FSA).[140]

The PYD abjured the opposition working in exile and instead joined the National Coordination Council, a consortium of leftist factions that the regime allowed to operate openly in Damascus. The council aimed to push reform through negotiation, without violence or foreign involvement.[141] In a 2011 interview PYD chairman Salih Muslim described the PYD's objectives using Ocalan's anarcho-Marxist argot. He refused "classical models like federalism, con-federalism, self-government, and autonomy." Instead, he focused on "democratic autonomy," through bottom-up cultural transformation. Muslim deemed Kurds who had aligned with the SNC the "henchmen" of Turkey.[142] By the autumn of 2011 the PYD launched what it called the People's Council for Rojava, deeming it part of the transition and reform process.[143] The opposition, in turn, accused the PYD of cooperating with the regime. There were widespread suspicions that the PYD killed Tammo in retaliation for his alignment with the SNC.[144]

The withering of state control, especially in the far northeast, provided the opportunity for the Kurdish groups to take power on the ground. By July 2012 government forces were falling back to protect the main metropolises of Aleppo and Damascus. The PYD's militia, the People's Protection Unit (YPG), took over towns and villages in the northeast and the north, establishing three distinctive cantons: Hasakah, the original area of the 1930s autonomous region, Kobani, and Afrin–Kurd Dagh.[145] To critics, the ascent of the PYD and Rojava confirmed the cooperation between the PYD and the regime. Syrian army troops remained garrisoned in Qamishli, unmolested by the PYD forces in the area.[146] Muslim acknowledged tactical coordination with the army but denied any strategic cooperation with Bashar.[147] Rojava became a conduit for cross-border smuggling of oil and other goods, migration of refugees, and humanitarian assistance for the war zone across the Syrian, Turkish, and Iraq borders.[148]

According to the PYD's public discourse, Rojava was not intended as the kernel of Kurdish statehood; indeed, it was hardly a state at all. The Rojava Social Contract, a quasi-constitutional document issued in 2013, contained no historical exposition on Kurdish national rights. Rather, it focused on a multiplicity of indigenous groups, "a confederation of Kurds, Arabs, Assyrians, Chaldeans, Arameans, Turkmen, Armenians and Chechens." The charter "protect[ed] fundamental human rights and liberties and reaffirms the peoples' right to self-determination," while affirming Syria's territorial integrity and its status as a "free, sovereign and democratic state, governed by a parliamentary system based on principles of decentralization and pluralism." Like the KRG in 1992, the PYD was proclaiming its allegiance to a hypothetical state.[149]

Regardless of ideological pretense, though, competition for territory and resources in the crucible of civil war molded Rojava into a state-like form. As

Michiel Leezenberg and Rana Khalaf have described, behind these commune-level committees was a centralized and hierarchical decision-making body dominated by the PYD. The YPG, which had grown to a significant twenty thousand people by 2014, including its famous women's battalions, remained under tight party control. The arrival of PKK guerrillas from outposts in southern Turkey and Qandil reinforced the PYD's military dominance. It also, however, created tensions between those focused on the Syrian front and those who prioritized the fight in Turkey. Just as in PKK-held areas of Iraq or Turkey, however, party propaganda, including hagiography of Ocalan himself, pervaded Rojava.[150]

There was immediate tension between the PYD and the KNC. Barzani initially tried to co-opt the PYD by seeking to create a common Syrian Kurdish front to manage affairs in Rojava. Barzani also interceded with Ankara, convincing Recep Tayyip Erdogan to allow the PYD to continue operating inside Syria so long as it refused PKK infiltration. When co-optation failed, Barzani turned to counterbalancing, trying to train a KNC militia force. There was no way for the KNC to match the PYD and PKK militarily, though. By the end of 2014 several thousand KDP–Syria members and other KNC affiliates had taken refuge in the KRG.[151]

From the inception of Rojava, the Islamic State was a mortal rival. As early as 2012 YPG and IS forces fought for control over the crucial border crossing, the smuggling and transit routes, oil depots, and the hydrological infrastructure. Battles for valuable rent-yielding real estate were hardly unusual in the war, but the conflict between PYD and IS had deeper ideological grounds. For reasons of avarice or cowardice, an Arab rebel or Syrian army soldier might offer the *baya'a* (oath of allegiance), grow an orthodox beard, and come to join IS. For Kurdish-speaking, Marxism-steeped men and women of the PYD, this was far less imaginable. The PYD propagandists depicted theirs as the struggle between Western enlightenment and retrograde Islamic fanaticism. IS's massacres and sexual enslavement, particularly the attack on the Yezidis in Sinjar and the siege of Kobani in 2014, solidified this framing and helped turn Rojava into a humanitarian case for the West.

The PYD became the most important element in the Western-backed Syrian Democratic Forces (SDF). The SDF took in FSA remnants, Arab tribal bands, and smaller militias that arrayed against IS. The YPG was always the largest and best-trained force under the SDF banner. At an estimated twenty-five thousand people, YPG comprised from half to three-quarters of the SDF's total contingent.[152] PYD forces played a crucial role in driving IS from the northern and northeast border. By late 2015 the PYD had created an unbroken zone of control all the way from the Iraqi border in the far east to the Euphrates, linking Rojava's Hasakah and Kobani cantons.

But the more territory and power PYD amassed, the more resistance it faced. Officially, Rojava was redubbed the Democratic Federation of Northern Syria

(DFNS) in 2016 in order to be more inviting to non-Kurdish groups and affirm a connection to Syria. Although Christians, Arabs, Turkmen, and others were involved at the commune level, the PYD still dominated the DFNS, just as it did the SDF. Human rights organizations reported patterns of forcible conscription, recruitment of child soldiers, ethnic cleansing, and other human rights abuses.[153] Some Arab and Turkoman militias refused to cooperate with the PYD, which they accused of seeking to agglomerate territory into Rojava. Indeed, the United States tried to constrain the PYD and to block the YPG from pushing into areas that lacked a Kurdish majority.

Nevertheless, the PYD took an increasingly unilateral stance, seizing territory first and asking permission later. In an interview in July 2015, Salih Muslim emphasized the PYD's independence and offered a significant rebuke to the man who had allowed the PYD to operate openly at the beginning of the war.

> I never believe[d] Syria will return to what it was; that is, to a country controlled by one party, one nationality, and one flag reflecting extremist approach[es]. We are working hard and sincerely for a democratic and decentralized Syria. . . . Personally, I do not think Assad's stay is possible. I don't think the Syrian people will accept [it] or that the war can stop if he stays.[154]

In the same interview Muslim criticized Iran, Bashar's strongest foreign backer, for its treatment of the Kurdish minority.

But what was Rojava's end? For Syrian-born members of the PYD, like Muslim himself, the goal may have been to solidify a Kurdish existence within a reformed Syrian state. As one Syrian PYD leader said in February 2017:

> Those who think that a society can exist without a state can keep on dreaming. We have to deal with the reality of the international system, which consists of states with borders. We should focus on getting Kurds recognised as an integral component of Syrian society whose rights are protected. It doesn't matter whether we do this via cantons or a federal region or whatever. I don't look at Iraqi Kurdistan as a positive example, but . . . we should not be pursuing utopia.[155]

But for the more doctrinaire of Ocalan's followers, statehood itself seemed counterrevolutionary and anachronistic. Those who had come up through the PKK regarded Rojava as a step toward a wider revolutionary campaign against Turkey. As the tentative truce between the PKK and the Turkish government unraveled at the end of 2015, the PYD seemed willing to sacrifice positions and alienate allies within Syria in order to carry the battle northward.[156]

Turkey, which had never made much distinction between the PYD and the PKK anyway, began taking steps to counter the PYD and dismember Rojava. Erdogan specifically warned against any moves to create a contiguous Kurdish-held territory across the Euphrates. In August 2016 SDF-affiliated PYD forces did cross the Euphrates to attack the IS-held city of Manbij. The United States had planned that the PYD would withdraw from the city in favor of local Arab troops once the battle ended. But PYD forces refused to relinquish their hold and seemed poised to push farther westward. In response, Turkish troops crossed the Syrian border into Jarabolous in Operation Euphrates Shield. Although the stated objective of the mission was to root out IS, the PYD was an obvious target as well. Parroting the US justification for the invasion of Iraq in 2003, Turkey claimed the old mid-century rules of territorial integrity no longer held. As an op-ed in a pro-Erdogan newspaper related:

> We're living in age of extraordinariness. . . . This is the complete disinte-gration and collapse of the international system, the fields of partner-ship being in disorder, alliance relations becoming meaningless, the trust ties between states and communities being destroyed and the start of systemic failure. . . . If this country is going to make it out alive—and in fact stronger—from the storm in question, the north of the Mosul-Aleppo line must urgently be turned into a safe zone and regardless of which organization, regardless of which map is being drawn, all the se-curity threats in this region must be eliminated.[157]

Turkish troops drove a wedge between the PYD positions in Kobani and Afrin. The United States and other Western powers tried to temper Turkey's response and urged the PYD to return east of the river. Almost simultaneous with the Turkish invasion, there were skirmishes between the PYD and regime-aligned fighters in city of Hasakah. This suggested that Damascus and Ankara, likely with Russian and Iranian approval, intended to block any further consolidation of Kurdish autonomy.[158]

The United States tried to shield the PYD from the Turkish advances, need-ing to preserve the SDF as a counterweight to Bashar, Iran, and Russia in the anti-IS coalition. Through a series of ceasefire agreements, the PYD forces were repositioned east of the Euphrates in preparation for the assault on Raqqa, the IS capital. Seizing the Tabqa and Ba'th Dams in the summer of 2017, along with the Tishrin Dam north of Lake Assad, the PYD effectively controlled the irrigation and electricity production for the entirety of eastern Syria.[159] PYD forces were at the front line in the conquest of Raqqa itself into the autumn of 2017.

In Iraq, as compared to Syria, the uprising and civil war had a more spas-modic rhythm. Both Baghdad and Erbil faced mounting popular disaffection over corruption, unemployment, and general maladministration through the end of the 2000s. Iraq lurched from emergency to emergency. After a constitutional crisis following the 2010 election, the 2011 protest wave gave voice to popular antipathy, especially among Sunni Arab communities that faced systematic exclusion. The Iraqi government's heavy-handed response further enflamed the situation. By December 2013 Fallujah and other cities in western and central Iraq were under IS control.

From Erbil's perspective, so long as IS was confined to western Iraq and Syria, it was the problem of the federal government. The Kurdish leaders had their own concerns with which to deal. By the end of the 2000s, it seemed that the KRG state-building project had stalled.[160] Barzani and Talabani were approaching their fifth decades as leaders of the KDP and PUK, respectively, and the twentieth year as effective co-rulers of the KRG. Below them in the party ranks, sons and nephews of their respective clans jockeyed for sinecures. Kurdish politics had become more deeply sultanistic.[161] Corruption and cronyism were especially apparent in the ranks of the Peshmerga and the intelligence services. Though technically part of Iraq's state security forces, most units operated under party control, allowing commanders to pursue private commercial fiefdoms.[162] The regional economy was weakening and overburdened by a bloated public sector.[163]

In the 2009 regional parliamentary elections, the Gorran ("change") Party, a protest movement led by Nashirwan Mustafa, a famed Peshmerga commander and ex-PUK official, won twenty-four seats.[164] Gorran activists eagerly fed the protest wave of 2011. PUK forces shot and killed demonstrators on the street of Sulaymaniyah. There was a general atmosphere of intimidation toward dissident activists and journalists.[165] The PUK bore the brunt of these challenges. After Talabani was incapacitated by a stroke in December 2012, debates about succession further crippled the party. In the 2013 regional elections Gorran surpassed the PUK to become the second-largest parliamentary bloc. Islamist parties also gained ground.[166] The erosion of the joint KDP-PUK alliance buffeted Barzani, even though the KDP gained seats. Barzani began his third term as KRG president in 2013, despite protests about the still unratified constitutional revisions. The KDP and the PUK were increasingly at odds and supported different candidates and factions. Internationally, the KDP pulled closer to Ankara and tried to prop up the Syrian KNC against the PYD. The PUK and Gorran, in turn, allied with the PYD and PKK and deepened ties to Iran.

Barzani raised the stakes in dealing with Baghdad. The KDP seemed to reach a kind of tacit alliance with Sunni Arab politicians who were pushing their own version of regional autonomy.[167] KDP parliamentarians backed efforts to counter or even oust Prime Minister Nuri al-Maliki. Barzani demanded new prerogatives, including the supremacy of the KRG over federal law, accommodations on

Kirkuk, and the right to sell oil directly to the international market.[168] Iraq's oil law permitted the KRG to manage new oil fields. The KRG leaders had been courting foreign oil companies for years. Most foreign firms, however, feared losing access to the much larger fields in southern Iraq by doing business with Erbil.[169]

Still, Barzani spoke optimistically about the chance of a referendum on KRG independence. Looking abroad, the international community seemed amenable to altering once sacrosanct international borders. Nechirvan Barzani, nephew of Massoud and KRG prime minister, cited South Sudan's vote for independence in 2011 as a warning to Iraq:

> Since 1992, as a part of its right to self-determination, the Iraqi Kurdistan region has decided to choose federalism. . . . Kurds have often been subject to oppression and mass murder throughout Iraq's history, which I don't think any Iraqi with conscience is happy about. Iraq can only progress if it solves its problems. Through war and oppression, it will end up like Sudan.[170]

With the civil war in Syria, it appeared that there might even be a possibility of Kurdish unification. In January 2014 the KRG announced its first unilateral oil sale through the pipeline to Turkey. The KRG tried to maintain the appearance of legal punctiliousness, earmarking 83 percent of the sale for the federal government. Still, the KRG officials refused to remit funds to the Iraqi national bank account, which they accused Maliki of misappropriating.[171]

This changed, however, when IS launched an offensive in the summer of 2014 on Mosul and the north. By August IS held territory from the outskirts of Aleppo to the entirety of Mosul. Neither the KRG nor federal forces had fared well at first. The Peshmerga retreated in disarray, struggling to defend their capital.[172] The Iraqi army performed even worse. Discredited by the losses, Maliki was forced to resign in favor of Haider al-Abadi, who seemed more conciliatory to Kurdish and Sunni demands and more tractable to the United States.[173]

Barzani saw a chance to bolt from the sinking Iraqi ship. Peshmerga forces moved on Kirkuk, the Nineveh Plains, and the other disputed territories. While Kurdish officials claimed this as a tactical maneuver to stem IS expansion, many saw a naked land grab. With the Kirkuk fields in hand, KRG oil sales quadrupled from the pre-June 2014 levels to some $4 billion in revenue.[174] Since the heyday of Mullah Mustafa, Kurdish leaders had considered oil a kind of diplomatic trump card that they could trade oil for political support from abroad. Accordingly, the KRG made sure that its closest allies received the benefits of support. Turkey, which operated the primary pipeline for KRG crude, took a cut.[175] Israel accepted Kurdish crude and the broader logic of the transaction. Israeli prime minister Benjamin Netanyahu said that Israel "should support the

Kurdish aspiration for independence, a nation of fighters [who] have proved political commitment and are worthy of independence."[176] Russian firms bought stakes in KRG oil pipelines.[177] This diplomatic strategy, though, came at significant economic costs, as global oil prices began to fall in 2015. Since most international firms feared being shut out by Baghdad, the KRG had to offer oil at a significant discount. Moreover, the federal government suspended financial allocation to the regional government once it began selling oil on its own, generating a net loss for the KRG economy.[178]

The disposition of Kurdistan, especially the territories captured since 2014, loomed as the global coalition moved to roll back the IS gain. Barzani insisted that KRG forces act as Baghdad's partner, not subordinate. The KDP and PUK forces, the Iraqi army, Iranian-backed Popular Mobilization Units militias, and Western military advisors and air support made an unwieldy alliance. Every territorial advance the KRG forces made expanded the territory they might incorporate into their future state. Though Baghdad grumbled, there was little choice but to placate Kurdish demands. Kurdish forces were the northern arm of the pincer closing on IS territories. Through 2015 and 2016 KRG forces played a major role in the capture of the Mosul Dam, Sinjar, and Mosul.[179]

The KRG intensified its outreach to the international community during the military campaign. In Washington it hired professional lobbyists to win favor in Congress and the White House.[180] Barzani argued that after fighting to oust IS, Kurds deserved the right to decide their own destiny through a referendum. Barzani blamed the problems of Iraq on its fundamentally artificial and illegitimate formation and, specifically, on the continuation of oppression by its Arab elite. The future, he said, was "a border drawn in blood" that would supersede the mistakes of the colonial era.[181] The point, though, was not just practical but also normative, referring back to the premise of the international system. "If any country does not back this referendum," Barzani told European Union officials in Brussels in July 2017, "then such a stance will contradict its democracy and its principles regarding the right of nations to self-determination."[182] At home, Barzani warned that Baghdad

> will take every right from us if they can. My beloved people, referendum is a means and not the end. Our goal is independence and determining our fate, so that Lausanne and Sykes-Picot cannot determine our fate anymore.[183]

Even so, the referendum stood on unsteady legal foundations. After Barzani dissolved parliament and expelled Gorran from the cabinet, there were doubts about the constitutionality of his presidency. Kurdish opposition figures accused him of using the referendum to distract from the problems of his own political leadership. Though few would openly question the Kurdish right to se-cession, many doubted the wisdom of proceeding with the vote. Barzani himself seemed hesitant to set a date for the voting. Even Nechirvan Barzani tried to downplay the referendum's significance, assuring an American journalist that "the outcome doesn't mean we will immediately embark [on independence] but it will show the international community what the population wants."[184]

For its part, the Iraq government maintained unequivocally that the vote would carry no legal weight and warned of a constitutional breach.[185] The inter-national community, including Iran and Turkey, signaled opposition and seemed to hope for a last-minute compromise.[186] Tensions were especially high in the Kurdish-held disputed territories, where the Kurdish demographic majority was most uncertain. Many minorities distrusted Barzani and the KDP, whom they blamed for leaving them undefended during the IS onslaught. They sought out alliances with Baghdad or, alternatively, the PKK and PUK. In the Nineveh Plains, the Assyrian Democratic Movement, one of the original IKF constitu-ents from the 1980s, mobilized its own militias in the hopes of blocking annexa-tion to the KRG.[187] The KRG, in turn, tried to entice Arabs, Turkmen, Yezidis, and Christians to support the referendum and made assurances that they could be full citizens of an independent Kurdistan.[188] In Kirkuk, however, the KRG took steps to ensure that only those who could prove residency prior the begin-ning of the Arabization campaign in 1957 could vote.[189] Although official data on voter turnout was questionable, enthusiasm for the referendum appeared highly uneven. In KDP-dominant areas like Dohuk, an estimated 80 to 95 per-cent cast ballots. In Sulaymaniyah and Halabja, turnout may have been as low as 50 percent.[190]

Regardless of the count, it was clear almost immediately following the refer-endum that Barzani had overplayed his hand. Baghdad banned international flights to Erbil and Sulaymaniyah. Iran and Turkey jointly expressed their com-mitment to preserving Iraq's territorial integrity and closed their borders with the KRG, pending the arrival of customs agents from Baghdad.[191] Iran began conducting joint military exercises with Iraqi troops. American secretary of state Rex Tillerson said that "the vote and the results lack legitimacy, and we continue to support a united, federal, democratic and prosperous Iraq."[192] Among the few voices of congratulation was the unrecognized Republic of Nagorno-Karabakh, which "welcome[d] the conduct of the referendum on independence in Iraqi Kurdistan, an act of exercising peoples' right to self-determination . . . upheld by the UN Charter and other fundamental international documents."[193]

Kirkuk, as always, was the epicenter of conflict. Iraqi security forces and mili-tias moved on the city, and protesters blocked the highway to Erbil.[194] Arrest warrants were issued for the members of the committee that had organized the referendum, as well as the KRG-appointed governor of Kirkuk, who had just a few days earlier opined confidently, "This is no different from Britain asking to get out of the European Union, or the Catalans asking for independence from Spain."[195] Kurdish residents fled northward. By mid-October about one hundred Peshmerga had died in sporadic fighting with the Iraqi security forces and militias. On October 15, PUK forces withdrew from Kirkuk, effectively ending the standoff. Kurdish forces began leaving other disputed areas shortly thereafter.[196] Announcing his resignation two weeks later, Barzani bitterly denounced the United States and the rest of the international community for betraying the Kurdish cause. He called the PUK's evacuation of Kirkuk an act of treason. "Nobody stood up with us," he said, "other than our mountains."[197]

Rojava suffered a similar fate. In late January 2018 Turkey launched another assault on the isolated canton of Afrin–Kurd Dagh. Arab and Turkmen militias, some former affiliates of the FSA, turned on the PYD. Kurdish civilians fled and the YPG fighters melted away. In March 2018 Turkish-backed troops entered the city of Afrin unopposed. They promptly toppled a statue of Kaveh, the mythical tyrant-slaying progenitor of the Kurds.[198]

## Conclusion

It is tempting to see Kurdish separatism in light of its most visible partisans. Outsized figures like Mullah Mustafa and Massoud Barzani, Talabani, and Ocalan dominated the landscape of Kurdish politics for generations. Their rivalries hampered intra-Kurdish coordination and left Kurds exposed to manipulation from outside. The KRG's failed independence push and the collapse of Rojava in 2017 and 2018 could be considered these gerontocrats' last gasp.

Such a view, however, misses the deeper historical processes that simultaneously fostered Kurdish claims to national self-determination and impeded their realization. As much as any other group in the Middle East, the Kurds were the direct heirs to Wilsonianism. The promise of self-determination for Kurds was intrinsic in the diplomatic and military unraveling of the Ottoman Empire. But the Kurds never had the opportunity to make it into a reality. Barzinji's Kingdom of Kurdistan, the autonomous zone in northeastern Syria, the KRM, and the intermittent civil war in Iraqi Kurdistan from 1963 to 1988 all met the same violent end. Their antagonists were not just titular states like Iraq, Syria, Turkey, or Iran but neighbors and great powers. Ultimately, states tended to protect their own; Kurds tended to turn on each other. The weight of the international system, which prioritized mid-century norms of sovereignty and territorial integrity, stifled the impetus for self-determination.

In the 1990s and 2000s Kurdish actors in Iraq felicitously found these barriers eroding. The global nation-state crisis began, in some respects, in Iraq.

Resolution 688 and the ensuing NFZ were essential for the emergence of the KRG in Iraq. In its corruption and patrimonialism, the KRG was not much different from most other unrecognized states to appear in the 1990s—and certainly no worse than the genocidal state of Saddam's Iraq. Barzani and Talebani refrained from making the ultimate legal break with Iraq. They clung to the limbs of legality, claiming to fulfill both international and Iraqi law. Despite its purgatorial juridical existence, the KRG was able to build the framework of cultural, political, and economic institutions necessary to join in the burgeoning process of globalization. It carried on the modernization process that the Ba'th had initiated but made sure that the beneficiaries were in Kurdistan, not Baghdad. The US invasion of 2003 was an unmistakable boon to the KRG. By the end of the 2010s, Barzani had chosen a path destined for confrontation. In the midst of Syria's civil war in 2011, Rojava followed a similar course at hastened speed. The PYD rhetorically avowed its loyalty to the abstract notion of Syrian sovereignty while overriding, destroying, or repurposing the real, concrete manifestations of the Syrian state on the ground. To legitimate their claims domestically and internationally, the leaders of the KRG and Rojava sought to reactivate the Wilsonian promise. Barzani's harangues about Sykes-Picot reminded audiences that self-determination was still the bedrock of the international system. Similarly, although ideologically skeptical of statehood, members of the PYD accepted the "reality" of the state system and tried to make themselves useful within it.

The battle against IS justified the continuation of Kurdish autonomy in both Iraq and Syria, but Kurdish claims to statehood rested on more than mere expediency. In many respects, the KRG and Rojava were models of rebel state making. They each amassed far more political and military power than either of their contemporaries in southern Yemen or eastern Libya. They controlled the key economic infrastructure of their region. Their political systems, though hardly liberal, were reasonably responsive to public pressures and demands. They enjoyed deep ties with the international community due to their position on the front line against IS. But ultimately, the KRG and Rojava were victims of their own success. Once IS was dispatched, the Kurds become dispensable. The international community, which had flouted norms of sovereignty in Iraq and Syria for over two decades, suddenly retrieved them, postponing the Wilsonian moment yet again.

# The Islamic State

Mosul, the Day of Prayer, Sixth of Ramadan 1435 AH
(Friday, July 4, 2014)

*The most distinguishing element in Mosul's skyline was the lopsided minaret known as the Hunchback (al-habda), rising sixty meters above the Grand Mosque of Nur al-Din on the west bank of the Tigris. Local lore held that it tilted because the Prophet Muhammad had used it as a stepping-stone on his way to heaven. In fact, wind erosion had caused the tower gradually to stoop.*

*The forces of the Islamic State (IS) assaulted Mosul, Iraq's second largest city, on June 5. Mosul yielded after only a few days of fighting. IS then made an earth-shattering declaration: The borders separating Iraq and Syria, indeed all borders dividing Muslim people, were canceled and the obligations of citizens to those states dissolved. The Islamic State was now a caliphate, in direct successorship to the Prophet Muhammad. Muslims around the world were obliged to offer the baya'a, the oath of allegiance, to IS and its new caliph, Abu Bakr al-Baghdadi.[1]*

*Few places in Mosul were more auspicious than the Grand Mosque to consummate this covenant. Mosul was known as a bastion of Sunni Islam, despite harboring pockets of Christians, Yezidis, Shabak, and other communities. Much of Mosul's religious infrastructure was devoted to saintly shrines like those to the prophet Jonah, Saint George, and local adepts revered across the region's religious communities. IS abhorred them. Adopting the puritanical Salafist theology, IS saw shrine veneration as idolatry and quickly demolished some of the city's most important sites.[2] The Grand Mosque, however, was spared. The mosque derived its name from its founding benefactor, Nur al-Din bin Imad al-Din al-Zangi, ancestral lord of the Zang (Zengid) dynasty. The Zang were part of a medieval resurgence of Sunni Islamic orthodoxy. During the twelfth and thirteenth centuries they ruled Syria and northern Mesopotamia with nominal allegiances to the Abbasid caliphate. In the name of the caliphate, which claimed legitimacy as the continuation of the Prophet Muhammad's polity, the Zang battled the Byzantines and the Crusader states, as well as the Shi'i Fatamids. Nur al-Din was renowned for his piety. He funded mosques, hospitals, and other public* works across the Levant, including a pulpit for Jerusalem's al-Aqsa Mosque. The endowment for Mosul, then part of his brother's domain while Nur al-Din ruled Aleppo, was a gesture of fraternity. Nur al-Din's mosque featured an intricate honeycombed dome (muqarnas) to complement its minaret. These structures, as the architectural historian Yasser Tabbaa put it, were intended to demonstrate Islam's dominance over Christianity and orthodoxy's triumph over schism and heresy.[3]

Baghdadi intended to surpass Nur al-Din and his dynasty. Standing beside the pulpit, with his black robes, turban, and fulsome beard, the forty-three-year-old had a messianic air. Mosul's city elders, civic leaders, tribal chieftains, and religious dignitaries assembled before him. Baghdadi cleaned his teeth with a sirwak, the same instrument the Prophet purportedly used, then mounted the podium. His sermon began as many others did during Ramadan, with the promise of mercy and forgiveness, but soon turned to martial themes. Mercy was impossible for polytheists. Baghdadi did not need to mention Shi'is, who ruled in Baghdad, or Christians, who had installed them. His selective recitations of the Quran were enough:

> Fight them until there is no sedition [fitna] and the religion, all of it, is for Allah. . . . . We sent down iron, wherein is great military might and benefits for the people, and so that Allah may make evident those who support Him and His messengers unseen. Indeed, Allah is Powerful and Exalted in Might.[4]

From jihad came the necessity and obligation of the caliphate, rule modeled upon the example of the Prophet and congruent with God's will. Here Baghdadi assumed false modesty: "I've been tested by Allah in my election as caliph. It is a heavy burden. I am no better than you. Advise me when I err and follow me if I succeed. And assist me against idol-worship."[5] By witnessing Baghdadi's leadership in such a historically significant and public forum and by offering prayers in his name, the assembled were already granting consent.

But the building in which Baghdadi stood was not the one that Nur al-Din had built. In fact, from its inception Mosul's Grand Mosque was a work in progress. In the late 1940s, the Iraqi Ministry of Religious Endowments razed the main mosque hall and shipped its original ornaments to a museum in Baghdad. They built a new structure of nondescript Andalusian style, with a hemispheric dome and flat concrete roof, lending the mosque a modern, sterile appearance. Before that, the Ottomans had repeatedly renovated the building, including transplanting a pulpit from a neighboring mosque in 1864.[6] As recently as 2010, UNESCO readied plans to repair the precarious minaret. The project was halted due to security concerns.

IS intended to highlight its ancient genealogy, but it could not blot out modernity. A wristwatch, once the emblem of the avant-garde in the Middle East, glinted on Baghdadi's arm.[7] An electric fan churned behind his head. Congregants surely noticed that cameras and microphones stood between themselves and the new caliph, although videographers edited this out of the footage that beamed out through IS social media organs. More significantly, the caliphate itself was enmeshed in the politics of the Wilsonian era. The Ottomans were the last credible claimants to the caliph, only relinquishing the title in 1924. The caliphate's demise, wrote one of the expert consultants to the King-Crane Commission, demonstrated the rejection of "backwardness" and a turn to "self-determination, constitutionalism, the separation of church and state, the desire to obtain the benefits of modern scientific advances" within the Muslim world.[8] The black IS banner, draped conspicuously in the mosque interior, was another unwitting gesture to recent Ottoman antecedents. The declaration of faith, "No God but God / Muhammad is the messenger of God," appeared in an archaic-looking script meant to evoke the Prophet's own banner. Yet, as William McCants notes, the image was neither ancient nor Arabian. Rather, it was a replica of the seal used in Istanbul's Topkapı Palace, itself recovered from a dubious relic.[9] After the Ottoman caliphate ended, twentieth-century Muslim intellectuals debated whether the caliphate would be reconstituted—and by whom. Faisal's Hashemite clan was among several dynasties that considered claiming the title.[10] The baya'a, meanwhile, became a common element of Arab political culture. In Syria and Iraq, citizens had once made similar oaths to Hafez al-Assad and Saddam Hussein.[11] As much as Baghdadi sought to supersede these illegitimate rulers, he could not help but follow them.

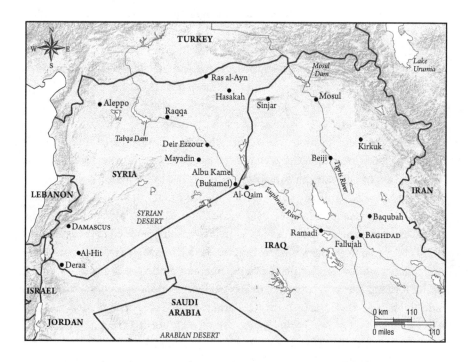

# Introduction

Of all the challengers to Arab statehood arising during the tumult of the Arab uprisings, the Islamic State (*ad-Dawla al-Islamiyya*) was the most astounding and alarming. IS seemed to explode on the scene with its blitzkrieg assault on Mosul and its declaration of the caliphal state. Yet from this summer 2014 peak, IS also suffered the worst collapse of any of the aspirants for territorial control. By 2016 IS was already in retreat, and by the following year it was in tatters.

IS represented a true revolutionary actor, challenging not just the territorial boundaries of a particular state but the foundations of sovereignty. Modern statehood and nationalism were alien and apostate. Anything that divided the *umma* (community) and prevented people from unifying around the true faith had to be broken. IS was hardly the first to espouse pan-Islam but was uniquely proactive in enacting its program.[12] It sought to overturn the entire normative structure of the international system. Ever remaining and expanding, as its pro-pagandists put it, IS attracted supporters and acolytes around the world and became the hub of a global insurgency.[13]

But IS was also a self-described state (*dawla*), a feature that distinguished it from other radical Islamic organizations and movements.[14] Before IS could supplant existing states, it first had to detach from them. The theatrics of IS's border breaking often elided its territorially specific practices meant to build a functioning Islamic state.[15] IS denied countries of origin any significance, but its leadership was divided by cliques of Iraqi, Syrian, and foreign nationals. Ideologues claimed to obliterate colonial boundaries, but their obsession with the "Sykes-Picot borders" granted these supposedly ephemeral demarcations new potency.[16] IS leaders dreamed of forming a transnational Islamic polity but were consumed with the day-to-day tasks of administering territories and ruling people that had very recently been Iraqis and Syrians.

The gap between IS's transnational reach and its limited geographic grasp is critical for understanding the rise and fall of IS. IS's protean territorial claims mirrored its frenetic search for historical predecessors. For IS ideologues, the Islamic State was legitimate because it fulfilled ancient prophesy. IS would make the umma dominant and whole, as it was in Muhammad's day. But this view ignores the mundane perspective of IS as an institution grounded in the context of Iraqi and Syrian territories.[17] More exactly, the Islamic State sank its roots at the inflection point of the Fertile Crescent, an area Islamic geographers called the Jazira ("island" or "peninsula").[18] Bracketed by the upper branches of the Tigris and Euphrates, the Jazira features semi-arid steppes, craggy mountains, and verdant riverbanks. Ottoman officials and Western Orientalists (including a young Mark Sykes) saw the Jazira as a functional region linked together by commerce in wool, foodstuffs, and textiles.[19] Its most important cities were Mosul, Deir

Ezzour, and Diyarbakir. Transhumant tribes, largely Arabic speaking in the south and Kurdish in the north, generated much of the raw material and protected—or, alternatively, pillaged—the caravansary. Trade flowed between Mosul and Aleppo, the gateway to the Syrian market. Although Sunni Islam predominated, the Jazira was a hodgepodge of sects and ethnicities. As Ali Nehme Hamdan points out, "as a region of lived experience—as a pragmatic geography—the politics of place in the Jazira have greatly shaped IS political practices more than its vision does."[20]

Within the spatial-historical context of the Jazira, IS appears not just as a terrorist super-group or a death cult but as a regional rebellion. It gestated in Iraq, spread into Syria, and then returned to capture the Mosul (Nineveh), Anbar, and Saladin governorates. Just as in the cases of separatism in Cyrenaica, South Yemen, and Kurdistan, IS capitalized on resentment toward the state centers, Baghdad and Damascus. In the midst of state crisis, it solidified territorial control in the Jazira by offering residents empowerment, security, and services.

To justify these efforts, IS also generated a narrative of grievance focused on the imposition of unjust, illegitimate, and foreign rule. The grist of these complaints dated back to the aftermath of World War I and the Wilsonian moment, when the region was divided between Syria and Iraq. Detractors constantly paint these states as artificial, colonially invented, and illegitimate. But ideas of "Syrian-ness" and "Iraqi-ness" were percolating already in the early twentieth century.[21] Faisal told world leaders at the Versailles Conference that "the various provinces of Arab Asia—Syria, Irak, Jezirah, Hejaz, Nejd, Yemen—are very different economically and socially, and it is impossible to constrain them into one frame of government." In contrapose to Syria, which was ready for immediate self-rule, "Jezirah and Iraq are two huge provinces, made up of three civilized towns, divided by large wastes thinly peopled by semi-nomadic tribes." A separate Arab monarchy, Faisal proposed, should incorporate Iraq and the Jazira, "buttressed by the men and material resources of a great foreign Power."[22] Of course, Faisal's plans collided with British and French designs. But the Arab nationalist agenda, premised on Wilsonian self-determination, also confronted obstacles from below. The drive to create Arab states did not necessarily accord with the wishes of the Jazira's inhabitants. State building in Iraq and Syria necessarily entailed encroachment from outside powers. The new borders deprived merchants in Mosul and Deir Ezzour of their usual markets and tribes of their customary pasturages and caravan routes. States demanded a kind of singular loyalty from their citizens that contradicted traditional systems of multivalent solidarity associated with clans, tribes, classes, sects, or ethnicity.[23] At the same time, the mandates splintered political authority and allowed Jazira tribes, merchants, and others to mount new claims that distanced them from state authority.[24] For several decades there was sporadic but violent contestation as local groups sought to resist or renegotiate their incorporation into the state. Yet no movement of national liberation raised a banner in the name of the Jazira's sovereignty, and no one could fix the region's territorial contours. The Jazira incorporates all or parts of today's Raqqa, Hasakah, and Deir Ezzour governorates in Syria and the Nineveh, Saladin, and Anbar governorates in Iraq.[25] Its integration into Syria and Iraq occurred by gradual subdual, co-optation, and accretion rather than formal unification or outright conquest. Many inhabitants welcomed the opportunities for social advancement through the military and the ruling party and the chance to gain from the expansion of irrigation and discovery of oil. By the turn of the twenty-first century, the Jazira's potential as the site of a distinctive political identity seemed forgotten.

Appearing on the scene after the US invasion of Iraq in 2003, al-Qaeda in Mesopotamia (AQI), IS's direct forbear, subsumed these modern displacements into a millenarian narrative in which Sunnis, champions of the true Islamic faith, battled multifarious deviancy. As a theater of cosmic strife, the Jazira's location in Syria and Iraq was moot. IS recast the Jazira's parochial conflicts—mercantile ambitions, competition for irrigation and pasturage, control over oil, and the recent humiliation of cashiered soldiers and civil servants—into an epochal struggle. As a messianic movement, IS was engaged in the concrete, terrestrial world while also being speculative, otherworldly, utopian, and universal.[26] IS reconstituted the Jazira as a sociopolitical entity only to transcend it. Accordingly, IS's appeal to outside actors differed from those of its contemporaries. Though IS capitalized on a political aspiration fostered by Wilsonianism, it looked past the principles of self-determination and the promises of contemporary international society. It turned instead to the norms of Islamic solidarity and the eternal and indivisible Sunni umma. The emancipation of the Jazira from apostates and imperialists was the emancipation of Muslims in general from unbelief.

## States, Boundaries, and Belonging in Syria and Iraq, c. 1880 to 2003

The transition of the Jazira from an interior domain of the Ottoman Empire into a frontier space separating the independent states of Iraq, Syria, and Turkey involved dramatic transformation in political and economic infrastructure. It also, however, carried on imperial traditions of dominance and hierarchy that had been nurtured at least since the days of the Zang. Taking control over the territory in the sixteenth century, the Ottomans assumed the banner of Sunni supremacy. Sunni rule, entailing allegiance to the Ottoman sultan-caliph, was right and enduring. Shi'i rule, usually suborned by Iran, was aberrant and ephemeral; Christian dominion, unthinkable.[27] Until the mid-nineteenth century, though, the empire was a distant overlord. The maintenance of peace, stability, and tax revenue was entrusted to tribal chiefs and local plenipotentiaries, many transplanted from elsewhere in the empire to serve as imperial lieges.[28] With their nineteenth-century reform, modernization, and centralization, the Ottomans took a more direct role in the affairs of the region. The Ottomans broke the power of the local dynasties and encouraged tribes to settle and farm, especially around the Euphrates. Over the course of the nineteenth century, the Ottomans tinkered repeatedly with the region's administrative boundaries.[29] European interest in extending economic influence, especially after the discovery of oil around Mosul in 1907, intensified and augmented the Ottomans' administrative reach. France planned to extend the Syrian railway past Palmyra to Deir Ezzour and Mosul.[30] Britain, aided by Ottoman administrators, tried to link to Mosul through the Tigris steamships.[31] Germany's Berlin-to-Baghdad railway had it terminus at Ras Ayn but promised to reach Mosul and Baghdad soon.[32] Until the eve of World War I, the Jazira was a pivot between Anatolia, the Levant, and the Persian Gulf. At war's end, the region become a buffer zone and battleground between Britain, France, and emergent Arab, Turkish, Armenian, and Kurdish nationalist movements.

Undergirding this competition was the ebb and flow of more local interests and competition. By November 1918 British colonial officers had already concluded that ruling the Jazira directly would be impossible:

No Government will exercise effective control over the Syrian Desert. Governments are concerned only with the administration of settled districts, and the relations of tribes to borders of cultivated land.[33]

French colonial administrators similarly determined that the physical geography of the Jazira steppe precluded a strong state hand. Instead, they focused on monitoring and controlling transit between the desert and the settled river regions.[34]

The Jazira frontier between Iraq and Syria remained a site of continual contestation through the 1920s. The mandates involved multiple competing sovereignties, including the nationalist factions operating in Damascus and Aleppo, then Baghdad, and the British and French colonial administrators, plus the League of Nations itself. Such circumstances allowed local actors, especially the tribes, opportunities to claim prerogatives that in many ways supplanted the state.[35]

Deir Ezzour, a kind of no-man's-land between the British and French zones of control, was a microcosm of how local objectives intersected with the national and imperial agendas. Between 1918 and 1920 the local Arabic-speaking tribes, primarily concerned with avoiding taxation or other forms of outside intrusion, repeatedly switched their allegiances between the Arab nationalist government in Damascus and the British colonial authorities in Baghdad. In the summer of

1919 a faction of Mesopotamian-born officials working in Damascus petitioned the King-Crane Commission for complete independence for Iraq. Iraq, they argued, should include Diyarbakir, Mosul, Baghdad, Basra, and Deir Ezzour. In September the British determined to use the Khabur River, east of the city of Deir Ezzour, as the demarcation between Iraq and Syria. The plan was a setback to the Arab nationalists and deleterious to the Shammar and Anaza tribal confederations, which migrated from the Jazira to the Arabian Peninsula. The nationalists reversed course; they now wanted Deir Ezzour and its downstream siblings removed from Iraq and attached to the Arab kingdom in Syria. In November 1919 Damascus dispatched Ramadan Shallash, the son of the local Albu Saraya sheikh from Deir Ezzour and an ex-Ottoman officer, to attack the small British garrisons. By exhortation and bribery, he rallied the Shammar and Anaza chiefs to storm Deir Ezzour, Mayadin, Albu Kamal, al-Qaim, and Ana. Eventually, the British were able to stymie Shallash by threatening aerial bombardment and peeling off his tribal allies one by one. Trying to stay in Britain's favor, Faisal repudiated Shallash's adventure. But the territorial change endured. Deir Ezzour, a district that most regarded as integral to Iraq, became instead part of Syria.[36]

Britain and France used similar strategies to coopt the Jazira's tribal magnates. They subsidized loyal tribal sheikhs and granted them broad authority to tax, administer justice according to tribal law, and maintain order in their designated area and among their tribal followers. Collective punishment was the rule. Tribal sheikhs converted massive tracts of tribal commons into private property, rendering the lesser tribesmen into sharecroppers. At the same time, the colonial authorities clamped down on internal migration, issuing passes and documentation designed to fix peripatetic tribes to certain specific territories. Britain and France tried to ply the loyalty of the sheikhs to gain leverage over the other mandatory power. The sheikhs, in turn, took advantage of the tenuous nature of state control to play off Britain and France against each other.[37] Becoming the state's intermediary granted tribal sheikhs unprecedented powers and increased intra-tribal tensions. Many tribes fractured into pro- and antistate wings. In the 1920s, for example, Ajil al-Yawer, the government-designated paramount of the Shammar in Iraq, faced a revolt within his own confederacy. The dissident faction refused to keep the peace and used Syrian territory as a base for its raids. Ultimately, the RAF was called to bring the rebels to heel. Raids and feuds persisted. Through the late 1920s and early 1930s tribal representatives, Iraqi and Syrian government officials, and British and French officers met repeatedly to negotiate plans for safe passage and demarcate borders across the Jazira.[38]

The Mosul province, site of the largest Jazira city and significant oil fields, was a much greater prize and evinced a similar contest between local, national, and colonial actors. In late 1918 France agreed to cede the provinces to Britain, a

modification of Sykes and Picot's original understanding. The British moved colonial officers to occupy the province but were blocked by Mustafa Kemal's
Nationalist Forces army and Sheikh Barzinji's Kurdish nationalist revolt. Thus,
the British kept Mosul out of their initial plans for Iraq.[39] In 1919 Arab nationalists in Mosul mobilized in anticipation of the King-Crane Commission, but the
Americans never arrived. Activists corresponded with the Arab government in
Damascus seeking military assistance to help drive out the British. They claimed
that Arab and Kurdish-speaking tribes were ready to rise against the British (although urban tradesmen and laborers were disengaged and apathetic). When
Damascus hesitated, the nationalists questioned whether they should continue
having faith in the principles of the Fourteen Points and considered joining the
Kemalist campaign. Moslawis celebrated the capture of Deir Ezzour by decorat-
ing the city with the Hashemite standard. Britain arrested student instigators
and conducted house-to-house searches to maintain order. Mosul's Arab nationalists continued to hope that the Hashemites might rescue them.[40]

With the cessation of hostilities in Anatolia and the Treaty of Lausanne in
1923, Turkey and Iraq both claimed Mosul as their own. Iraq, newly established
two years earlier and under League mandate, alleged that Mosul was primarily
Arab. Turkey, just recognized by the international community, asserted that
Turkish and Kurdish speakers were the majority. In 1924 the League of Nations
dispatched an investigatory commission, precipitating a mobilization in the city
reminiscent of King and Crane's arrival in Syria in 1919. Faisal, crowned king of
Iraq after his expulsion from Syria, rallied pro-Iraqi public opinion and argued
that self-determination dictated Mosul's attachment to Iraq. Britain helped the
Iraqi claim by tightening its de facto administrative control in the city. The
League delegates tried to escape the Anglo-Iraqi-orchestrated echo chamber. Yet
they still assumed that ethnic and linguistic affiliation would determine popular
will, and thus a simple head count of Arabs, Kurds, Turks, and others would suf-
fice. Instead, they heard a multitude of voices expressing demands that did not
correspond with these simple categories. Some residents favored Iraq or Turkey.
Others wanted Arab rule, but not under the British thumb. Some held out hope
for a Kurdish kingdom. Some complained that attachment to Iraq would force
them to turn toward Baghdad and Basra, when their natural inclinations—and
markets—remained in Syria. Considerations were even more complicated for
the smaller communities in the province. Refugees from the Ottoman genocide,
Assyrian Christians feared Muslim domination in a state and instead sought to
maximize their territorial autonomy in Iraq or Anatolia. The Yezidis had long
faced Ottoman oppression and were suspicious of any state that might impose
conscription upon them. Ultimately, the League awarded Mosul to Iraq in 1926,
but only after Britain cut a side deal granting Ankara a portion of the area's oil
proceeds.[41]

As much as Syrian and Iraqi statehood introduced novel ideas of citizenship and imposed new territorial delimitations to the Jazira, one aspect of the previous Ottoman era remained intact: the presumption of Sunni supremacy. This was no longer a matter of theology but of social capital. The Ottoman education system had systematically cultivated the Sunnis as officers and administrators while neglecting Shi'is and other minorities. This imbued the Sunni community with a sense of entitlement to rule, as they alone had accumulated the skills necessary to lead a modern state. Yet, as recently converted Arab nationalists, they regarded sectarianism (*ta'ifiyya*) as retrograde and inimical to national unity.[42] The tendency to downplay sectarian cleavages was even more pronounced among the most radical proponents of pan-Arabism in the 1950s. Paradoxically, national minorities were often attracted to pan-Arabism because it allowed them to obscure their own precarious domestic positions. Nevertheless, every substantive step toward the unification of Arab states necessarily entailed enhancement of the Sunni position, a fatal flaw in many unification schemes.[43]

In Iraq the British directly encouraged Sunni supremacy. The 1920 revolt, instigated by the Shi'i clerical leadership and waged primarily by the Shi'i tribes in the south, convinced the British of the need to install a reliable—and Sunni—figure in Iraq. Faisal's entourage, Arabic-speaking ex-Ottoman officers and veterans from the failed Syrian Arab kingdom, solidified Sunni Arab control over the state.[44] The British and the Iraqi leadership knew that Shi'is outnumbered Sunnis. Echoing the arguments the mandatory powers had used to deny Arab statehood, they justified minority rule by describing the Shi'is as yet unfit for rule. Faisal privately reflected in 1932:

> Iraq is a kingdom governed by a Sunni Arab government established on the ruins of Ottoman rule. This government rules over a Kurdish part, most of which consists of a majority of ignorant people . . . and an ignorant Shi'i majority that belongs racially to the same [ethnicity as] the government. But the oppression they had under the Turkish rule did not enable them to participate in the governance or give them training to do so.[45]

The situation remained roughly the same for the next seventy decades. The organs of Iraqi statehood reinforced Sunni hegemony without mentioning it explicitly. Iraq adopted Ottoman designations that distinguished between inhabitants of Iraqi and Iranian origins, an effort to deny Shi'is citizenship in the new Iraqi state.[46] As the Iraqi government recruited Arabic-speaking civil servants from Syria, Yemen, or Egypt, native-born Iraqis of Iranian origins were excluded or sidelined. Iraqi schoolbooks tried to offer an ecumenical account of Arab-Islamic history but generally ignored Shi'i religious customs or treated them as unseemly and backward. Badly needed development projects for the south came with unvarnished paternalism. For their part, Iraqi Shi'is responded with a more overtly sectarian vision. Iraq, they argued, rightfully belonged to its majority population. The collusion of Sunni despots and imperialists prevented Shi'i leadership.⁴⁷

Implicit but persistent Sunni supremacism in Iraq helped integrate the Jazira region into the Iraqi state. One of the reasons Britain and Faisal wanted to add the Mosul territory to Iraq and encouraged the migration of tribes from the Syrian side of the Jazira was to bolster Sunni Arab demography.⁴⁸ At least ten of the sixty-six ex-Ottoman officials who joined Faisal in Iraq originated from the Upper Euphrates or Mosul. Some were the sons of landed aristocrats or tribal leaders, others from more modest circumstances. All, however, came to Baghdad confident in their destiny to govern.⁴⁹ Patterns of recruitment and advancement with the military and civil services helped induct the Sunni Arabs of the Jazira into the ruling elite. Moreover, state policies that allowed the tribal elite to accrue economic and political power locally further enhanced the ties between center and periphery. By 1958 an estimated one-quarter to one-third of the Iraqi officer corps hailed from the Mosul area, and Ahmed Ajil al-Yawer, the son of Ajil al-Yawer, was the country's single largest landowner.⁵⁰ Iraq's public health statistics from the mid-1960s show that the Ramadi, Mosul, and Saladin governorates far outperformed the southern provinces in terms of infant mortality and access to healthcare, suggestive of the concentration of government investment in these areas.⁵¹

Pan-Arabism and its promise of returning to more organic and authentic borders had a strong attraction in the Jazira, where many residents retained familial or tribal ties in Syrian territory.⁵² In March 1959 a faction of pro-unification officers led by Abd al-Wahhab al-Shawwaf staged an insurrection in Mosul against Abd al-Karim al-Qassem. Qassem had led a group of Free Officers in deposing the Hashemite monarchy the previous year. Unlike most of his co-conspirators, Qassem was close to the Iraqi Communists, was disinclined toward pan-Arabism, and generally seemed to champion Iraqi Shi'is and Kurds. Yawer, along with much of Mosul's mercantile and landed elite, backed Shawwaf. Gemal abd al-Nasser and the United Arab Republic (UAR) offered air support from Syria. Underlying these national and even regional concerns, though, was a local context of rivalry and feud. Qassem's plans for land reform and civil law threatened the region's conservative Sunni Arab elites. For almost a decade, the Shammar chieftain-landlords had been embroiled in a bloody feud with the Communists. Kurds and some Christians joined the Communist's Peace Partisans or the Popular Resistance Forces, pro-government militias. When the UAR air support failed to materialize, the insurrection degenerated into brawls, looting, and killing. The Shammar were driven from the city. In 1963, when Qassem was deposed in a right-wing coup, the Shammar joined in running down suspected Communist sympathizers.[53]

The ascent of Saddam Hussein and the Ba'th Party in Iraq in 1968 continued the tradition of Sunni dominance and anchored Iraq's ruling elite in the Jazira region between Baghdad and Mosul. Such domination was enacted in different ways over time. Like its predecessors, the Ba'th saw itself as a non-sectarian, unifying force in Iraq. Especially in the 1970s and 1980s, the era of "High Ba'thism," the Iraqi state tried to articulate a notion of Iraqi national identity acceptable to both Sunnis and Shi'is (often to the detriment of pan-Arab principles and neglect of the Kurds).[54] Officials hardly ever mentioned the Sunni-Shi'a sectarian divide, even in private. With massive oil wealth at its disposal, the regime built loyal and disciplined citizenry through spending on education, public health, infrastructure, and agriculture across the country.[55] At the same time, though, the regime's inner core was deeply patrimonial. Saddam surrounded himself with his closest kin from Tikrit, a small Jazira city north of Baghdad. Tikritis had gravitated toward the Iraqi army since the mandate era. Relying on tribal affinities and solidarity, the most sensitive positions in the party apparatus and security sectors were dominated by members of Saddam's Al Bu Nasir tribe and neighboring tribes in the Saladin and Anbar provinces. Although the regime's inner workings were difficult to decipher, Saddam seemed to favor specific tribal branches and sub-branches from among the Ubayd, Jubur, Azza, Tayy, Khazraj, Dulaymi, and Shammar. Once elevated, regime elites tried both to remain in Saddam's good graces and to hoard opportunities and resources for themselves and their families.[56]

Saddam was acutely aware of (and somewhat embarrassed by) his narrow, patrimonial social base. Doctrinally, the Ba'th equated tribalism with feudalism. The regime once even banned surnames indicative of tribal or place origins. Nonetheless, tribalism became a key element in Saddam's strategy of rule, especially (although not exclusively) in the Jazira. Reversing the land reform drive of the 1960s, the regime encouraged tribal elites to accumulate large holdings. Economic liberalization and new investments in hydrological infrastructure in the 1980s spurred large-scale commercial farming. A hydroelectric dam was built at Haditha and an irrigation barrage at Fallujah. The largest project was the Saddam Hydroelectric Dam upstream from Mosul (commonly referred to as the Mosul Dam). Due to design and building flaws, the dam immediately showed signs of erosion and stress, necessitating a backup facility at Badush. The dam's massive reservoir also fouled the downstream drinking water.[57] Still, with state-subsidized electricity and water, tribal landlords across the Jazira partnered with urban contractors in investments in agricultural equipment and livestock. The Ugail tribe, which had once dominated the Jazira caravansary, emerged as the largest landholding family north of Mosul, a status they had likely tried to hide in prior decades. Mosul became Iraq's breadbasket. The transformation of tribal sheikhs into capitalists exacerbated intra-tribal tensions. Peasants and small farmers increasingly encountered sheikhs less as familial patrons and more as creditors or landlords.[58] From the perspective of the government, tribes also served a military purpose, supplementing the party militias. The Shammar tribe was granted arms and organized its own militias to fight the Kurdish insurrection in the 1960s and 1970s.

Precisely because tribes were so tightly tied to the regime, they required special scrutiny. Just as he did for other parts of the country, Saddam used tactics of divide-and-rule and collective punishment to keep enemies at bay. Tribal leaders were replaced if they could not control their charges. Tribal lands could be confiscated and tribe members purged. This included capital punishment. Even members of Saddam's own Al Bu Nasir tribe were not exempt from such recrimination. After the 1991 March uprisings the regime also became more overtly reliant on tribal leaders and tribal norms to make up for the weaknesses of the Iraqi state. In some respects, this was an inspired choice. Some of Iraq's largest tribal confederations had both Sunni and Shi'i components, giving Saddam added sway in the south. Tribal leaders had new positions in the government and access to Saddam himself. For the first time since the 1930s, the state openly devolved coercive authority to tribal leaders, allowing them to bear arms and administer justice in their domains. But tribal leaders had their own agendas for their newfound autonomy. As Iraqis suffered under debilitating international sanctions, tribes along the Syrian and Jordanian borders became even more involved in smuggling consumer goods, pharmaceuticals, and oil. This type of transit often required partnership with regime figures. More ominously, the regime faced periodic revolts from Jazira tribes that sensed Saddam's control was slipping.[59]

Concurrent (although not always concordant) with Saddam's neotribalism, the regime also relied on religion as a means of social control. The Faith Campaign placed new emphasis on Islam in public life, especially schools and universities. The presidential office directly oversaw this initiative, with the involvement of senior Ba'th figures like Izzat Ibrahim al-Douri. The campaign was meant to be ecumenical and build a basis for social cohesion in the midst of economic degradation. Yet it often gave voice to Sunni chauvinism that had hovered in the background of the regime. Already during the Iran-Iraq War (1980–88), regime propaganda used thinly veiled code words to disparage the Shi'is as an Iranian fifth column. The regime forbade or discouraged marriages between Shi'i men and Sunni women, unions that would presumably yield children who ascribed to the Shi'a sect. The government also deported tens of thousands of people whose documents identified their ancestors as Iranian.[60] After 1991 and the crushing of the southern uprisings, attacks on Shi'is become more overt. The

Faith Campaign also yielded space for grassroots religiosity, including Salafism and other conservative Islamist tendencies. Though the Ba'th discouraged unauthorized zealotry, they could not stamp it out.[61] Sectarian affinity was an important element in yoking the Jazira into the Iraqi state, but it alone was not sufficient. Neo-tribalism helped to protect the regime but undercut the integration of Jazira under the Iraqi state. It made the Jazira into a separate reserve where tribal authority and power prevailed and, at times, could challenge the state.

Sunni supremacy manifested differently on the Syrian side of the border. The French presumed that Sunnis were entitled to rule Syria by virtue of demography and experience but tried to thwart the bequest of state power. French divide-and-rule stratagems instead hived off minority ethno-sectarian enclaves.[62] The creation of Christian-dominated Lebanon was the most obvious example. Within Syria itself this policy led to the construction of the separate Alawite State, the Jabal Druze State, the State of Aleppo and the State of Damascus, and the Hasakah autonomy experiment. In the Ottoman era, groups like the Alawis, Druze, and Ismailis were regarded as heretics and social outcasts, brigands, vagabonds, peasants, or servants in the great Sunni estates. While the British sought to recruit the sons of the Sunni Arab elite into the Iraqi army, the French relied on bringing these compact minorities into the colonial army.[63] The Syrian Arab nationalists, mainly hailing from the Sunni-dominated merchant and landed classes, decried these policies as contrary to the premise of self-determination. When independence arrived, the nationalists immediately set about to reverse French policies and reinstate the dominance of the urban elite—which coincidentally happened to be largely Sunni.[64]

The Jazira was a peripheral zone at the inception of the Syrian state and, compared to Iraq, remained relatively marginal through the twentieth century. The tribes around Deir Ezzour, whether Arabic or Kurdish speaking, were economically and culturally distinct from the urban core, despite a common Sunni confession. Tribal policies effectively exempted the tribes from state control, creating an unofficial tribal state within the state. As an incentive for quiescence, the French allowed tribal leadership to enclose previously communal lands and accumulate private holdings. Parliamentary seats were reserved for tribal representatives, who consistently voted against the National Bloc.[65]

When the nationalists took power in Syria in 1937 they rescinded much of the tribal leaders' political autonomy but hastened their economic integration. The French had already laid some of this groundwork by extending the railway and encouraging settlements in Hasakah and Qamishli to make up for the loss of the Iraqi and Turkish markets. Deir Ezzour became the effective capital of the northeast, the hub between the city, agricultural areas, and the nomadic zone, and the conduit between the region and Damascus.[66] In the late 1940s Shammar tribal chiefs worked with urban speculators to grab up pasturages and convert them into farmland. Contractors, many hailing from Christian or other minority back-grounds, rented out combines, tractors, trucks, drills, and pumps. The state made little effort to regulate this concentration of wealth. As in Iraq, lesser-ranking tribesmen and clients found themselves reduced to sharecroppers and tenants. Many were attracted to socialist ideas of land reform and redistribution. Moreover, due to poor land management, much of the Jazira soil verged on exhaustion.[67]

In 1963 a military cabal of Ba'th-associated officers seized power in Damascus. The group was dominated by officers from minority backgrounds, particularly Ismaili Shi'is, Druze, Christians, and Alawis. As Nikolaos van Dam put it, more than just overturning the regime, the Ba'th coup reversed the traditional domi-nance of the Sunni magnates over the peripheral minorities in Syria.[68] The Ba'th touted plans for a socialist revolution, including secular civil law, land reform, collectivization, and nationalization. Although the rise of Hafez al-Assad within the Ba'th and the 1970s "corrective movement" blunted this radicalism, the relo-cation of political power in Syria was unmistakable. Assad was an Alawi, a stig-matized sect from rural Latakia, known pejoratively as Nusayris.[69] The Alawis had gained prominence by serving in the French-backed military. As president, Assad tried to elide his sectarian background and cultivated an image as a mod-erate, ecumenical, and modern Muslim leader.[70] Market reforms helped the regime earn some allies among the old industrial and mercantile elite and inau-gurated a distinctive form of crony capitalism.[71] Nevertheless, Assad, like Saddam, kept the most important positions of rule for his closest Alawi kin. The opposition to the Ba'th, therefore, tended to accentuate sectarianism. The 1982 Muslim Brotherhood uprising, centered in the staunchly Sunni mercantile cities of Aleppo, Hama, and Homs, combined economic grievances with a sense that apostates had usurped Sunni supremacy.[72]

A regime of sectarian interlopers shorn of animating ideology, Ba'th control in the Syrian side of the Jazira rested on patron-client networks. Because of its scarcity, water was a key element of political and social power. The state co-opted local leaders by allocating access to irrigation and pumps. The Tabqa Dam, near Raqqa, and the smaller installations on the Balikh and Khabur Rivers, were em-blems of state power. Beginning in 1968 with Soviet assistance, the irrigation scheme induced dramatic social change. To supply the construction, railroads extended from Latakia and Aleppo to Raqqa, Deir Ezzour, Hasakah, and Qamishli. Thousands of technocrats, engineers, skilled laborers, support staff, and their families moved to the Raqqa area for the projects. Ancillary party orga-nizations, labor unions, and women's groups emerged. New schools, hospitals, and dispensaries followed.[73] The discovery of modest oil fields near Deir Ezzour in the 1980s increased the economic bonanza.

Tribal leaders, eager to put the mid-1960s era of collectivization behind them, looked to partner with the state. They built ties with urban capitalists and received

state subsidies. Reversing a century-long push for sedentarization, the government also opened up land for grazing among certain favored tribes. In the discourse of international development consultants, tribal leaders became local
"stakeholders" in state-controlled natural resources.[74] Especially in the smaller
towns and villages, the state acted through its tribal intermediaries, and, in turn,
tribal chiefs became the face of the state.[75] Assad mobilized the Arab tribes to
fight the Muslim Brotherhood revolt in the 1980s and encouraged the tribes to
migrate into the "Arab Belt" as part of his effort to break up Kurdish demographic
weight along the Iraq and Turkish border. To demonstrate their pro-regime
bona fides, the Hadidiyin tribe, a part of the Shammar confederacy, managed to
"discover" an ancient Alawi ancestry.[76] Additionally, in the 1980s the regime allowed Iranian-backed Shi'i religious organizations to proselytize among the
tribes of Deir Ezzour, particularly those claiming descent from the Shi'i saints.
Some elements of the Baggara converted to Shi'ism.[77]

But development also brought dislocation. Few of the Euphrates agro-irriga-
tion projects actually met their output targets. Dams and reservoirs inundated
villages and forced residents from their homes. Moreover, these large-scale ventures in human and ecological engineering took a long-term toll on society and
the environment. Drought was a constant concern. Many lesser tribesmen saw
their relationship transformed into a purely clientelist exchange with few reciprocal obligations of protection. Rivalry between cultivators and pastoralists over
land use intensified, and there was an increasing urban-rural divide. Some described the city of Raqqa as an internal colony of transmigrants from elsewhere
in Syria.[78]

Despite three decades of development, northeastern Syria remained comparatively backward. Even as irrigation, education, and healthcare expanded in
the area, regional inequalites were stark. Between 1964 and 1977 the number of
schools, doctors, and hospitals doubled or better in Raqqa, Deir Ezzour, and
Hasakah, but these governorates lagged behind Damascus and Aleppo in terms
of access to schools and medicine.[79] As late as 1990 Damascus had twice as many
hospital beds per capita as Raqqa and Deir Ezzour and three times more than
Hasakah.[80] This trend continued, or even worsened, into the 2000s, according to
government statistics.[81] The Syrian Jazira, then, remained far more tangential to
the regime than its Iraqi counterpart.

## "Iraq Is Our Iraq"

The Islamic State first took root in the unsettled soil of the Jazira following the
US invasion of Iraq in 2003. The invasion marked a multifold cataclysm. It broke
the juridical and empirical sovereignty of the Iraqi state. Iraq's army, police, and

other key institutions of coercion and governance were eviscerated. The invasion also inverted Iraq's traditional ethnosectarian hierarchy, ending the presumption of Sunni predominance. The United States had hoped to devise some form of power sharing through federalist institutions. Ghazi al-Yawer, yet another scion of the Shammar tribe from Mosul, was named to the transitional Iraqi Governing Council and served briefly in the ceremonial presidency in 2004. Still, the newly installed Iraqi political elite, with strong backing from Tehran, was more or less explicit about empowering Iraq's Shi'i majority. Iraqis were caught in an ethno-sectarian security dilemma. One community's ascent could only come at the cost of the other; losing power meant falling victim to all manner of violence.[82] Saddam's ouster was an immediate blow to the Jazira tribes and clans that had specially benefited from his rule. But the conditions of state failure also offered opportunities to contest political authority and deploy new local, sectarian, and supra-national identities that challenged Syria and Iraq's incorporation of the Jazira.

With the United States unready to take control over the entirety of the country, Iraqis had to find other sources of security and protection. Violence escalated quickly in the Jazira, and insurgency took hold. The uprising harbored a mélange of groups with differing motivations and agendas. Some were criminals trying to extort protection from locals. Some were smugglers. Others were tribal leaders, eager for a chance to expand their authority. Tribal leadership often overlapped with holdovers from the Ba'th regime and its security apparatus, which the United States had unceremoniously dissolved. There were also Arab nationalists, claiming to defend Iraq from a joint US- and Iranian-backed invasion. Salafi Islamist groups also emerged, mixing the newly religious and those who had toiled in the underground of the Ba'th state. They dismissed secular Ba'thism but reviled the US occupation and its Iraqi supporters.[83] Undergirding all of these elements was an increasingly overt and sectarian notion of Sunni identity. The arrival of a Shi'i-dominated government in Baghdad, backed by the two countries Saddam deemed mortal enemies, crystallized the sense of displacement. Such commonality bridged the gaps of ideology, as well as tribal and local affiliation (i.e., Tikritis, Moslawis, etc.) within the Sunni community.[84]

The emergence of Sunni sectarianisms brought Iraqis into the broader currents of Sunni sectarianist revival. In August 2003 AQI attacked Shi'i religious figures and shrines, U.N. and Red Cross buildings, US installations, foreign embassies, and other high-profile targets. AQI had originated as Jama'at at-Tawhid wa Jihad (the Monotheism and Jihad Group) under the leadership of Abu Musab al-Zarqawi. A Jordanian-born Palestinian and once a petty criminal, Zarqawi had fought in Afghanistan and joined the vanguard of the global jihad. In 2004 Zarqawi pledged allegiance to Osama bin Laden, changing his group into al-Qaeda in Mesopotamia (*al-Qaeda fi Bilad ar-Rafidayn*). As the local affiliate of the transnational al-Qaeda organization, AQI sought to subsume Iraq into a global and cosmic battle. Iraq was a front in which to strike a blow against the "far enemy"—the Western powers, which had systematically blocked Islamic ascendance. Iraq's state sovereignty was insignificant. Few of AQI's leaders were born in Iraq. Many of its rank and file were also foreign fighters. Analysis of captured AQI documents from August 2006 to August 2007 detailed some 248 Saudis, 112 Libyans, and 49 Algerians who infiltrated Iraq through Syria.[85] In fact, even use of the moniker Mesopotamia—in lieu of Iraq—was meant to signal objection to illegitimate colonial borders. As Zarqawi's successor, the Egyptian Abu Ayyub al-Masri (Abu Hamza al-Hijri, "the Migrant"), put it, "We are not the sons of Sykes-Picot."[86] Zarqawi was adamant about the necessity of Sunni supremacy and regarded the Shi'is as heretics that had to be eradicated. Many Iraqis saw Zarqawi's brutal attacks on Shi'is as divisive. Even Osama bin Laden deemed them excessive and counterproductive. For Zarqawi, though, they were an essential part of a master plan. As Zarqawi described in his letter to al-Qaeda's central command:

> If we are able to deal them [the Shi'as] blow after painful blow so that they engage in a battle, we will be able to reshuffle the cards so there will remain no value or influence for the ruling council, or even for the Americans who will enter into a second battle with the Shi'a. This is what we want. Then, the Sunnis will have no choice but to support us in many of the Sunni regions. When the Mujahidin would have secured a land they can use as a base to hit the Shi'a inside their own lands, with a directed media and a strategic action, there will be a continuation between the Mujahidin inside and outside of Iraq.[87]

The goal was to spark Sunni-Shi'i civil war, draw in the United States and Iran, and precipitate a global conflagration between unbelievers and the galvanized Sunni umma.

But even as Zarqawi positioned AQI for a global struggle, he and the AQI leadership discussed the possibility of establishing some form of territorial state (*dawla*) that could be the seat of a restored Sunni caliphate.[88] Beyond its spectacular mass-casualty terrorism, AQI also set out to control the insurgency in the Jazira, especially along the border areas. In 2004 AQI tried to exploit tension between the US occupation forces and Kurdish regional forces encroaching southward to gain a foothold in Mosul.[89] Through 2004 and 2005 AQI combined coercion and enticements to draw in or destroy the Jazira tribes. It cemented blood alliances though arranged and forced marriages to the daughters of tribal sheikhs. It took control over key smuggling routes by bribing border guards for information about licit and contraband traffic, including the crucial refined gasoline. AQI became so financially successful that al-Qaeda headquarters even requested that it make a loan back to the central command.[90] Anbar cities like Ramadi and Fallujah became effectively no-go zones for US troops.

AQI's metamorphosis into an Islamic state occurred after Zarqawi was killed by US forces in June 2006. First, al-Masri, a former member of Ayman al-Zawahiri's Egyptian Islamic Jihad group, was designated minister of war and overall commander by al-Qaeda's central leadership. In October the AQI consultative council named Abu Umar al-Baghdadi (Hamid Dawud Mohamed Khalil al-Zawi), a former police officer from Haditha, as "commander of the faithful," an appellation that portended caliphal status. His personal background and role remained mysterious, but there was some suggestion that he merely served as an Iraqi front for a still foreign organization.

The initial announcements of the establishing of a caliphal Islamic state in Iraq betray marked ambivalence toward Iraqi sovereignty. Early on some called the group the Islamic State in Iraq (*ad-Dawla al-Islamiyya fi'l-'Iraq*); others, the Islamic State of Iraq (*Dawlat al-'Iraq al-Islamiyya*).[91] This seemingly minor difference in prepositions had substantive implication. The designation of "in Iraq" implied that Iraq was nothing but a spatial or territorial referent, a synonym for Mesopotamia. In contrast, "of Iraq" suggested that Iraq as a polity retained political significance. IS claimed to incorporate areas of Iraq where Sunni Arabs held (or thought they held) demographic predominance—Baghdad, Anbar, Nineveh, Kirkuk, Saladin, and parts of the Babil and Wasit provinces. Baquba was named the IS capital.[92] IS spokesman Muharab al-Juburi (the scion of one of the most powerful Jazira tribes) likened IS to the Kurdish Region in Iraq, which had been granted formal autonomy in Iraq's 2005 constitution.

> After the Kurds have taken possession of a state in the north, and the Shi'a have been established in a federal state in the middle and south . . . it has become necessary for the honorable and free Sunnis among the mujahidin and engaged scholars and notables to give something [comparable] to their brothers and their sons . . . especially in light of the farcical drama known as "Maliki's state," in which, sadly, traitorous Sunnis have played roles.[93]

Most of IS's leadership, though, rejected any connection to Iraqi statehood and the analogy of IS to Iraq's federal entities. Abu Umar retorted, "We are not fighting for patriotism but rather for God's word." In January 2007 IS published a treatise arguing that it had gained legitimacy as a caliphal state through the consent of Iraq's communal and religious leaders, known as *ahl al-hall wa al-'aqd* ("people who loosen and bind"). It was obligatory for all mujahideen to renounce previous claims of allegiance and acknowledge the caliphate of Abu

Umar through the baya'a.[94] Although the relationship between al-Qaeda and the IS leadership was fraying, al-Qaeda backed the new entity. Al-Qaeda media publicized the issuance of the infamous IS black banner, and bin Laden urged Iraqis to swear allegiance to IS. Still, some of the world's most influential ideologues of jihad questioned whether an "imaginary" or "paper" state could really demand such singular loyalty.[95]

Just as IS failed to get legitimation from the external, transnational arena, it also failed to solidify a following within Iraq itself. Like other insurgent groups, AQI wanted to make Iraq ungovernable for the United States and its Shi'i and Kurdish allies. Iraqi insurgents may have seen themselves in explicitly sectarian terms, but they still harbored a sense of Iraqi patriotism. This presumption of Sunni privilege to rule contributed to the general Sunni rejection of federalism, at least initially. About three-quarters of Iraqi Sunnis boycotted the elections to select delegates to the 2005 constitutional convention. In Anbar, turnout was in the single digits. To accept federalism was to concede relegation to a minority status.[96] These groups wanted to regain Iraq, not splinter or dissolve it. In contrast, AQI stretched Sunni sectarian identity to its de-territorialized breaking point. Its ferocious anti-Shi'i violence alienated many Iraqis (and other Arabs) and made it harder to create alliances that might resist the United States.[97] The Council of Muslim Clerics, the main political front for the Sunni rejectionists, regarded AQI as beyond the pale.[98] Militants like the 1920 Revolution Brigade, Jaysh Islami, and Jaysh Rijal Tariqat Naqshbandi (JRTN), a Ba'thist front group led by Izzat Ibrahim al-Douri, coalesced against the foreign insurgents.[99]

Perhaps the most aggrieved were the Jazira tribes. Under al-Masri especially, IS bullied fellow Sunnis.[100] Even before AQI's hegemony over the Upper Euphrates region, some Anbar tribal leaders had contacted US field commanders proposing to help root out insurgents if the United States guaranteed the tribes autonomy and immunity from Baghdad. In 2003 and 2004 Washington was still committed to rebuilding the Iraqi state and would not countenance devolving power to armed non-state actors. Moreover, the nascent Iraqi government did not trust tribes that had so recently aligned with Saddam and the Ba'th. As the security situation worsened, however, cooperating with armed non-state actors proved necessary. The formal resumption of Iraqi sovereignty in June 2004 only highlighted the disparities between juridical and de facto power. Interior Ministry forces collaborated with militias of the Supreme Council for Islamic Revolution in Iraq to wage a dirty war against Sunnis. State forces and militias abducted, imprisoned, raped, tortured, and summarily executed thousands of suspected terrorists.[101]

Unable to stem the proliferation of state-sponsored militias or the slide toward civil war, the United States returned to the idea of alliance with the Sunni tribes, leading to the emergence of the Anbar Awakening. The Awakening began in November 2005 when tribal leaders met in Ramadi to discuss assisting the United States to reestablish order in Anbar. Although the Awakening leaders would sometimes refer to themselves as the Sons of Iraq (*ibna al-'Iraq*), the relationship between the movement, the state of Iraq, and the US occupation authority was complicated and contingent. Tribal sheikhs framed their alliance with the United States as serving Iraq, but their decisions often reflected the realities of local grievances and greed. Many of these tribal leaders had past connections to the Ba'th regime or even backed the insurgency. Abd al-Sattam al-Rishawi (Abu Risha), a minor sheikh of the Dulaymi confederation and notorious smuggler, emerged among the leading figures of the Awakening. Abu Risha was wary of AQI's puritanical ideology and of its attempts to muscle in on regional smuggling and displace tribal leadership. In return for setting up a tribal militia and keeping order in his tribal territory, the United States offered to pay tribal fighters $300 per month, grant the sheikhs bonuses in reconstruction aid, and allow the reassertion of tribal law and dominion.[102]

While the tribes were cutting ties with the insurgency and aligning with the United States, AQI was trying to turn itself into a caliphal state. AQI tried to kill off the movement's tribal leaders and intimidate the remainder of the sheikhs to repent and return to the fold. Abu Risha died in a bombing near his home in September 2007. Some Islamist and ex-Ba'th insurgent groups, like the JRTN, opposed both AQI and the pro-US tribes.[103] Yet the enlistment of the tribal militias and the surge in US troop levels proved ineluctable. By March 2007 the movement had drawn in twenty-nine thousand men in Anbar alone, stretching from Fallujah to al-Qaim.[104] Ramadi and other hotbeds of insurgency became suddenly quiet. The United States launched similar measures along the Tigris in Nineveh, Saladin, and Tamim, as well as in Babil, Diyala, and Baghdad.[105]

In some respects, the Awakening movement affirmed the Jazira's attachment to the Iraq state and the tribes' rejection of the transnational notions of sectarian identity AQI had championed. Ahmad Naji Jibarah al-Juburi of the Saladin Tribal Council said in September 2006:

> Iraq is our Iraq. It does not belong to the leaders of the al-Qaeda organization who came and entered Iraq to liberate it from occupation. He didn't come to liberate Iraq from its own people. We are the people of Iraq and he wants to liberate us, which means that he wants to eliminate us and make Iraq a wasteland void of its people and citizens. . . . Al-Qaeda helps the occupation to divide and tear Iraq to shreds.[106]

On the other hand, the Awakening also effectuated a de facto separation. The United States played the role of guarantor of regional autonomy in this extraconstitutional devolution. Government troops were effectively barred from areas of

Anbar and Saladin where the Awakening forces ruled. As power in Iraq was allocated explicitly along ethnosectarian lines, there was a logical symmetry to this
arrangement. Defense Minister Sa'adon ad-Dulaymi funneled weapons and
money to help set up these tribal militias.[107] As one Anbar businessmen put it,
"The Shi'a have the army and the militias. We just want a Sunni army to balance
them."[108] Like the insurgency from which it emerged, the Awakening was a
hodgepodge of disparate forces launched by local leaders for parochial purposes.
Authority remained fragmented. Some of the Awakening sheikhs had little legitimacy or support. People saw them only as purveyors of American patronage.
A 2007 poll in Anbar showed that fewer than a quarter of respondents were confident in their local leaders. Moreover, there were constant concerns that empowered militias would backslide to realign with al-Qaeda.[109]

The gains in security and stability of 2007 and 2008 came largely at the ex-
pense of the central government.[110] Prime Minister Nuri al-Maliki regarded the
Awakening as an American plot to weaken his authority and empower the
Sunnis. As the United States readied to withdraw from Iraq, Sunni militia leaders
demanded induction into the state security services as a reward for their service
against AQI and guarantee of their autonomy. Maliki moved adroitly to divide
and rule the Sunni opposition. The government purged, arrested, and even killed
the Awakening leadership on grounds of supporting terrorism, while at the same
time co-opting individual Sunni leaders.[111] The Sunni leadership fragmented.
On one hand, Iyyad Allawi's Iraqiyya party coalition won strong support in
Sunni areas during the 2010 parliamentary election, focusing on creating a coherent, centralized, and secular (non-sectarian) Iraqi state. On the other hand,
once Maliki had effectively stymied the Iraqiyya initiative in parliament, there
was more and more demand to devolve power to the individual governorates.[112]
In September 2013 Nineveh governorate's council voted to grant itself the power
to negotiate with international oil companies, a move that Maliki quickly
quashed. There were also demands to create a Sunni regional bloc analogous to
the Kurdish Regional Government.[113]

Ultimately, IS ended the decade of the 2000s battered but not broken. In
order to survive, it gave up pretensions to statehood and reverted to its insurgent
instincts. Although IS maintained nominal ties with al-Qaeda, it was no longer
the front of global jihad that it had been under Zarqawi. Its leadership was now
comprised overwhelmingly of born and bred Iraqis, not foreigners. The case in
point was the ascent of Abu Bakr al-Baghdadi. Born Ibrahim Awad Ibrahim al-
Badri in 1971, Baghdadi hailed from the Qurayshi branch of the Albu Badr tribe
of Samarra, meaning he was a direct descendent of the Prophet Muhammad.
Baghdadi earned a PhD in religious sciences from Saddam Islamic University.
After the US invasion of 2003 he helped found a militant group that eventually
aligned with AQI. He was captured and imprisoned at the US base at Camp

Bucca, where he made further contact with several of the future IS leaders. Abu Bakr al-Baghdadi became spiritual leader of IS after an air strike killed Abu Umar in April 2011.[114] Several emergent IS leaders had served in the Ba'th military and security establishment and were probably only recently converted to Salafism, such as top military commander Samir Abd Muhammed al-Khlifawi (Haji Bakr). The exact number, role, and impact of ex-Ba'thist leaders in this new generation of IS leadership are difficult to estimate.[115] However, it seems probable that their training and experience shaped IS's organizational and military capacities. More diffusely, even those IS members who had not been party members still came of age in the era of the sanctions and Saddam's Faith Campaign and then experienced the upheaval of the US occupation.[116] As the United States hastened its withdrawal from 2008 to 2011 and Maliki systematically undercut the Awakening's tribal leadership, IS lurked in the shadows. By the end of the decade IS operatives were entrenched in Mosul, where Maliki had blocked efforts to promulgate Awakening-style militias, in addition to Ramadi, Fallujah, and other cities. With IS ranks coming increasingly from the sons of Iraq's Jazira soil, IS operatives were in good position to extort smugglers and local businesses. Even police and government employees had to kick back for "protection."[117]

The collapse of the Iraqi state in the mid-2000s reverberated across the Syrian border. The political opening following the death of Hafez in 2000 and the ascent of his son Bashar had ended quickly. While Bashar was more market oriented and technocratic than his father, he was no less concerned about regime survival. The American invasion, therefore, posed a complex challenge. On one hand, there had always been a rivalry between the Syrian and Iraqi branches of the Ba'th. Syria had allied with Tehran during the Iran-Iraq War and stood aside during the 1990–91 Gulf War. On the other hand, Syria did not want to see the US plan for forced regime change succeed either. Assad dissembled and temporized. He allowed some elements of the Iraq Ba'th to relocate to Syrian territory. US officials accused Damascus of failing to patrol the frontier and cut off infiltration.[118] The six-hundred-kilometer frontier was badly unmanned. The most important crossings were at Yarubiyya/Rabia, which linked by road to Mosul, at at-Tanf/al-Walid, which linked to Iraq's Highway 1 and ran through the desert to Ramadi, and at Albu Kamal/al-Qaim, which followed the course of the Euphrates in the heart of the Jazira.[119] The Americans tried to reinforce the border by strengthening the Iraqi border patrol and erecting an earthen barrier, at some points fifteen feet high and topped with electric or razor wire. As the insurgency continued and Bashar began to worry about his own vulnerability to radical Sunni actors, he cooperated more readily with the United States.[120]

Viewed at ground level from the Syrian side of the Jazira, the situation was even more complicated. In the mid-2000s drought struck the entire region. In the driest period of 2007 and 2008, wheat and barley yields fell by 47 and 67 percent, respectively. In these dire circumstances, Bashar's form of corrupt and crony capitalism worsened matters. Cuts to the diesel subsidy made it impossible to get crops to market. Poverty and malnutrition rates in the region skyrocketed. Residents fled rural areas to become laborers elsewhere in Damascus, Beirut, or the Persian Gulf states. The UN estimated that by 2009 some three hundred thousand people had left the northeast and that some 60 to 70 percent of the villages of Hasakah and Deir Ezzour were abandoned.[121]

Tribes of Deir Ezzour still maintained ties with their kin in Iraq. The relative prosperity of the Iraqi side of the Jazira and the intensity of government investment probably incited some envy through the 1990s.[122] As violence engulfed the once privileged Iraqi sections of the Jazira (as well as Baghdad and the south), hundreds of thousands of Iraqis fled into Syria.[123] The Syrian government tried to impound these Iraqi refugees, keeping them clustered in neighborhood pockets in Damascus or Aleppo, or in the northeast close to the Iraqi border. Syria refused to issue work visas for the refugees, consigning Iraqis to the informal sectors, including sex work. But the refugee enclaves also created a more complex jurisdictional conundrum, since the operations of international aid agencies, donors, and the UN granted these Iraqi enclaves a kind of extra-territorial presence within Syria.[124]

Ultimately, occupation, war, and counterinsurgency transformed both sides of the Syrian-Iraqi frontier into a region of contested, layered, and multiple sovereignties. Cross-border trafficking had played a role in the regional economy since the advent of the Syria-Iraq boundary and became even more important during the sanctions era of the 1990s. Building on these preexisting networks, Jazira tribes mobilized to take advantage of the new war economy. There was an active trade in livestock, cigarettes, pharmaceuticals, consumer goods, refined fuel, alcohol, gold, and light weapons. Syrian border guards, many reassigned from the lucrative Lebanese border, routinely took a "tax" on smuggled goods, which reached 30 percent by 2007.[125]

Along with these banal trespasses, the insurgency also turned the Jazira into a conduit for a more valuable and sensitive good: foreign fighters. So many smugglers and prospective foreign jihadis sought accommodations in Deir Ezzour that the city experienced a spike in housing prices. AQI ran a minibus from the city to Albu Kamal. From there, infiltrators crossed the border by foot and rendezvoused in al-Qaim. When the United States tried to shut this passage, the infiltration route shifted toward Mosul.[126] Multiple factors drew Syrians into the Iraqi crucible. For some, this was a chance to defend and avenge Sunni supremacy. As in Iraq, Salafism and other forms of Islamic conservatism were taking root in Syria's Sunni Arab community generally. The Salafis adopted AQI's framing of the conflict as a global jihad against unbelief.[127] Others, though, had more parochial interests tied to the kinship-based loyalties that spanned the Syria-Iraq border. Captured documents from 2006 to 2007 show that the preponderance of AQI's Syrian recruits (twelve of forty-nine total) originated in Deir Ezzour.[128] For the Jazira tribes in particular, involvement with the insurgency may have had less to do with unifying the global umma than with restoring the tribal contiguity and autonomy that the states of Syria and Iraq had disrupted.

## The Jazira Caliphate, 2011–2017

The demonstrations that began in early 2011 in Syria and Iraq focused initially on issues of broad national concern, such as corruption, accountability, and repression. The heavy-handed government responses escalated a cycle of protest and repression that heightened sectarian tensions and Sunnis' sense of victimhood.[129] Yet neither Damascus nor Baghdad could concentrate enough force to deter or defeat rebellion. With states weakened, IS renewed its bid to break the borders. Theoretically, this was to be the first step toward reasserting Sunni Muslim orthodoxy. But this overarching sectarian grievance was refracted through the kaleidoscope of parochial interests, fears, and ambitions within the Jazira.[130] Substantively, the restoration of the global umma required self-rule for the Jazira.

Maliki regarded the protests as a front for Sunni terrorists and used them as a pretext to continue his assault on Iraq's Sunni leadership. Iraqi security forces shot and killed protesters in Fallujah, Mosul, and Baghdad during the nationwide "Day of Rage" on February 25, 2011. Vice President Tariq al-Hashemi, scion of the Mahshadani tribe from Baghdad and Haditha, was indicted for supporting terrorism and eventually fled the country. In 2012 the personal guard of Finance Minister Rafi al-Isawwi of Fallujah's Albu Isawwi tribe were arrested and Isawwi was targeted for assassination. Other parliamentarians and dignitaries faced harassment, trumped-up charges, and arrest. The purge of Awakening-associated police continued, with some six thousand cashiered in Anbar.[131] IS built new tactical alliances with other insurgent groups, like the ex-Ba'thist JRTN.[132] On August 15, 2011, IS coordinated twenty-two bombings around Iraq, a show of strength meant to demoralize the security forces. In July 2012 IS struck a prison in Tikrit, the first in a yearlong campaign to free incarcerated IS figures, as well as hundreds of other inmates. With IS's prominence rising, establishment Sunni leaders who had accommodated Maliki appeared as stooges and traitors. On December 30, 2012, a mob in Ramadi assaulted Deputy Prime Minister Saleh Mutlaq, an ex-Ba'thist and member of the Jubur tribe.[133]

Bashar, too, blamed outsiders and Islamic radicals for the crisis. The regime's use of lethal force, torture, imprisonment, sexual violence, and extra-judicial executions, though, quickly reinforced the sectarian framing of the conflict.[134] Bashar tried to keep the opposition divided. Protests began in Mayadin, downstream from Deir Ezzour, in late March, two weeks after the government crackdown in Deraa. Bashar turned to the regional tribal leadership to manage the situation in the northeast. He established the semi-official Syrian Arab Tribes and Clan Forum and distributed millions of dollars to loyal sheikhs. In November 2011 Bashar celebrated Eid al-Adha with tribal sheikhs in Raqqa. Raqqa in particular seemed immune to the unrest that took hold elsewhere in the country. The tribes, he said, were "a national repository of the traditions and authentic position in their patriotism [*wataniyya*] and Arab nationalism [*qawmiyya*]."[135] The opposition, too, tried to woo the tribes. Tribal representatives and organizations were granted seats in the Syrian National Council (SNC). Arab tribal leaders, though, quickly began to spar with Kurdish factions over the disposition of Hasakah.[136]

The tribes in northeastern Syria fragmented amid the crosscurrents of regime and rebel pressures. Elements of the Shammar and Fadhl tribes remained in the regime camp. The Nu'im and Aqaydat tribes joined the resistance. In some cases, younger dissident members rejected their elders' pro-regime stance, effectively breaking tribal cohesion. The Shi'i subsections of the Baggara tribe relocated to government-controlled areas around Aleppo. By the summer of 2011 an estimated fifty thousand tribesmen in and around Deir Ezzour had joined the resistance, and by late 2012 the government controlled only a few pockets within the city of Deir Ezzour itself. There was an efflorescence of local committees and councils devoted to managing security, welfare, and schooling in the absence of the state. Many of these were tied to tribes and clans. Leaders of the Mashahda, Bakir, and Shaytat clans within the Aqaydat tribe tried to establish their own umbrella opposition organization mobilized on a unified idea of tribal identity. Such efforts to assert tribal autonomy on a grand scale proved unworkable. Most councils and militias came about through smaller-scale mobilization of neighborhoods, districts, and municipalities.[137]

IS and al-Qaeda moved to insert themselves within the emerging melee of armed groups. In August 2011 Abu Bakr al-Baghdadi dispatched Abu Muhammed al-Joulani (Ahmed Hussein al-Shar'a) to make contact with the Syrian resistance. The Syrian-born Joulani had worked closely with Zarqawi and rose through the ranks of IS, even during its turn toward Iraq-ization in the late 2000s. Joulani was from a small town in the Golan Heights, close to the disengagement line with Israel.[138] In January 2012 Joulani announced the formation of Jubhat al-Nusra (the Victory Front, JAN). Joulani built alliances with Ahrar ash-Sham, the most formidable Islamic fighting groups nationwide, and with the Syrian Islamic Front umbrella. In Aleppo JAN also worked with the local forces, like the Harakat Nur al-Din al-Zangi militia (named for the twelfth-century ruler). JAN kept an arm's-length distance from the SNC-affiliated Free Syrian Army (FSA) but seemed willing to coexist with rebels of all stripes. It propped up relief efforts and humanitarian assistance to war-affected areas. For JAN there was no inherent contradiction between asserting Sunni supremacy and seeking to maintain Syria's territorial integrity. As Joulani would relate in a subsequent interview, while many Syrians had joined the jihad in Iraq during the 2000s, "Our bodies were there but our hearts were attached to the land of al-Sham [the Levant]."[139] JAN leaned toward Syrian nationalism, in deed if not in word.[140]

Although the northern cities of Hama, Homs, and Aleppo were the most valuable targets for opposition mobilization, the northeast was still Syria's main agricultural zone and had Syria's largest oil fields. With the breakdown of the state, the area descended into a free-for-all. Loyalist tribes and remnants of the Ba'th Party formed pro-government militias around the inner cities of Deir Ezzour and Raqqa. Kurdish fighters were concentrating up the Khabur and along the northern border. Around Deir Ezzour, local security was often in the hands of brigands and tribal chieftains. In the fall of 2012 and winter of 2013, JAN, Ahrar ash-Sham, and other rebel groups made a concerted campaign to establish firmer control over the area, particularly the oil fields and their estimated $1–$3 million in daily revenue. JAN set up its administrative and judicial center downstream in ash-Shuhayl, near Mayadin. By early March 2013 JAN, Ahrar ash-Sham, and FSA forces had taken Raqqa. JAN sidelined many of the local councils and seized control over the oil and gas infrastructure.[141] IS supported JAN from the Iraqi side of the border. When rebels assaulted the northern border post of Yarubiya, Syrian troops retreated into Iraq. Iraqi authorities took custody of the Syrians and arranged to transfer them to al-Walid, where they could then cross safely back into Syria. But IS, likely with support from local tribes, ambushed the convoy in the desert south of al-Qaim, killing over fifty Syrians and a dozen Iraqi soldiers on March 4. IS deemed this troop transfer evidence of collusion between the "Safavid army of Iraq and Syria."[142]

Rebel success in Syria delighted Abu Bakr al-Baghdadi. On April 9, Baghdadi revealed that JAN was an IS front organization. It was now time, he announced, to absorb JAN back into IS. As Baghdadi described it, the Islamic State "crossed the boundaries that despicable hands demarcated between Islamic states to thwart our movement. This is the state for which Sheikh Abu Musab al-Zarqawi paved the way."[143] Joulani, however, rejected Baghdadi's demands and turned to al-Qaeda's central command for support. Zawahiri tried to mediate the dispute. He reminded both camps of their common enemies, namely, unbelievers and apostates. He designated JAN as the sole al-Qaeda affiliate for Syria and IS the standard-bearer for Iraq. But Baghdadi refused these ministrations. By effectively conceding to illegitimately drawn international borders, al-Qaeda had forfeited leadership of the pan-Islamic revolution. It was IS's turn at the vanguard.[144]

Al-Khlifawi, the onetime Iraqi military officer turned IS commander, led assaults on JAN positions across northern and northeastern Syria.[145] About half of JAN's fighting force defected to IS. Although IS was able to launch bombings and assassinations across Syria, it was in Raqqa that it had the chance to enact its plan for rule. The city was effectively pacified by June, with IS pushing out JAN, the FSA, and others. Local tribes granted allegiance to IS. The police station was painted black and became the new IS headquarters.

IS also accelerated its operations on the Iraqi side of the border. There were attacks on al-Qaim, al-Hit, ar-Rawa, and Haditha.[146] In December 2013 and January 2014 IS forces, backed by segments of the Dulaymi and JRTN, took over Ramadi and Fallujah.[147] Maliki tried belatedly to co-opt Sunni tribal leaders. The new tribal military councils concentrated naturally in the Jazira regions of Anbar, Saladin, and Mosul, plus Baghdad and Diyala, and featured many of the same tribal sheikhs and ex-Ba'thists who had joined the Awakening in 2005 and 2006.[148] But those willing to work with the state, such as Ahmed Sitar, the brother of Abu Risha, were often too compromised to garner much support. Police and tribal militias splintered and dissolved.[149] Distrust of Maliki drove many tribal leaders to back IS. This was often less about commitment to religious ideology than about repelling government abuses.[150] Nineveh governor Atheel al-Nujaifi reflected:

> People were under the heavy pressure of the army and the regime. They didn't like the army and they needed someone to protect them from the army. Also, the police and the army resorted to sectarian attitudes when doing their duties.[151]

IS's apparent momentum changed the grim calculus of fear and security within the Sunni community. One Juburi sheikh from Anbar explained that the Sunni community could "fight against ISIS and allow Iran and its militias to rule us, or do the opposite. We chose ISIS for only one reason. ISIS only kills you. The Iraqi government kills you and rapes your women."[152]

On June 5, 2014, an IS force of some fifteen hundred assaulted Mosul, the most ambitious gambit yet. The Mosul garrison was a formidable twenty thousand men, commanded by a former Republican Guard officer who was a close ally of Maliki. But training, equipment, and morale had lapsed. Some units were dealing with the crisis in Anbar. IS and JRTN operatives had already infiltrated the city, creating a fifth column. By June 10 the security forces were retreating in disarray.[153] The JRTN sought to claim Mosul as its own, hoisting placards of Saddam and Douri. In a matter of weeks, though, IS forces purged the Ba'thist element and took sole possession of the city.[154] Their offensive extended down the Tigris and Euphrates, all the way to the outskirts of Baghdad. By the end of the month the Albu Mahal tribe at al-Qaim had yielded the last border post to IS.[155] To commemorate its erasure of the border, IS released one of its most widely viewed videos, entitled "Break All the Borders." The video showed IS soldiers walking through the empty border posts, executing several prisoners, and announcing "the end of Sykes-Picot." Said one Syrian, "Now I can enter Iraq without a passport."[156]

The tribal underpinnings of the IS rebellion were readily apparent. Ali Hatim al-Suleimani, emir of the Dulaymi confederacy, related in June,

> It is the tribal rebels who are in control of the situation in Mosul. It is not reasonable to say that a group like ISIS, which has a small number of men and vehicles, could be in control of a large city like Mosul. Therefore, it is clear that this is a tribal revolution, but the government is trying to force us all to wear the robe of the terrorists and ISIS. . . . When we get rid of the government, we will be in charge of the security file [portfolio] in the regions, and then our objective will be to expel terrorism—the terrorism of the government and that of ISIS. . . . The revolution does not belong to anyone, but the tribal revolutionaries are the masters of the scene. Iraq is heading towards partition. There are two choices: either Iraq becomes a sea of blood, or each community rules itself. Central government is not the solution. We do not want an Iraq that fails to respect our dignity and religion.[157]

The conquest of Mosul marked the second coming of IS as a state. IS was no longer an underground insurgent group or one of al-Qaeda's franchises. It ruled a territory of some 90,000 square miles (23,000 km²). Nearly all of this was territory hugging the Tigris and Euphrates and their intercostal byways. On the Euphrates, it held from Jarabolous, on the Syria-Turkish border, all the way to Fallujah. On the Tigris, IS held from the Mosul Dam all the way to Balad, less than 60 miles (100 km) from Baghdad. Within these territories there were some five to seven million inhabitants.[158] No one could accuse IS of being mere "paper" now. The demonstrable ability to govern enabled Abu Bakr al-Baghdadi to take the pulpit in Mosul on July 4, 2014, publicly accept the pledge of allegiance, and substantiate the caliphate.[159]

Paradoxically, the substantiation of a territorialized caliphal state also thrust IS into the transnational arena. IS needed acknowledgment from the global Islamic public spheres to legitimate their state. Most Islamic leaders were aghast at IS's brutality and its perversion of the caliphal ideal. Al-Qaeda-associated theoreticians criticized IS for different reasons. The announcement of the caliphate and the demand for singular allegiance divided the global jihadist front. Abu Muhammed Maqdisi, the Jordanian-Palestinian theologian who had tutored

Zarqawi, belittled the "Islamic State organization" (*tanzim ad-dawla al-islami-yya*) and questioned whether it was any more than a battlefield command.[160] Moreover, Baghdadi had betrayed al-Qaeda, which had made a binding baya'a to the Taliban's Mullah Umar. Joulani and JAN pledged allegiance to al-Qaeda and, by extension, Mullah Umar. Joulani indirectly rebuked IS as a group which "exaggerated in labeling others as infidels." Syria, he said, was a "generally Muslim community," as were Egypt and Turkey. Within liberated territories, Syrian people actively choose to follow Islamic law. Minorities, he added, were integral to Syrian society and had to be protected. Still, despite his efforts at ecumenism, Joulani could not avoid the sectarian frame, saying:

> The conflict has long been a sectarian one. It is a natural conflict on which the almighty God has created people and they struggled between truth and falsehood. Rule in Syria was by the Nusayri sect, that is known as the Alawite sect. More than ninety percent of the security and army officers were in the hands of this regime. The regime climbed [to power] only after sacrificing the Sunnis.[161]

In lieu of the caliphate, he offered plans to establish an Islamic emirate in the Levant, including Idlib, Aleppo, Dar'a, and Ghouta. Most other Syrian revolutionaries, though, disregarded the idea.[162]

Still, IS set off messianic anticipation across the Islamic world. Eschatological speculation had become more common in radical Islamic circles after 2001. IS propagandists fanned these flames, depicting the campaign in Syria and Iraq as part of an apocalyptic struggle heralding the arrival of the Mahdi and the restoration of Sunni Islamic dominance. In the wake of the conquest of Mosul, an IS spokesman announced on July 3, "The Islamic State has no borders, and its conquest will continue with God's permission."[163] Although estimates are fuzzy, tens of thousands of foreign fighters from dozens of countries traveled to Syria and Iraq to join the revolution. Some of these were veteran jihadists. Others were adventurers, thugs, and the recently radicalized.[164] In addition, fighting groups from around the Islamic world offered the baya'a to IS and Baghdadi, including in Yemen, Libya, Afghanistan, and Egyptian Sinai.[165] In Europe and North America, IS-inspired terrorists made secret plans to carry out jihad individually.

IS's global and messianic airs, though, often complicated its mission to rule on the ground. Most of these far-flung IS "provinces" failed to materialize. Others quickly died off. Some of the offers were unsuitable because they came from dilettante organizations that were not up to the IS standard.[166] The foreign fighters arriving in Syria and Iraq were useful as fodder in military campaigns, but they had to be trained, fed, and armed. They were not always welcomed by the locals. IS did not subscribe to al-Qaeda's idea of launching a transnational, global insurgency to fight the "far enemy."[167] Rather, IS envisioned a totalizing mode of governance based on the example of the Prophet Muhammad and his early companions. As Charles Lister explains, within its base of operations, IS sought to "provide the same services that a nation-state offers its citizens, but according to the group, in a more ethical manner."[168] Beginning in the proving grounds of Raqqa and spreading across the Jazira and other caliphal domains, IS sought to eliminate the traces of the old regime and install an overtly sectarian version of Sunni supremacy. In Raqqa, one of the first acts of IS rule was to execute Alawis. The tiny Yezidi community was subject to genocidal extermination. Shi'is were heretics, rejecters of God's unity and sowers of sedition. They either converted or were killed. In accordance with the example of the seventh-century caliphate, Christians were afforded the chance to accept subordination to Islamic rule and declare their loyalty to IS. Sufi shrines, ancient antiquities, and posters bearing human likenesses were destroyed as objects of idolatry.[169]

For all of its stringency, though, IS followed a conventional form of state building. Upon taking power in a city, IS's top priority was to disarm residents and eliminate unauthorized or rival clerics, effectively consolidating the monopoly over the legitimate and legal use of force.[170] IS saw itself as governing by popular will. The baya'a was a kind of social contract, specifying the obligations of both ruler and ruled. The "Charter for the City" document, first promulgated in Raqqa in September 2014 and duplicated in other IS-held cities, further enunciated the idea of reciprocal obligations and entitlements. The charter derived its name from the agreement the Prophet Muhammad had made with the residents of Medina. But the content was very different, effectively pledging IS to fulfill the functions of a modern state. IS set up bureaucracies to manage public health, welfare, education, and information. Of course, IS's demands were stringent and its punishments brutal. Some of these had clear Islamic precedents, such as amputation or stoning. Others, like defenestration and crucifixion, were more bizarre and seemed intended to impress more in their savagery than in their fidelity to sharia. Additionally, IS used collective punishment, often videotaped and broadcast on social media, as a warning to recalcitrants. Hundreds of members of the Albu Nimr tribe in al-Hit and the ash-Sheitat tribe near Deir Ezzour were massacred to avenge tribal rebellions.[171] Mirroring the ways the Maliki and Assad regimes used sexual violence to degrade, dishonor, and demoralize opposition, IS used sexual violence to enforce its own prescribed hierarchy. This was most apparent in the case of the Yezidi women. Since Yezidis were heretics, they were not entitled to protection from the state. Their bodies were deemed legitimate spoils of war, and several thousand were taken as sex slaves in IS camps. IS in this way asserted control over the most basic biological power of reproduction.[172] Over two million people left their homes to escape IS's approach, but some three to four million remained, trying to survive and maneuver within the IS system.

Even those who fled appreciated the public safety and regularity that IS ensured. Unlike the Syrian and Iraqi states, IS appeared to take seriously complaints about corruption and official malfeasance.[173]

Beyond crime and punishment, IS also set about to remold everyday life to match its vision of piety. This went beyond the injunctions forbidding alcohol, music, smoking, and unveiled women. The zakat, a mandatory 2.5 to 5 percent tax, was taken from all citizens. Other taxes applied to war booty and other realms of economic activity.[174] Civil servants, who continued to receive salaries from the central governments of Iraq and Syria through 2015, transferred a portion of their salaries to IS coffers. IS introduced its own school curriculum, emphasizing the necessity of jihad and seeking to nurture the next crop of fighters. References to the Western (Gregorian) calendar were forbidden. Instead, IS authorized a committee of observers and experts to measure lunar movements, necessary to fix the Islamic calendar and mark the date of holidays like Ramadan.[175]

A key element in IS's power was mastery of natural resources. In the oil fields around Deir Ezzour, IS backed dissidents within the ash-Sheitat tribe angry about JAN's allocation of oil and gas revenue to a rival sub-clan. IS used the dispute to mobilize tribal supporters and oust JAN from the area.[176] Funds from smuggling oil and refined products to Kurdistan, Turkey, and other rebel-held areas allowed IS to pay its fighters in Syria around $400 per month, with additional stipends for wives and children.[177] In Iraq, it also gained control over some of the smaller fields around Mosul. IS also controlled substantial cement factories and phosphate mines.

Equally importantly, by controlling the region's hydrology, IS oversaw electrification and irrigation. Engineers and technicians at the Tabqa Dam stayed at their post under IS supervision. IS even sold electricity back to the Assad government for the Syrian national grid. The Mosul Dam also remained intact, with IS apparently keeping up critical maintenance (belying predictions that IS would sabotage the dam in a fit of apocalyptic pique). Thanks to increased rainfall, agricultural production in Deir Ezzour and Nineveh rebounded in 2014 and 2015. The IS territories were self-sufficient for grain and could trade with other rebel groups or in Turkey, the KRG, or Iraq. Taxes on cereals alone could have generated $56 million in 2015, around 40 percent of IS's revenue stream.[178]

The cancellation of the Syrian-Iraqi border fundamentally altered the flows of Jazira's political economy. With the price gradient for diesel gone, there was less market for fuel smuggling within IS areas. Syrian herders had access to new markets in Nineveh. IS took customs duties from goods entering and exiting IS-controlled areas from Turkey, Kurdistan, and rebel enclaves in Syria.[179] To displace the common use of US dollars, Iraqi dinars, or other foreign currency, IS issued gold dirham coins (a name derived from the ancient Greek drachma, but a design purportedly based on coins issued by the Caliph Uthman).[180]

The physical elimination of the Syrian-Iraqi border could not eradicate the social manifestations of Syrian and Iraq identity, however. Citizens of the IS still saw themselves (and their neighbors) in terms of the prior nationalities. As Hadi al-Faysal, a Deir Ezzour journalist, observed, "In Furat [Euphrates] province of the Islamic State, residents of Bukamal [Albu Kamal] are still Syrian and residents of al-Qaim are still Iraqi."[181] The apostasy of national identity proved stubborn and reached all the way to the top IS leadership. Though IS touted the equality of (male) Sunnis within the caliphal state, operationally, Abu Bakr al-Baghdadi and his inner circle had a hard time trusting anyone who had not passed through the gauntlet of the previous decade's insurgency in Iraq.[182] Consequently, the IS's upper-echelon commanders were a who's who of the Sunni tribes from northern and western Iraq. There was no single dominant clan or tribe in IS. The most conspicuous were members of the relatively small Rawa tribe from Ana and Sunni Turkmen from Tel Afar. Other notables included the Jubur (of Mosul and Kirkuk), Jaimalla (Fallujah), Albu Bali (Ramadi), Albu Issa (Fallujah), and Dulaymi (Anbar). The common use of tribal surnames as noms de guerre indicates the pride IS leaders took in their tribal heritages.[183]

IS often positioned itself as a kind of super-tribe. According to Ronen Zeidel, about half of IS commanders in Iraq were assigned to territories outside their tribal domains.[184] This allowed IS to act as mediator for tribal feuds and to leverage and manipulate local animosities for its own ends.[185] Just as sexual coercion was a means to subjugate, arranged marriages were an important tool for cementing tribal alliances within the Sunni community, especially in a polygamous culture. War widows were encouraged to remarry fighters as quickly as possible. Abu Bakr al-Baghdadi took as his second wife a member of the Dulaymi, the widow of another insurgent.[186] When al-Khlifawi ventured into Syria following the split with JAN, he married IS recruits into the local clans, building consanguine networks that IS could then mobilize and draw upon.[187]

IS's stance in Iraq, therefore, differed significantly from its position in Syria. In Iraq, IS had effectively marginalized most other Sunni insurgent groups. It controlled some of the most important cities in the predominantly Sunni regions, including Mosul (2 million residents), and the provincial capitals of Ramadi (1 million) and Tikrit (900,000). In Syria, IS was but one of dozens of armed groups, and its territorial holdings were more thinly populated. Raqqa and Deir Ezzour combined had fewer than 2 million residents. The most significant of Syria's cities, including the Sunni strongholds of Aleppo, Hama, and Homs, were not under its control.[188]

Given the obvious but unacknowledged dominance of Iraqis within the movement, IS could at times seem like a movement of colonization within Syria. In fighting off the IS incursion and continuing the campaign against Assad, Joulani and JAN became progressively more Syrian in identification. In early

2015 Zawahiri instructed JAN to concentrate its efforts on the Syrian campaign and disregard the "far enemy." In 2016 JAN formally severed its relationship with al-Qaeda. Renaming itself Jabhat Fateh al-Sham (Front for the Conquest of the Levant), it became even more firmly planted in Syrian soil.[189]

The immediate response to IS's eruption in 2013 and 2014 was badly disjointed. The Syrian military left IS's position in the north and northeast unmolested, focusing on the more immediate threat from JAN and other rebel groups. Syrian Kurdish militias blocked IS encroachment into Hasakah and the Turkish border region. The Iraqi military proved in no condition to fight back. Grand Ayatollah Ali al-Sistani and other senior Shi'i authorities in Iraq and Iran called for a popular mobilization (*hashid sha'bi*), essentially the formation of state-sponsored militias, to defend Baghdad and the south.[190] KRG forces initially buckled but then moved opportunistically in the disputed regions of Kirkuk, Nineveh, and Diyala.

Gradually, though, an ad hoc anti-IS coalition emerged. Iran was the lynchpin, providing the most direct backing to both Damascus and Baghdad. Iran's expeditionary Quds Force trained and regularized the Popular Mobilization Units (PMU) in Iraq and the shabiha militias in Syria. Tehran also helped recruit fighters from Lebanese Hezbollah and elsewhere to augment Syrian ground forces. The United States initially dithered in Iraq but eventually found an effective division of labor, providing training, equipment, air support, intelligence, and targeted drone strikes while Iran handled the ground war. The situation in Syria was even more complicated. Russia provided significant air and ground support to Syrian operations. Additionally, Turkey, Jordan, the Gulf states, and European powers all committed funds or forces to help beat back IS.

Constant military pressure compelled IS to devote enormous resources to defense. According to captured documents, about two-thirds of IS's budget went to pay soldiers. Healthcare, schools, food support, and municipal upkeep were constantly strapped.[191] The revenue from taxes and plunder left IS well-off for an insurgent group, but were far from adequate for an operational state. IS's payments to soldiers declined as fighting wore on. In the first months of IS rule in Mosul, IS handed out free grain and bread to civilians. Yet the basic food subsidy that the Iraqi and Syrian governments had offered for decades proved too costly, causing consumer prices to rise in IS-held areas. Technical issues also proved daunting. Turkey embargoed the Euphrates waters heading to the Tabqa Dam, forcing IS to ration water and electricity.[192] Farmers complained that IS seized their produce and did not provide credit to invest in the new machinery necessary to ensure long-term agricultural stability.[193]

Ultimately, IS's retreat left the Jazira a landscape of ashes and mud. Committed to fighting to the death, IS soldiers killed suspected spies and took civilians as human shields. For their part, the allies tended to use indiscriminate force against IS-held cities and towns. Homes and businesses were leveled. Sectarian militias, operating under the aegis of the PMU in Iraq or the shabiha in Syria, executed suspected IS collaborators. Tens of thousands became refugees, sparking renewed concerns about retaliation against Sunnis that would only deepen the humanitarian disaster.[194] In October 2015 Iraqi forces took back the oil refinery at Beiji. Ramadi and Fallujah fell in the first half of 2016. Iraqi and Kurdish forces encircled Mosul in October 2016, making slow but steady progress through the summer of 2017. On June 21 desperate IS fighters blew up the Nur al-Din Mosque and toppled its famous leaning minaret. The demolition of the very site in which the caliphate had been enunciated three years earlier coincided with Laylat al-Qadr, the date Islamic tradition holds the Angel Gabriel revealed the Quran to Mohammad. Abadi deemed this "a formal declaration of [IS's] defeat."[195] In Syria US-aligned Kurdish forces retook Raqqa that same month. Government troops, backed by Iran and Russia, took Deir Ezzour that autumn. By the end of the year IS was reduced to pockets between the Khabur River and the Iraq border and to the area downstream between Mayadin and Albu Kamal. Losing land by the day, IS leaders seemed to give up on the idea of territorial control. IS spokesman Abu Mohammed Adnani stated: "O America, would we be defeated and you be victorious if you were to take Mosul or Sirte [in Libya] or Raqqa? . . . Certainly not! We would be defeated and you victorious only if you were able to remove the Koran from Muslims' hearts."[196] Although IS leaders suggested that their losses in Syria and Iraq were just tactical retreats, they focused again on IS's ability to wage war globally through networks of loosely coordinated sleeper cells and self-radicalized terrorists. The IS caliphate had become more virtual than real.

Baghdadi's message of September 2017, the first issuance in a year, delved further into the eschatological. It began with discussion of the expulsion of Satan, banishment from Eden, Noah and the Flood, and then the redemption of Islam and the Islamic State:

> Campaigns by the nations of disbelief continued against the lands of the Muslims, and that which was impermissible became permissible. Religion was lost and Muslims descended into chaos, pulled in all directions by their whims and desires. The Arab and Persian tyrants, the minions of the Jews and servants of the Cross, beleaguered and besieged them, but the mercy of God and His blessings upon this umma are truly great. He brought together the sons of Islam from among the tribes, who are connected by none of the vanities of this fleeting world. They reinvigorated the world with jihad, and gave new life to those who studied the principals of the righteous religion and the sharia of the Lord of all creation. They battled against the nations of disbelief in the east and the west, in the north and the south.[197]

Baghdadi further asserted that IS had become the "authoritative" religious source for Islam:

> The sons of Islam in the caliphate state have proven, thanks to God's grace, that they, with their steadfastness and firmness in facing the instruments of the enemy and their deadly arsenal, that they are the ummah's fortress, its solid shield, its blazing hope, and its first line of defense against the rejectionist [i.e., Shi'is], Houthi [of Yemen], Magi [Zoroastrians/Iranians], Nusayri enemy, which has begun to foster hopes of placing its grip on the Sunnis' lands, with unparalleled support from the Cross's apostate servants and minions.

As the battle reached an apocalyptic crescendo, Mosul became the physical site of Armageddon:

> What proves this is the perseverance of the ummah's men in this age in which they remained steadfast in Mosul, refusing to turn over the land that was ruled by God's sharia to the infidels and the Crusader nations, except with death and bloodshed, taking pride in their religion, elevating their faith, certain and perseverant, awaiting their reward. They fulfilled their pledge and their word, refusing to turn it over except over their skulls and limbs. They are excused, after nearly a year of fighting and battle, as we reckon them, though God is the final judge. This is despite the fact that the spiteful Crusaders, as is their nature with the Muslims in Mosul and the other areas in the abode of Islam, left no deadly and destructive weapon unused. Nothing they claim was forbidden to them went unused. They burned people, trees, and everything on the earth. May God give them what they deserve. This did not deter the mujahideen from their jihad. The lives of the sons of Islam shall remain cheap in the cause of their Creator the Exalted. As they seemed to say: Say: Can you expect for us (any fate) other than one of two most glorious things [i.e., martyrdom or victory]? But we can expect for you either that Allah will send his punishment from Himself, or by our hands. So wait; we too will wait with you.[198]

While IS's territorial hold receded, the power of tribes endured in the Jazira. In both Syria and Iraq, the government inducted tribal leaders and militias into anti-IS forces. In Iraq, some tribal forces were incorporated into the PMU. The Upper Euphrates Regiment contained several tribesmen from the al-Qaim area and received training with Danish special forces.[199] In Syria, the Tribal Army initially cooperated, but later clashed, with Kurdish militias fighting against IS.[200]

The Iraqi government, especially, recognized the pivotal role that tribes and tribal leaders could play in stabilization and reconstruction in the Jazira. With support from the international community, Baghdad empowered tribal leaders to maintain peace and stability and manage reconciliation. Yet these tribal leaders still retained their own ambitions and agendas. With tacit approval, they retaliated against suspected IS collaborators under tribal law. Without due process, those who had joined the caliphate, as well as their tribal relatives and kin, were subject to tribal retribution, including demolition of homes, banishments, and even execution.[201] The Jazira remained a space where state control was only tenuous and indirect.

## Conclusion

IS was the most disruptive claimant to sovereign statehood to emerge after 2011. Unlike other rebels in the Arab world, IS refused to ingratiate itself with the international community. IS's derisions of international norms and its terrorist threats were intended to affront and intimidate. Baghdadi, like Zarqawi before him, wanted to shake the international system to its core. IS aimed to overturn the international system's Western-dominated hierarchy and surpass the territorial nation-state, its key constitutive element. Islam, rightly guided by the IS caliph and modeled on the example of seventh-century Arabia, would be universal and triumphant. There would be no need, therefore, for artificial territorial demarcations.

In practical terms, though, IS was inscribed in specific spatial and temporal bounds. Within the Jazira, IS offered more than just millenarian promises about the caliphate and a return to Sunni supremacy.[202] To individuals and communities that had suffered dire setbacks in the prior decade, it provided protection, security, and empowerment. IS gained support by blocking rapacious state authority, providing for public welfare, and honoring tribal autonomy. These ideas appeared ancient—eternal and divinely ordained, according to IS—but they stemmed from particular histories of state formation in Syria and Iraq. Likewise, IS's repertoires of coercion, from its extortion of smugglers to its sexual violence and mass killings, echoed the governance of the Syrian and Iraqi states.

It was not accidental that IS emerged in the peripheries of the collapsed states of Syria and Iraq. As soon as Iraq and Syria gained sovereignty, the Jazira stood out as a zone of exception, "semi-civilized," in the parlance of the Wilsonian era. The Jazira was socially, economically, and politically distinctive. But unlike for the Kurds, Cyrenaicans, Zionists, Armenians, or Arabs, no one lobbied for the region's independence. No one claimed it as a national homeland worthy of self-determination at Versailles and San Remo, or subsequently petitioned the

League of Nations. No map delineated the Jazira's boundaries. A coherent notion of Jazira identity never congealed. Nevertheless, the space between the Upper Euphrates and Tigris Rivers remained a hotbed of anti-state resistance. At every opportunity local tribal leaders agitated for greater autonomy and exemption from the rules and regulations of the centralizing state. Brigandage, diffuse uprisings, and general unruliness characterized the area for much of the twentieth century. Though not articulated as secessionist, these efforts amounted to campaigns to separate the Jazira from Syria and Iraq and reconnect the severed ligatures of tribal and kin relations. Damascus and Baghdad both mixed repression with policies of co-optation and accommodation to respond to the challenges. Especially in Saddam's Iraq, the affinities of Sunni sectarianism and calibrated enticement helped to yoke the Iraq tribal leadership to the national elite.

The collapse of the Iraqi state in 2003, though, threw this arrangement into disarray. It overturned the premise of Sunni supremacy. It also unfettered those who imagined a return to tribal supremacy in the Jazira. AQI enlisted the habits of local rebellion in its campaign against Baghdad and the United States. But treating northwestern Iraq as an arena of global conflict ultimately alienated many Sunni Arab tribal leaders, who resented foreigners usurping their local dominance. Sponsoring the Awakening militias in 2006, the United States undercut the insurgency by offering the tribal leaders a better deal. By the end of the decade, though, Maliki's drive toward centralizing power effectively reneged on this offer.

The 2011 uprisings provided an opportunity to transmute the otherworldly, the global, and the local dimensions of IS's agenda. IS's appeal to outsiders, including its assumption of caliphal authority, were part of a messianic and apocalyptic program. Yet these endeavors were inextricable from the effort to detach the Jazira from the misshapen borders of Syria and Iraq. IS did not break all the borders, just the ones that impinged on the Jazira. Moreover, IS's mission to form a state indicated a distinctly modernist sensibility that meshed, sometimes uncomfortably, with its purported medievalism and messianic pretensions. If anyone was citizens and constituents of IS's rebel state, it was the Jazira tribes. Just as other separatists had, IS set about to establish a better-functioning and more legitimate political entity worthy of the promise of Wilsonianism.

# Conclusion

## The Ends of Separatism in the Arab World

Scattered across eastern and southeastern Europe are numerous monuments dedicated to the memory of Woodrow Wilson. As the Habsburg Empire broke down, Bratislava was even briefly renamed Wilson City in gratitude for the president's efforts for Czechoslovakian independence. Some of these commemorations were later expunged or effaced. The Nazis demolished the statue of Wilson at Prague's main rail terminal, the Croatian fascists rechristened Sarajevo's Wilson Promenade for Mussolini, and Warsaw's Wilson Square was named for the Paris Commune under Communist rule. Since 1991, however, many states have restored Wilson to a place of honor, a kind of national foster father.[1]

This book is about Wilson's less happy admirers in the Middle East and North Africa. Part I examined how state-building elites in the region adopted Wilson's discourse about self-determination to gain footing in the international system in the post–World War I era. Yet statehood also brought subordination, paternalistic mandates, and continual neo-imperialist interjections. The result was congenitally defective Arab states. They retained juridical status and territorial integrity by dint of international recognition. Yet they proved unequal to the challenge of providing security and welfare to their own citizens or physically controlling their allotted space. The global nation-state crisis cast an enormous shadow over the 2011 Arab uprisings. The acceleration of state deaths, state births, and the appearance of spectral-like unrecognized de facto states through the 1990s and 2000s signaled a breakdown in the consensus of mid-century liberal internationalism. In the Arab world, what began with demands for reform or regime change devolved into civil wars that tore apart the already fragile states. Outside intervention further upended de jure notions of sovereignty.[2]

Part II examined those groups that sought to break the borders of the existing regional structures during the 2011 conflagration—the federalist movement in Cyrenaica, the Southern Movement (SM) in South Arabia, the Kurds in Iraq and Syria, and the Islamic State (IS). Each of these separatists claimed, in various ways, to be the orphans of Wilsonianism. These nations, too, deserved recognition, self-determination, and statehood. Yet they had suffered setbacks and frustrations at critical junctures of state formation during the twentieth century. The 2011 uprisings provided another opportunity, a sudden slackening in the restraints that had held contemporary states together. It was a fresh chance to break away. The Kurdish Regional Government in Iraq, the federalists in Cyrenaica, and the SM explicitly framed their efforts as restoring lost autonomy and sovereignty. Rojava's linkages to past Kurdish autonomy movements in Turkey and Syria were less explicit but no less pertinent. IS defined itself as the continuation of the Ottomans' legacy of Sunni supremacy, felled by European intrusion after World War I. The failure of regional states was an occasion to correct these mistakes.

The possibilities of restoring a lost twentieth-century birthright gave separatists a ready script for collective action. This script designated—although not always definitively—a national community and territory. Equally importantly, it specified who the nation's antagonists were and why victory was necessary and just. As states collapsed, separatists seized control over oil depots, dams, border crossings, ports, airstrips, and other infrastructure. They operated schools, court systems, police, and agricultural co-ops. They provided the benefits of statehood to those whom the titular state had excluded or denied.

Reclaiming self-determination also affected engagement with the international society. The Kurds in Syria and Iraq, the South Yemenis, and the Cyrenaicans all looked to the United States, the European powers, and the UN to gain material support and moral legitimacy. Much as the prior generations of state builders had addressed the gatekeepers of international society, they portrayed themselves as future pillars of stability. IS, the black sheep in the separatist flock, defied the global community and touted itself as a global revolutionary actor. Still, it also sought the affirmation of the global Islamic umma and could not help but define itself as a state nonetheless.

In emphasizing long temporal horizons, the individuation and singularity of specific countries and groups, and their interconnectedness in a global system, this book is wary of generalizing or forecasting. Nevertheless, the findings add to scholarly and policy discussions about the origins of separatist conflicts, how the international community responds to separatist claims, and the future of statehood in the MENA region and the wider world.

## The Tenacious Power of Dead States

Thomas Hobbes famously described life without the state as "solitary, poor, nasty, brutish, and short," but the evidence is not on his side. The recent studies of rebel governance have given new insights into the kinds of political order that arise when states recede. This order can range from the predatory to the reciprocal, including new kinds of social contracts between rebel rulers and civilians. Still, rebel rulers are often seen as rote utility maximizers, pursing rational strategies to maintain and expand their physical power. But by excising identity, culture, or history, these theories cannot explain what distinguishes rebels' agenda, what shapes their vision for the future, or why some seek to displace a particular regime while others aim for secession or separatism.[3]

This book explains how repertoires of contention and violence, accumulated during prior drives for sovereignty, propel rebels toward centrifugal, separatist strategies.[4] This argument complements hypotheses about the impact of segmented state institutions in generating new separatist claims. Segmented institutional systems, like the USSR's ethno-federalist structure, offered a pre-fabricated platform for political actors looking to break away. In the MENA region, besides Iraqi Kurdistan, there are few federalist segmented institutions from which to start a rebellion. Instead, rebels used dead or conquered states as the starting point for their engagement.

These prior identities are not essential, innate, or even ancient. In the case of the Arab world, they largely originated with the construction of the regional system after the world wars. These identities were tenacious, as Allan Hoben and Robert Hefner put it, because they were "renewed, modified, and remade with each generation."[5] Incumbent Arab states tried to negate or appropriate the memories of their historical competitors. Separatists, in turn, tried to revive and reclaim them. IS was most radical in this respect, demanding that citizens forget their respective experience of statehood in Iraq and Syria and revert to an Edenic age of Sunni supremacy. At the same time, however, IS drew directly from repertoires of the Sunni dominance articulated by twentieth-century states. The KRG quasi-state, beginning in 1991, made sure that Kurds in Iraq knew of Sèvres, Mahabad, the aborted 1970 autonomy plan, and Halabja, emphasizing the divergent course of Kurdish and Iraqi history. Similarly, the SM in Yemen kept alive memories of southern independence, although the leadership disagreed about which political entity—the People's Democratic Republic of Yemen, the Aden city-state, or Hadramawt and the sultanates—was its progenitor. The weakness of the incumbent state allowed these separatists a long latency period. In other cases, activating these supposedly essential identities happened much more rapidly, concomitant with the collapse of the state. At the time of revolution, few Cyrenaicans (much less Libyans in general) likely remembered or cared about the intricacies of 1950s monarchical federalism or the brief emirate that preceded it. There had been few visible signs of an ethnic or quasi-ethnic divide between the east and Tripolitania. But there were memories of families, tribes, and clans that had perceived themselves satisfied or dissatisfied with their inclusion and provision from the state. The task of the separatists, therefore, was to pursue a claim for Cyrenaica that was morally assuasive and materially viable. Similarly, the PYD was a minor actor in Syrian politics before 2011. Its efforts to solidify Rojava in the midst of civil war represented an open-ended reinterpretation of what it meant to be Kurdish and Syrian. Ultimately, Rojava raised the question of whether it was possible to be both at once. But there was always some portion (possibly a majority) of the purported national community that avoided the dangerous and uncertain path of separation. To the separatists' frustration, these detractors—traitors, if you like—were blind to the cleavages that demarcated them from other citizens of the nominal state and disinterested in the prior struggles of failed state building.

In response, separatists strove to emphasize authenticity and historical rootedness, but also contemporaneousness and adaptability. For decades states had sought to impose socioeconomic modernization as a means of political control. In Kurdistan, Cyrenaica, South Yemen, and the Jazira, land reform (whether socialist or capitalist in bent), detribalization, and ecological engineering were inextricable from state building and subordination. The separatists did not disavow these measures. Rather, they repurposed them, promising to turn modernization into liberation.

The importance of prior statehood becomes even clearer when comparing cases of uprisings and revolution where separatism did not appear. Tunisia and Egypt, the earliest revolutionary states of 2011, are also two of the most coherent and long-standing states in the Arab world. In both countries, the uprising heightened ethno-sectarian tensions, specifically between Arabs and Berbers in Tunisia and between Muslims and Christians in Egypt. However, in both cases, contention was vertical, aiming to influence the central state, not to separate horizontally. In Bahrain, the divide between Sunnis and Shi'is was much starker, but there was no call for a separate and independent Shi'a state. On the contrary, Bahrain's Arab Shi'is consider themselves an indigenous group that had suffered disenfranchisement at the hands of the Sunni al-Khalifa monarchy. During the popular uprising, Bahraini Shi'is demanded equitable access to the state and its resources, not to hive off a new territorial entity.[6]

Examining the sedimented history of state formation in the MENA region and the legacies of dead states is suggestive of where separatist conflicts are likely to emerge if there is another breakdown in state power. In North Africa, Berber minorities have periodically demanded greater political rights and inclusion, although they rarely sought full territorial separation.[7] In 2016 activists in Morocco's Rif region appropriated the flag and memory of the short-lived Rif Republic in protests demanding economic development, language rights, and an end to political repression. With the Moroccan state functionally intact, however, there was little hope to gain autonomy unilaterally. Berbers living in the Netherlands and other parts of the diaspora, however, cited the history of the Rif Republic to bolster their plan for separatism.[8] Elsewhere, dead states appear to be more thoroughly buried, such as the Imamate of Nizwan (now part of Oman) or the Hejaz and Asir (both part of Saudi Arabia). Their resurrection may still only await a groundswell strong enough to shake the state's coercive grip.

## Separatism and the Disorganized Hypocrisy of Proxy Wars

The distance between the presumption of de jure sovereignty and de facto control among developing states was never a secret. Yet this did not diminish enthusiasm for sovereign statehood as an ideal form of political organization. Through most of the twentieth century, the adduction of sovereignty and statehood was considered key to global order. Accordingly, members of the international community affirmed these principles, despite apparent deficits of certain countries. Territorial boundaries had to be preserved in law, even if they were violated periodically in action. This is the essence of what Stephen Krasner calls sovereignty's "organized hypocrisy," the ability to maintain a general normative protocol and codes of conduct notwithstanding shortcomings in specific practices.[9]

IS refused to play this game. It decried the international system as illegitimate and apostate. It denounced the hypocrisies of an international society that claimed to provide for the equality of members but allowed greater powers to dominate the weaker. It asked how an international society committed to humanitarianism could condone the oppression and murder of Muslims. IS thus confronted the entire global system.[10]

The other separatist groups, meanwhile, followed the rules of international society, or at least pretended to. The Cyrenaican, South Arabian, and Kurdish separatists knew that their demands for territorial adjustment broke fundamental tenets of the global order, but they promised that this would be their only trespass. They glommed onto the idea of self-determination as an alternative constitutive norm in their acts of self-creation. Wilsonianism was a trump card to justify the breaking of borders.[11] At the same time, they depicted themselves as reliable and ready candidates for admission to the club of states. They signaled acceptance of international law, democracy, and humanitarian responsibility. They tried to leverage their de facto control over oil, dams, ports, and airspace to entice outside sponsors and investment. Independence would improve global security. Most importantly, separatists served as the spearheads of campaigns against IS and al-Qaeda, whose anti-system agitation made them an immediate target for repression.

The members of the international community eagerly inducted separatist movements as proxies in their campaigns. Proxy wars appeared to be a cheaper and less risky alternative to the kinds of direct intervention the United States undertook in Iraq in 2003. Just like their predecessors after World War I, state-aspirants were caught in the tumult of conflicting regional and geopolitical agendas. The UAE and Saudi Arabia determined the fate of South Arabia's bid for independence. Cyrenaica separatists, locked in a mortal embrace with Haftar, became dependent on the whims of Egypt, the UAE, Russia, and the United States. The Kurds' foreign patrons, including Turkey, Iran, and the United States, were also their greatest impediment in their bid to realize self-determination. In each case, outside powers exploited their proxies' ability to operate on the ground and abandoned them when the immediate threat dissipated.[12] No group, so far, has seen its bids rewarded. In effect, the separatists were forced to remain within states that were either functionally moribund or overtly murderous toward their own people.

This does not bode well for the substantiation of new rules and norms. The problem was not that aspiring state builders challenged the principles of sovereignty and statehood. Rather, the shortsighted and cynical policies of existing states, recognized members of the international society, hurt the chances of retaining a meaningful commitment to statehood. Proxy warfare succeeded in containing and degrading IS, at least temporarily. But the solemn avowals of respect for territorial integrity after IS's defeat in 2017, for example, were risible coming from actors that had so little concern for norms of nonintervention five years earlier. Touched by the global nation-state crisis, Yemen, Libya, Iraq, and Syria may well endure but cannot prevail. The normative protocols that keep them intact are less consistent and more ambiguous—a manifestly disorganized kind of hypocrisy.[13] Though Western policy makers recite the mantra that state building is essential for regional order, their actions further reduced statehood to a hollow territorial shell. In Yemen, Syria, Iraq, and Libya, the international community missed the chance to mitigate or resolve conflicts through negotiated secession, ethnofederal confederation arrangements, or tacit arrangements for de facto statehood.[14] The more states and their outside backers rely on naked coercion to maintain power, the more their moral authority recedes. Cooperation becomes harder, domestic peace more tenuous, international stability more fragile.[15] Weakened states are poor partners in campaigns against global jihad and weak pillars for global order. Separatists, meanwhile, who had demonstrated capacities for governance and the desire to enter international society, were left to cope with a new round of repression. They still bide their time for the next Wilsonian moment.

# What Is a State Worth?

In the midst of the 2011 uprisings, the Palestinian philosopher Sari Nusseibeh posed a provocative question:

> I began asking myself what the state we were fighting for is worth. How much killing can a group suffer or commit before the suffering and the loss of life outweigh the values on whose behalf the killing is being committed—before the situation reaches to tragic absurdity?[16]

The Palestinian national movement shares many characteristics with the separatist movements in southern Arabia, Kurdistan, Cyrenaica, and the Jazira. Palestinians, too, claimed to have been orphaned by Wilsonianism, denied the legacy of self-determination. Over the course of decades, they have struggled to bring an end to the Israeli occupation and gain international recognition. Modest successes, such as the emergence of the Palestinian Authority and the 2011 bid for UN membership, though, punctuated general failures.[17] Now, Nusseibeh reluctantly suggested, the enormous costs of attaining statehood made the pursuit foolhardy. Nusseibeh's questions pertain equally to Cyrenaica, South Arabia, Kurdistan, and IS.

Some observers are ready to write-off statehood generally as an outdated or failed political experiment.[18] Why strive to emulate a model that is already heading to the dustbin of history? Yet, the fact that so many people continue to sacrifice (often times in vain) in separatists conflicts indicates that some still see moral or material value in statehood. Beyond the active separatist movements in MENA, contemporaries in Catalonia and Scotland, and the recent examples of Kosovo, East Timor, and South Sudan, suggests that statehood remains an attractive mode for organizing political life and critically important to global order.[19] Each of the separatist movements discussed in this book aimed to "earn" sovereign statehood by attaining physical control on the ground and support abroad. If states have responsibilities, then those political entities that meet those responsibilities ought to be rewarded and recognized. Sovereignty can be both the carrot and stick for getting separatists groups to abide by the rules of the international system. However, many aspiring state-builders may conclude that such a rigged game is not worth playing after the debacles of the 2010s. Whatever the benefits of statehood and whatever the motivation of separatists to attain them, the international community may still never be forthcoming.

If the bid to correct the mishaps of the Wilsonian-era state making goes unrequited, then alternative arrangements must be found. Surveying development and governance in the MENA region, Ellen Lust notes the prominence of "competing authorities [that] are not incidental or subordinate to the state, but rather are critical, enduring actors."[20] States in MENA often overlay or mask the more formidable power of transnational religious communities, clans, tribes, neighborhood and village councils, trading networks, and corporations. Unlike states and state-aspirants, these entities do not necessarily seek to monopolize violence, set broad developmental goals, or demand singular allegiance and loyalty. Yet they often do provide security, foster economic development, and serve as focal points of identity. Their scope is more limited, their coverage uneven. Their governance may not allow the full extent of human flourishing, but they are good enough to provide basic requisites of human security. They are therefore a more promising option than sticking with decrepit or abusive states.[21]

With the path of breaking away to form a new statehood blocked, citizens may opt to let states atrophy and fade away. Rebellion and resistance will take the form of withdrawal, not confrontation. From the perspective of the international community, such an adaptation holds promise and peril. These non-state actors, unlike separatists, are seldom eager for attention from the international community. They operate outside of the usual diplomatic custom and procedure. This makes them hard to manipulate or even engage from without. Yet they may still deliver a more stable political order than what the last century of Arab statehood has afforded.

# NOTES

## Introduction

1. Islamic State of Iraq and al-Sham, "The End of Sykes-Picot," *Al-Hayat* (Iraq), uploaded on June 29, 2014, by Aaron Y. Zelin to his Jihadology website, http://jihadology.net/2014/06/29/al-%E1%B8%A5ayat-media-center-presents-a-new-video-message-from-the-islamic-state-of-iraq-and-al-sham-the-end-of-sykes-picot/.
2. Declaration of the Caliphate, https://ia902505.us.archive.org/28/items/poa_25984/EN.pdf (accessed May 30, 2018).
3. Ian Black, "Isis Breach of Iraq-Syria Border Merges Two Wars into One 'Nightmarish Reality,'" *Guardian*, June 19, 2014, http://www.theguardian.com/world/2014/jun/18/isis-iraq-syria-two-wars-one-nightmare.
4. James Gelvin, "Obsession with Sykes-Picot Says More about What We Think of Arabs than History," *The Conversation*, May 12, 2016, http://theconversation.com/obsession-with-sykes-picot-says-more-about-what-we-think-of-arabs-than-history-58775 (accessed May 30, 2018); Louise Fawcett, "States and Sovereignty in the Middle East: Myths and Realities," *International Affairs* 93.4 (2017): 789–780.
5. Ghusan Sharbek, "Barzani li'l hayat: Harit saykes-picot mustina'h wa al hudud al-jadid turasmim bi al-dam" [Barzani to al-Hayat: The Sykes-Picot map is artificial and the new borders are drawn in blood], *Al-Hayat*, February 8, 2015, http://www.alhayat.com/Articles/7243606
6. Benjamin Miller, "Balance of Power or the State-to-Nation Balance: Explaining Middle East War-Propensity," *Security Studies* 15.4 (2006): 658–705; Michael C. Hudson, *Arab Politics: The Search for Legitimacy* (New Haven, CT: Yale University Press, 1977).
7. Iliya Harik, "The Origins of the Arab State System," in *The Arab State*, ed. G. Luciani (Berkeley: University of California Press, 1990), 1–28; Lisa Blaydes, "State Building in the Middle East," *Annual Review of Political Science* 20 (2017): 487–504; Raffaella A. Del Sarto, "Contentious Borders in the Middle East and North Africa: Context and Concepts," *International Affairs* 93.4 (2017): 772.
8. George Antonius, *The Arab Awakening: The Story of the Arab National Movement* (New York: Simon Publishing, 1938).
9. Kevin M. Woods, David D. Palkki, and Mark E. Stout, eds., *The Saddam Tapes: The Inner Workings of a Tyrant's Regime, 1978–2001* (New York: Cambridge University Press, 2011), 124.
10. Osama bin Laden, "The World Islamic Front," February 23, 1998, in *Messages to the World*, ed. Bruce Lawrence (New York: Verso, 2005), 60.
11. Osama bin Laden, "Among a Band of Knights," February 14, 2013, in Lawrence, *Messages to the World*, 18.

12. Cited in James Gelvin, "Don't Blame Sykes-Picot," *OUPblog*, February 7, 2015, http://blog.oup.com/2015/02/dont-blame-sykes-picot/.
13. Jeffrey Goldberg, "After Iraq," *Atlantic*, January/February 2008.
14. Robin Wright, "How 5 Countries in the Middle East Could Become 14," *New York Times*, September 28, 2013.
15. Yaroslav Trofimov, "Would New Borders Mean Less Conflict in the Middle East?" *Wall Street Journal*, April 10, 2015, https://www.wsj.com/articles/would-new-borders-mean-less-conflict-in-the-middle-east-1428680793.
16. Donald L. Horowitz, "Patterns of Ethnic Separatism," *Comparative Studies in Society and History* 23.2 (1981): 165–195; John R. Wood, "Secession: A Comparative Analytical Framework," *Canadian Journal of Political Science* 14.1 (1981): 107–134; Kristin M. Bakke, "State, Society and Separatism in Punjab," *Regional & Federal Studies* 19.2 (2009): 291–308.
17. Gelvin, "Obsession with Sykes-Picot"; Fawcett, "States and Sovereignty in the Middle East".
18. Erez Manela, *The Wilsonian Moment: Self-determination and the International Origins of Anticolonial Nationalism* (New York: Oxford University Press, 2007).
19. David Patrick Houghton, "The Role of Self-Fulfilling and Self-Negating Prophecies in International Relations," *International Studies Review* 11.3 (2009): 552–584; Harry Verhoeven, "The Self-Fulfilling Prophecy of Failed States: Somalia, State Collapse and the Global War on Terror," *Journal of Eastern African Studies* 3.3 (2009): 405–425.
20. On the proxy war dynamics, see Bassel F. Salloukh, "The Arab Uprisings and the Geopolitics of the Middle East," *International Spectator* 48.2 (2013): 32–46; Andreas Krieg, "Externalizing the Burden of War: The Obama Doctrine and US Foreign Policy in the Middle East," *International Affairs* 92.1 (2016): 97–113; Marc Lynch, *The New Arab Wars: Uprisings and Anarchy in the Middle East* (New York: Public Affairs, 2016); Amr Yossef and Joseph Cerami, *The Arab Spring and the Geopolitics of the Middle East: Emerging Security Threats and Revolutionary Change* (New York: Palgrave Pivot, 2015).
21. Paul R. Williams and Francesca Jannotti Pecci, "Earned Sovereignty: Bridging the Gap between Sovereignty and Self-determination," *Stanford Journal of International Law* 40 (2004): 347; Paul R. Williams, Michael P. Scharf, and James R. Hooper, "Resolving Sovereignty-Based Conflicts: The Emerging Approach of Earned Sovereignty," *Denver Journal of International Law & Policy* 31 (2002): 349; Milena Sterio, *The Right to Self-determination under International Law: "Selfistans," Secession, and the Rule of the Great Powers* (New York: Routledge, 2013).
22. Raymond Hinnebusch, "Order and Change in the Middle East: A Neo-Gramscian Twist on the International Society Approach," in *International Society and the Middle East*, ed. Barry Buzan and Ana Gonzalez-Pelaez (London: Palgrave, 2009), 202–203.
23. Max Weber, "Politics as Vocation," in *From Max Weber: Essays in Sociology*, ed. H. H. Gerth and C. Wright Mills (New York: Oxford University Press, 1958), 78(italics in original).
24. John Breuilly, *Nationalism and the State* (Manchester: Manchester University Press, 1993). For a general survey, see Craig Calhoun, "Nationalism and Ethnicity," *Annual Review of Sociology* 19.1 (1993): 211–239.
25. Rogers Brubaker and Frederick Cooper, "Beyond 'Identity,'" *Theory and Society* 29.1 (2000): 1–47.
26. Jordan Branch, "Territory as an Institution: Spatial Ideas, Practices and Technologies," *Territory, Politics, Governance* 5.2 (2017): 131–144; Boaz Atzili and Burak Kadercan, "Territorial Designs and International Politics: The Diverging Constitution of Space and Boundaries," *Territory, Politics, Governance* 5.2 (2017): 115–130.
27. Anthony Smith, "State-Making and Nation-Building," in *States in History*, ed. John A. Hall (London: Blackwell, 1986); Michael Mann, *The Sources of Social Power*, vol. 1, *A History of Power from the Beginning to A.D. 1760* (New York: Cambridge University Press, 1986), 7–8.
28. Marta Reynal-Querol, "Ethnicity, Political Systems, and Civil Wars," *Journal of Conflict Resolution* 46.1 (2002): 29–54; Rogers Brubaker and David D. Laitin, "Ethnic and Nationalist Violence," *Annual Review of Sociology* 24.1 (1998): 423–452; Andreas Wimmer, Lars-Erik Cederman, and Brian Min, "Ethnic Politics and Armed Conflict: A Configurational Analysis of a New Global Data Set," *American Sociological Review* 74.2 (2009): 316–337.

29. James D. Fearon and David D. Laitin, "Ethnicity, Insurgency, and Civil War," *American Political Science Review* 97.1 (2003): 75–90. See also Cullen S. Hendrix, "Head for the Hills? Rough Terrain, State Capacity, and Civil War Onset," *Civil Wars* 13.4 (2011): 345–370.

30. Michael L. Ross, "How Do Natural Resources Influence Civil War? Evidence from Thirteen Cases," *International Organization* 58.1 (2004): 35–67; Ibrahim Ahmed Elbadawi and Raimundo Soto, "Resource Rents, Institutions, and Violent Civil Conflicts," *Defence and Peace Economics* 26.1 (2015): 89–113.

31. Zachariah Cherian Mampilly, *Rebel Rulers: Insurgent Governance and Civilian Life during War* (Ithaca, NY: Cornell University Press, 2011); Ana Arjona, Nelson Kasfir, and Zachariah Mampilly, eds., *Rebel Governance in Civil War* (New York: Cambridge University Press, 2015); Thomas Risse and Eric Stollenwerk, "Legitimacy in Areas of Limited Statehood," *Annual Review of Political Science* 21 (2018): 403–418; Ana Arjona, *Rebelocracy* (New York: Cambridge University Press, 2016).

32. Harris Mylonas and Nadav Shelef, "Which Land Is Our Land? Domestic Politics and Change in the Territorial Claims of Stateless Nationalist Movements," *Security Studies* 23.4 (2014): 754–786; Harris Mylonas and Nadav Shelef, "Methodological Challenges in the Study of Stateless Nationalist Territorial Claims," *Territory, Politics, Governance* 5.2 (2017): 145–157; Ariel Zellman, "Uneven Ground: Nationalist Frames and the Variable Salience of Homeland," *Security Studies* 27.3 (2018): 485–510.

33. Nils B. Weidmann, "Geography as Motivation and Opportunity: Group Concentration and Ethnic Conflict," *Journal of Conflict Resolution* 53.4 (2009): 526–543; Nicholas Sambanis, "Do Ethnic and Nonethnic Civil Wars Have the Same Causes? A Theoretical and Empirical Inquiry (Part 1)," *Journal of Conflict Resolution* 45.3 (2001): 259–282.

34. Päivi Lujala, "The Spoils of Nature: Armed Civil Conflict and Rebel Access to Natural Resources," *Journal of Peace Research* 47.1 (2010): 15–28; Jason Sorens, "Mineral Production, Territory, and Ethnic Rebellion: The Role of Rebel Constituencies," *Journal of Peace Research* 48.5 (2011): 571–585.

35. Tim C. Wegenast and Matthias Basedau, "Ethnic Fractionalization, Natural Resources and Armed Conflict," *Conflict Management and Peace Science* 31.4 (2014): 432–457; Matthias Basedau and Thomas Richter, "Why Do Some Oil Exporters Experience Civil War but Others Do Not? Investigating the Conditional Effects of Oil," *European Political Science Review* 6.4 (2014): 549–574.

36. Peter Krause, *Rebel Power: Why National Movements Compete, Fight, and Win* (Ithaca, NY: Cornell University Press, 2017); Kathleen Gallagher Cunningham, *Inside the Politics of Self-determination* (New York: Oxford University Press, 2014); Kathleen Gallagher Cunningham, Kristin M. Bakke, and Lee J. M. Seymour, "Shirts Today, Skins Tomorrow: Dual Contests and the Effects of Fragmentation in Self-determination Disputes," *Journal of Conflict Resolution* 56.1 (2012): 67–93; Bethany Lacina, "Periphery versus Periphery: The Stakes of Separatist War," *Journal of Politics* 77.3 (2015): 692–706.

37. Nelson Kasfir, "Rebel Governance: Constructing a Field of Inquiry: Definitions, Scope, Patterns, Order, Causes," in *Rebel Governance in Civil War*, ed. Ana Arjona, Nelson Kasfir, and Zachariah Mampilly (New York: Cambridge University Press, 2015), 40.

38. K. J. Holsti, *Taming the Sovereigns: Institutional Change in International Politics* (New York: Cambridge University Press, 2004), 113.

39. Stephen M. Saideman, "Explaining the International Relations of Secessionist Conflicts: Vulnerability versus Ethnic Ties," *International Organization* 51.4 (1997): 721–753; Viva Ona Bartkus, *The Dynamic of Secession* (New York: Cambridge University Press, 1999); Bridget Coggins, *Power Politics and State Formation in the Twentieth Century: The Dynamics of Recognition* (New York: Cambridge University Press, 2014).

40. Harris Mylonas, *The Politics of Nation-Building: Making Co-Nationals, Refugees, and Minorities* (New York: Cambridge University Press, 2013).

41. Reyko Huang, "Rebel Diplomacy in Civil War." *International Security* 40.4 (2016): 89–126; Hyeran Jo, *Compliant Rebels* (New York: Cambridge University Press, 2015); Bridget L. Coggins, "Rebel Diplomacy: Theorizing Violent Non-State Actors' Strategic Use of Talk," in *Rebel Governance in Civil War*, ed. Ana Arjona, Nelson Kasfir, and Zachariah Mampilly (New York: Cambridge University Press, 2015).

42. James Ker-Lindsay, *The Foreign Policy of Counter Secession: Preventing the Recognition of Contested States* (New York: Oxford University Press, 2012).

43. Robert H. Jackson, *Quasi-States: Sovereignty, International Relations and the Third World* (New York: Cambridge University Press, 1993); Robert H. Jackson, *The Global Covenant: Human Conduct in a World of States* (New York: Oxford University Press, 2000). For application to Africa, see Jeffrey Herbst, *States and Power in Africa: Comparative Lessons in Authority and Control* (Princeton, NJ: Princeton University Press, 2014).

44. Pierre Englebert, *Africa: Unity, Sovereignty, and Sorrow* (Boulder, CO: Lynne Rienner Publishers, 2009).

45. Michael W. Doyle, *The Question of Intervention: John Stuart Mill and the Responsibility to Protect* (New Haven, CT: Yale University Press, 2015); Han Liu, "Two Faces of Self-determination in Political Divorce," *ICL Journal* 10.4 (2016): 355–385.

46. Elisabeth S. Clemens, "Toward a Historicized Sociology: Theorizing Events, Processes, and Emergence," *Annual Review of Sociology* 33 (2007): 527–549; Jack A. Goldstone, "Initial Conditions, General Laws, Path Dependence, and Explanation in Historical Sociology, 1," *American Journal of Sociology* 104.3 (1998): 829–845; Paul Pierson, *Politics in Time: History, Institutions, and Social Analysis* (Princeton, NJ: Princeton University Press, 2004).

47. Charles Tilly, *Coercion, Capital, and European States, ad 990–1992* (Oxford: Blackwell, 1992); Thomas Ertman, *Birth of the Leviathan: Building States and Regimes in Medieval and Early Modern Europe* (New York: Cambridge University Press, 1997); Hendrik Spruyt, *The Sovereign State and Its Competitors: An Analysis of Systems Change* (Princeton, NJ: Princeton University Press, 1996).

48. For a general discussion, see Brian D. Taylor and Roxana Botea, "Tilly Tally: War-Making and State-Making in the Contemporary Third World," *International Studies Review* 10.1 (2008): 27–56; Georg Sørensen, "War and State-Making: Why Doesn't It Work in the Third World?" *Security Dialogue* 32.3 (2001): 341–354. For region-specific examples, see Jeffrey Herbst, *States and Power in Africa: Comparative Lessons in Authority and Control.* (Princeton, NJ: Princeton University Press, 2014); Miguel Angel Centeno, *Blood and Debt: War and the Nation-State in Latin America* (State College, PA: Penn State Press, 2002); Dan Slater, *Ordering Power: Contentious Politics and Authoritarian Leviathans in Southeast Asia* (New York: Cambridge University Press, 2010), 37–38.

49. Yuri Slezkine, "The USSR as a Communal Apartment; or, How a Socialist State Promoted Ethnic Particularism," *Slavic Review* 53.2 (1994): 414–452.

50. Philip G. Roeder, "Soviet Federalism and Ethnic Mobilization," *World Politics* (1991): 196–232; Mark R. Beissinger, *Nationalist Mobilization and the Collapse of the Soviet State* (New York: Cambridge University Press, 2002); Georgi M. Derluguian, *Bourdieu's Secret Admirer in the Caucasus: A World-System Biography* (Chicago: University of Chicago Press, 2005).

51. Ryan D. Griffiths, "Between Dissolution and Blood: How Administrative Lines and Categories Shape Secessionist Outcomes," *International Organization* 69.3 (2015): 731–751; Monica Duffy Toft, *The Geography of Ethnic Violence: Identity, Interests, and the Indivisibility of Territory* (Princeton, NJ: Princeton University Press, 2005).

52. Michael Hechter, *Containing Nationalism* (New York: Oxford University Press, 2000), 25. See also Ted Robert Gurr and Will H. Moore, "Ethnopolitical Rebellion: A Cross-Sectional Analysis of the 1980s with Risk Assessments for the 1990s," *American Journal of Political Science* (1997): 1079–1103.

53. Benjamin Smith, "Separatist Conflict in the Former Soviet Union and Beyond: How Different Was Communism?" *World Politics* 65.2 (2013): 350–381; David S. Siroky and John Cuffe, "Lost Autonomy, Nationalism and Separatism," *Comparative Political Studies* 48.1 (2015): 3–34; Lars-Erik Cederman et al., "Territorial Autonomy in the Shadow of Conflict: Too Little, Too Late?" *American Political Science Review* 109.2 (2015): 354–370; Adrian Florea, "De Facto States: Survival and Disappearance (1945–2011)" *International Studies Quarterly* 61.1 (2017): 337–351.

54. Christoph Zurcher, *The Post-Soviet Wars: Rebellion, Ethnic Conflict, and Nationhood in the Caucasus* (New York: NYU Press, 2007).

55. Roeder finds that the impact of prior statehood is roughly of the same magnitude as the impact of segmentation in generation of separatist impulses. See Philip G. Roeder, *Where*

*Nation-States Come From: Institutional Change in the Age of Nationalism* (Princeton, NJ: Princeton University Press, 2007), 208.

56. Alberto Simpser, Dan Slater, and Jason Wittenberg, "Dead but Not Gone: Contemporary Legacies of Communism, Imperialism, and Authoritarianism," *Annual Review of Political Science* 21 (2018): 419–439.

57. Allan Hoben and Robert Hefner, "The Integrative Revolution Revisited," *World Development* 19.1 (1991): 18. See also Joseph Ruane and Jennifer Todd, "The Roots of Intense Ethnic Conflict May Not in Fact Be Ethnic: Categories, Communities and Path Dependence," *European Journal of Sociology/Archives Européennes de Sociologie* 45.2 (2004): 209–232.

58. This is similar to the argument about the default meeting at Grand Central Station. See Lee Cronk and Beth L. Leech, *Meeting at Grand Central: Understanding the Social and Evolutionary Roots of Cooperation* (Princeton, NJ: Princeton University Press, 2012); Michael Suk-Young Chwe, *Rational Ritual: Culture, Coordination, and Common Knowledge* (Princeton, NJ: Princeton University Press, 2013).

59. Michael C. Hudson, *Arab Politics: The Search for Legitimacy* (New Haven, CT: Yale University Press, 1977), 3–5; Iliya F. Harik, "The Ethnic Revolution and Political Integration in the Middle East," *International Journal of Middle East Studies* 3.3 (1972): 303–323.

60. Iraq and Sudan are both qualified exceptions. See Chibli Mallat, "Federalism in the Middle East and Europe," *Case Western Reserve Journal of International Law* 35 (2003): 1–14.

61. Sean Yom, *From Resilience to Revolution: How Foreign Interventions Destabilize the Middle East* (New York: Columbia University Press, 2015); Rolf Schwarz, *War and State Building in the Middle East* (Gainesville: University of Florida Press, 2012); Thierry Gongora, "War Making and State Power in the Contemporary Middle East," *International Journal of Middle East Studies* 29 (1997): 323–340.

62. Boaz Atzili, *Good Fences, Bad Neighbors: Border Fixity and International Conflict* (Chicago: University of Chicago Press, 2011); Keith Krause, "State-Making and Region-Building: The Interplay of Domestic and Regional Security in the Middle East," *Journal of Strategic Studies* 26.3 (2003): 99–124; Ian S. Lustick, "The Absence of Middle Eastern Great Powers: Political 'Backwardness' in Historical Perspective," *International Organization* 51.4 (1997): 653–683.

63. Nazih N. Ayubi, *Over-Stating the Arab State: Politics and Society in the Middle East* (New York: I. B. Tauris, 1996).

64. Eva Bellin, "Reconsidering the Robustness of Authoritarianism in the Middle East: Lessons from the Arab Spring," *Comparative Politics* 44.2 (2012): 127–149; Marc Morjé Howard and Meir R. Walters, "Explaining the Unexpected: Political Science and the Surprises of 1989 and 2011," *Perspectives on Politics* 12.2 (2014): 394–408; Raymond Hinnebusch, "Introduction: Understanding the Consequences of the Arab Uprisings—Starting Points and Divergent Trajectories," *Democratization* 22.2 (2015): 205–217; Frédéric Volpi, "Explaining (and Re-Explaining) Political Change in the Middle East during the Arab Spring: Trajectories of Democratization and of Authoritarianism in the Maghreb," *Democratization* 20.6 (2013): 969–990; Jason Brownlee, Tarek E. Masoud, and Andrew Reynolds, *The Arab Spring: Pathways of Repression and Reform* (New York: Oxford University Press, 2014).

65. Marc Lynch, *The Arab Uprising: The Unfinished Revolutions of the New Middle East* (New York: PublicAffairs, 2013), 12.

66. Marc Lynch, "Failed States and Ungoverned Spaces," *Annals of the American Academy of Political and Social Science* 668.1 (2016): 24–35; Mehran Kamrava, "Weak States in the Middle East," in *Fragile Politics: Weak States in the Greater Middle East*, ed. Mehran Kamrava (New York: Oxford University Press, 2016), 1–29; Fawcett, "States and Sovereignty in the Middle East," 789–807; Lorenzo Kamel, ed., *The Frailty of Authority: Borders, Non-State Actors and Power Vacuums in a Changing Middle East* (Rome: Edizioni Nuova Cultura, 2017); Ibrahim Fraihat, *Unfinished Revolutions: Yemen, Libya, and Tunisia after the Arab Spring* (New Haven, CT: Yale University Press, 2016).

67. For a handful of exceptions, see Lisa Anderson, "Demystifying the Arab Spring: Parsing the Differences between Tunisia, Egypt, and Libya," *Foreign Affairs* 90.3 (2011): 2–7;

Ariel I. Ahram and Ellen Lust, "The Decline and Fall of the Arab State," *Survival* 58.2 (2016): 7–34; I. William Zartman, "States, Boundaries and Sovereignty in the Middle East: Unsteady but Unchanging," *International Affairs* 93.4 (2017): 937–948.

68. David Patel, "Remembering Failed States in the Middle East," POMEPS, May 2015, http://pomeps.org/2015/05/04/remembering-failed-states-in-the-middle-east/#_ftn 1.

69. Email communication with Sean Yom, October 8, 2015.

70. Cf. Joshua Teitelbaum, *The Rise and Fall of the Hashemite Kingdom of Arabia* (London: Hurst, 2001); William Eagleton, *The Kurdish Republic of 1946* (New York: Oxford University Press, 1963); Avi Shlaim, "The Rise and Fall of the All-Palestine Government in Gaza," *Journal of Palestine Studies* 20 (1990): 37–53; Madawi Al-Rasheed, *Politics in an Arabian Oasis: The Rashidi Tribal Dynasty* (New York: I. B. Tauris, 1991).

71. Bernhard Ebbinghaus, "When Less Is More: Selection Problems in Large-N and Small-N Cross-National Comparisons," *International Sociology* 20.2 (2005): 133–152.

72. Anna Gordon and Sarah Parkinson, "How the Houthis Became 'Shi'a,'" *Middle East Report Online*, January 27, 2018, https://www.merip.org/mero/mero012718.

73. Charles Tilly, *Big Structures, Large Processes, Huge Comparisons* (Thousand Oaks, CA: Russell Sage Foundation, 1984), 124–144.

74. Philip McMichael, "Incorporating Comparison within a World-Historical Perspective: An Alternative Comparative Method," *American Sociological Review* 55 (1990): 385–397.

75. On the tension between generalization and specificity in comparative work, see Theda Skocpol and Margaret Somers, "The Uses of Comparative History in Macrosocial Inquiry," *Comparative Studies in Society and History* 22.2 (1980): 174–197; Kathleen Thelen, "Historical Institutionalism in Comparative Politics," *Annual Review of Political Science* 2.1 (1999): 369–404.

76. David Collier and James Mahoney, "Insights and Pitfalls: Selection Bias in Qualitative Research," *World Politics* 49.1 (1996): 56–91; Ryan Saylor, "Why Causal Mechanism and Process Tracing Should Alter Case Selection Guidance," *Sociological Methods & Research* (2018), doi/10.1177/0049124118769109.

77. Rudra Sil, "Triangulating Area Studies, Not Just Methods: How Cross-Regional Comparisons Aids Qualitative and Mixed-Methods Research," in *Comparative Area Studies: Methodological Rationales and Cross-Regional Applications*, ed. Ariel I. Ahram, Patrick Köllner, and Rudra Sil (New York: Oxford University Press, 2018), 237, 242; Michael Mann, "In Praise of Macro-Sociology: A Reply to Goldthorpe," *British Journal of Sociology* 45.1 (1994): 37–54; Ian S. Lustick, "History, Historiography, and Political Science: Multiple Historical Records and the Problem of Selection Bias," *American Political Science Review* 90.3 (1996): 605–618; Cameron G. Thies, "A Pragmatic Guide to Qualitative Historical Analysis in the Study of International Relations," *International Studies Perspectives* 3.4 (2002): 351–372.

78. Daniel Chernilo, "Social Theory's Methodological Nationalism: Myth and Reality," *European Journal of Social Theory* 9.1 (2006): 5–22; Harris Mylonas, "Methodological Problems in the Study of Nation-Building: Behaviorism and Historicist Solutions in Political Science," *Social Science Quarterly* 96.3 (2015): 740–758.

## Chapter 1

1. For discussion of itinerary and luggage, see Harry Howard, *The King-Crane Commission* (Beirut: Khayats, 1963).

2. Woodrow Wilson, Address to Congress, February 11, 1918, https://wwi.lib.byu.edu/index.php/President_Wilson's_Address_to_Congress,_Analyzing_German_and_Austrian_Peace_Utterances.

3. Robert Lansing, *The Peace Negotiations: A Personal Narrative* (New York: Houghton Mifflin, 1921), 97.

4. For comparisons of Lenin and Wilson's approaches to self-determination, see Arno J. Mayer, *Wilson vs. Lenin: Political Origins of the New Diplomacy, 1917–1918* (New Haven, CT: Yale University Press, 1959).

5. Siba N'Zatioula Grovogui, *Sovereigns, Quasi Sovereigns, and Africans: Race and Self-determination in International Law* (Minneapolis: University of Minnesota Press, 1996), 120–3.

6. Allen Lynch, "Woodrow Wilson and the Principle of 'National Self-determination': a reconsideration." *Review of International Studies* 28.2 (2002): 419–436; Michla Pomerance, "The United States and Self-determination: Perspectives on the Wilsonian Conception," *American Journal of International Law* 70.1 (1976): 1–27.

7. Victor Mamatey, *The United States and East Central Europe, 1914–1918* (Princeton, NJ: Princeton University Press, 1957), 310.

8. Erez Manela, "A Man ahead of His Time? Wilsonian Globalism and the Doctrine of Preemption," *International Journal* 60.4 (2005): 1115–1124; Patrick Cottrell, *The Evolution and Legitimacy of International Security Institutions* (New York: Cambridge University Press, 2016), 71–77.

9. Gerrit W. Gong, *The Standard of Civilization in International Society* (New York: Oxford University Press, 1984); Richard S. Horowitz, "International Law and State Transformation in China, Siam, and the Ottoman Empire during the Nineteenth Century," *Journal of World History* 15.4 (2004): 445–486; Eugene Rogan, "The Emergence of the Middle East into the Modern State System," in *International Relations of the Middle East*, ed. Louise Fawcett (New York: Oxford University Press, 2013), 37–59; Nuri Yurdusev, "The Middle East Encounter with the Expansion of European International Society," in *International Society and the Middle East*, ed. Barry Buzan and Ana Gonzalez-Paelev (New York: Palgrave Macmillan, 2009).

10. Erez Manela, *The Wilsonian Moment: Self-determination and the International Origins of Anticolonial Nationalism* (New York: Oxford University Press, 2007), 141.; Arnulf Becker Lorca, "Petitioning the International: A 'Pre-history' of Self-determination," *European Journal of International Law* 25.2 (2014): 497–523.

11. Stuart Schaar, "President Woodrow Wilson and the Young Tunisians," *Maghreb Review: Majallat al-Maghrib* 31.1 (2006): 129–144.

12. Lisa Anderson, "The Tripoli Republic, 1918–1922," in *Social and Economic Development of Libya*, ed. E. George H. Joffe and Keith Stanley McLachlan (Boulder, CO: Westview, 1982), 43–66; Saad Bugaighis, "The Italian Invasion of Libya and the Nineteen Years of Libyan Resistance" (PhD diss., University of Washington, 2011).

13. Rogan, "The Emergence of the Middle East into the Modern State System," 37–39.

14. Ali A. Allawi, *Faisal I of Iraq* (New Haven, CT: Yale University Press, 2014), 234.

15. James L. Gelvin, *Divided Loyalties: Nationalism and Mass Politics in Syria at the Close of Empire* (Berkeley: University of California Press, 1998), 161.

16. Allawi, *Faisal*, 198–199. For a report on the meeting, see Statements for the Hedjaz by Emir Faisal," February 6, 1919, 185/5138/4, US State Department Files, NARA, RG 356, M820, Roll 544, 395–401.

17. Tom Segev, *One Palestine, Complete: Jews and Arabs under the British Mandate*, tr. Haim Watzman (New York: Henry Holt, 1999), 38, 196.

18. Meir Zamir, *The Formation of Modern Lebanon* (London: Croom Helm, 1985), 56–57, 62–67; Asher Kaufman, *Reviving Phoenicia: The Search for Identity in Lebanon* (New York: I. B. Tauris, 2004), 85–87.

19. Margaret MacMillan, *Paris 1919: Six Months That Changed the World* (New York: Random House, 2007), 377. See also Mark Malkasian, "The Disintegration of the Armenian Cause in the United States, 1918–1927," *International Journal of Middle East Studies* 16.3 (1984): 352.

20. Leonard V. Smith, "Wilsonian Sovereignty in the Middle East: The King-Crane Commission Report of 1919," in *The State of Sovereignty: Territories, Laws, Populations*, ed. Douglas Howland and Luise White (Bloomington: Indiana University Press, 2009), 59.

21. Andrew Patrick, *America's Forgotten Middle East Initiative: The King-Crane Commission of 1919* (New York: I. B. Tauris, 2015), 105–107, 261.

22. Allawi, *Faisal*, 244–245.

23. Howard, *King-Crane Commission*, 107–108.

24. Keith David Watenpaugh, *Being Modern in the Middle East: Revolution, Nationalism, Colonialism, and the Arab Middle Class* (Princeton, NJ: Princeton University Press, 2014), 126, 149.

25. Damascus Declaration," July 2, 1919, reproduced in William Yale, "Recommendation as to the Future Disposition of Palestine, Syria, and Mount Lebanon," July 26, 1919, 867N.00/102, Records of the American Commission to Negotiate Peace, NARA, RG 256, M820, Roll 544, 0366–0402.

26. Howard, *King-Crane Commission*, 99.

27. James L. Gelvin, *Divided Loyalties: Nationalism and Mass Politics in Syria at the Close of Empire* (Berkeley: University of California Press, 1998): 34–35. See also Patrick, *America's Forgotten Middle East Initiative*, 261; Michael Reimer, "The King-Crane Commission at the Juncture of Politics and Historiography," *Critique: Critical Middle Eastern Studies* 15.2 (2006): 129–150.

28. William Yale, "Report on the Details of Interviews in London (Sept. 27, 1919, to Oct. 14, 1919"), Records of the American Commission to Negotiate Peace, NARA, RG 256, MG 820, Roll 544, 0220. See also Max Reibman, "The Case of William Yale: Cairo's Syrians and the Arab Origins of American Influence in the Post-Ottoman Middle East, 1917–19," *International Journal of Middle East Studies* 46.4 (2014): 681–702.

29. William Yale, "Recommendation as to the Future Disposition of Palestine, Syria, and Mount Lebanon," July 26, 1919, 867N.00/102, Records of the American Commission to Negotiate Peace, NARA, RG 256, M820, Roll 544, 0366–0402.

30. Ussama Makdisi, *Faith Misplaced: The Broken Promise of US-Arab Relations, 1820–2001* (New York: PublicAffairs, 2011), 126–127; Michael Oren, *Power, Faith, Fantasy: America in the Middle East, 1776 to the Present* (New York: Norton, 2007), 373–375, 389–396; Matthew F. Jacobs, *Imagining the Middle East: The Building of an American Foreign Policy, 1918–1967* (Chapel Hill: University of North Carolina Press, 2011), 99.

31. Erez Manela, "Dawn of a New Era: The 'Wilsonian Moment' in Colonial Contexts and the Transformation of World Order, 1917–1920," in *Competing Visions of World Order*, ed. Sebastian Conrad and Dominic Sachsenmaier (New York: Palgrave Macmillan, 2007), 126.

32. Manela, "Dawn of a New Era"; Leonard V. Smith, *Sovereignty at the Paris Peace Conference of 1919* (New York: Oxford University Press, 2018); Elizabeth Borgwardt, *A New Deal for the World* (Cambridge, MA: Harvard University Press, 2007).

33. Robert Lansing, "A Definition of Sovereignty," *Proceedings of the American Political Science Association* 10 (1914).

34. Importantly, William H. Buckler, one of the US commission, made a note that Yale's minority report was the "most interesting and one that the Dept. should have." See handwritten note, September 10, 1919, US State Department Files, NARA, RG 256, M820, Roll 544, 0479.

35. Reprinted in Walter Laqueur and Dan Schueftan, eds., *The Israel-Arab Reader: A Documentary History of the Middle East Conflict*, 8th ed., rev. and updated (New York: Penguin, 2016), 22.

36. Allawi, *Faisal*, 262–263.

37. For more on the fate of the Syrian Arab Kingdom, see Philip Shukry Khoury, *Syria and the French Mandate: The Politics of Arab Nationalism, 1920–1945* (Princeton, NJ: Princeton University Press, 2014); Elizabeth Thompson, *Colonial Citizens: Republican Rights, Paternal Privilege, and Gender in French Syria and Lebanon* (New York: Columbia University Press, 2000); Daniel Neep, *Occupying Syria under the French Mandate: Insurgency, Space and State Formation* (New York: Cambridge University Press, 2012).

38. David E. Omissi, *Air Power and Colonial Control: The Royal Air Force, 1919–1939* (Manchester: Manchester University Press, 1990); Priya Satia, "The Defense of Inhumanity: Air Control and the British Idea of Arabia," *American Historical Review* 111.1 (2006): 16–51.

39. Peter Sluglett, *Britain in Iraq: Contriving King and Country* (New York: I. B. Tauris, 2007); Reeva S. Simon, *Iraq between the Two World Wars* (New York: Columbia University Press, 1986).

40. Erez Manela, "The Wilsonian Moment and the Rise of Anticolonial Nationalism: The Case of Egypt," *Diplomacy and Statecraft* 12.4 (2001): 114.
41. Bugaighis, "The Italian Invasion of Libya in 1911."
42. Joel Beinin, *Workers and Peasants in the Modern Middle East* (New York: Cambridge University Press, 2001), 1–71; Nathan Brown, "Brigands and State Building: The Invention of Banditry in Modern Egypt," *Comparative Studies in Society and History* 32.2 (1990): 258–281; Juan R. Cole, "Of Crowds and Empires: Afro-Asian Riots and European Expansion, 1857–1882," *Comparative Studies in Society and History* 31.1 (1989): 106–133.
43. Nikki R. Keddie, "The Revolt of Islam, 1700 to 1993: Comparative Considerations and Relations to Imperialism," *Comparative Studies in Society and History* 36.3 (1994): 463–487.
44. Occasionally indigenous leaders did try to enlist support from outside powers by making grandiose claims about their status and prestige. For example, Abd al-Qadir dispatched a letter to British consular officials asking the king of England for support against the French in return for access to Algerian ports. Abd al-Qadir assumed the title of "sultan" of Algiers, Oran, and Tlemcen but made no claim to speak on behalf of a people or community. In general, these efforts were received with disdain and puzzlement. See Raphael Danziger, "Abd al-Qadir's First Overtures to the British and Americans (1835–1836)," *Revue de l'Occident musulman et de la Méditerranée* 18 (1974): 45–63.
45. Israel Gershoni and James P. Jankowski, *Egypt, Islam, and the Arabs: The Search for Egyptian Nationhood, 1900–1930* (New York: Oxford University Press, 1986), 5–11.
46. For a discussion of how Middle East actors engaged the Great Powers and the League, see Leonard V. Smith, "Drawing Borders in the Middle East after the Great War: Political Geography and 'Subject Peoples,'" *First World War Studies* 7.1 (2016): 5–21.
47. Adria Lawrence, *Imperial Rule and the Politics of Nationalism: Anti-Colonial Protest in the French Empire* (New York: Cambridge University Press, 2013).
48. David S. Woolman, *Rebels in the Rif: Abd el Krim and the Rif Rebellion* (Stanford, CA: Stanford University Press, 1968).
49. National Archives (UK), FO 371/9474, Government of the Riff Republic, "Declaration of State and Proclamation to All Nations," reissued at Ajdir, July 1, 1923.
50. Anna Chotzen, "Beyond Bounds: Morocco's Rif War and the Limits of International Law," *Humanity: An International Journal of Human Rights, Humanitarianism, and Development* 5.1 (2014): 33–54.
51. Rashid Khalidi, *The Iron Cage: The Story of the Palestinian Struggle for Statehood* (Boston: Beacon Press, 2007), 33–35.
52. Othman Ali, "The Kurds and the Lausanne Peace Negotiations, 1922–23," *Middle Eastern Studies* 33.3 (1997): 521–534.
53. Isam Ghanem, "The Legal History of Asir (Al-Mikhlaf Al-Sulaymani)," *Arab Law Quarterly* 5.3 (1990): 211; John E. Peterson, *Yemen: The Search for a Modern State* (New York: Routledge, 1982), 58.
54. On the Armenians and Assyrians, see Khoury, *Syria and the French Mandate*, 527–531; Khaldun S. Husry, "The Assyrian Affair of 1933 (I)," *International Journal of Middle East Studies* 5.2 (1974): 161–176. For a comparative overview, see Laura Robson, *States of Separation: Transfer, Partition, and the Making of the Modern Middle East* (Berkeley: University of California Press, 2017).
55. Michelle Burgis-Kasthala, "Mandated Sovereignty? The Role of International Law in the Construction of Arab Statehood during and after Empire," in *Sovereignty after Empire: Comparing the Middle East and Central Asia*, ed. Sally Cummings and Raymond Hinnebusch (Edinburgh: Edinburgh University Press, 2011) 104–126.
56. Mikulas Fabry, *Recognizing States: International Society and the Establishment of New States since 1776* (New York: Oxford University Press, 2010), 12–13.
57. For arguments about the novelty of the mandate structure and its empowerment of mandatory leaders, particularly for those deemed "Class A," see Susan Pedersen, "The Meaning of the Mandates System: An Argument," *Geschichte und Gesellschaft* (2006): 560–582; Peter Sluglett, "An Improvement on Colonialism? The 'A' Mandates and Their Legacy in the Middle East," *International Affairs* 90.2 (2014): 419–420; David Fieldhouse, *Western*

*Imperialism in the Middle East,* 1914–1958 (New York: Oxford University Press, 2006), 340–8.

58. Sluglett, *Britain in Iraq,* chapter 7.
59. Manley O. Hudson, "Admission of Egypt to Membership in the League of Nations," *American Journal of International Law* 31.4 (1937): 681–683
60. Importantly, while the Hejaz had been considered a potential member of the League, it had never exercised that option by taking positive steps to join. It therefore remained outside of international society. Clive Leatherdale, *Britain and Saudi Arabia, 1925–1939: The Imperial Oasis* (Totowa, NJ: Frank Cass, 1983), chapter 7.
61. Marika Sherwood, "'Diplomatic Platitudes': The Atlantic Charter, the United Nations and Colonial Independence," *Immigrants & Minorities* 15.2 (1996): 135–150; Edward A. Laing, "The Norm of Self-determination, 1941–1991," *California Western International Law Journal* 22 (1991): 209; Antonio Cassese, *Self-determination of Peoples: A Legal Reappraisal* (New York: Cambridge University Press, 1995), 37.
62. Fred H. Lawson, "Westphalian Sovereignty and the Emergence of the Arab States System: The Case of Syria," *International History Review* 22.3 (2000): 529–556; Salma Mardam Bey, *Syria's Quest for Independence* (Reading, Eng.: Ithaca Press, 1994), 79, 108, 148.
63. Benjamin Rivlin, "The United States and Moroccan International Status, 1943–1956: A Contributory Factor in Morocco's Reassertion of Independence from France," *International Journal of African Historical Studies* 15.1 (1982): 64–82; David Stenner, "Did Amrika Promise Morocco's Independence? The Nationalist Movement, the Sultan, and the Making of the 'Roosevelt Myth,'" *Journal of North African Studies* 19.4 (2014): 524–539.
64. Yemen would follow in 1947.
65. Martin Thomas, "France Accused: French North Africa before the United Nations, 1952–1962," *Contemporary European History* 10.1 (2001): 91–121; Scott L. Bills, *The Libyan Arena: The United States, Britain, and the Council of Foreign Ministers, 1945–1948* (Kent, OH: Kent State University Press, 1995).
66. Matthew Connelly, *A Diplomatic Revolution: Algeria's Fight for Independence and the Origins of the Post-Cold War Era* (New York: Oxford University Press, 2002), 5. See also Martin Alexander and John F. V. Keiger, "France and the Algerian War: Strategy, Operations and Diplomacy," *Journal of Strategic Studies* 25.2 (2002): 1–32.
67. Cited in Hanna Batatu, *The Old Social Classes and the Revolutionary Movements of Iraq: A Study of Iraq's Old Landed and Commercial Classes and of its Communists, Ba'thists and Free Officers* (London: Saqi, 2012), 25–26.
68. Memorandum by Emir Faisal," January 1, 1919, 185.5138/2, US State Department Files, NARA, RG 356, M820, Roll 544, 0382.
69. Cited in Batatu, *The Old Social Classes,* 25–26.
70. For a general overview on the expansion of the intelligence and security services in the 1960s, see Elizabeth Picard, "State and Society in the Arab World: Towards a New Role for the Security Services?" in *The Many Faces of National Security in the Arab World,* ed. Bahgat Korany, Paul Noble, and Rex Brynen (New York: Palgrave Macmillan, 1993), 258–274. On the Egyptian mukhabarat, see Owen L. Sirrs, *The Egyptian Intelligence Service: A History of the Mukhabarat, 1910–2009* (New York: Routledge, 2010). On Syria, see Andrew Rathmell, "Syria's Intelligence Services: Origins and Development," *Journal of Conflict Studies* 16.2 (1996); Carl Anthony Wege, "Assad's Legions: The Syrian Intelligence Services," *International Journal of Intelligence and CounterIntelligence* 4.1 (1990): 91–100. On Iraq, see Joseph Sassoon, *Saddam Hussein's Ba'th Party: Inside an Authoritarian Regime* (New York: Cambridge University Press, 2011, chapter 4; Ibrahim Al-Marashi, "The Family, Clan, and Tribal Dynamics of Saddam's Security and Intelligence Network," *International Journal of Intelligence and CounterIntelligence* 16.2 (2003): 202–211. On Jordan, see Nawaf Tell, "Jordanian Security Sector Governance: Between Theory and Practice," Geneva Centre for the Democratic Control of Armed Forces, Working Paper 145 (2004), 6.
71. Tarik Yousef, "Development, Growth and Policy Reform in the Middle East and North Africa since 1950," *Journal of Economic Perspectives* 19.3 (2004): 91–116; Steve Heydemann, "Social Pacts and the Persistence of Authoritarianism in the Middle East," in *Debating*

*Authoritarianism: Dynamics and Durability in Nondemocratic Regimes*, ed. Oliver Schlumberger (Stanford, CA: Stanford University Press, 2007); Stephen King, *The New Authoritarianism in the Middle East and North Africa* (Bloomington: Indiana University Press, 2009).

72. Sami Zubaida, "The Fragments Imagine the Nation: The Case of Iraq," *International Journal of Middle East Studies* 34.2 (2002): 211. See also Jacqueline S. Ismael and Tareq Y. Ismael, "The Social Contract and the Iraqi State," *International Journal of Contemporary Iraqi Studies* 9.3 (2015): 225–245.

73. William Lancaster and Fidelity Lancaster, "Integration into Modernity: Some Tribal Rural Societies in the Bilād ash-Shām," in *Nomadic Societies in the Middle East and North Africa: Entering the 21st Century*, ed. Dawn Chatty (Leiden: Brill, 2006), 341. For larger discussion, see Philip Shukry Khoury and Joseph Kostiner, eds., *Tribes and State Formation in the Middle East* (Berkeley: University of California Press, 1990).

74. Elie Podeh, *The Politics of National Celebrations in the Arab Middle East* (New York: Cambridge University Press, 2011).

75. On cults of personality, see Roger Owen, *The Rise and Fall of Arab Presidents for Life: With a New Afterword* (Cambridge, MA: Harvard University Press, 2014), 31–36; Joseph Sassoon, *Anatomy of Authoritarianism in the Arab Republics* (New York: Cambridge University Press, 2016), 199–215.

76. Malik Mufti, *Sovereign Creations: Pan-Arabism and Political Order in Syria and Iraq* (Ithaca, NY: Cornell University Press, 1996); Adeed Dawisha, *Arab Nationalism in the Twentieth Century: From Triumph to Despair*, 2nd ed. (Princeton, NJ: Princeton University Press, 2016); Eberhard Kienle, *Ba'th v. Ba'th: The Conflict between Syria and Iraq, 1968–1989* (New York: I. B. Tauris, 1990).

77. Malcolm H. Kerr, *The Arab Cold War: Gamal 'Abd al-Nasir and His Rivals, 1958–1970* (New York: Oxford University Press, 1971); John F. Devlin, "The Baath Party: Rise and Metamorphosis," *American Historical Review* (1991): 1396–1407.

78. On the Berbers in Algeria and Morocco, see Bruce Maddy-Weitzman, *The Berber Identity Movement and the Challenge to North African States* (Austin: University of Texas Press, 2011). On the Shi'is of Iraq, Lebanon, and Bahrain, see Yitzhak Nakash, *Reaching for Power: The Shi'a in the Modern Arab World* (Princeton, NJ: Princeton University Press, 2011). On the Kurds, see Edmund Ghareeb, *The Kurdish Question in Iraq* (Syracuse, NY: Syracuse University Press, 1981), 148; Dana Adams Schmidt, "Recent Developments in the Kurdish War," *Journal of the Royal Central Asian Society* 53.1 (1966): 26, 30. On Sudan, see Ann Mosely Lesch, "Confrontation in the Southern Sudan," *Middle East Journal* 40.3 (1986); Francis Mading Deng, "War of Visions for the Nation," *Middle East Journal* 44.4 (1990): 596–609.

79. Eckart Woertz, *Oil for Food: The Global Food Crisis and the Middle East* (New York: Oxford University Press, 2013), 25–104.

80. For a comparative case study on Egypt, see John Waterbury, *Exposed to Innumerable Delusions: Public Enterprise and State Power in Egypt, India, Mexico, and Turkey* (New York: Cambridge University Press, 1993).

81. On passive and hidden resistance, see Asef Bayat, *Life as Politics: How Ordinary People Change the Middle East* (Stanford, CA: Stanford University Press, 2013); Charles Tripp, *The Power and the People: Paths of Resistance in the Middle East* (Cambridge: Cambridge University Press, 2013).

82. Janine A. Clark, *Islam, Charity, and Activism: Middle-Class Networks and Social Welfare in Egypt, Jordan, and Yemen* (Bloomington: Indiana University Press, 2004); Asef Bayat, "Activism and Social Development in the Middle East," *International Journal of Middle East Studies* 34.1 (2002): 1–28.

83. Charles Tilly, "Does Modernization Breed Revolution?" *Comparative Politics* 5.3 (1973): 439.

84. Oren Barak, *The Lebanese Army: A National Institution in a Divided Society* (Albany, NY: SUNY Press, 2009).

85. Boaz Atzili, "State Weakness and 'Vacuum of Power' in Lebanon," *Studies in Conflict & Terrorism* 33.8 (2010): 757–782.

86. On the idea of final homeland for Shi'is, see Fouad Ajami, *The Vanished Imam: Musa al Sadr and the Shia of Lebanon* (Ithaca, NY: Cornell University Press, 1987) 62; Farah Kawtharani, "A Shi'i Religious Perspective on Lebanese Sectarianism: The Islamic Shi'i Supreme Council under Shaykh Muhammad Mahdi Shams al-Din (1978–2001)," *Journal of Shi'a Islamic Studies* 8.2 (2015): 159–191; Waleed Hazbun, "Assembling Security in a 'Weak State:' The Contentious Politics of Plural Governance in Lebanon since 2005," *Third World Quarterly* 37.6 (2016): 1053–1070.

87. Cheryl A. Rubenberg, "The Civilian Infrastructure of the Palestine Liberation Organization: An Analysis of the PLO in Lebanon until June 1982," *Journal of Palestine Studies* 12.3 (1983): 54–78.

88. Doyle McManus, "All the Elements of a State—Except Land: PLO Taking On Look of a Government," *Los Angeles Times*, June 25, 1981; Rosemary Sayigh, "A House Is Not a Home: Permanent Impermanence of Habitat for Palestinian Expellees in Lebanon," *Holy Land Studies* 4.1 (2005): 17–39; Nora Stel, "Mediated Stateness as a Continuum: Exploring the Changing Governance Relations between the PLO and the Lebanese State," *Civil Wars* (2017): 1–29.

89. Paul Thomas Chamberlin, *The Global Offensive: The United States, the Palestine Liberation Organization, and the Making of the Post–Cold War Order* (New York: Oxford University Press, 2012), 238.

90. David Hirst, *Beware of Small States: Lebanon, Battleground of the Middle East* (New York: Nation Books, 2010), 97. See also Samir Khalaf, *Civil and Uncivil Violence in Lebanon: A History of the Internationalization of Communal Conflict* (New York: Columbia University Press, 2002), 35.

91. Speech by Yasser Arafat, UN General Assembly, November 13, 1974, *Le Monde diplomatique*, http://mondediplo.com/focus/mideast/arafat74-en.

92. Thomas D. Musgrave, *Self-determination and National Minorities* (New York: Oxford University Press, 2000), 180–237; Uriel Abulof, "We the Peoples? The Strange Demise of Self-determination," *European Journal of International Relations* 22.3 (2016): 536–565.

93. Steven R. Ratner, "Drawing a Better Line: *Uti Possidetis* and the Borders of New States," *American Journal of International Law* (1996): 590–624; , Uriel Abulof, "The Confused Compass: From Self-determination to State-determination," *Ethnopolitics* 14.5 (2015): 488–497.

94. "Confrontation in the Gulf; Excerpts from Iraq's Statement on Kuwait," *New York Times*, August 9, 1990, http://www.nytimes.com/1990/08/09/world/confrontation-in-the-gulf-excerpts-from-iraq-s-statement-on-kuwait.html .

95. Clovis Maksoud, "Diminished Sovereignty, Enhanced Sovereignty: United Nations–Arab League Relations at 50," *Middle East Journal* 49 (1995): 582–594; Gamil Matar and Ali al-Din Hilal, *Al-nizam al- iqlimi al-arabi* [The Arab regional system] (Beirut: Dar al-Mustaqbal al-Arabi, 1983). This was even more explicit in the Cairo Proclamation issued by the African Union in Cairo in 1964. See Saadia Touval, "The Organization of African Unity and African Borders," *International Organization*, 21.1 (1967): 102–127.

96. On the prominence and disappointment of pan-Arabism in regional politics, see Fred Lawson, *Constructing International Relations in the Arab World* (Stanford, CA: Stanford University Press, 2006); Michael N. Barnett, *Dialogues in Arab Politics: Negotiations in Regional Order* (New York: Columbia University Press, 1998).

97. Boaz Atzili, *Good Fences, Bad Neighbors: Border Fixity and International Conflict* (Chicago: University of Chicago Press, 2011); Ian S. Lustick, "The Absence of Middle Eastern Great Powers: Political 'Backwardness' in Historical Perspective," *International Organization* 51.4 (1997): 653–683.

98. Anouar Boukhars, "Simmering Discontent in the Western Sahara," Carnegie Endowment for International Peace, March 12, 2012, http://carnegieendowment.org/2012/03/12/simmering-discontent-in-western-sahara# (accessed June 8, 2018); David Lynn Price, *The Western Sahara* (Beverly Hills, CA: SAGE, 1979): 30.

99. Christopher Maynard, *Out of the Shadow: George H. W. Bush and the End of the Cold War* (College Station: Texas A&M University Press, 2008), 90.

100. Cf. Resolution 686 (1991) of March 2, 1991, https://undocs.org/S/RES/686(1991).

101. Daniel Schorr, "Ten Days That Shook the White House," *Columbia Journalism Review* 30.2 (1991): 21–3.
102. Resolution 688 (1991) of April 5, 1991, http://unscr.com/en/resolutions/688.
103. Alison Williams, "Hakumat al Tayarrat: The Role of Air Power in the Enforcement of Iraq's Boundaries," *Geopolitics* 12.3 (2007): 505–528.
104. Ofra Bengio, *Saddam Speaks on the Gulf Crisis: A Collection of Documents* (Tel Aviv: Moshe Dayan Center for Middle East and African Studies, Tel Aviv University, 1992), 209.
105. Philip G. Roeder, *Where Nation-States Come From: Institutional Change in the Age of Nationalism* (Princeton, NJ: Princeton University Press, 2007), 163. UN Secretary General and former Egyptian diplomat Boutros Boutros-Ghali described the crisis in more general terms as a "Grotian moment"; see Boutros Boutros-Ghali, "A Grotian Moment," *Fordham International Law Journal* 18 (1994): 1609–1616.
106. Bridget Coggins, *Power Politics and State Formation in the Twentieth Century: The Dynamics of Recognition* (New York: Cambridge University Press, 2014). For a discussion about its implications for Africa, see Lee J. M. Seymour, "Sovereignty, Territory and Authority: Boundary Maintenance in Contemporary Africa," *Critical African Studies* 5.1 (2013): 17–31.
107. For the text of the speech, see "Remarks to the Supreme Soviet of the Republic of the Ukraine in Kiev, Soviet Union," August 1, 1991, http://www.presidency.ucsb.edu/ws/?pid=19864. For more on US equivocation on the breakup of the USSR, see Stuart Elden, *Terror and Territory: The Spatial Extent of Sovereignty* (Minneapolis: University of Minnesota Press, 2009), 150–151.
108. Juan J. Linz and Alfred Stepan, *Problems of Democratic Transition and Consolidation: Southern Europe, South America, and Post-Communist Europe* (Baltimore, MD: Johns Hopkins University Press, 1996), chapter 2. See also Jørgen Møller and Svend-Erik Skaaning, "Stateness First?" *Democratization* 18.1 (2011): 1–24.
109. Jonathan Paquin, *A Stability-Seeking Power: US Foreign Policy and Secessionist Conflicts* (Montreal: McGill-Queen University Press, 2010), 6, 179–181.
110. Jonathan D. Caverley, "Power and Democratic Weakness: Neoconservatism and Neoclassical Realism," *Millennium* 38.3 (2010): 593–614; G. John Ikenberry et al., *The Crisis of American Foreign Policy: Wilsonianism in the Twenty-First Century* (Princeton, NJ: Princeton University Press, 2009), 67.
111. Georg Sørensen, "After the Security Dilemma: The Challenges of Insecurity in Weak States and the Dilemma of Liberal Values," *Security Dialogue* 38.3 (2007): 357–378.
112. Ryan D. Griffiths, *Age of Secession* (New York: Cambridge University Press, 2016).
113. Mikulas Fabry, *Recognizing States: International Society and the Establishment of New States since 1776* (New York: Oxford University Press, 2010), 180.
114. Pål Kolstø and Helge Blakkisrud, "Living with Non-Recognition: State- and Nation-Building in South Caucasian Quasi-States," *Europe-Asia Studies* 60.3 (2008): 483–509.
115. Bruno de Witte, "Sovereignty and European Integration: The Weight of Legal Tradition," *Maastricht Journal of European and Comparative Law* 2 (1995); Tanja E. Aalberts, "The Future of Sovereignty in Multilevel Governance Europe: A Constructivist Reading," *JCMS: Journal of Common Market Studies* 42.1 (2004): 23–46.
116. Luke Glanville, *Sovereignty and the Responsibility to Protect: A New History* (Chicago: University of Chicago Press, 2013).
117. Barry Buzan and George Lawson, *The Global Transformation: History, Modernity and the Making of International Relations* (New York: Cambridge University Press, 2015), 212; Toby Dodge, "Intervention and Dreams of Exogenous Statebuilding: The Application of Liberal Peacebuilding in Afghanistan and Iraq," *Review of International Studies* 39.5 (2013): 1189–1212.
118. Robert G. Rabil, "The Iraqi Opposition's Evolution: From Conflict to Unity?" *Middle East Review of International Affairs* 6.4 (2002): 1–17.
119. Cited in Michael Gunter, "The Iraqi National Congress (INC) and the Future of the Iraqi Opposition," *Journal of South Asian and Middle Eastern Studies* 19.3 (1996), 9. See also Rabil, "The Iraqi Opposition's Evolution".
120. On Chalabi's career, see Aram Roston, *The Man Who Pushed America to War: The Extraordinary Life, Adventures and Obsessions of Ahmad Chalabi* (New York: Nation Books,

2008); Richard Bonin, *Arrows of the Night: Ahmad Chalabi and the Selling of the Iraq War* (New York: Anchor, 2012). On the role of exiles, see Walt Vanderbush, "Exiles and the Marketing of US Policy toward Cuba and Iraq," *Foreign Policy Analysis* 5.3 (2009): 287–306.

121. Sarah Graham-Brown, "Intervention, Sovereignty and Responsibility," *Middle East Report* 193 (1995): 2–32; Tim Niblock, *"Pariah States" and Sanctions in the Middle East: Iraq, Libya, Sudan* (Boulder, CO: Lynne Rienner Publishers, 2002), 118; Geoff Simons, *The Scourging of Iraq* (New York: St. Martin's, 1996), 110–111.

122. Jareer Elass, "Sovereignty Issue Seen as Roadblock as U.N., Iraq Resume Oil Sale Talks," *Oil Daily*, April 9, 1996.

123. For general discussion of the sanctions, see Joy Gordon, *Invisible War: The United States and the Iraq Sanctions* (Cambridge, MA: Harvard University Press, 2010); Amatzia Baram, "The Effect of Iraqi Sanctions: Statistical Pitfalls and Responsibility," *Middle East Journal* 54.2 (2000): 194–223. On public health, see Mohamed M. Ali and Iqbal H. Shah, "Sanctions and Childhood Mortality in Iraq," *Lancet* 355.9218 (2000): 1851–1857; Alberto Ascherio et al., "Effect of the Gulf War on Infant and Child Mortality in Iraq," *New England Journal of Medicine* 327.13 (1992): 931–936.

124. Niblock, *Pariah States*; Ian Hurd, "The Strategic Use of Liberal Internationalism: Libya and the UN Sanctions, 1992–2003," *International Organization* 59.3 (2005): 495–526.

125. Glanville, *Sovereignty and the Responsibility to Protect*, 327.

126. Barak Mendelsohn, *Combating Jihadism: American Hegemony and Interstate Cooperation in the War on Terrorism* (Chicago: University of Chicago Press, 2009).

127. Tanisha M. Fazal, *State Death: The Politics and Geography of Conquest, Occupation, and Annexation* (Princeton, NJ: Princeton University Press, 2011), 238.

128. Francis Fukuyama, " 'Stateness' First," *Journal of Democracy* 16.1 (2005): 84–88.

129. Ariel I. Ahram, "Returning Exiles to Iraqi Politics," *Middle East Review of International Affairs* 9.1 (2005): 71; John McGarry and Brendan O'Leary, "Iraq's Constitution of 2005: Liberal Consociation as Political Prescription," *International Journal of Constitutional Law* 5.4 (2007): 670–698.

130. Eric Herring and Glen Rangwala, *Iraq in Fragments: The Occupation and Its Legacy* (Ithaca, NY: Cornell University Press, 2005); Ahmed Hashim, *Insurgency and Counter-Insurgency in Iraq* (Ithaca, NY: Cornell University Press, 2005).

131. Roy Allison, *Russia, the West, and Military Intervention* (New York: Oxford University Press, 2013); Gerard Toal, *Near Abroad: Putin, the West, and the Contest over Ukraine and the Caucasus* (New York: Oxford University Press, 2017).

132. See the special issue "Major Powers and the Contested Evolution of a Responsibility to Protect," ed. Philipp Rotmann, Gerrit Kurtz, and Sarah Brockmeier, *Conflict, Security & Development* 14.4 (2014); Miles Kahler, "Rising Powers and Global Governance: Negotiating Change in a Resilient Status Quo," *International Affairs* 89.3 (2013): 718.

133. On Iran, see Joel S. Migdal, *Shifting Sands: The United States in the Middle East* (New York: Columbia University Press, 2014), 196–208. On the more general rise of regional powers, see Buzan and Lawson, *The Global Transformation*, 297.

## Chapter 2

1. Mehran Kamrava, *Qatar: Small State, Big Politics* (Ithaca, NY: Cornell University Press, 2015).

2. Marc Lynch, *Voices of the New Arab Public: Iraq, al-Jazeera, and Middle East Politics Today* (New York: Columbia University Press, 2006).

3. Stephen Brook, "Al-Jazeera Is World's Fifth Top Brand," *Guardian*, February 1, 2005, https://www.theguardian.com/media/2005/feb/01/marketingandpr.broadcasting.

4. James Mann, *The Obamians: The Struggle inside the White House to Redefine American Power* (New York: Penguin, 2012), 258.

5. Clinton Says U.S. Seeks to Broaden Relationship with Yemen," State Department Press Release and Documents, January 11, 2011.

6. Forum for the Future: Partnership Dialogue Panel Session, January 13, 2011, https://2009-2017.state.gov/secretary/20092013clinton/rm/2011/01/154595.htm (accessed May 14, 2018).

7. Lee Jones, "Sovereignty, Intervention, and Social Order in Revolutionary Times," *Review of International Studies* 39.5 (2013): 1149–1167. See also George Abu Ahmad, "Order, Freedom and Chaos: Sovereignties in Syria," *Middle East Policy* 20.2 (2013): 47–54.

8. Jillian Schwedler, "Spatial Dynamics of the Arab Uprisings," *PS: Political Science & Politics* 46.2 (2013): 230–234.

9. Observed Jean-Pierre Filiu: "The Arab revolutions rejuvenate a nationalist narrative that is beefed up through its very dynamics. The regimes whose overthrow is called for are portrayed as alien to their own nation and people, as legitimate targets in a genuine fight for self-determination. The fascinating part of the process is not only that this nationalist movement remains delimited by the post-colonial borders, but also that there has been so far no anti-Western outburst." Jean-Pierre Filiu, *The Arab Revolution: Ten Lessons from the Democratic Uprising* (New York: Oxford University Press, 2011), 93; see also Laurence Louër, "A Decline of Identity Politics," *International Journal of Middle East Studies* 43.3 (2011): 389–390.

10. Lin Noueihed and Alex Warren, *The Battle for the Arab Spring: Revolution, Counter-Revolution and the Making of a New Era* (New Haven, CT: Yale University Press, 2012), 109.

11. Sharon Erickson Nepstad, "Nonviolent Resistance in the Arab Spring: The Critical Role of Military-Opposition Alliances," *Swiss Political Science Review* 17.4 (2011): 485–491.

12. Glen Rangwala, "The Creation of Governments-in-Waiting: The Arab Uprisings and Legitimacy in the International System," *Geoforum* 66 (2015): 215–223. See also Uriel Abulof, " 'The People Want(s) to Bring Down the Regime': (Positive) Nationalism as the Arab Spring's Revolution," *Nations and Nationalism* 21.4 (2015): 658–680; John Agnew, "Rethinking Popular Sovereignty in Light of the Arab Awakening," *Arab World Geographer* 15.2 (2012): 82–90.

13. Susan Woodward, *The Ideology of Failed States* (New York: Cambridge University 2017), 123–131. On the historical comparison, see Leonard V. Smith, *Sovereignty at the Paris Peace Conference of 1919* (New York: Oxford University Press, 2018), 132.

14. Robert Marquand, "Amid BRICS' Rise and 'Arab Spring,' a New Global Order Forms," *Christian Science Monitor*, October 18, 2011.

15. Andrew Fitzmaurice, "Sovereign Trusteeship and Empire," *Theoretical Inquiries in Law* 16.2 (2015): 447–472; Mahmood Mamdani, "Responsibility to Protect or Right to Punish?" *Journal of Intervention and Statebuilding* 4.1 (2010): 53–67.

16. Ibrahim Raslan, "Sovereignty and Intervention in the Middle East: From the Fall of the Ottoman Empire to the Arab Spring" (PhD diss., University of Denver, 2014), 184; Asli Bali and Aziz Rana, "Pax Arabica? Provisional Sovereignty and Intervention in the Arab Uprisings," *California Western International Law Journal* 42 (2011): 323.

17. Ethan Chorin, *Exit the Colonel: The Hidden History of the Libyan Revolution* (New York: PublicAffairs, 2012), 204–205.

18. Yousef Sawani, "Dynamics of Continuity and Change," in *The 2011 Libyan Uprisings and the Struggle for the Post-Qadhafi Future*, ed. Jason Pack (New York: Palgrave MacMillan, 2013), 73; Sean Kane, "Barqa Reborn? Eastern Regionalism and Libya's Political Transition," in *The Libyan Revolution and Its Aftermath*, ed. Peter Cole and Brian McQuinn (New York: Oxford University Press, 2015), 221.

19. William Taylor, *Military Responses to the Arab Uprisings and the Future of Civil-Military Relations in the Middle East: Analysis from Egypt, Tunisia, Libya, and Syria* (New York: Palgrave Macmillan, 2014), 148–151. On the emergence of the militias, see Jihad Awdeh, Mahmud Khalifa Jawdeh, and Ahmed abd al-tawbi al-Khatib, *Militishiyat wa al-Harakat al-Musallahah fi Libya* (Cairo: Maktab al-Arabi lil tarouf, 2015).

20. Taylor, *Military Responses*, 152–154.

21. Gaddafi's Son: 'There Will Be Rivers of Blood in Libya,' " February 21, 2011, https://www.youtube.com/watch?v=Z9SJc1PcOfE (accessed March 17, 2018).

22. Gadhafi's Speech Transcript," February 26, 2011, https://petewarden.com/2011/02/26/gadhafis-speech-transcript/ (accessed March 17, 2018).

23. "Gadhafi's Speech Transcript," February 26, 2011.

24. "Libya Defectors: Pilots Told to Bomb Protesters Flee to Malta," *Guardian*, February 21, 2011, https://www.theguardian.com/world/2011/feb/21/libya-pilots-flee-to-malta.
25. Alan Kuperman argues that the TNC and others overreacted and indeed inflated concerns. See Alan J. Kuperman, "A Model Humanitarian Intervention? Reassessing NATO's Libya Campaign," *International Security* 38.1 (2013): 105–136; Saskia van Genugten, *Libya in Western Foreign Policies, 1911–2011* (London: Palgrave McMillan, 2016), 148.
26. President Obama Speaks on the Turmoil in Libya: 'This Violence Must Stop,'" February 23, 2011, https://obamawhitehouse.archives.gov/blog/2011/02/23/president-obama-speaks-turmoil-libya-violence-must-stop (accessed March 17, 2018).
27. Christopher S. Chivvis, *Toppling Qaddafi: Libya and the Limits of Liberal Intervention* (New York: Cambridge University Press, 2013), 29–31; Luke Glanville, "Intervention in Libya: From Sovereign Consent to Regional Consent," *International Studies Perspectives* 14.3 (2013): 333.
28. For complete text, see "Declaration of the Establishment of the National Transitional Temporary Council," in Jean-Pierre Filiu, *The Arab Revolution: Ten Lessons from the Democratic Uprising* (New York: Oxford University Press, 2011), 163–167.
29. Chivvis, *Toppling Qaddafi*, 32–33.
30. Kareem Fahim and David D. Kirkpatrick, "Libyan Rebels Said to Debate Seeking U.N. Airstrikes," *New York Times*, March 1, 2011, http://www.nytimes.com/2011/03/02/world/africa/02libya.html.
31. Libyan Opposition Council Chairman Comments on Remarks by British PM," BBC Monitoring, al-Arabiya TV on March 14, 2011, Document 135FD2984B257460.
32. Chivvis, *Toppling Qaddafi*, 52.
33. Steven Erlanger, "By His Own Reckoning, One Man Made Libya a French Cause," *New York Times*, April 1, 2011, https://www.nytimes.com/2011/04/02/world/africa/02levy.html; Christopher Dickey, "Why Sarkozy Went to War," *Newsweek*, April 13, 2011, http://www.newsweek.com/why-sarkozy-went-war-66463.
34. Arab League, "The Outcome of the Council of the League of Arab States Meeting at the Ministerial Level in Its Extraordinary Session on the Implications of the Current Events in Libya and the Arab Position," March 12, 2011, http://responsibilitytoprotect.org/Arab%20League%20Ministerial%20level%20statement%2012%20march%202011%20-%20english(1).pdf (accessed March 17, 2018).
35. Glanville, "Intervention in Libya," 333–336; Ranj Alaadin, "Libya & the Arab League," in *Political Rationale and International Consequences of the War in Libya*, ed. Dag Henriksen and Ann Karin Larssen (New York: Oxford University Press, 2016).
36. Ethan Bronner and David D. Sanger, "Arab League Endorses No-Flight Zone over Libya," *New York Times*, March 13, 2011, http://www.nytimes.com/2011/03/13/world/middleeast/13libya.html?pagewanted=all.
37. The Outcome of the Council of the League of Arab States Meeting, Cairo, March 12, 2011," available at http://responsibilitytoprotect.org/Arab%20League%20Ministerial%20level%20statement%2012%20march%202011%20-%20english(1).pdf (accessed September 12, 2018).
38. Kristian Ulrichsen, "The Rationale and Implications of Qatar's Intervention in Libya," in *Political Rationale and International Consequences of the War in Libya*, ed. Dag Henriksen and Ann Karin Larssen (New York: Oxford University Press, 2016), 126.
39. Mary Beth Sheridan and Scott Wilson, "U.S. Actions in Libya May Speak Louder than Words," *Washington Post*, March 19, 2011, https://www.washingtonpost.com/world/us-actions-may-speak-louder-than-words/2011/03/19/ABVWsZx_story.html?utm_term=.6b4acb3bc8b4.
40. Chivvis, *Toppling Qaddafi*, 54, 60–62.
41. Libyan Rebels 'Disappointed' by NATO," Al-Jazeera, April 6, 2011, http://www.aljazeera.com/news/africa/2011/04/201145191641347449.html (accessed march 23, 2018).
42. Nic Robertson, Reza Sayah, Ben Wedeman, Brian Todd, and Yousef Basil, "Libyan Rebel Leaders Say They Are 'Disappointed' by NATO's Efforts," CNN, April 5, 2011, http://www.cnn.com/2011/WORLD/africa/04/05/libya.war/index.html (accessed March 23, 2018); "Libyan Rebels 'Disappointed' by NATO.

43. Kuperman, "A Model Humanitarian Intervention?" 124.
44. Kuperman, "A Model Humanitarian Intervention?" 114.
45. Kristian Ulrichsen, *Qatar and the Arab Spring* (New York: Oxford University Press, 2014), 127; Sam Dagher, Charles Levinson, and Margaret Coker, "Tiny Kingdom's Huge Role in Libya Draws Concern," *Wall Street Journal*, October 17, 2011, https://www.wsj.com/articles/SB10001424052970204002304576627000922764650 .
46. Chivvis, *Toppling Qaddafi*, 105–108, 154–156.
47. William Hague, "Chair's Statement," April 13, 2011, http://www.nato.int/nato_static/assets/pdf/pdf_2011_04/20110926_110413-Libya-Contact_-Group-Doha.pdf (accessed May 18, 2018); Stefan Talmon, "De-Recognition of Colonel Qaddafi as Head of State of Libya?" *International and Comparative Law Quarterly* 60.03 (2011): 759–767.
48. Ulrichsen, "The Rationale and Implications of Qatar's Intervention in Libya," 126; Leonardo Bellodi, "Libya's Assets and the Question of Sovereignty," *Survival* 54.2 (2012): 39–45.
49. Jacob Sullivan to Hillary Clinton, "Fwd UNSC/Libya: Readout of 4/4 Briefing and Consultations," April 4, 2011, US State Department, Case No. F-2014-20439, Doc. No. C05779774, http://graphics.wsj.com/hillary-clinton-email-documents/pdfs/C05779774.pdf (accessed May 14, 2018).
50. Chorin, *Exit the Colonel*, 242.
51. Libyan Premier Says Territorial Integrity, Al-Qadhafi Non-Negotiable," BBC Monitoring, Al-Jamahiriyah TV, Tripoli, on June 16, 2011, Document BBCMNF0020110616e76g0035x.
52. Libyan PM Al-Mahmudi Interviewed on Ways to Solve Crisis, Talks with Opposition," BBC Monitoring, Al-Arabiya TV, Dubai, on July 3, 2011.
53. For instance, see Jean Ping, "Fallait-il tuer Kadhafi?" *Le Monde diplomatique*, August 2014, https://www.monde-diplomatique.fr/2014/08/PING/50709 (accessed October 17, 2017); Sri Lankan Daily Slams NATO for Backing 'War Crimes' of Rebels in Libya," BBC Monitoring, September 1, 2011, Document BBCSAP0020110901e791000ul.
54. Russian FM Discontent over Libyan Contact Group Ambitions," ITAR-TASS, May 6, 2011.
55. Taylor, *Military Responses*, 156–158.
56. Chivvis, *Toppling Qaddafi*, 145–153.
57. Cited in Ulrichesen, *Qatar and the Arab Spring*, 128.
58. Al-Arabiya Interviews Libya's Mahmud Jibril on Resignation, Domestic Issues," BBC Monitoring, November 11, 2011, Document BBCMEP0020111111e7bb003jt.
59. Charles Levinson, "Minister in Tripoli Blasts Qatari Aid to Militia Groups," *Wall Street Journal*, October 12, 2011, https://www.wsj.com/articles/SB10001424052970203499704576625441762600166.
60. Chorin, *Exit the Colonel*, 244–248.
61. Samer N. Abboud, *Syria* (Malden, MA: Polity, 2016), 67–69.
62. Christopher Phillips, *The Battle for Syria: International Rivalry in the New Middle East* (New Haven, CT: Yale University Press, 2016), 106.
63. Profile: Syria's Burhan Ghalioun," Al-Jazeera, April 1, 2012, http://www.aljazeera.com/news/middleeast/2012/04/201241184026297247.html (accessed March 23, 2018).
64. Phillips, *The Battle for Syria*, 108–109.
65. Philips, *The Battle for Syria*, 65–66.
66. Elizabeth O'Bagy, "Syria's Political Opposition," Institute for the Study of War, Middle East Security Report 4, April 2012, 16–18, http://www.understandingwar.org/sites/default/files/Syrias_Political_Opposition.pdf (accessed March 17, 2018).
67. Jonas Bergan Draege, "The Formation of Syrian Opposition Coalitions as Two-Level Games," *Middle East Journal* 70.2 (2016): 197–198, 201; Abboud, *Syria*, 101–104. See also Mustafa Menshawy, "Constructing State, Territory, and Sovereignty in the Syrian Conflict," *Politics* (2018): 0263395718770348.
68. Phillips, *The Battle for Syria*, 84–85.
69. Scott Pedersen, "Syrian Opposition Forms Unity Council, Hoping to y Arab Spring," *Christian Science Monitor*, October 4, 2011, https://www.csmonitor.com/World/Middle-East/2011/1004/Syrian-opposition-forms-unity-council-hoping-to-continue-Arab-Spring ; Phillips, *The Battle for Syria*, 113.

70. Alexandra Zavis and Rima Marrouch, "Syria Opposition Groups Agree to Coordinate Efforts," *Los Angeles Times*, December 1, 2011, http://articles.latimes.com/2011/dec/01/world/la-fg-syria-accord-20111202. Philips, *The Battle for Syria*, 114–115.

71. Taylor, *Military Responses*, 97–99; Phillips, *The Battle for Syria*, 126–127

72. Phillips, *The Battle for Syria*, 113.

73. Cited in David W. Lesch, *Syria: The Fall of the House of Assad* (New Haven, CT: Yale University Press, 2013), 199.

74. Cf. Anne-Marie Slaughter, "We Will Pay a High Price if We Do Not Arm Syria's Rebels," *Financial Times*, July 31, 2012, https://www.ft.com/content/a03392ce-da35-11e1-b03b-00144feab49a; Helene Cooper, "U.S. Quietly Getting Ready for Syria without Assad," *New York Times*, September 19, 2011, http://www.nytimes.com/2011/09/20/world/middleeast/us-is-quietly-getting-ready-for-a-syria-without-an-assad.html.

75. Phillips, *The Battle for Syria*, 110.

76. Ulrichsen, *Qatar and the Arab Spring*, 135, 142–143; Phillips, *The Battle for Syria*, 67–73.

77. James Harkin, "Syria's Opposition Should Be Careful Not to Overplay Its Hand," *Guardian*, December 16, 2011, https://www.theguardian.com/commentisfree/2011/dec/16/syria-opposition-media-war.

78. "The New Face of Syria," *Majalla Magazine*, January 3, 2012, http://eng.majalla.com/2012/01/article55228695/the-new-face-of-syria (accessed March 23, 2018).

79. President Bashar al-Assad's Speech at the People's Assembly, March 30, 2011," http://www.presidentassad.net/index.php?option=com_content&view=article&id=305:president-bashar-al-assad-s-a-speech-at-the-people-s-assembly-march-30-2011&catid=117&Itemid=496 (accessed May 14, 2018).

80. Emile Hokayem, "'Assad or We Burn the Country': Misreading Sectarianism and the Regime in Syria," War on the Rocks, August 24, 2016, https://warontherocks.com/2016/08/assad-or-we-burn-the-country-misreading-sectarianism-and-the-regime-in-syria/ (accessed March 17, 2018).

81. Taylor, *Military Responses*, 97–99; Dorothy Ohl, Holger Albrecht, and Kevin Koehler, "For Money or Liberty? The Political Economy of Military Desertion and Rebel Recruitment in the Syrian Civil War," Carnegie Middle East Center, November 24, 2015, http://carnegieendowment.org/files/ACMR_AlbrechtKoehlerOhl_SyrianRebel_English_final.pdf (accessed March 17, 2018).

82. Phillips, *The Battle for Syria*, 164.

83. President al-Assad's 2012 Damascus University Speech," http://www.presidentassad.net/index.php?option=com_content&view=article&id=274:president-al-assad-s-2012-damascus-university-speech&catid=118&Itemid=496 (accessed May 14, 2018).

84. Ulrichsen, *Qatar and the Arab Spring*, 131.

85. Speech Delivered by H. E. President Bashar al-Assad at the People's Assembly," June 4, 2012, http://www.presidentassad.net/index.php?option=com_content&view=article&id=276:speech-delivered&catid=118&Itemid=496 (accessed May 14, 2018).

86. "In Syria, Death of Tourism Most Visible Sign of Major Economic Damage," *Washington Post*, June 8, 2011, https://www.washingtonpost.com/world/middle-east/in-syria-the-death-of-tourism/2011/05/30/AGrTguLH_story.html?utm_term=.e28881b629dd.

87. Syria Opposition Presses for 'Serious Action,'" Al-Jazeera, April 1, 2012, http://www.aljazeera.com/news/asia-pacific/2012/04/2012412022613580.html (accessed March 23, 2018).

88. Phillips, *The Battle for Syria*, 129–131, 137, 143.

89. Cited in O'Bagy, "Syria's Political Opposition," 20.

90. Jonathan Head, "Syrian National Council Head Burhan Ghalioun to Resign," BBC News, May 17, 2012, http://www.bbc.com/news/world-middle-east-18106592 (accessed March 23, 2018); "Syria Opposition Rift Widens with Resignation of Burhan Ghalioun," *Guardian*, May 17, 2012, https://www.theguardian.com/world/2012/may/17/syria-opposition-rift-burhan-ghalioun.

91. Neil MacFarquhar and Michael R. Gordon, "As Fighting Rages, Clinton Seeks New Syrian Opposition," *New York Times*, October 31, 2012, http://www.nytimes.com/2012/11/01/

world/middleeast/syrian-air-raids-increase-as-battle-for-strategic-areas-intensifies-rebels-say.html.

92. Cited in Talmon, "De-Recognition," 230.

93. Draege, "Formation of Syrian Opposition," 206–207.

94. Philips, *Battle for Syria*, 126–129, 163.

95. Taylor, *Military Responses*, 100.

96. Abdul Wahab Badrakhan, "Raising the Ceiling: Syria's Inside Opposition Not Ready to Give Up," Al-Arabiya, February 22, 2013, http://english.alarabiya.net/en/views/2013/02/22/Raising-the-ceiling-Syria-s-inside-opposition-not-ready-to-give-up.html (accessed March 17, 2018).

97. Bashar al-Assad's January 6th, 2013 Speech," http://www.presidentassad.net/index.php?option=com_content&view=article&id=273:president-bashar-al-assad-s-january-6th-2013-speech&catid=119&Itemid=496 (accessed May 14, 2018).

98. Reinoud Leenders and Antonio Giustozzi, "Outsourcing State Violence: The National Defence Force, 'Stateness' and Regime Resilience in the Syrian War," *Mediterranean Politics* (2017): 1–24; Oxford Analytica, "Syria: Foreign Aid Will Keep War Economy Afloat," July 15, 2013; Economist Intelligence Unit, "Syria Economy: Regime Talks Up Reconstruction," July 14, 2014.

99. For the complete speech, see Aron Lund, "Falling Back, Fighting On: Assad Lays Out His Strategy," Carnegie Middle East Center, *Diwan*, July 27, 2015, http://carnegieendowment.org/syriaincrisis/?fa=60857 (accessed May 15, 2018); Agence France Presse, "Assad Regime 'to Accept Syria's De Facto Partition,' " *Arab News*, May 25, 2015, http://www.arabnews.com/world/news/751681 (accessed May 15, 2018).

100. Tom Perry and Patricia Zengerle, "Kerry Issues Warning as Syrian Parties Back Halt to Fighting," Reuters, February 24, 2016, http://www.reuters.com/article/mideast-crisis-syria/kerry-issues-warning-as-syrian-parties-back-halt-to-fighting-idUSKCN0VW1K8 (accessed May 14, 2018).

101. Philipp Casula, "Russia between Diplomacy and Military Intervention," *Russian Analytical Digest* 175, November 16, 2015, 10; Samer Araabi, "Syria's Decentralization Roadmap," Carnegie Endowment for International Peace, March 23, 2017, http://carnegieendowment.org/sada/68372 (accessed November 7, 2017).

102. Laurent Bonnefoy and Marine Poirier, "La structuration de la révolution yéménite," *Revue française de science politique* 62.5 (2012): 895–913.

103. On the strategic stakes in Yemen, see Christopher Boucek and Marina Ottaway, eds., *Yemen on the Brink* (Washington, DC: Carnegie Endowment, 2010); Sarah Phillips, *Yemen and the Politics of Permanent Crisis* (New York: Routledge, 2011).

104. Yemeni Leader Interviewed on Domestic Issues, Foreign Ties, Fighting Terrorism," BBC World Monitoring, *Asharq al-Awsat* website, London, on March 4, 2012, Document BBCMEP0020120308e838001p5.

105. Paper Calls on Yemeni Government to Acknowledge North-South Secession," BBC World Monitoring, Yemen Fox, Sana'a, on September 14, 2013, Document BBCMEP0020130914 e99e002jq. On the NDC process, see Erica Gaston, "Process Lessons Learned in Yemen's National Dialogue," US Institute of Peace Special Report 342, February 2014, https://www.usip.org/sites/default/files/SR342_Process-Lessons-Learned-in-Yemens-National-Dialogue.pdf (accessed May 22, 2018).

106. Success of National Dialogue 'Key to Yemen's Future,' Says Foreign Minister," BBC World Monitoring, *Asharq al-Awsat* website, London, on September 29, 2013, Document BBCMEP20130930e99u004ed.

107. For a general discussion of the shortcomings of the Yemen transition, see Stacey Philbrick Yadav, "The 'Yemen Model' as a Failure of Political Imagination," *International Journal of Middle East Studies* 47.1 (2015): 144–147.

108. Statement by Saudi Ambassador Al-Jubeir on Military Operations in Yemen," March 25, 2015, www.operationrenewalofhope.com/statement-by-saudi-ambassador-al-jubeir-on-military-operations-in-yemen/ (accessed May 15, 2018).

109. Drew Thompson, "Responsibility While Protecting (RwP) and the Intervention in Yemen," *Ethics & International Affairs* blog, January 25, 2017, https://www.ethicsandinternation-

alaffairs.org/2017/responsibility-protecting-intervention-yemen/#fn-11962-1 (accessed May 15, 2018). See also Tom Ruys and Luca Ferro, "Weathering the Storm: Legality and Legal Implications of the Saudi-Led Military Intervention in Yemen," *International & Comparative Law Quarterly* 65, no. 1 (2016): 61–98.

110. Kristian Coates Ulrichsen, "Endgames for Saudi Arabia and the United Arab Emirates in Yemen," in *Politics, Governance, and Reconstruction in Yemen*, POMEPS Studies 29, January 2018, 31–33, https://pomeps.org/wp-content/uploads/2018/02/POMEPS_Studies_29_Yemen_Web-REV.pdf (accessed May 23, 2018).

111. Anthony Hardwood, "Saudi Arabia Using Famine as Weapon in War," *Newsweek*, November 28, 2017, http://www.newsweek.com/saudi-arabia-using-famine-weapon-war-724680; Kate Lyons, "Yemen's Cholera Outbreak Now the Worst in History as Millionth Case Looms," *Guardian*, October 12, 2017, https://www.theguardian.com/global-development/2017/oct/12/yemen-cholera-outbreak-worst-in-history-1-million-cases-by-end-of-year.

112. Saudi Arabia Keeping Yemen President Hadi 'under House Arrest,'" Alaraby, November 7, 2017, https://www.alaraby.co.uk/english/news/2017/11/7/yemeni-president-hadi-under-house-arrest-in-riyadh (accessed May 14, 2018).

113. Ray Takeyh, "A United Libyan Nation Can Avoid Partition," *Financial Times*, April 18, 2011, https://www.ft.com/content/4ec3f2ba-6a08-11e0-86e4-00144feab49a; Federica Saini Fasanotti, "A Confederal Model for Libya," Brookings *Order from Chaos* blog, August 2, 2016, https://www.brookings.edu/blog/order-from-chaos/2016/07/06/a-confederal-model-for-libya (accessed May 14, 2018); Stephanie Kirchgaessner and Julian Borger, "Trump Aide Drew Plan on Napkin to Partition Libya into Three," *Guardian*, April 10, 2017, https://www.theguardian.com/world/2017/apr/10/libya-partition-trump-administration-sebastian-gorka; Jonathan Stevenson, "The Dangerous Allure of a Syrian Partition," *New York Times*, March 17, 2016, https://www.nytimes.com/2016/03/18/opinion/the-dangerous-allure-of-a-syrian-partition.html; Noah Browning, "War Pushes Yemen to Partition, Thwarting Peace Efforts," Reuters, October 30, 2016, https://www.reuters.com/article/us-yemen-security-partition/war-pushes-yemen-to-partition-thwarting-peace-efforts-idUSKBN12U06J (accessed May 14, 2018).

## Chapter 3

1. Freya Stark, *The Coast of Incense* (London: J. Murray, 1953), 162–163.

2. On Idris's personal interactions with the British military administration, see Richard Synge, *Operation Idris* (London: Society for Libyan Studies, 2015).

3. Text available in Mohammed Bashir al-Mughayribi, *Watha'iq jami'yat 'Umar al-Mukhtar* [Documents of the Omar al-Mukhtar Group] (Cairo: n.p., 1993), 114–116.

4. On the declaration, see Majid Khadduri, *Modern Libya: A Study in Political Development* (Baltimore, MD: Johns Hopkins University Press, 1963), 73; E. A. V. De Candole, *The Life and Times of King Idris* (London: published privately by Mohamed Ben Ghalbon, 1990), 98.

5. On the origins and outlook of the Omar al-Mukhtar Club, see Anna Baldinetti, "Libya's Refugees, Their Places of Exile, and the Shaping of Their National Idea," *Journal of North African Studies* 8.1 (2003): 72–86.

6. Youssef Sawani and Jason Pack, "Libyan Constitutionality and Sovereignty Post-Qadhafi: The Islamist, Regionalist, and Amazigh Challenges," *Journal of North African Studies* 18.4 (2013): 535.

7. Ali Abdullatif Ahmida, *The Making of Modern Libya: State Formation, Colonization, and Resistance, 1830–1932* (Albany, NY: SUNY Press, 1994).

8. Hadi M. R. Bulugma, "The Urban Geography of Benghazi" (PhD diss., University of Durham, 1964), 284. On the progress of urbanization, see Ahmed A. Mahmood-Misrati, "Land Conversion to Urban Use: Its Impact and Character in Libya," *Ekistics* (1983): 183–194.

9. For a discussion of tribalism in Cyrenaica as a fictive descent, see Emrys L. Peters, Jack Goody, and Emanuel Marx, *The Bedouin of Cyrenaica: Studies in Personal and Corporate Power* (New York: Cambridge University Press, 1990).

10. Iliya Harik, "The Origins of the Arab State System," In *The Arab State*, ed. G. Luciani (Berkeley: University of California Press, 1990), 1–28.

11. Nicola A. Ziadeh, *Sanūsīyah: A Study of a Revivalist Movement in Islam* (Leiden: Brill, 1958), 113–117.

12. John Wright, *Libya: A Modern History* (London: Taylor & Francis, 1982), 28–30; Ziadeh, *Sanūsīyah*, 51–58, Ahmeida, *Making of Modern Libya*, 100. On Senussi-Ottoman relations, see Mostafa Minawi, *The Ottoman Scramble for Africa: Empire and Diplomacy in the Sahara and the Hijaz* (Stanford, CA: Stanford University Press, 2016).

13. Dirk Vandewalle, *A History of Modern Libya* (New York: Cambridge University Press, 2012), 26–28.

14. Lisa Anderson, "The Tripoli Republic, 1918–1922," in *Social and Economic Development of Libya*, ed. E. George H. Joffe and Keith Stanley McLachlan (Boulder, CO: Westview, 1982), 43–66; Saad Bugaighis, "The Italian Invasion of Libya and the Nineteen Years of Libyan Resistance" (PhD diss., University of Washington, 2011).

15. Douglas L. Johnson, *Jabal al-Akhdar, Cyrenaica: An Historical Geography of Settlement and Livelihood* (Chicago: University of Chicago Press, 1973), 169; Wright, *Libya*, 3–22; Lisa Anderson, *The State and Social Transformation in Tunisia and Libya, 1830–1980* (Princeton, NJ: Princeton University Press, 1987), 200–202, 208.

16. Anderson, *State and Social Transformation*, 214. See also Bugaighis, "The Italian Invasion of Libya."

17. E. E. Evans-Pritchard, *The Senussi of Cyrenaica* (London: Oxford University Press, 1954), 153–155; Anderson, *State and Social Transformation*, 251–252; Anna Baldinetti, *The Origins of the Libyan Nation: Colonial Legacy, Exile and the Emergence of a New Nation-State* (New York: Routledge, 2014), chapter 4.

18. Ahmida, *The Making of Modern Libya*, 136–140; Hala Khamis Nassar and Marco Boggero, "Omar al-Mukhtar: The Formation of Cultural Memory and the Case of the Militant Group That Bears His Name," *Journal of North African Studies* 13.2 (2008): 201–217.

19. Bulugma, "The Urban Geography of Benghazi," 59–62, 86.

20. Anderson, *State and Social Transformation*, 217. For an extended discussion, see Claudio G. Segrè, *Fourth Shore: The Italian Colonization of Libya* (Chicago: University of Chicago Press, 1974).

21. Wright, *Libya*, 44–45; Anderson, *State and Social Transformation*, 221.

22. E. E. Evans-Pritchard, one of the foremost anthropologists of Libya but also a colonial official at the time, said credulously that at the end of the war the Senussis directed, "administratively, economically, and militarily, the entire Bedouin population, and morally the entire population, Bedouin and townsmen alike." Evans-Pritchard, *The Senussi*, 227.

23. Anderson, *State and Social Transformation*, 252–259; Vandewalle, *A History of Modern Libya*, 37–40.

24. Khadduri, *Modern Libya*, 72; Adrian Pelt, *Libyan Independence and the United Nations: A Case of Planned Decolonization* (New Haven, CT: Yale University Press, 1970), 46–47.

25. Salaheddin Salem Hasan, "The Genesis of the Political Leadership of Libya, 1952–1969: Historical Origins and Development of Its Component Elements" (PhD diss., George Washington University, 1973), 164–168; Bulugma, "The Urban Geography of Benghazi," 96–97.

26. UN General Assembly Resolution 289 (IV), Question of the Disposal of the Former Italian Colonies, https://documents-dds-ny.un.org/doc/RESOLUTION/GEN/NR0/051/08/IMG/NR005108.pdf?OpenElement (accessed May 15, 2018).

27. Pelt, *Libyan Independence and the United Nations*, 46–49; Khadduri, *Modern Libya*, 168.

28. Hasan, "Genesis of the Political Leadership of Libya," 165–167.

29. Wright, *Libya*, 46–50, 73.

30. Wright, *Libya*, 79; Anderson, *State and Social Transformation*, 256–257.

31. Hasan, "Genesis of the Political Leadership of Libya," 167–168, 443.

32. Bulugma, "The Urban Geography of Benghazi," 67–68, 284.

33. Wright, *Libya*, 101–102; Omar Fathalay, "The Historical, Social, Economics, and Historical Milieus," in *Political Development and Bureaucracy in Libya*, ed. Omar Fathalay et al. (Lexington, MA: Lexington Books, 1977), 24.

34. Hasan, "Genesis of the Political Leadership of Libya," 187–189.

35. On the transformation of Benghazi, see Bulugma, "The Urban Geography of Benghazi," 85, 100.

36. On social change in Cyrenaica, see Johnson, *Jabal al-Akhdar, Cyrenaica*; Musa S. Khalidi, "Dilemmas of Rural Development in Cyrenaica, Libya," *Studies in Comparative International Development* 20.2 (1985): 48–64; Thomas Hüsken, "Tribes, Revolution, and Political Culture in the Cyrenaica Region of Libya," in *Local Politics and Contemporary Transformations in the Arab World: Governance beyond the Center*, ed. Malika Bouziane, Cilja Harders, and Anja Hoffmann (New York: Palgrave Macmillan, 2013), 215–216.

37. Bulugma, "The Urban Geography of Benghazi," 252–253, 265–267. Davis's study of Cyrenaica from the late 1970s confirms this assessment. See John Davis, *Libyan Politics: Tribe and Revolution: An Account of the Zuwaya and Their Government* (Berkeley, CA: University of California Press, 1988).

38. Bulugma, "The Urban Geography of Benghazi," 203–204, 267.

39. Hasan, "Genesis of the Political Leadership of Libya," 185–186, 189.

40. Mansour O. El-Kikhia, *Libya's Qaddafi: The Politics of Contradiction* (Gainesville: University Press of Florida, 1997), 37; Frank Ralph Golino, "Patterns of Libyan National Identity," *Middle East Journal* 24.3 (1970): 351.

41. Lisa Anderson, "Qadhdhafi and His Opposition," *Middle East Journal* 40.2 (1986): 229.

42. Anderson, *State and Social Transformation*, 261; Hasan, "Genesis of the Political Leadership of Libya," 186–187.

43. El-Kikhia, *Libya's Qaddafi*, 88–90, 163; Hanspeter Mattes, "Formal and Informal Authority in Libya since 1969," in *Libya since 1969*, ed. Dirk Vandewalle (New York: Palgrave Macmillan, 2008), 70–73; Wright, *Libya*, 136.

44. John Anthony Allan, "Water Resource Evaluation and Development in Libya—1969–1989," *Libyan Studies* 20 (1989): 235–242.

45. George Joffe, "Islamic Opposition in Libya," *Third World Quarterly* 10.2 (1988): 627; Yehudit Ronen, "Qadhafi and Militant Islamism: Unprecedented Conflict," *Middle Eastern Studies* 38.4 (2002): 7–8; Hüsken, "Tribes, Revolution, and Political Culture," 224.

46. Alia Brahimi, "Islam in Libya," in *Islamist Radicalisation in North Africa: Politics and Process*, ed. George Joffé (New York: Routledge, 2012), 23.

47. For details on LIFG, see Omar Ashour, "Post-Jihadism: Libya and the Global Transformations of Armed Islamist Movements," *Terrorism and Political Violence* 23.3 (2011): 377–397.

48. Amal Obeidi, *Political Culture in Libya* (London: Curzon, 2001), 118–119; Hüsken, "Tribes, Revolution, and Political Culture," 217–218.

49. Obeidi, *Political Culture*, 119.

50. Obeidi, *Political Culture*, 221; Igor Cherstich, "When Tribesmen Do Not Act Tribal: Libyan Tribalism as Ideology (Not as Schizophrenia)," *Middle East Critique* 23.4 (2014): 412.

51. Nasser and Boggero, "Omar al-Mukhtar," 203–204.

52. Ethan Chorin, *Exit the Colonel: The Hidden History of the Libyan Revolution* (New York: PublicAffairs, 2012), 179–180; Hüsken, "Tribes, Revolution, and Political Culture," 219–221.

53. Frederic Wehrey, "The Struggle for Eastern Libya," Carnegie Endowment for International Peace, September 2012, 8, http://carnegieendowment.org/files/libya_security_2.pdf (accessed May 15, 2018).

54. Chorin, *Exit the Colonel*, 191–192.

55. On the emergence of the militias, see Jihad Awdeh, Mahmud Khalifa Jawdeh, and Ahmed abd al-tawbi al-Khatib, *Militishiyat wa al-Harakat al-Musallahah fi Libya* (Cairo: Maktab al-Arabi lil tarouf, 2015).

56. On the international politics surrounding the TNC, see Christopher S. Chivvis, *Toppling Qaddafi: Libya and the Limits of Liberal Intervention* (New York: Cambridge University Press, 2013); Stefan Talmon, "De-Recognition of Colonel Qaddafi as Head of State of Libya?" *International and Comparative Law Quarterly* 60.3 (2011): 759–767; Leonardo Bellodi, "Libya's Assets and the Question of Sovereignty," *Survival* 54.2 (2012): 39–45.

57. For a biography of Buera, see Buera…Khabir al-idarat al-lathy qad al-barliman l'tahqid ahlam al-libeen" [Buera…expert on administration that comes to parliament to fulfill the dreams of Libyans], *Al-Wasit*, August 4, 2014, http://alwasat.ly/ar/news/libya/29795/ (accessed May 15, 2018).

58. For a comparison, Mustafa Abd al-Jalil, chairman of the TNC, was born in 1952. See also Buera's comments on the history of the Libyan flag and anthem. "Nawab yabdoon ara-him bi shu'n taghayer al-'alm wa al-nishad al-watani" [MPs seem to change their views about the national flag and anthem], *Al-Wasit*, January 15, 2017, http://alwasat.ly/ar/news/libya/130149/ (accessed May 15, 2018).

59. Awdeh, Jawdeh, and al-Khatib, *Militishiyat wa al-Harakat al-Musallahah fi Libya*, 23–25.

60. On the comparative salience of tribalism in the east, see Peter Cole, "Tribe, Security, Justice and Peace in Libya Today," US Institute of Peace, *PeaceWorks* 118, August 2016, https://www.usip.org/publications/2016/09/tribe-security-justice-and-peace-libya-today (accessed March 13, 2017); Hüsken, "Tribes, Revolution, and Political Culture," 224–225.

61. Sean Kane, "Barqa Reborn? Eastern Regionalism and Libya's Political Transition," in *The Libyan Revolution and Its Aftermath*, ed. Peter Cole and Brian McQuinn (New York: Oxford University Press, 2015), 229–231.

62. Kane, "Barqa Reborn?" 228. For example, Fathi al-Sha'iri, one of the leaders of Islamist militias in Derna, hailed from one of city's leading tribes. See Wehrey, "Struggle for Eastern Libya," 11.

63. Mary Fitzgerald, "Finding Their Place: Libya's Islamists during and after the Revolution," in *The Libyan Revolution and Its Aftermath*, ed. Peter Cole and Brian McQuinn (New York: Oxford University Press, 2015), 211, 217; Wehrey, "Struggle for Eastern Libya," 9.

64. Wehrey, "Struggle for Eastern Libya," 13.

65. Fitzgerald, "Finding Their Place," 201.

66. Kane, "Barqa Reborn?" 231–232.

67. Human Rights Watch, "Stop Attacks on Sufi Shrines," August 31, 2012, https://www.hrw.org/news/2012/08/31/libya-stop-attacks-sufi-sites (accessed May 15, 2018).

68. Wehrey, "Struggle for Eastern Libya," 11, 13

69. The anthem can be heard at https://www.youtube.com/watch?v=RK81-H9O580 (accessed May 15, 2018).

70. Wehrey, "Struggle for Eastern Libya," 8; Kane, "Barqa Reborn?" 231–234.

71. Kane, "Barqa Reborn?" 239.

72. Kane, "Barqa Reborn?" 233, 235–238.

73. Libyan NTC Leader Says Move to Partition Country Dangerous," BBC Monitoring, sec. ALERT, March 6, 2012, NewsBank, infoweb.newsbank.com/apps/news/document-view?p=AWNB&docref=news/13D5D45DBB216BB0 (accessed 1 June 1, 2018).

74. AFP, "Libya Leader Vows to Halt Autonomy Bid," Al-Jazeera, March 7, 2012, http://www.aljazeera.com/news/africa/2012/03/201237103524945859.html (accessed May 15, 2018).

75. Jacob Sullivan to Hillary Clinton, "Fwd: Latest from HRC Friend," April 23, 2012, US State Department, Case No. F-2015–04841, Doc. No. C05792069, http://graphics.wsj.com/hillary-clinton-email-documents/pdfs/C05792069.pdf (accessed May 15, 2018).

76. Sawani and Pack, "Libyan Constitutionality and Sovereignty Post-Qadhafi," 527; Kane, "Barqa Reborn?" 236.

77. See comments in the post-election focus groups run by International Foundation for Electoral Systems, "Voters' Opinions of the Election Process in Libya," March 2013, 20, https://www.ifes.org/sites/default/files/libya_fg_report_final_2.pdf (accessed May 15, 2018).

78. Chorin, *Exit the Colonel*, 299; Wehrey, "Struggle for Eastern Libya," 6.

79. Lisa Anderson, "'They Defeated Us All': International Interests, Local Politics, and Contested Sovereignty in Libya," *Middle East Journal* 71.2 (2017): 241–242.

80. Gaith Shennib and Marie-Louise Gumuchian, "UAE Embassy Compound Attacked in Libyan Capital," Reuters, July 25, 2013, http://www.reuters.com/article/us-libya-uae-attack-idUSBRE96O04J20130725 (accessed May 15, 2018).

81. Irfan Al-Alawi, "More Destruction of Sufi Tombs Shows Islamists Are Not Defeated," Lapidomedia: Centre for Religious Literacy in Journalism, July 25, 2012, http://www. lapidomedia.com/libya-more-destruction-sufi-tombs-shows-islamists-are-not-defeated (accessed May 15, 2018); Libya Clashes Break Out over Sufi Shrine Attack," BBC, September 7, 2012, http://www.bbc.com/news/world-africa-19522215 (accessed May 15, 2018); Human Rights Watch, "Stop Attacks on Sufi Shrines."

82. Anthony Loyd, "Rebel Choking Libya's Oil Exports Steps Up His Bid for Power; Libya," *Times* (London), October 30, 2013, http://www.thetimes.co.uk/article/rebel-choking-libyas-oil-exports-steps-up-his-bid-for-power-rl2g53db38z.

83. Will Crisp, "Tripoli Has Only One Option—It Must Free Us, Says Jadhran," *Petroleum Economist*, October 8, 2013, http://www.petroleum-economist.com/articles/politics-economics/africa/2013/tripoli-has-only-one-option-it-must-free-us-says-jadhran (accessed May 15, 2018).

84. Andrew McGregor, "Autonomy Campaign in Cyrenaica Brings Libya's Oil Industry to a Halt," *Jamestown Foundation Terrorism Monitor* 11.20 (October 31, 2013), https:// jamestown.org/program/autonomy-campaign-in-cyrenaica-brings-libyas-oil-industry-to-a-halt/ (accessed May 15, 2018).

85. Ahmed Obeidi, "Cyrenaica Tribal Elders Reaffirm Support for Jadhran, Promise to Export Oil," *Libya Herald*, December 22, 2013, https://www.libyaherald.com/2013/12/22/cyre-naica-tribal-elders-reaffirm-support-for-jedhran-promise-to-export-oil/ (accessed May 15, 2018); Ashraf Abdul-Wahab and Houda Mzioudet, "Mixed Messages from Ajdabiya as Maghraba Tribe Try to Negotiate Misrata Pullback from Sirte," *Libya Herald*, March 14, 2014, https://www.libyaherald.com/2014/03/14/mixed-messages-from-ajbabiya-as-maghraba-tribe-try-to-negotiate-misrata-pullback-from-sirte/ (accessed May 15, 2018); Kane, "Barqa Reborn?" 242–243.

86. Wolfram Lacher, "Libya's Local Elites and the Politics of Alliance Building," *Mediterranean Politics* 21.1 (2016), 78; Hüsken, "Tribes, Revolution, and Political Culture," 224.

87. Esam Mohamed, "Eastern Libya's Self-Declared Government Forms Regional Oil Company in Challenge to Tripoli," Associated Press, November 11, 2013.

88. Brian Hutchinson, "Notorious Canadian Lobbyist Signs $2M Contract to Promote Libya Militants Aiming to Divide Country," *National Post*, January 6, 2014, http://news.nationalpost. com/news/notorious-canadian-lobbyist-hired-by-militants-seeking-breakaway-from-libya.

89. David Kirkpatrick, "SEAL Team Raids a Tanker and Thwarts a Militia's Bid to Sell Libyan Oil," *New York Times*, March 17, 2014, https://www.nytimes.com/2014/03/18/world/ middleeast/libya-oil-tanker.html.

90. Khalid Mahmoud, "Tarablus tu'talib rasmi al-mujtama' ad-dawli bimusa'adatiha fi tamin am al-bilad" [Security council officially requests the international community intervene to secure national security], *Asharq al-Awsat*, March 22, 2014, http://aawsat.com/home/ article/61051 (accessed May 15, 2018); Khalid Mahmoud, "Majlis al-Amn yufardh 'aqubat ala muharbi an-naft al-libi" [Security Council imposes sanctions on Libyan oil smugglers], *Asharq al-Awsat*, March 21, 2014, http://aawsat.com/home/article/60186 (accessed May 15, 2018).

91. International Crisis Group, "The Prize: Fighting for Libya's Energy Wealth," International Crisis Group Report 163, December 3, 2015, 10–11, https://www.crisisgroup.org/middle-east-north-africa/north-africa/libya/prize-fighting-libya-s-energy-wealth (accessed March 10, 2017).

92. Federalism in Libya: The Never-Ending Debate," Al-Jazeera, May 9, 2014, http:// www.aljazeera.com/news/middleeast/2014/04/federalism-east-libya-debate-201442493215796441.html (accessed May 15, 2018).

93. Frederic Wehrey, *The Burning Shores: Inside the Battle for the New Libya* (New York: Farrar, Straus & Giroux, 2018), 196, 200.

94. Thomas Hüsken, "The Practice and Culture of Smuggling in the Borderland of Egypt and Libya," *International Affairs* 93.4 (2017): 897–915; Maha Salem, "Adel Al-Fidi: Unifier les tribus est la seule garantie pour la réussite de tout accord de paix en Libye," *Al-Ahram hebdo*,

June 3, 2015, http://hebdo.ahram.org.eg/NewsContent/1078/2/8/11676/Adel-AlFidi%E2%80%93Unifier-les-tribus-est-la-seule-garan.aspx (accessed July 13, 2017).

95. Wolfgang Mühlberger, "Egypt's Foreign and Security Policy in Post-R2P Libya," *International Spectator* 51.2 (2016): 99–112; Frederic Wehrey, David Bishop, and Ala' Al-Rababa'h, "Backdrop to an Intervention: Sources of Egyptian-Libyan Border Tension," Carnegie Endowment for International Peace, August 27, 2014, http://carnegieendowment.org/2014/08/27/backdrop-to-intervention-sources-of-egyptian-libyan-border-tension-pub-56475 (accessed May 15, 2018).

96. Ali Shu'ab, "Intihabat ra'isa al-barlman al-libi tudha'f al-islamiyyeen wa al-federaliyyeen" [Elections for Libyan parliamentary leader weaken Islamists and Federalists], *Al-Hayat*, August 6, 2014, http://www.alhayat.com/Articles/3986312/%D8%A7%D9%86%D8%AA%D8%AE%D8%A7%D8%A8%D8%A7%D8%AA-%D8%B1%D8%A6%D8%A7%D8%B3%D8%A9-%D8%A7%D9%84%D8%A8%D8%B1%D9%84%D9%85%D8%A7%D9%86-%D8%A7%D9%84%D9%84%D9%8A%D8%A8%D9%8A-%D8%AA%D8%B6%D8%B9%D9%81-%D8%A7%D9%84%D8%A5%D8%B3%D9%84%D8%A7%D9%85%D9%8A%D9%8A%D9%86-%D9%88%D8%A7%D9%81%D9%8A%D8%AF%D9%8A%D8%B1%D8%A7%D9%84%D9%8A%D9%8A%D9%86 (accessed May 15, 2018).

97. "Buera: al-muatamar al-watani as-sabiq ya'da'm taqseem Libya" [Buera: The former National Congress is supporting the breakup of Libya], *Al-Wasat*, August 25, 2014, http://alwasat.ly/ar/news/libya/33244/ (accessed May 15, 2018).

98. Kamal Abdullah, "Libya Teeters Further," *Al-Ahram Weekly*, November 13, 2014, http://weekly.ahram.org.eg/News/7723/19/Libya-teeters-further.aspx (accessed May 15, 2018).

99. Libya's Oil to Flow Despite Struggle between Rival Governments," Reuters, October 24, 2014, http://www.reuters.com/article/us-libya-oil-idUSKCN0IC18520141023 (accessed May 15, 2018).

100. International Crisis Group, "The Prize: Fighting for Libya's Energy Wealth," International Crisis Group Report 163, December 3, 2015, 23, https://www.crisisgroup.org/middle-east-north-africa/north-africa/libya/prize-fighting-libya-s-energy-wealth (accessed March 10, 2017).

101. Oxford Analytical Division, "Divisions Plague Financial Institutions," December 29, 2016, https://dailybrief.oxan.com/Analysis/DB216939/Divisions-plague-Libyas-financial-institutions (accessed September 8, 2018).

102. International Crisis Group, "The Prize," 23.

103. Human Rights Watch, "Libya: War Crimes as Benghazi Residents Flee," March 22, 2017, https://www.hrw.org/news/2017/03/22/libya-war-crimes-benghazi-residents-flee (accessed May 15, 2018); Economist Intelligence Unit, "Libya Politics: Powerful Anti-Haftar Faction Emerges in the East," August 19, 2016.

104. Kamal Abdallah, "Doves and Hawks," *Al-Ahram Weekly*, January 29, 2015, http://weekly.ahram.org.eg/News/10295.aspx (accessed May 15, 2018); Karim Mezran, "The Skhirat Agreement Represents a Positive Step for Libya," *Daily Star* (Lebanon), August 25, 2015, http://www.dailystar.com.lb/Opinion/Commentary/2015/Aug-25/312580-the-skhirat-agreement-represents-a-positive-step-for-libya.ashx (accessed May 15, 2018).

105. Kamal Abdallah, "Libya's Darkest Year," *Al-Ahram Weekly*, December 18, 2014, http://weekly.ahram.org.eg/News/7967/19/Libya%E2%80%99s-darkest-year.aspx (accessed May 15, 2018).

106. Abd al-Sattar Hitayti, "Ashbah Ajdabiyya" [Ghosts of Ajdabiya], *Asharq al-Awsat*, January 27, 2016, http://aawsat.com/home/article/553601/%D9%8A%D9%88%D9%85%D9%8A%D8%A7%D8%AA-%D8%A7%D9%84%D9%88%D8%B6%D9%89-%D9%81%D9%8A-%D9%84%D9%8A%D8%A8%D9%8A%D8%A7-1-%D9%85%D9%86-5-%C2%AB%D8%A3%D8%B4%D8%A8%D8%A7%D8%AD-%D8%A5%D8%AC%D8%AF%D8%A7%D8%A8%D9%8A%D8%A7%C2%BB-%D9%8A%D8%AB%D9%8A%D8%B1%D9%88%D9%86-%D8%A7%D9%84%D9%81%D8%B2%D8%B9-%D9%81%D9%8A-%D9%85%D9%86%D8%B7%D9%82%D8%A9-%D8%A7%D9%84%D9%87%D9%84%D8%A7%D9%84 (accessed May 15, 2018).

107. Kamal Abdallah, "Benghazi: Road to Stability," *Al-Ahram Weekly*, December 14, 2015, http://weekly.ahram.org.eg/News/15012/19/Benghazi--Road-to-stability.aspx (accessed May 15, 2018).

108. "LNA Commander Quits Saying Hafter's Men Raided His Beida Home," *Libya Herald*, February 13, 2017, https://www.libyaherald.com/2017/02/13/lna-commander-quits-saying-hafters-men-raided-his-beida-home/ (accessed May 15, 2018).

109. "Al-Jaysh al-libi yu'ana kitiba at-tawhid al-salafi" [The Libyan Army mourns the commander of the Salafi Tawhid battalion], *Al-Wasat*, February 9, 2015, http://alwasat.ly/ar/news/libya/60535/ (accessed May 15, 2018).

110. Abdulkader Assad, "Cyrenaica Threatens Separation from Libya," *Libya Observer*, April 2, 2016, https://www.libyaobserver.ly/news/cyrenaica-threatens-separation-libya (accessed May 15, 2018); Wolfgang Pusztai, "Does Federalism Have a Future in Libya?" Atlantic Council *MENASource* blog, August 22, 2016, http://www.atlanticcouncil.org/blogs/menasource/does-federalism-have-a-future-in-libya (Accessed May 15, 2018).

111. Hisham Matar, *In the Country of Men* (New York: Dial Press, 2007), 183.

112. Lisa Anderson, "Tribe and State: Libyan Anomalies," In *Tribes and State Formation in the Middle East*, ed. Philip Khoury and Joseph Kostiner (Berkeley: University of California Press, 1990), 292.

113. Nicholas Pelham, "Libya against Itself," *New York Review of Books*, February 19, 2015, http://www.nybooks.com/articles/2015/02/19/libya-against-itself/.

114. Sawani and Pack, "Libyan Constitutionality and Sovereignty Post-Qadhafi," 537–539; Ines Kohl, "Libya's 'Major Minorities.' Berber, Tuareg and Tebu: Multiple Narratives of Citizenship, Language and Border Control," *Middle East Critique* 23.4 (2014): 423–438.

115. Associated Press, "Libyan Tabu Tribe Threatens Election Boycott," July 2, 2012, http://gulfnews.com/news/mena/libya/libyan-tabu-tribe-threatens-election-boycott-1.1043460 (accessed May 15, 2018).

116. Brian McQuinn, "History's Warriors: The Emergence of Revolutionary Battalions in Misrata," in *The Libyan Revolution and Its Aftermath*, ed. Peter Cole and Brian McQuinn (New York: Oxford University Press, 2015), 244.

117. M. Dumas, "Southern Libya Awaits Another Spring," Inter Press Service, September 25, 2013, http://www.ipsnews.net/2013/09/southern-libya-awaits-another-spring/ (accessed May 15, 2018); Borzou Daragahi, "Libya's Badlands," *Financial Times*, January 10, 2014, https://www.ft.com/content/e5881820-78c4-11e3-a148-00144feabdc0 .

118. Matteo Capasso and Igor Cherstich, "The Libyan Event and the Part for the Whole," *Middle East Critique* 23.4 (2014): 383

119. Matteo Capasso and Karim Mezran, "The Idea of the Islamic State in Libyan Politics since Independence," *Storia del pensiero politico* 3 (2014): 423–438.

## Chapter 4

1. For visuals, see South Yemen Officials Form Breakaway Council to Defy Hadi," Middle East Eye, May 12, 2017, http://www.middleeasteye.net/news/south-yemen-forms-own-leadership-defiance-hadi-1347164242 (accessed May 23, 2018).

2. On the health crisis in Aden, see Zeyad Sallami et al., "Impact of the Armed Conflict of 2015–2016 in Aden on Health Services and the Availability of Medicines," *Health* 9.4 (2017): 685–696.

3. Kevin Davis, "From Collective Memory to Nationalism: Historical Remembrance in Aden" (MA thesis, Georgetown University, 2014), 32–33. For more on Khormakasar as a "new" district in Aden, see Susanne Dahlgren, *Contesting Realities: The Public Sphere and Morality in Southern Yemen* (Syracuse, NY: Syracuse University Press, 2010), 35, 51–54.

4. For the Arabic text of the Aden Historic Declaration, see Qiyada janubiyya bi'raisa al-luwa aydarous zubaidi yudeer shu'un al-janub" [Southern Command headed by Major General Aidarous Zubaidi manages affairs of the south], http://tajaden.org/spot/4622.html (accessed June 14, 2017). For English, see . http://www.southernhirak.org/2017/06/aden-historic-declaration.html (accessed July 31, 2017).

‹

5. Lisa Wedeen, *Peripheral Visions: Publics, Power, and Performance in Yemen* (Chicago: University of Chicago Press, 2009). See also Robert Burrowes, "The Republic of Yemen: The Politics of Unification and Civil War, 1989–1995," in *The Middle East Dilemma: The Politics and Economics of Arab Integration*, ed. Michael C. Hudson (New York: Columbia University Press, 1999), 188–189.

6. On geology and tectonics, see William Bosworth, Philippe Huchon, and Ken McClay, "The Red Sea and Gulf of Aden Basins," *Journal of African Earth Sciences* 43.1 (2005): 334–378; Ian Davison et al., "Geological Evolution of the Southeastern Red Sea Rift Margin, Republic of Yemen," *Geological Society of America Bulletin* 106.11 (1994): 1474–1493.

7. For a description of the geopolitics of the era, see Giancarlo Casale, *The Ottoman Age of Exploration* (New York: Oxford University Press, 2010).

8. J. Richard Blackburn, "The Collapse of Ottoman Authority in Yemen, 968/1560–976/1568," *Die Welt des Islams* 19.1/4 (1979): 119–176.

9. On the British entry to Yemen, see R. J. Gavin, *Aden under British Rule* (New York: Harper & Row, 1975).

10. Paul Dresch, *A History of Modern Yemen* (New York: Cambridge University Press, 2000), 120–123; Linda Boxberger, *On the Edge of Empire: Hadhramawt, Emigration, and the Indian Ocean, 1880s–1930s* (Albany, NY: SUNY Press, 2002), 183, 208.

11. John M. Willis, "Making Yemen Indian: Rewriting the Boundaries of Imperial Arabia," *International Journal of Middle East Studies* 41.1 (2009): 23–38.

12. For discussion of Britain's form of indirect rule, see Susanne Dahlgren, *Contesting Realities*, chapters 2 and 3.

13. Thomas Kühn, "Shaping and Reshaping Colonial Ottomanism: Contesting Boundaries of Difference and Integration in Ottoman Yemen, 1872–1919," *Comparative Studies of South Asia, Africa and the Middle East* 27.2 (2007): 315–331.

14. On nineteenth-century Ottoman rule in Yemen, see Caesar E. Farah, *The Sultan's Yemen: Nineteenth-Century Challenges to Ottoman Rule* (New York: I. B. Tauris, 2002).

15. Robert D. Burrowes, *The Yemen Arab Republic: The Politics of Development, 1962–1986* (New York: Routledge, 2016), 16.

16. Manfred W. Wenner, *Modern Yemen, 1918–1966* (Baltimore, MD: Johns Hopkins University Press, 1967) 50–1, 168.

17. Robin Bidwell, *The Two Yemens* (Boulder, CO: Westview, 1983), 104.

18. Frank W. Brecher, "Charles R. Crane's Crusade for the Arabs, 1919–39," *Middle Eastern Studies* 24.1 (1988): 47; David Hapgood, *Charles R. Crane: The Man Who Bet on People* (Washington, DC: Institute for Current World Affairs, 2001), 78.

19. Wenner, *Modern Yemen*, 75, 158–159, 166.

20. A. Z. al-Abdin, "The Free Yemeni Movement (1940–48) and Its Ideas on Reform," *Middle Eastern Studies* 15.1 (1979): 36–48; Dresch, *History of Modern Yemen*, 56–58.

21. On the role of the United Nations, see King-Yuh Chang, "The United Nations and Decolonization: The Case of Southern Yemen," *International Organization* 26.1 (1972): 37–61.

22. Alexander Knysh, "The Cult of Saints in Hadramawt: An Overview," *New Arabian Studies* 1 (1993): 137–152; Abdalla S. Bujra, "Political Conflict and Stratification in Hadramaut—I: Nationalism and the Yemeni Revolution: Their Effects on Hadramaut," *Middle Eastern Studies* 3:4 (1967): 355–375.

23. Spencer Mawby, *British Policy in Aden and the Protectorates, 1955–67: Last Outpost of a Middle East Empire* (New York: Routledge, 2005), 39.

24. For a survey of the complicated politics of the era, see Fred Halliday, *Arabia without Sultans* (London: Saqi, 2013).

25. Halliday, *Arabia without Sultans*, 157. See also A. S. Bujra, "Urban Elites and Colonialism: The Nationalist Elites of Aden and South Arabia," *Middle Eastern Studies* 6.2 (1970): 191

26. Mawby, *British Policy in Aden*, 21, 34–43, 100–107.

27. Alec Cumming-Bruce, "Federation of South Arabia (Lecture)," *Journal of the Royal United Service Institution* (1965): 113. For broader discussion of the federation, see Karl Pieragostini, *Britain, Aden and South Arabia: Abandoning Empire* (New York: St. Martin's, 1991).

28. Noel Brehony, "Explaining the Triumph of the National Liberation Front," *Middle Eastern Studies* 53.1 (2017): 37; Bujra, "Urban Elites and Colonialism," 190; Simon C. Smith, "Revolution and Reaction: South Arabia in the Aftermath of the Yemeni Revolution," *Journal of Imperial and Commonwealth History* 28.3 (September 1, 2000): 195–196.

29. Pieragostini, *Britain, Aden and South Arabia,* 222

30. Halliday, *Arabia without Sultans,* 218; Helen Lackner, *PDR Yemen: Outpost of Socialist Development in Arabia* (London: Ithaca Press, 1985), 46–47.

31. Wedeen, *Peripheral Visions,* 37, 55.

32. Tareq Y. Ismael and Jacqueline S. Ismael, *The People's Democratic Republic of Yemen: Politics, Economics, and Society: The Politics of Socialist Transformation* (London: Pinter Publishers, 1986), 79–80

33. F. Gregory Gause, "Yemeni Unity: Past and Future," *Middle East Journal* 42.1 (1988): 36–37.

34. Noel Brehony, *Yemen Divided: The Story of a Failed State in South Arabia* (New York: I. B. Tauris, 2011), 41, 74; Lackner, *PDR Yemen,* 59–60.

35. Geraint Hughes, "A Proxy War in Arabia: The Dhofar Insurgency and Cross-Border Raids into South Yemen," *Middle East Journal* 69.1 (2015): 91–104; Richard Schofield, "The Last Missing Fence in the Desert: The Saudi-Yemeni boundary," *Geopolitics and International Boundaries* 1.3 (1996): 247–299.

36. Cited in Lackner, *PDR Yemen,* 60.

37. Brehony, *Yemen Divided,* 74.

38. Lackner, *PDR Yemen,* 61–62; Brehony, *Yemen Divided,* 66–67.

39. Lackner, *PDR Yemen,* 163. For a broad discussion of development under the PDRY, see Ismael and Ismael, *The People's Democratic Republic of Yemen.*

40. Lackner, *PDR Yemen,* 111; Brehony, *Yemen Divided,* 69–71.

41. Brehony, *Yemen Divided,* 69–71.

42. Lackner, *PDR Yemen,* 109–110, 114–118; Norman Cigar, "Islam and the State in South Yemen: The Uneasy Coexistence," *Middle Eastern Studies* 26.2 (1990): 185–203; Dahlgren, *Contesting Realities,* 83–84.

43. Brehony, *Yemen Divided,* 58–59.

44. Brehony, *Yemen Divided,* 70; Norman Cigar, "South Yemen and the USSR: Prospects for the Relationship," *Middle East Journal* 39.4 (1985): 795–796.

45. Brehony, *Yemen Divided,* 75, 93–94.

46. Brehony, *Yemen Divided,* 169–170.

47. On the Soviet-PDRY relationship, see Cigar, "South Yemen and the USSR," 778; Norman Cigar, "Soviet–South Yemeni Relations: The Gorbachev Years," *Journal of South Asian and Middle Eastern Studies* 12.4 (1989): 5–16.

48. Brehony, *Yemen Divided,* 169–170.

49. Yemen President and Vice-President Address Unity Day Ceremony," Republic of Yemen Radio, Sana'a, 0920 GMT, May 22, 1990, from BBC Summary of World Broadcasts, May 24, 1990.

50. Dresch, *History of Modern Yemen,* 135; Sheila Carapico, "The Economic Dimension of Yemeni Unity," *Middle East Report* 184 (1993): 9–14.

51. AliZayn ibn Shanzūr Yāfiʿī, 'Sirāʿ al-muzmin wa-mutaṭallabāt al-khurūj al-āmin: khulāṣah lil-qaḍīyah al-Janūbīyah wa-taḥaddiyāt al-fidrālīyah al-Yamanīyah [The perpetual conflict and objectives beyond security: Summary on the southern issue and the federalist plan in Yemen] (Sana'a: Maktabat Khaldi ibn al-Walid, 2015), chapter 3.

52. Stephen Day, "The Federal Plan in Yemen: History of an Idea and Its Current Development," in *Rebuilding Yemen: Political, Economic and Social Challenges,* ed. Noel Brehony and Saud Al-Sarhan (Berlin: Gerlach Press, 2015), 35.

53. Paul Dresch and Bernard Haykel, "Stereotypes and Political Styles: Islamists and Tribesfolk in Yemen," *International Journal of Middle East Studies* 27.4 (1995): 408.

54. Group Declares 'Holy War' on PDRY 'Pagans,'" FBIS, AFP on April 15, 1990, Document AB1604220190. For a discussion of the tendency to frame the YSP as apostate or atheistic, see Stacey Philbrick Yadav, *Islamists and the State: Legitimacy and Institutions in Yemen and Lebanon* (New York: I. B. Tauris, 2013), chapter 5.

55. Dresch and Haykal, "Stereotypes," 424–425; Victoria Clark, *Yemen: Dancing on the Heads of Snakes* (New Haven, CT: Yale University Press, 2010), 161–163.

56. "A Real Arab Revolution," *New York Times*, May 8, 1993, http://www.nytimes.com/1993/05/08/opinion/a-real-arab-revolution.html.

57. Sheila Carapico, "Elections and Mass Politics in Yemen," *Middle East Report* 185 (1993): 2; Stephen W. Day, *Regionalism and Rebellion in Yemen: A Troubled National Union* (New York: Cambridge University Press, 2012), 118–120.

58. Day, "The Federal Plan," 32.

59. Salih, al-Bid Discuss Present 'Crisis,' " FBIS, MBC Television in Arabic on December 7, 1993, Document NC0812211593.

60. Reform Grouping's Al-Ahmar Rejects Federalism," FBIS, *Asharq al-Awsat*, London, in Arabic on December 8, 1993, Document PM0912155293.

61. Day, *Regionalism and Rebellion*, 126–127.

62. Day, *Regionalism and Rebellion*, 131–133, 148.

63. Brehony, *Yemen Divided*, 196–198; Day, *Regionalism and Rebellion*, 131–133; Ashraf Fouad, "S. Yemen on Diplomatic Offensive to Stop Civil War," Reuters, June 17, 1994.

64. Salih Says Bid and His Supporters Never Believed in Yemeni Unity," BBC World Monitoring, Yemeni Republic Radio, Sana'a, May 26, 1994.

65. Day, *Regionalism and Rebellion*, 130, 137.

66. Day, *Regionalism and Rebellion*, 130, 137.

67. Wedeen, *Peripheral Visions*, 59–63. See also Susanne Dahlgren, "The Snake with a Thousand Heads: The Southern Cause in Yemen," *Middle East Report Online* (2010), https://www.merip.org/mer/mer256/snake-thousand-heads; Day, *Regionalism and Rebellion*, 147–157.

68. Iain Walker,"Hadrami Identities in Saudi Arabia," in *Rebuilding Yemen: Political, Economic and Social Challenges*, ed. Noel Brehony and Saud Al-Sarhan (Berlin: Gerlach Press, 2015), 55; Day, *Regionalism and Rebellion*, 155–157.

69. Sheila Carapico, "Yemen and the Aden-Abyan Islamic Army," *Middle East Report Online* (2000), https://www.merip.org/mero/mero101800.

70. Peter Salisbury, "The Sad Decline of Aden's Once-Thriving Port," *Financial Times*, March 6, 2013.

71. Day, *Regionalism and Rebellion*, 143–151; Human Rights Watch, "Yemen," 1997, https://www.hrw.org/reports/1997/WR97/ME-10.htm (accessed June 13, 2017).

72. Daniel Corstange, *The Price of a Vote in the Middle East* (New York: Cambridge University Press, 2016), 103; Day, *Regionalism and Rebellion*, 146–148.

73. Brehony, *Yemen Divided*, 210–1.

74. Corstange, *Price of a Vote*, 100–101; Shelagh Weir, "A Clash of Fundamentalisms," *Middle East Report Online* (1997), https://www.merip.org/mer/mer204/clash-fundamentalisms.

75. On the Houthis, see Stacey Philbrick Yadav, "Sectarianization, Islamists Republicanism, and International Misrecognition in Yemen," in *Sectarianization: Mapping the New Politics of the Middle East*, ed. Nader Hashemi and Danny Postel (New York: Oxford University Press, 2017), 188–189; Marieke Brandt, *Tribes and Politics in Yemen: A History of the Houthi Conflict* (New York: Oxford University Press, 2017); Jack Freeman, "The al Houthi Insurgency in the North of Yemen: An Analysis of the Shabab al Moumineen," *Studies in Conflict & Terrorism* 32.11 (2009): 1008–1019.

76. Susanne Dahlgren, "The Southern Movement in Yemen," *ISIM Review* 22 (2008): 50–51; Brehony, *Yemen Divided*, 211.

77. International Crisis Group, "Breaking Point? Yemen's Southern Question," Report 114, October 20, 2011, 6, https://www.crisisgroup.org/middle-east-north-africa/gulf-and-arabian-peninsula/yemen/breaking-point-yemen-s-southern-question; Stephen W. Day, *Regionalism and rebellion in Yemen: A troubled national union* (New York: Cambridge University Press, 2012), 227–233.

78. Human Rights Watch, "In the Name of Unity: The Yemeni Government's Brutal Response to Southern Movement Protests," December 15, 2009, 54–56, https://www.hrw.org/report/2009/12/15/name-unity/yemeni-governments-brutal-response-southern-movement-protests.

79. International Crisis Group, "Breaking Point?" 8.

80. Day, *Regionalism and Rebellion,* 267.

81. Human Rights Watch, "In the Name of Unity," 18–19.

82. International Crisis Group, "Breaking Point?" 8; Yāfiʿī, *ʿSirāʿ al-muzmin wa-mutaṭallabāt al-khurūj al-āmin,* chapter 4.

83. Cited in Dahlgren, "The Snake with a Thousand Heads" ; available on YouTube, https://www.youtube.com/watch?v=2YeAw2PRZUc.

84. Brehony, *Yemen Divided,* 201–202; Day, *Regionalism and Resistance,* 247–263; Yemeni Jihadist Leader Joins Southern Movement, Favours Independence," *Asharq al-Awsat,* May 14, 2009, LexisNexis (accessed March 2, 2017).

85. Human Rights Watch, "In the Name of Unity," 23–24.

86. Day, *Regionalism and Rebellion,* 245.

87. For biographical details, see "Hassan Baoum: an-nidhal bi al-kalima wa bi as-sumt" [Hassan Baoum: The struggle with words and with silence], *Al-Arabi,* February 16, 2017, https://www.al-arabi.com/Faces/10459/%D8%AD%D8%B3%D9%86-%D8%A8%D8%A7%D8%B9%D9%88%D9%85-%D8%A7%D9%84%D9%86%D8%B6%D8%A7%D9%84-%D8%A8%D8%A7%D9%84%D9%83%D9%84%D9%85%D8%A9-%D9%88%D8%A8%D8%A7%D9%84%D8%B5%D9%85 (accessed June 12, 2017).

88. Day, *Regionalism and Rebellion,* 246–247, 260–263.

89. Human Rights Watch, "In the Name of Unity," 36.

90. April Longley Alley, "Assessing (In)security after the Arab Spring: The Case of Yemen," *PS: Political Science & Politics* 46.4 (2013): 721–726.

91. Human Rights Watch, "Days of Bloodshed in Aden," March 2011, https://www.hrw.org/sites/default/files/reports/yemen0311webwcover.pdf.

92. International Crisis Group, "Breaking Point?" 9; Day, *Regionalism and Rebellion,* 280; Join Anti-Salih Protests, South Yemen Activists Told," Agence France Presse, March 2, 2011, Factiva (accessed March 15, 2017); Rights Group Says Yemen Used Deadly Force in Aden." Voice of America Press Releases and Documents, March 9, 2011, Factiva (accessed March 15, 2017).

93. International Crisis Group, "Yemen's Southern Question: Avoiding a Breakdown," Report 145, September 25, 2013, 11–12, https://www.crisisgroup.org/middle-east-north-africa/gulf-and-arabian-peninsula/yemen/yemen-s-southern-question-avoiding-breakdown (accessed May 22, 2018).

94. Yemen's Separatists Stage Anti-Election Rallies amid Violence," Xinhua News Agency, February 16, 2012, Factiva (accessed March 15, 2017).

95. Yemen Election Ends Saleh's 33-Year Rule," al-Jazeera, February 21, 2012, http://www.aljazeera.com/news/middleeast/2012/02/201222117511739757.html (accessed June 6, 2017); USAID, "IFES Yemen Survey Briefing Report," April 2012, https://www.ifes.org/sites/default/files/ifes_yemen_march_survey_final_report_jm_dm_sm_jm2_bd_sm_2.pdf (accessed June 6, 2017).

96. Peter Salisbury, "Southern Movement Stages Mass Rally in Yemen," al-Jazeera, October 14, 2014, http://www.aljazeera.com/news/middleeast/2014/10/southern-movement-stages-mass-rally-yemen-20141014113118895623.html; Abdulkawi Mohammed Rashad Al-Shabei to the Yemen Times: The Southern Movement Was the First One to Reject Injustice and Humiliation," *Yemen Times,* January 21, 2013, Factiva (accessed March 15, 2017); Anne-Linda Amira Augustin, "'Spaces in the Making': Peripheralization and Spatial Injustice in Southern Yemen," *Middle East—Topics & Arguments* 5 (2015): 47–55; Ibrahim Fraihat, *Unfinished Revolutions: Yemen, Libya, and Tunisia after the Arab Spring* (New Haven, CT: Yale University Press, 2016), 42–43, 237.

97. Walker, "Hadrami Identities," 54–55.

98. "Unrest in Hadramout: 'We Hold the State Accountable,'" *Yemen Times,* December 31, 2013, Factiva (accessed March 15, 2017).

99. Of 565 NDC seats, 112 went to the GPC, 50 to Islah, 35 to the Houthis. Additionally, each part was required to have at least 50 percent of its delegates from the south. See ICG, "Yemen's Southern Question," 3; Erica Gaston, "Process Lessons Learned in Yemen's National Dialogue," US Institute of Peace Special Report 342, February 2014, https://

www.usip.org/sites/default/files/SR342_Process-Lessons-Learned-in-Yemens-National-Dialogue.pdf (accessed May 22, 2018).

100. Tanja Granzow, "Violent vs. Non-Violent Struggle: Investigating the Impact of Frames on Movement Strategies in Yemen," *Civil Wars* 17.2 (2015): 174; for video, see https://www.youtube.com/watch?v=15HALdkuIbo.

101. Tobias Thiel, "Yemen's Imposed Federal Boundaries," *Middle East Report Online* (2015), https://www.merip.org/yemens-imposed-federal-boundaries; Day, "The Federal Plan," 24–25, 34; Fraihat, *Unfinished Revolutions*, 42–43, 237.

102. Anne-Linda Amira Augustin, "'Tawra Tawra Yā Ğanūb': Slogans as Means of Expression of the South Arabian Independence Struggle," in *Romano-Arabica XV: Graffiti, Writing and Street Art in the Arab World* (Bucharest: University of Bucharest Center for Arab Studies, 2015), 49.

103. Granzow, "Violent versus Non-Violent," 174–175.

104. Augustin, "Slogans as Means of Expression," 49, 53.

105. Day, "The Federal Plan," 32; Fraihat, *Unfinished Revolutions*, 48–50

106. The Houthis, too, rejected the 4+2 plan. See Theil, "Yemen's Imposed Federal Borders"; Fraihat, *Unfinished Revolutions*, 46–47; Peter Salisbury, "Yemen's Southerners See Hope in Houthis' Rise," al-Jazeera, October 20, 2014, http://www.aljazeera.com/news/middleeast/2014/10/yemen-southerners-see-hope-houthis-rise-2014102052535893759.html (accessed June 12, 2017).

107. Yadav, "Sectarianization," 196–197.

108. Day, "The Federal Plan," 33; Fraihat, *Unfinished Revolutions*, 48–50; Haykal Bafna, "Hadhramaut: Rebellion, Federalism, or Independence in Yemen," Muftah, April 22, 2014, https://muftah.org/hadhramaut-rebellion-federalism-independence/#.WX81IseGM2x (accessed July 31, 2017).

109. Fraihat, *Unfinished Revolutions*, 48–50.

110. Arab Central Banks Endorse Relocation of Yemen's Central Bank," *Asharq al-Awsat*, September 23, 2016, https://english.aawsat.com/asharq-al-awsat-english/news-middle-east/arab-central-banks-endorse-relocation-yemens-central-bank (accessed June 8, 2017).

111. AFP, "Hadi Appoints Aidarus Al Zubaidi Governor of Aden," December 8, 2015, http://www.emirates247.com/news/region/hadi-appoints-aidarus-al-zubaidi-governor-of-aden-2015-12-08-1.613188 (accessed June 8, 2017).

112. For more on Bin Brik, see Laurant Bonnefoy, "Sunni Islamist Dynamics in Context of War: What Happened to al-Islah and the Salafis?" in *Politics, Governance, and Reconstruction in Yemen*, POMEPS Studies 29, January 2018, 23–26, https://pomeps.org/wp-content/uploads/2018/02/POMEPS_Studies_29_Yemen_Web-REV.pdf (accessed May 23, 2018).

113. Fuad Rajeh and Tamsin Carlisle, "South Yemen Separatists Vow to Escalate Protests if Oil, Gas Exports Continue," *Platts Commodity News*, October 16, 2014.

114. Abigail Fielding-Smith, "Kidnapped and Never Seen Again: UAE Accused of Forced Disappearances in Yemen," Bureau for Investigative Journalism, June 8, 2017, https://www.thebureauinvestigates.com/stories/2017-06-08/disappearance-and-torture-uae-forces-accused-of-widespread-abuse-in-yemen (accessed June 11, 2017); Human Rights Watch, "Yemen: UAE Backs Abusive Local Forces," June 22, 2017, https://www.hrw.org/news/2017/06/22/yemen-uae-backs-abusive-local-forces (accessed May 23, 2018).

115. On the rumors, see Augustin, "'Spaces in the Making,'" 3. On repression, see Al Hakm al-fa'ily fi 'aden Hani bin breik" [The real ruler of Aden, Hani bin Brik], Yemennewsgate, May 3, 2016 http://www.yemennewsgate.net/news19174.html (accessed June 7, 2017; Ashraf al-Falahi, "Why Yemen May Not Be Heading for a Split," *Al-Monitor*, February 10, 2016, http://www.al-monitor.com/pulse/originals/2016/02/yemen-president-hadi-southern-mobility-movement-secession.html (accessed June 7, 2017); "Muaskar 20 fi 'aden" [Camp 20 in Aden], *al-Arabi*, May 19, 2017, https://www.alaraby.co.uk/politics/2017/5/18/%D9%85%D8%B9%D8%B3%D9%83%D8%B1-20-%D9%81%D9%8A-%D8%B9%D8%AF%D9%86-%D8%B3%D9%84%D9%88%D9%83%D8%AF%D8%A7%D8%B9%D8%B4%D9%8A-%D8%A8%D8%B1%D8%B3%D9%85-%D8%A7%D9%84%D8%AD%D8%B2%D8%A7%D9%85-%D8%A7%D9%84%D8%A3%D9%85%D9%86%D9%8A-1 (accessed June 8, 2017).

116. "Hisar dukhul al-qat ila 'aden bi yomieen fi al-usbua'…I'mara al-awal fi 26 'ama" [Restricting the entry of *qat* to Aden to weekends…the first time in 26 years], *Al-Hayat*, May 15, 2016, http://www.alhayat.com/Articles/15616188/صرخدولالدقا ….

117. "UAE Donates 50 Generators to Yemeni Authorities," *Construction Week Online*, July 18, 2016, http://www.constructionweekonline.com/article-40085-uae-donates-50-generators-to-yemeni-authorities/ (accessed June 19, 2017).

118. Haykal Bafna, "Hadhramaut: Rebellion, Federalism, or Independence in Yemen," Muftah, April 22, 2014, https://muftah.org/hadhramaut-rebellion-federalism-independence/#.WX81IseGM2x (accessed July 31, 2017).

119. Yara Bayoumy, Noah Browning, and Mohammed Ghobari, "How Saudi Arabia's War in Yemen Has Made al Qaeda Stronger—and Richer," Reuters, April 8, 2017, https://www.reuters.com/investigates/special-report/yemen-aqap/.

120. Saeed Al-Batati, "Yemen: The Truth behind al-Qaeda's Takeover of Mukalla," al-Jazeera. September 16, 2015, http://www.aljazeera.com/news/2015/09/yemen-truth-al-qaeda-takeover-mukalla-150914101527567.html (accessed May 23, 2018); International Crisis Group, "Yemen's al-Qaeda: Expanding the Base," Report 174 (February 2, 2017), https://www.crisisgroup.org/middle-east-north-africa/gulf-and-arabian-peninsula/yemen/174-yemen-s-al-qaeda-expanding-base (accessed May 23, 2018).

121. Michael Horton, "AQAP in Southern Yemen: Learning, Adapting and Growing," *Jamestown Foundation Terrorism Monitor* 14.2 (2016): 7–11, https://jamestown.org/program/aqap-southern-yemen-learning-adapting-growing/ (accessed June 8, 2017).

122. "Hani bin brek al-wazir al-aqwa fi al-'asimah 'aden mahal at-tahqeeq…" [Hani Bin Brik is the strongest minister in the capital Aden, reveals an investigation], *Yemen Press*, April 28, 2017, http://yemen-press.com/news95615.html (accessed June 12, 2017).

123. For Arabic text of the Aden Historic Declaration, see Qiyada janubiyya bi'raisa al-luwa aydarous zubaidi yudeer shu'un al-janub" [Southern Command headed by Major General Aidarous Zubaidi manages affairs of the south], http://tajaden.org/spot/4622.html (accessed June 14, 2017).

124. Aden Historic Declaration, Article 1.

125. "Al-A'laf yuthahroon l'mutaliba lil istiqlal al-junub" [Thousands demonstrate demanding independence for the South], *As-safir*, May 22, 2017, http://assafir.com/article/351678 (accessed June 8, 2017); Susan Dahlgren, "Popular Revolutions Advances toward State Building in Southern Yemen," in *Politics, Governance, and Reconstruction in Yemen*, POMEPS Studies 29, January 2018, 17–22, https://pomeps.org/wp-content/uploads/2018/02/POMEPS_Studies_29_Yemen_Web-REV.pdf (accessed May 23, 2018).

126. Saeed al-Batati, "One Yemeni Governor Wants Trump to Know: You're Fighting al Qaeda All Wrong," *Foreign Policy*, June 8, 2017, http://foreignpolicy.com/2017/06/06/one-yemeni-governor-wants-trump-to-know-youre-fighting-al-qaeda-all-wrong/ (accessed June 19, 2017); Dahlgren, "Popular Revolutions Advances toward State Building in Southern Yemen," 18.

127. "Tayar za'im al-junubi yatabra' min 'alan 'aden at-tarikhi" [The southern leader Hassan Baoum disavows the Aden Historic Declaration], *Al-Mashhad al-Yemeni al-Awal*, May 4, 2017, http://www.almshhadalyemeni.com/40070# (accessed June 12, 2017).

128. Aden Declaration, Article IV.

129. "GCC: Aden-Based Southern Transitional Council 'Doomed to Fail,'" *The New Arab*, May 16, 2017, https://www.alaraby.co.uk/english/news/2017/5/16/gcc-aden-based-southern-transitional-council-doomed-to-fail (accessed May 16, 2018).

130. Dahlgren, "Popular Revolutions Advances toward State Building in Southern Yemen," 18.

131. Augustin, "Slogans as Means of Expression," 49, 53.

132. The logical flaws of this sectarian perspective are manifest. Saleh was of Zaydi descent but had been a fierce foe to the Houthis during the Saadeh war and turned against them again in 2017. Similarly, many tribes aligned with the Houthi not out of ideological conviction but because of local rivalries and because of harms suffered at the hands of the central government. For their part, Houthis claimed that their military campaign aimed to save Yemen from American domination and the scourge of Sunni jihadists.

133. Lisa Wedeen, "Seeing like a Citizen, Acting like a State: Exemplary Events in Unified Yemen," *Comparative Studies in Society and History* 45.4 (2003): 680–713.


## Chapter 5

1. Isabel Coles and Ali A. Nabhan, "Iraqi Kurds Vote in Independence Referendum Despite Warnings from Baghdad, U.S.," *Wall Street Journal*, September 25, 2017. https://www.wsj.com/articles/iraqi-kurds-vote-in-independence-referendum-despite-warnings-from-baghdad-u-s-1506328499.

2. Campbell Macdiarmid, "'I Want to Die in the Shadow of the Flag of an Independent Kurdistan," *Foreign Policy*, June 15, 2017, http://foreignpolicy.com/2017/06/15/i-want-to-die-in-the-shadow-of-the-flag-of-an-independent-kurdistan/ (accessed April 15, 2018).

3. Martin Chulov, "Kurdish Independence Closer than Ever, Says Massoud Barzani," *Guardian*, January 22, 2016, https://www.theguardian.com/world/2016/jan/22/kurdish-independence-closer-than-ever-says-massoud-barzani.

4. Iraqi Kurd Leader Slams Sykes-Picot 'Catastrophic' Deal," Anadolu Agency, May 16, 2016, InfoTrac Newsstand, http://link.galegroup.com/apps/doc/A452455455/STND?u=viva_vpi&sid=STND&xid=de93e5c2 (accessed March 19, 2018.

5. Ari Khalidi, "Kurds Do Not Need A State: PKK Leader," *Kurdistan24*, June 20, 2017, http://www.kurdistan24.net/en/news/ebeff9b0-893d-4893-9514-c76496cdb746 (accessed June 1, 2018); Sangar Ali, "PKK Leader: Referendum a Democratic Right, No One Should Stand against It," *Kurdistan24*, June 13, 2017, http://www.kurdistan24.net/en/news/1ba4d164-3e06-431d-9a14-e83370cb869a (accessed June 1, 2018).

6. "Kurds in Rojava Show Support for Kurdistan Region Referendum," *Rudaw*, September 26, 2017, http://www.rudaw.net/english/middleeast/syria/26092017.

7. "Iran's Kurds Are Growing Restless, Too," *Economist*, September 30, 2017, https://www.economist.com/news/middle-east-and-africa/21729790-referendum-held-iraqi-kurds-revving-up-their-iranian-cousins-irans-kurds.

8. Dina al-Shibeeb, "Big 'Yes' from Kurdish Diaspora Likely in Independence Vote," *al-Arabiya*, September 25, 2017, http://english.alarabiya.net/en/perspective/features/2017/09/25/Big-yes-from-Kurdish-diaspora-likely-in-independence-vote.html; Baxtiyar Goran, "Kurdistan Diaspora March for Independence Referendum in Geneva, Vienna, Oslo, San Diego," *Kurdistan24*, September 10, 2017, http://www.kurdistan24.net/en/news/e4d1e117-1806-4e11-9fc7-42f401559e95.

9. Sherif Pasha, "Memorandum on the Claims of the Kurd People," *International Journal of Kurdish Studies* 15.1/2 (2001): 131.

10. Maria T. O'Shea, "Between the Map and the Reality: Some Fundamental Myths of Kurdish Nationalism," *Peuples Méditerranéens* 68–69 (1994): 173.

11. Denise Natali, *The Kurds and the State: Evolving National Identity in Iraq, Turkey, and Iran* (Syracuse, NY: Syracuse University Press, 2005), xvii; H. Akin Ünver, "Schrödinger's Kurds: Transnational Kurdish Geopolitics in the Age of Shifting Borders," *Journal of International Affairs* 69.2 (2016): 67–70.

12. Turan Keskin, "The Impact of the Arab Uprisings on the Kurds," in *Authoritarianism in the Middle East: Before and after the Arab Uprisings*, ed. J. Karakoç Bakis and Jülide Karakoç (New York: St. Martin's, 2015), 127–149.

13. Rupert Emerson, "Self-determination," *American Journal of International Law* 65.3 (1971): 459–475; Eduard Beneš, "The Position of the Small Nation in Post-War Europe," *American Journal of Sociology* 49.5 (1944): 390–396; Benyamin Neuberger, "National Self-determination: Dilemmas of a Concept," *Nations and Nationalism* 1.3 (1995): 297–325.

14. Martin van Bruinessen, "Nationalisme kurde et ethnicités intra-kurdes," *Peuples Méditerranéens* 68–69 (1994): 11–37; Philip G. Kreyenbroek, "On the Kurdish Language," in *The Kurds*, ed. Philip G. Kreyenbroek and Stefan Sperl (London: Routledge, 2005), 62–73; Amir Hassanpour, "The Indivisibility of the Nation and Its Linguistic Divisions," *International Journal of the Sociology of Language* 217 (2012): 49–73.

15. Resat Kasaba, *A Moveable Empire: Ottoman Nomads, Migrants, and Refugees* (Seattle: University of Washington Press, 2011); Michael Eppel, *A People without a State: The Kurds from the Rise of Islam to the Dawn of Nationalism* (Austin: University of Texas Press, 2016), 239–251.

16. Eppel, *A People without a State*, 239; David McDowall, *A Modern History of the Kurds* (New York: I. B. Tauris, 2003), 51–53.

17. Eppel, *A People without a State*, 248–251.

18. McDowall, *Modern History of the Kurds*, 53.

19. For discussion of the Hamidiyya, see Janet Klein, *The Margins of Empire: Kurdish Militias in the Ottoman Tribal Zone* (Stanford, CA: Stanford University Press, 2011).

20. Joyce Blau and Yasir Suleiman, "Language and Ethnic Identity in Kurdistan: An Historical Overview," in *Language and Identity in the Middle East and North Africa*, ed. Yasir Suleiman (New York: Routledge, 2013), 153–164.

21. John Limbert, "The Origins and Appearance of the Kurds in Pre-Islamic Iran," *Iranian Studies* 1.2 (1968): 41–51; Mahmud Omidsalar, "Kāva," *Encyclopaedia Iranica*, http://www.iranicaonline.org/articles/kava-hero (accessed May 16, 2018).

22. Janet Klein, "Kurdish Nationalists and Non-Nationalist Kurdists: Rethinking Minority Nationalism and the Dissolution of the Ottoman Empire, 1908–1909," *Nations and Nationalism* 13.1 (2007): 137–138, 142–143.

23. Hakan Özoğlu, "'Nationalism' and Kurdish Notables in the Late Ottoman–Early Republican Era," *International Journal of Middle East Studies* 33.3 (2001): 386.

24. V. Minorsky, "Sulaymāniyya," in *Encyclopaedia of Islam, Second Edition*, ed. P. Bearman, Th. Bianquis, C. E. Bosworth, E. van Donzel, and W. P. Heinrichs, http://dx.doi.org/10.1163/1573-3912_islam_COM_1113.

25. Wadie Jwaideh, *The Kurdish National Movement: Its Origins and Development* (Syracuse, NY: Syracuse University Press, 2006), 197–198; Natali, *The Kurds and the State*, 30–31.

26. Cecil John Edmonds, "Kurdish Nationalism," *Journal of Contemporary History* 6.1 (1971): 96.

27. Jordi Tejel Gorgas, "Urban Mobilization in Iraqi Kurdistan during the British Mandate: Sulaimaniya, 1918–30," *Middle Eastern Studies* 44.4 (2008): 540; Eden Naby, "The First Kurdish Periodical in Iran," *International Journal of Kurdish Studies* 20.1/2 (2006): 215–235.

28. David E. Omissi, *Air Power and Colonial Control: The Royal Air Force, 1919–1939* (Manchester: Manchester University Press, 1990), chapter 2; Priya Satia, "The Defense of Inhumanity: Air Control and the British Idea of Arabia," *American Historical Review* 111.1 (2006): 16–51.

29. Natali, *The Kurds and the State*, 37.

30. Sherko Kirmanj, "Kurdish History Textbooks: Building a Nation-State within a Nation-State," *Middle East Journal* 68.3 (2014): 370.

31. Denise Natali, *The Kurdish Quasi-State: Development and Dependency in Post–Gulf War Iraq* (Syracuse, NY: Syracuse University Press, 2010), 5–10; Michiel Leezenberg, "Urbanization, Privatization, and Patronage: The Political Economy of Iraqi Kurdistan," in *The Kurds: Nationalism and Politics*, ed. Faleh Abd al-Jabar and Hosham Dawod (London: Saqi, 2006), 155–156.

32. Arbella Bet-Shlimon, "The Politics and Ideology of Urban Development in Iraq's Oil City: Kirkuk, 1946–58," *Comparative Studies of South Asia, Africa and the Middle East* 33.1 (2013): 26–40.

33. Martin van Bruinessen, *Agha, Shaikh and State: The Social and Political Structures of Kurdistan* (London: Zed, 1992), 190.

34. Amir Hassanpour, "State Policy on the Kurdish Language: The Politics of Status Planning," *Kurdish Times* 4 (1991): 43–50.

35. On minority treaties, see Blanche E. C. Dugdale and Wyndham A. Bewes, "The Working of the Minority Treaties," *Journal of the British Institute of International Affairs* (1926): 79–95; Leonard Smith, *Sovereignty at the Paris Peace Conference of 1919* (New York: Cambridge University Press, 2018), 240–250.

36. Edmonds, "Kurdish Nationalism," 94–95; Sarah Shields, "Mosul, the Ottoman legacy and the League of Nations," *International Journal of Contemporary Iraqi Studies* 3.2 (2009): 217–

230; Susan Pedersen, "Getting Out of Iraq—in 1932: The League of Nations and the Road to Normative Statehood," *American Historical Review* 115.4 (2010): 975–1000; Peter Sluglett, *Britain in Iraq: Contriving King and Country* (New York: I. B. Tauris, 2007), 129–131, 150–151.

37. Andrew Mango, "Atatürk and the Kurds," *Middle Eastern Studies* 35.4 (1999): 1–25; Ugur Ümit Üngör, *The Making of Modern Turkey: Nation and State in Eastern Anatolia, 1913–1950* (New York: Oxford University Press, 2012).

38. For an overview of the repression in Turkey, see McDowall, *Modern History of the Kurds*, 186–211. For specific cases, see Robert Olson, "The Kurdish Rebellions of Sheikh Said (1925), Mt. Ararat (1930), and Dersim (1937–8): Their Impact on the Development of the Turkish Air Force and on Kurdish and Turkish Nationalism," *Die Welt des Islams* 40.1 (2000): 67–94.

39. On the issue of minorities in the French mandate, see Benjamin Thomas White, *The Emergence of Minorities in the Middle East: The Politics of Community in French Mandate Syria* (Edinburgh: Edinburgh University Press, 2011). For general discussion of French policies, see Philip Shukry Khoury, *Syria and the French Mandate: The Politics of Arab Nationalism, 1920–1945* (Princeton, NJ: Princeton University Press, 2014).

40. Eva Savelsberg, "The Syrian-Kurdish Movements: Obstacles rather than Driving Forces for Democratization," in *Conflict, Democratization, and the Kurds in the Middle East*, ed. David Romano and Mehmet Gurses (New York: Palgrave Macmillan, 2014), 88.

41. Ismet Cheriff Vanly, "The Kurds in Syria and Lebanon," in *The Kurds*, ed. Philip G. Kreyenbroek and Stefan Sperl (New York: Routledge, 2005), 141, 148–149.

42. Savelsburg, "The Syrian-Kurdish Movements," 87; Harriet Allsopp, *The Kurds of Syria: Political Parties and Identity in the Middle East* (New York: I. B. Tauris, 2016), 58–59; Jordi Tejel Gorgas, "The Terrier Plan and the Emergence of a Kurdish Policy under the French Mandate in Syria, 1926–1936," *International Journal of Kurdish Studies* 21.1/2 (2007): 93.

43. Gorgas, "The Terrier Plan," 99–100; Vanly, "The Kurds in Syria and Lebanon," 149; Jordi Tejel, *Syria's Kurds: History, Politics and Society* (New York: Routledge, 2008), 18–19.

44. Daniel Neep, *Occupying Syria under the French Mandate: Insurgency, Space and State Formation* (New York: Cambridge University Press, 2012), 142–145; Savelsberg, "The Syrian-Kurdish Movements," 87–89; Allsopp, *The Kurds of Syria*, 58–59. On cultural efforts, see Jordi Tejel Gorgas, "The Kurdish Cultural Movement in Mandatory Syria and Lebanon: An Unfinished Project of 'National Renaissance,' 1932–46," *Iranian Studies* 47.5 (2014): 839–855.

45. Tejel, *Syria's Kurds*, 34–36.

46. This novel claim required recruiting Iran's Lurs and Bakhtiaris as branches of the Kurdish nation.

47. O'Shea, "Between the Map and Reality," 176, 181. See also Zeynep Kaya, "Maps into Nations: Kurdistan, Kurdish Nationalism and International Society" (PhD thesis, London School of Economics and Political Science, 2012).

48. Tejel, *Syria's Kurds*, 42; Borhanedin Yassin, *Vision or Reality? The Kurds in the Policy of the Great Powers, 1941–1947* (Lund: Lund University Press, 1995), 159–160.

49. Adeeb Khalid, "Backwardness and the Quest for Civilization: Early Soviet Central Asia in Comparative Perspective," *Slavic Review* 65.2 (2006): 231–251.

50. Nader Entessar, *Kurdish Politics in the Middle East* (Lanham, MD: Lexington Books, 2009), 22–24; Yassin, *The Kurds in the Policy of the Great Powers*, 144–148.

51. Yassin, *The Kurds in the Policy of the Great Powers*, 152–153, 159–160.

52. William Eagleton, *The Kurdish Republic of 1946* (London: Oxford University Press, 1963), 62–63; Entessar, *Kurdish Politics in the Middle East*, 25.

53. Edmonds, "Kurdish Nationalism," 99; Jwaideh, *The Kurdish Nationalist Movement*, 253; Yassin, *The Kurds in the Policy of the Great Powers*, 163; Eagleton, *The Kurdish Republic of 1946*, 91.

54. Edmonds, "Kurdish Nationalism," 95; Olson, "Kurdish Rebellions," 403.

55. Yassin, *The Kurds in the Policy of the Great Powers*, 167–169, 172–180; Jwaideh, *The Kurdish Nationalist Movement*, 253–254.

56. On the larger geopolitical dimensions of the crisis, see Louise Fawcett, *Iran and the Cold War: The Azerbaijan Crisis of 1946* (New York: Cambridge University Press, 2009); Stephen L. McFarland, "A Peripheral View of the Origins of the Cold War: The Crises in Iran, 1941–47," *Diplomatic History* 4.4 (1980): 333–352.

57. Yassin, *The Kurds in the Policy of the Great Powers*, 215–217.

58. Jwaideh, *The Kurdish Nationalist Movement*, 260–263; Yassin, *The Kurds in the Policy of the Great Powers*, 153, 211–212; Eagleton, *The Kurdish Republic of 1946*, 121–122.

59. Allsop, *The Kurds of Syria*, 59–61; Savelsberg, "The Syrian-Kurdish Movements," 89.

60. Peter Fragiskatos, "The Stateless Kurds in Syria: Problems and Prospects for the Ajanib and Maktumin Kurds," *International Journal of Kurdish Studies* 21.1/2 (2007), fn. 3; Gary C. Gambill, "The Kurdish Reawakening in Syria," *Middle East Intelligence Bulletin* 6.4 (2004): 5; Hanna Batatu, *Syria's Peasantry, the Descendants of its Lesser Rural Notables, and Their Politics* (Princeton, NJ: Princeton University Press, 1999), 119–120.

61. Gambill, "The Kurdish Reawakening in Syria."

62. Vanly, "The Kurds in Syria and Lebanon," 151.

63. Fragiskatos, "The Stateless Kurds in Syria," 112; Kerim Yildiz, *The Kurds in Syria: The Forgotten People* (Ann Arbor, MI: Pluto Press, 2005), 33.

64. Gambill, "The Kurdish Reawakening in Syria."

65. Yildiz, *The Kurds in Syria*, 36–37. For more on agricultural reform, see Raymond A. Hinnebusch, *Peasant and Bureaucracy in Ba'thist Syria: The Political Economy of Rural Development* (Boulder, CO: Westview, 1989); Robert Springborg, "Baathism in Practice: Agriculture, Politics, and Political Culture in Syria and Iraq," *Middle Eastern Studies* 17.2 (1981): 191–209.

66. Middle East Watch, *Syria Unmasked: The Suppression of Human Rights by the Assad Regime* (New Haven, CT: Yale University Press, 1991), 98–99.

67. On the PKK in Turkey, see Aysegul Aydin and Cem Emrence, *Zones of Rebellion: Kurdish Insurgents and the Turkish State* (Ithaca, NY: Cornell University Press, 2015).

68. Yildiz, *The Kurds in Syria*, 58; Tejel, *Syria's Kurds*, 78.

69. Ofra Bengio, *Saddam's Word: Political Discourse in Iraq* (New York: Oxford University Press, 1998), 112.

70. "Program and Administrative Regulations of the Democratic Party of Kurdistan (1960)," *Middle East Journal* 15.4 (1961): 445.

71. Edmund Ghareeb, *The Kurdish Question in Iraq* (Syracuse, NY: Syracuse University Press, 1981), 39–40; Natali, *The Kurds and the State*, 41–50.

72. McDowall, *Modern History of the Kurds*, 306–310; Avshalom H. Rubin, "Abd al-Karim Qasim and the Kurds of Iraq: Centralization, Resistance and Revolt, 1958–63," *Middle Eastern Studies* 43.3 (2007): 353–382.

73. On military performance, see Kenneth M. Pollack, *Arabs at War: Military Effectiveness, 1948–1991* (Lincoln: University of Nebraska Press, 2004), 156–180.

74. Martin Van Bruinesses, "Kurds, States, and Tribes," in *Tribes and Power: Nationalism and Ethnicity in the Middle East*, ed. Faleh Abdul Jabar and Hosham Dawod (London: Saqi, 2003), 172–173; McDowall, *Modern History of the Kurds*, 312, 355–357.

75. Liam Anderson and Gareth Stansfield, *Crisis in Kirkuk: The Ethnopolitics of Conflict and Compromise* (Philadelphia: University of Pennsylvania Press, 2009), 34–40.

76. Ghareeb, *The Kurdish Question*, 40; Natali, *The Kurds and the State*, 52–55. For a description of the impact of leftism on the new generation of Kurdish nationalism, see Jalal Talebani's interview in "Iraqi President Interviewed on Early Political Life, Memories—Part 3," BBC World Monitoring, *Asharq al-Awsat* website on August 11, 2009, Document 12A24EF1C9AE8018. Iraqi Kurdish PUK Leader Talabani Says 'Kirkuk Is Jerusalem of Kurdistan,'" BBC Monitoring, Kurdistani Nuwe, Al-Sulaymaniyah, on December 26, 2001, Document 0F97A79187E689E0.

77. Ghareeb, *The Kurdish Question*, 58–64; McDowall, *Modern History of the Kurds*, 317–324.

78. Bengio, *Saddam's Word*, 110–112.

79. Kirmanj, "Kurdish History Textbooks," 370.

80. Ofra Bengio, *The Kurds of Iraq: Building a State within a State* (Boulder, CO: Lynne Rienner Publishers, 2012), 51–55.

81. Ghareeb, *The Kurdish Question*, 73–78, 88, 112–114; Yaniv Voller, "Identity and the Ba'th Regime's Campaign against Kurdish Rebels in Northern Iraq," *Middle East Journal* 71.3 (2017): 389–390; McDowall, *Modern History of the Kurds*, 327; Anderson and Stansfield, *Crisis in Kirkuk*, 28–29.

82. Voller, "Identity and the Ba'th Regime's Campaign against Kurdish Rebels in Northern Iraq," 391–396.

83. Saad B. Eskander, "Fayli Kurds of Baghdad and the Ba'ath Regime," In *The Kurds: Nationalism and Politics*, ed. Faleh Abd al-Jabar and Hosham Dawod (London: Saqi Books, 2006), 180–202.

84. Ghareeb, *The Kurdish Question*, 112–114.

85. Ghareeb, *The Kurdish Question*, 133–134.

86. Bengio, *Saddam's Word*, 114.

87. Ghareeb, *The Kurdish Question*, 147–149, 156; McDowall, *Modern History of the Kurds*, 334

88. Ghareeb, *The Kurdish Question*, 151.

89. McDowall, *Modern History of the Kurds*, 337–338; Ghareeb, *The Kurdish Question*, 158–159.

90. Ghareeb, *The Kurdish Question*, 9, 175–176.

91. McDowall, *Modern History of the Kurds*, 335–340; Ghareeb, *The Kurdish Question*, 162–165.

92. Ghareeb, *The Kurdish Question*, 176–178; Natali, *The Kurds and the State*, 56–58.

93. Ghareeb, *The Kurdish Question*, 181–183; McDowall, *Modern History of the Kurds*, 344–346.

94. Dina Rizk Khoury, *Iraq in Wartime: Soldiering, Martyrdom, and Remembrance* (New York: Cambridge University Press, 2013), 110–122; McDowall, *Modern History of the Kurds*, 340. For a broader discussion of authoritarian modernization in Iraqi Kurdistan, see Leszek Dzięgiel, *Rural Community of Contemporary Iraqi Kurdistan Facing Modernization* (Krakow: Agricultural Academy in Krakow, Institute of Tropical and Subtropical Agriculture and Forestry, 1981).

95. Leezenberg, "Urbanization, Privatization, and Patronage," 158; Ghareeb, *The Kurdish Question*, 179–181; Robert Springborg, "Infitah, Agrarian Transformation, and Elite Consolidation in Contemporary Iraq," *Middle East Journal* 40.1 (1986): 33–52; McDowall, *Modern History of the Kurds*, 354.

96. Natali, *The Kurds and the State*, 62.

97. Martin van Bruinessen, "Kurdish Paths to Nation," in *The Kurds: Nationalism and Politics*, ed. Faleh Abd al-Jabar and Hosham Dawod (London: Saqi Books, 2006), 35.

98. McDowall, *Modern History of the Kurds*, 347–349, 355.

99. Human Rights Watch, *The Anfal Campaign in Iraqi Kurdistan* (New York: Human Rights Watch, 1993), 41–44.

100. Ariel I. Ahram, "Development, Counterinsurgency, and the Destruction of the Iraqi Marshes," *International Journal of Middle East Studies* 47.3 (2015): fn. 58.

101. Bengio, *Saddam's Word*, 182–191.

102. Kevin M. Woods, David D. Palkki, and Mark E. Stout, eds., *The Saddam Tapes: The Inner Workings of a Tyrant's Regime, 1978–2001* (New York: Cambridge University Press, 2011), 231–234.

103. Human Rights Watch, *The Anfal Campaign*. For overviews of the genocide and the international reaction, see Joost R. Hiltermann, *A Poisonous Affair: America, Iraq, and the Gassing of Halabja* (New York: Cambridge University Press, 2007).

104. Talabani, at least, anticipated that regardless of Saddam's fate, the Kurds would have new opportunities for autonomy or even independence. See Michael M. Gunter, *The Kurds of Iraq: Tragedy and Hope* (New York: St. Martin's, 1992), 41.

105. Bengio, *The Kurds of Iraq*, 205.

106. Kurdistan: Constitution of the Iraqi Kurdistan Region," http://www.unpo.org/article/538 (accessed May 29, 2018).

107. Michael M. Gunter, "Federalism and the Kurds of Iraq: The Solution or the Problem?" in *The Kurds: Nationalism and Politics*, ed. Faleh Abd al-Jabar and Hosham Dawod (London: Saqi, 2006): 235–236.

108. Bengio, *The Kurds of Iraq*, 217.

109. On the Iraqi opposition politics, see Robert G. Rabil, "The Iraqi Opposition's Evolution: From Conflict to Unity?" *Middle East Review of International Affairs* 6.4 (2002): 1–17; Michael Gunter, "The Iraqi National Congress (INC) and the Future of the Iraqi Opposition," *Journal of South Asian and Middle Eastern Studies* 19.3 (1996): 1–20.
110. Leezenberg, "Urbanization, Privatization, and Patronage," 172–175; Gareth Stansfield, "Finding a Dangerous Equilibrium: The Kurds in Post-Saddam Iraq," in *The Kurds: Nationalism and Politics*, ed. Faleh Abd al-Jabar and Hosham Dawod (London: Saqi, 2006), 265–266.
111. Leezenberg, "Urbanization, Privatization, and Patronage," 170–174; Ronald Ofteringer and Ralf Bäcker, "A Republic of Statelessness: Three Years of Humanitarian Intervention in Iraqi Kurdistan," *Middle East Report* 187/188 (1994): 40–45.
112. Bengio, *The Kurds of Iraq*, 200.
113. Johannes Jüde, "Contesting Borders? The Formation of Iraqi Kurdistan's De Facto State," *International Affairs* 93.4 (2017): 853.
114. Kirmanj, "Kurdish History Textbooks," 371.
115. Natali, *The Kurdish Quasi-State*, 46.
116. Leezenberg, "Urbanization, Privatization, and Patronage," 161–162, 173–174; Natali, *The Kurdish Quasi-State*, 49.
117. Iraqi Kurdish PUK Leader Talabani Says 'Kirkuk Is Jerusalem of Kurdistan,'" BBC Monitoring.
118. Glen Rangwala, "The Creation of Governments-in-Waiting: The Arab Uprisings and Legitimacy in the International System," *Geoforum* 66 (2015): 215–223.
119. Jüde, "Contesting Borders?" 853.
120. Ashley S. Deeks and Matthew D. Burton, "Iraq's Constitution: A Drafting History," *Cornell International Law Journal* 40 (2007): 1–89; Andrew Arato, *Constitution Making under Occupation: The Politics of Imposed Revolution in Iraq* (New York: Columbia University Press, 2009). For discussion on federalism, see John McGarry and Brendan O'Leary, "Iraq's Constitution of 2005: Liberal Consociation as Political Prescription," *International Journal of Constitutional Law* 5.4 (2007): 670–698; Karna Eklund, Brendan O'Leary, and Paul R. Williams, "Negotiating a Federation in Iraq," in *The Future of Kurdistan in Iraq*, ed. Brendan O'Leary, John McGarry, and Khaled Salih (Philadelphia: University of Pennsylvania Press, 2006), 235–250.
121. Article 121.
122. Aram Rafaat, "Kirkuk: The Central Issue of Kurdish Politics and Iraq's Knotty Problem," *Journal of Muslim Minority Affairs* 28.2 (2008): 256–259; Anderson and Stansfield, *Crisis in Kirkuk*, 190–192; Quil Lawrence, "A Precarious Peace in Northern Iraq," *Middle East Report Online*, October 1, 2009, https://www.merip.org/mero/mero100109.
123. Stansfield, "Finding a Dangerous Equilibrium," 270; The Kurdistan Referendum Movement from an Arab Point of View," BBC Monitoring, Al-Ta'akhi, Baghdad, on December 28, 2004, Document 10764C9185B236DC.
124. Kirmanj, "Kurdish History Textbooks," 372–381.
125. Diane E. King, *Kurdistan on the Global Stage: Kinship, Land, and Community in Iraq* (New Brunswick, NJ: Rutgers University Press, 2013), 212.
126. Yasmin Mousa, "It's Iraq but It's Not, Part 1," *New York Times, At War* blog, January 6, 2011, https://atwar.blogs.nytimes.com/2011/01/06/its-iraq-but-its-not-part-1/. Kira Walker, "Knowledge of Arabic Fading among Iraq's Kurds," *Rudaw*, November 22, 2015, http://www.rudaw.net/english/kurdistan/221120131 (accessed May 31, 2018).
127. Jaffer Sheyholislami, "Identity, Language, and New Media: The Kurdish Case," *Language Policy* 9.4 (2010): 289–312; King, *Kurdistan*, 215–216.
128. Kurdish Writer Considers Kosovo Independence, Kurdish Leaders' Failings," BBC Monitoring, Awene, Sulaymaniyah, on February 19, 2008, Document 11EF5AD7E41FD550; Iraqi Politicians Discuss Impact of Kosovo's Independence," BBC Monitoring, Al-Sharqiyah TV, Dubai, on February 19, 2008, Document 11EF5AD558A58648.
129. Natali, *The Kurdish Quasi-State*, 120–121.
130. My Iraq: Kurdish Businessman," BBC, March 21, 2007, http://news.bbc.co.uk/2/hi/middle_east/6467659.stm; Philip Shishkin, "Kurdish Rivalries Play Out on Cellphones," *Wall Street Journal*, November 24, 2007, https://www.wsj.com/articles/SB119586996079802804.

131. Tejel, *Syria's Kurds*, 108–112; Yildiz, *The Kurds in Syria*, 41.

132. Allsop, *The Kurds of Syria*, 104–105; Tejel, *Syria's Kurds*, 113–114.

133. Christian Sinclair and Sirwan Kajjo, "The Evolution of Kurdish Politics in Syria," Middle East Research and Information Project, August 31, 2011, https://www.merip.org/mero/mero083111.

134. Savelsberg, "The Syrian-Kurdish Movements," 91–93; Brian Whitaker, "Clashes between Syrian Kurds and Arabs Claim More Victims," *Guardian*, March 16, 2004, https://www.theguardian.com/world/2004/mar/17/syria.brianwhitaker; Hassan M. Fattah, "Kurds, Emboldened by Lebanon, Rise Up in Tense Syria," *New York Times*, July 2, 2005, https://www.nytimes.com/2005/07/02/world/middleeast/kurds-emboldened-by-lebanon-rise-up-in-tense-syria.html.

135. Fragiskatos, "The Stateless Kurds in Syria," 116.

136. Tejel, *Syria's Kurds*, 132.

137. Ünver, "Schrödinger's Kurds," 74.

138. Barak Mendelsohn, "God vs. Westphalia: Radical Islamist Movements and the Battle for Organising the World," *Review of International Studies* 38.3 (2012): 589–613.

139. Savelsberg, "The Syrian-Kurdish Movements," 94; Robert Lowe, "The Emergence of Western Kurdistan and the Future of Syria," in *Conflict, Democratization, and the Kurds in the Middle East*, ed. David Romano and Mehmet Gurses (New York: Palgrave Macmillan, 2014): 234–235.

140. Savelsberg, "The Syrian-Kurdish Movements," 94–97; Lowe, "The Emergence of Western Kurdistan," 227; "The Kurdish National Council in Syria," *Diwan*, Carnegie Middle East Center, February 15, 2012, http://carnegie-mec.org/diwan/48502?lang=en.

141. Jonas Bergan Draege, "The Formation of Syrian Opposition Coalitions as Two-Level Games," *Middle East Journal* 70.2 (2016): 197–198, 201.

142. Interview: Salih Muslim Muhammad," KurdWatch, November 8, 2011, http://www.kurdwatch.org/html/en/interview6.html.

143. Lowe, "The Emergence of Western Kurdistan," 227.

144. Lowe, "The Emergence of Western Kurdistan," 230–232; Qamishli: Ightiyal Mish'al at-Tamo [Qamishli: Assassination of Mishal Tammo], KurdWatch, October 10, 20122, http://www.kurdwatch.org/index.php?aid=2079&z=ar.

145. Michael M. Gunter, "The Kurdish Spring," *Third World Quarterly* 34.3 (2013): 452; Lowe, "The Emergence of Western Kurdistan," 228–9.

146. Savelsberg, "The Syrian-Kurdish Movements," 97–99; Lowe, "The Emergence of Western Kurdistan," 228–230.

147. Syrian Kurdish Leader on Fight against Islamic State, Role in Turkey, Syria," BBC Monitoring, *Al-Hayat* website, London, on July 25–28, 2015, Document 156ED8DCE 988FAF8.

148. Benoît Montabone, "The Wartime Emergence of a Transnational Region between Turkey and Syria (2008–2015)," in *The Transnational Middle East: People, Places, Borders*, ed. Leïla Vignal, 181.

149. For further description, see Ayman al-Tamimi, "A Visit to the Jazeera Canton: Report and Assessment," *Pundicity*, February 22, 2018, http://www.aymennjawad.org/20873/a-visit-to-the-jazeera-canton-report (accessed May 29, 2018).

150. Michiel Leezenberg, "The Ambiguities of Democratic Autonomy: The Kurdish Movement in Turkey and Rojava," *Southeast European and Black Sea Studies* 16.4 (2016): 671–690; Rana Khalaf, "Governing Rojava: Layers of Legitimacy in Syria," Chatham House, December 2016, https://syria.chathamhouse.org/research/governing-rojava-layers-of-legitimacy-in-syria

151. Lowe, "The Emergence of Western Kurdistan," 227–229.

152. Kyle Orton, "The Coalition's Partner in Syria: The Syrian Democratic Forces," *Kyle Orton's Blog*, July 9, 2017, https://kyleorton1991.wordpress.com/2017/07/09/the-coalitions-partner-in-syria-the-syrian-democratic-forces/ (accessed May 29, 2018); Molly Hennessy-Fiske, "Confused by All Those Groups Fighting in Syria? We Break It Down with Arm Patches," *Los Angeles Times*, July 23, 2017, http://www.latimes.com/world/middleeast/la-fg-syria-opposition-patches-2017-htmlstory.html.

153. Human Rights Watch, "Under Kurdish Rule: Abuses in PYD-Run Enclaves of Syria," June 19, 2014, https://www.hrw.org/report/2014/06/19/under-kurdish-rule/abuses-pyd-run-enclaves-syria (accessed May 29, 2018); Amnesty International, "Syria: 'We Had Nowhere to Go,'" October 13, 2015, https://www.amnesty.org/en/documents/mde24/2503/2015/en/ (accessed May 29, 2018).

154. BBC Monitoring, *Al-Hayat* website, London, on July 25–28, 2015, Record 156ED8DCE988FAF8.

155. International Crisis Group, "The PKK's Fateful Choice in Northern Syria," Middle East Report 176, May 4, 2017, https://www.crisisgroup.org/middle-east-north-africa/eastern-mediterranean/syria/176-pkk-s-fateful-choice-northern-syria (accessed May 29, 2018), 5.

156. Aaron Stein and Michelle Foley, "The YPG-PKK Connection," *MENASource*, January 26, 2016, http://www.atlanticcouncil.org/blogs/menasource/the-ypg-pkk-connection (accessed May 29, 2018); International Crisis Group, "The PKK's Fateful Choice in Northern Syria."

157. "Turkish Editorial Foresees Collapse of International System," BBC Monitoring, *Yeni Safak* website on November 21, 2016, Document 160D1E74294F5140.

158. Barak Barfi, "Assad Bombs the Kurds: Implications for U.S. Strategy in Syria," Washington Institute, *Policywatch* 2678, August 23, 2016, http://www.washingtoninstitute.org/policy-analysis/view/assad-bombs-the-kurds-implications-for-u.s.-strategy-in-syria (accessed May 29, 2018); W. van Wilgenberg, "Kurdish 'Capital' Erupts in Battle between Assad Militias and Kurds," *Middle East Eye*, April 21, 2016, http://www.middleeasteye.net/news/kurds-syria-confront-syrian-regime-their-unofficial-capital-880343545 (accessed May 29, 2018).

159. Syria's Major Water Resources Controlled by PKK's Syria Affiliate," *Daily Sabah*, June 15, 2017, https://www.dailysabah.com/war-on-terror/2017/06/15/syrias-major-water-resources-controlled-by-pkks-syria-affiliate (accessed May 14, 2018).

160. Stansfield, "Finding a Dangerous Equilibrium," 267–268

161. Kawa Hassan, "Kurdistan's Politicized Society Confronts a Sultanistic System," Carnegie Endowment for International Peace, 2015, http://carnegieendowment.org/files/CMEC_54_Hassan_11.pdf (accessed May 16, 2018).

162. Jüde, "Contesting Borders?" 854; Natali, *The Kurdish Quasi-State*, 106; Mario Fumerton and Wladimir van Wilgenburg, "Kurdistan's Political Armies: The Challenge of Unifying the Peshmerga Forces," Carnegie Endowment for International Peace, https://carnegieendowment.org/2015/12/16/kurdistan-s-political-armies-challenge-of-unifying-peshmerga-forces-pub-61917 (accessed May 16, 2018).

163. Fumerton and van Wilbenburg, "Kurdistan's Political Armies"; Paul Rivlin, "Kurdistan's Economic Woes," *Iqtisadi: Middle East Economy*, Moshe Dayan Center, Tel Aviv University, October 30, 2017, https://dayan.org/content/kurdistan-economic-woes (accessed May 16, 2018).

164. Iraqi Kurdish Website Carries Programme of Democratic Change Trend," BBC Monitoring, Sbay media website on October 8, 2008, Document 123CCB7221C1B558.

165. Human Rights Watch, "Iraq: Widening Crackdown on Protests," April 21, 2011,https://www.hrw.org/news/2011/04/21/iraq-widening-crackdown-protests (accessed May 16, 2018).

166. Jüde, "Contesting Borders?" 857.

167. Jacob Sullivan to Hillary Clinton, "Maliki, " December 21, 2011, US State Department, Case No. F-2014–20438, Doc. No. C05785715, http://graphics.wsj.com/hillary-clinton-email-documents/pdfs/C05785715.pdf (accessed May 16, 2018).

168. Michael Kelly, "The Kurdish Regional Constitution within the Framework of the Iraqi Federal Constitution: A Struggle for Sovereignty, Oil, Ethnic Identity, and the Prospects for a Reverse Supremacy Clause," *Penn State Law Review* 114.3 (2010): 707–808.

169. David Romano, "Iraq's Descent into Civil War: A Constitutional Explanation," *Middle East Journal* 68.4 (2014): 536–538.

170. Kurdistan Former PM Says 'Iraq Will End Up like Sudan' if Kurd Rights Ignored," BBC Monitoring, *Rudaw*, Arbil, on January 17, 2011, Document 134F06F45CAA64E8.

171. Romano, "Iraq's Descent," 560.

172. Kenneth Pollack, "Iraq: Understanding the ISIS Offensive against the Kurds," Brookings Institution, *Markaz*, August 11, 2014, https://www.brookings.edu/blog/markaz/2014/08/11/iraq-understanding-the-isis-offensive-against-the-kurds/ (accessed May 16, 2018).

173. Not incidentally, it was Fuad Masum, the second Kurd to serve as president of Iraq and another senior PUK official, who granted Abadi his mandate to form a new government. See Bill Chappell, "New Leader of Iraq Is Nominated, but Maliki Insists He'll Stay in Office," NPR, August 11, 2014, https://www.npr.org/sections/thetwo-way/2014/08/11/339522191/new-leader-of-iraq-is-nominated-as-maliki-insists-hell-stay-in-office (accessed May 18, 2018).

174. Omar Al-Nidawi, "How ISIL Changed the Oil Map of Iraq," al-Jazeera, December 1, 2017, https://www.aljazeera.com/indepth/opinion/isil-changed-oil-map-iraq-171130151714129.html (accessed May 18, 2018).

175. Jüde, "Contesting Borders?" 854–859. For insights on the KRG-Turkey's energy relationship, see Jacob Sullivan to Hillary Clinton, "Readout from Kurdistan Trip," April 1, 2012, US State Department, Case No. F-2014–20439, Doc. No. C05790032, http://graphics.wsj.com/hillary-clinton-email-documents/pdfs/C05790032.pdf (accessed May 18, 2018).

176. "Israel's Prime Minister Backs Kurdish Independence," *Guardian*, June 29, 2014, https://www.theguardian.com/world/2014/jun/29/israel-prime-minister-kurdish-independence.

177. Selina Williams, "Oil Companies' Bet on Kurdistan Turns Sour," *Wall Street Journal*, April 26, 2016, https://www.wsj.com/articles/oil-companies-bet-on-kurdistan-turns-sour-1461708524.

178. Al-Nidawi, "How ISIL Changed the Oil Map of Iraq."

179. Stephen Kalin and Dmitry Zhdannikov, "U.S. Helped Clinch Iraq Oil Deal to Keep Mosul Battle on Track," Reuters, October 3, 2016, https://www.reuters.com/article/us-mideast-crisis-usa-mosul-exclusive-idUSKCN12314Z (accessed May 18, 2018).

180. Eric Lipton, "Iraqi Kurds Build Washington Lobbying Machine to Fund War against ISIS," *New York Times*, May 6, 2016, https://www.nytimes.com/2016/05/07/us/politics/iraqi-kurds-build-washington-lobbying-machine-against-isis.html .

181. Ghusan Sharbek, "Barzani li'l hayat: harit saykes-picot mustina'h wa al hudud al-jadid turasmim bi al-dam" [Barzani to al-Hayat: The Sykes-Picot Map is artificial and the new borders are drawn in blood], *Al-Hayat*, February 8, 2015, http://www.alhayat.com/Articles/7243606 (accessed May 18, 2018).

182. Barzani in Brussels Says Kurds will Secede from Iraq," BBC Monitoring, July 12, 2017, Document 165983D90685F3D0.

183. President Barzani: Without a Better Alternative That Can Convince the Kurdistan People, We Will Hold the Referendum, Whatever the Consequences Are," Kurdish Democratic Party official website, September 14, 2017, http://www.kdp.info/a/d.aspx?l=13&a=103097 (accessed May 29, 2018).

184. Trudy Rubin, "Time for Kurdish Independence?" *Philadelphia Inquirer*, March 23, 2017, http://www.philly.com/philly/columnists/trudy_rubin/20170323_Worldview__Rubin__Time_for_Kurdish_independence_.html (accessed May 16, 2018).

185. Iraqi PM Abadi Says Kurdish Independence Referendum 'Unconstitutional,'" Reuters, September 12, 2017, https://www.reuters.com/article/us-mideast-crisis-iraq-kurds-abadi/iraqi-pm-abadi-says-kurdish-independence-referendum-unconstitutional-idUSKCN1BN2FK (accessed May 18, 2018)

186. Laura Bröker, "Any Hope for a Kurdish State?" Heinrich Böll Stiftung–North America, 2017, 16–17, https://www.boell.de/sites/default/files/any_hope_for_a_kurdish_state.pdf.

187. Tamer el-Ghobashy, "Christians and Yazidis See a Bleak Future in a Proposed Independent Kurdish State," *Washington Post*, October 7, 2017, https://www.washingtonpost.com/world/middle_east/christians-and-yazidis-see-a-bleak-future-in-a-proposed-independent-kurdish-state/2017/10/06/f15d2176-a2d3-11e7-b573-8ec86cdfe1ed_story.html; Michael Knights, "Turkey's Waiting Game in Sinjar," *TurkeyScope* 1.8 (2017), http://www.washingtoninstitute.org/uploads/Knights20170622-Turkeyscope.pdf (accessed May 16, 2018). On the Assyrians, see Gregory J. Kruczek, "Christian Minorities and the Struggle

for Nineveh: The Assyrian Democratic Movement in Iraq and the Nineveh Plains Protection Units" (PhD diss., Virginia Polytechnic Institute and State University, 2018).

188. Nineveh Tribes Call for Their Areas to Join Kurdistan Region," BBC Monitoring, *Rudaw* website on June 21, 2017, Document 165459F679178A20.

189. Isabel Coles and Ali A. Nabhan, "Iraqi Kurds Vote in Independence Referendum Despite Warnings from Baghdad, U.S.," *Wall Street Journal*, September 27, 2017, https://www.wsj.com/articles/iraqi-kurds-vote-in-independence-referendum-despite-warnings-from-baghdad-u-s-1506328499.

190. Christine McCaffray Van Den Toorn, "Internal Divides behind the Kurdistan Referendum," Carnegie Endowment for International Peace, October 11, 2017, http://carnegieendowment.org/sada/73359 (accessed June 12, 2018).

191. Rouhani, Erdogan Discuss Iraqi Kurdish Referendum by Phone," Xinhua News Agency, September 25, 2017, http://www.xinhuanet.com/english/2017-09/25/c_136636764.htm (accessed May 18, 2018).

192. Mustafa Salim, Karen DeYoung, and Tamer El-Ghobashy, "Tillerson Says Kurdish Independence Referendum Is Illegitimate," *Washington Post*, September 29, 2017, https://www.washingtonpost.com/world/middle_east/iraq-bans-flights-to-kurdish-region-as-rift-grows-over-independence-bid/2017/09/29/860e326e-a532-11e7-b573-8ec86cdfe1ed_story.html?utm_term=.133cd2fdfc32.

193. Karabakh Hails Iraqi Kurdish Referendum," BBC Monitoring, Azatutyn.am on September 27, 2017, Document 16734729F8724588. Flanders also sent a delegation of support; see Alan Hope, "Flanders Follows Cuban Mission with Visit to Iraqi Kurdistan," *FlandersToday*, May 16, 2018, http://www.flanderstoday.eu/politics/flanders-follows-cuban-mission-visit-iraqi-kurdistan (accessed May 16, 2018).

194. Rod Nordland and David Zucchino, "As Kurdish Borders Close, Region's Leader Warns Iraq," *New York Times*, September 30, 2017, https://www.nytimes.com/2017/09/29/world/middleeast/iraq-kurds-referendum.html.

195. D. Soguel, "Defiant, Kurds Vote in Northern Iraq, Seeking Path to Independence," *Christian Science Monitor*, September 25, 2017, https://www.csmonitor.com/World/Middle-East/2017/0925/Defiant-Kurds-vote-in-northern-Iraq-seeking-path-to-independence.

196. "Bafel Talabani: PUK Chose 'Tactical Withdrawal' from Kirkuk after Casualties," *Rudaw*, October 21, 2017, http://www.rudaw.net/english/kurdistan/211020179.

197. 'Nobody Stood with the Kurds' Says Bitter Barzani," Reuters, October 29, 2017, https://www.reuters.com/article/us-mideast-crisis-iraq-kurds-speech/nobody-stood-with-the-kurds-says-bitter-barzani-idUSKBN1CY0RU (accessed May 16, 2018).

198. Molly Crabapple, "How Turkey's Campaign in Afrin Is Stoking Syrian Hatreds," *New York Review of Books*, April 11, 2018, http://www.nybooks.com/daily/2018/04/11/how-turkeys-campaign-in-afrin-is-stoking-syrian-hatreds/. On the toppling of the statue, see https://www.youtube.com/watch?v=c_LnzGYWJS0.

## Chapter 6

1. On the history of the baya'a, see Andrew Marsham, "Bayʿa," in *Encyclopaedia of Islam, Three*, ed. Kate Fleet, Gudrun Krämer, Denis Matringe, John Nawas, and Everett Rowson (Brill Online, accessed January 11, 2018).

2. Miroslav Melčák, and Ondřej Beránek, "ISIS's Destruction of Mosul's Historical Monuments: Between Media Spectacle and Religious Doctrine," *International Journal of Islamic Architecture* 6.2 (2017): 389–415.

3. Yasser Tabbaa, "The Mosque of Nūr al-Dīn in Mosul, 1170–1172," *Annales Islamologique* 36 (2002): 351. See also Yasser Tabbaa, "The Muqarnas Dome: Its Origin and Meaning," *Muqarnas* 3 (1985): 61–74. For more on the career of Nur al-Din, see Yaacov Lev, "The Social and Economic Policies of Nūr al-Dīn (1146–1174): The Sultan of Syria," *Der Islam* 81.2 (2004): 218–242.

4. Surat Al-Anfal 8:39; Surat al-Hadid 57:25.

5. Translation of the Khutbah of Commander of the Faithful, Caliph of the Muslims, Abu Bakr al-Husayni al-Qurayshi al-Baghdadi (may Allah protect him) Ramadan 6th 1435 in Mosul, Iraq," https://azelin.files.wordpress.com/2014/07/abc5ab-bakr-al-e1b8a5ussayn-c4ab-al-qurayshc4ab-al-baghdc481dc4ab-22khue1b9adbah-and-jumah-prayer-in-the-grand-mosque-of-mc5abe1b9a3ul-mosul22-en.pdf.

6. Tabbaa, "The Mosque of Nūr al-Dīn in Mosul," 340; Saïd Diywahji, "Jama'a an-Nuri fi al-Mawsil," *Sumer* 5 (1949); Dina Rizk Khoury, *State and Provincial Society in the Ottoman Empire: Mosul,* 1540–1834 (New York: Cambridge University Press, 2002): 35–36.

7. Avner Wishnitzer, *Reading Clocks, Alla Turca: Time and Society in the Late Ottoman Empire* (Chicago: University of Chicago Press, 2015); Mehmet Bengü Uluengin, "Secularizing Anatolia Tick by Tick: Clock Towers in the Ottoman Empire and the Turkish Republic," *International Journal of Middle East Studies* 42.1 (2010): 17–36.

8. Albert Howe Lybyer, "Recent Political Changes in the Moslem World," *American Political Science Review* 18.3 (1924): 513–514. See also Elie Kedourie, "The End of the Ottoman Empire," *Journal of Contemporary History* 3.4 (1968): 19–28.

9. William McCants, *The ISIS Apocalypse: The History, Strategy, and Doomsday Vision of the Islamic State* (New York: Macmillan, 2015), 20, 122.

10. Mona Hassan, *Longing for the Lost Caliphate: A Transregional History* (Princeton, NJ: Princeton University Press, 2017), chapter 7; Vernie Liebl, "The Caliphate," *Middle Eastern Studies* 45.3 (2009): 373–391.

11. Ariel I. Ahram, "Iraq and Syria: The Dilemma of Dynasty," *Middle East Quarterly* 9.2 (2002): 33–42; Elie Podeh, "The Bay'a: Modern Political Uses of Islamic Ritual in the Arab World," *Die Welt des Islams* 50.1 (2010): 117–152.

12. Richard Nielsen, "Does the Islamic State Believe in Sovereignty?" in *Islamism in the IS Age,* POMEPS Studies No. 12, March 2015, 28–30, https://pomeps.org/wp-content/uploads/2015/03/POMEPS_Studies_12_ISAge_Web.pdf (accessed March 3, 2018); Charles R. Lister, *The Islamic State: A Brief Introduction* (Washington, DC: Brookings Institution Press, 2015), 34.

13. Tanisha M. Fazal, "Religionist Rebels & the Sovereignty of the Divine," *Dædalus* 147.1 (2018): 25–35; Matthieu Rey, "L'état islamique, terre de frontières?" in *Les frontières mondialisées,* ed. Sabine Dullin and Etienne Forestier-Peyrat (Paris: Presses Universitaires de France, 2015).

14. Quinn Meacham, "How Much of a State Is the Islamic State?" in *Islamism in the IS Age,* POMEPS Studies 12, March 2015, 20–24, https://pomeps.org/wp-content/uploads/2015/03/POMEPS_Studies_12_ISAge_Web.pdf (accessed March 3, 2018).

15. On IS's claims to be post-territorial, see Yosef Jabareen, "The Emerging Islamic State: Terror, Territoriality, and the Agenda of Social Transformation," *Geoforum* 58 (2015): 51–55.

16. Peter Harling and Alex Simon, "Erosion and Resilience of the Iraqi-Syrian Border," European University Institute, RSCAS Working Paper 2016/61 (2015), http://cadmus.eui.eu//handle/1814/37015 (accessed March 3, 2018).

17. Fawaz Gerges, *ISIS: A History* (Princeton, NJ: Princeton University Press, 2016), 6.

18. For a discussion of the Islamic conquest of the Jazira, see Ahmad ibn Yahya Baladhuri, *Futuh al-buldān* (Cairo: Shurkah Tabba al-Kitab al-Arabiyyah, 1901), 179–181, 194.

19. For Sykes's impressions, see Mark Sykes, "Journeys in North Mesopotamia," *Geographical Journal* 30.3 (1907): 237–254; Mark Sykes, "Journeys in North Mesopotamia (Continued)," *Geographical Journal* 30.4 (1907): 384–398.

20. Ali Nehme Hamdan, "Breaker of Barriers? Notes on the Geopolitics of the Islamic State in Iraq and Sham," *Geopolitics* 21.3 (2016): 621.

21. On Syria, see Butrus Abu-Manneh, "The Christians between Ottomanism and Syrian Nationalism: The Ideas of Butrus al-Bustani," *International Journal of Middle East Studies* 11.3 (1980): 287–304. On Iraq, see Reidar Visser, "Proto-Political Conceptions of Iraq in Late Ottoman Times," *International Journal of Contemporary Iraqi Studies* 3.2 (2009): 143–154; Fanar Haddad, "Political Awakenings in an Artificial State: Iraq, 1914–20," *International Journal of Contemporary Iraqi Studies* 6.1 (2012): 3–25; Nabil Al-Tikriti, "Was

There an Iraq before There Was an Iraq?" *International Journal of Contemporary Iraqi Studies* 3.2 (2009): 133–142.

22. Eliezer Tauber, *The Formation of Modern Iraq and Syria* (New York: Routledge, 2013), 328–329.

23. Sarah D. Shields, *Mosul before Iraq: Like Bees Making Five-Sided Cells* (Albany, NY: SUNY Press, 2000), 165.

24. Robert Fletcher, "The ʿAmārāt, Their Sheikh, and the Colonial State: Patronage and Politics in a Partitioned Middle East," *Journal of the Economic and Social History of the Orient* 58.1/2 (2015): 165.

25. I will leave apart areas of Jazira around Diyarbakir that eventually became Turkey. For discussion, see Ugur Ümit Üngör, *The Making of Modern Turkey: Nation and State in Eastern Anatolia, 1913–1950* (New York: Oxford University Press, 2012).

26. Yonina Talmon, "Millenarian Movements," *European Journal of Sociology/Archives Européennes de Sociologie* 7.2 (1966): 159–200.

27. Kamal S. Salibi, "Middle Eastern Parallels: Syria—Iraq—Arabia in Ottoman Times," *Middle Eastern Studies* 15.1 (1979): 70–81; Selim Deringil, "The Struggle against Shiism in Hamidian Iraq: A Study in Ottoman Counter-Propaganda," *Die Welt des Islams* (1990): 45–62. For the ways Ottoman rule solidified Sunni hegemony through family law, see Karen M. Kern, *Imperial Citizen: Marriage and Citizenship in the Ottoman Frontier Provinces of Iraq* (Syracuse, NY: Syracuse University Press, 2011).

28. Cf. Khoury, *State and Provincial Society in the Ottoman Empire*; Shields, *Mosul before Iraq*; Frank Stewart, "A Bedouin Proto-State in Late Ottoman Syria: The Jubur on the Khabur in 1914," *Jerusalem Studies in Arabic and Islam* 33 (2007): 343–374; Stefan H. Winter, "The Province of Raqqa under Ottoman Rule, 1535–1800: A Preliminary Study," *Journal of Near Eastern Studies* 68.4 (2009): 253–268.

29. At the turn of the twentieth century, Raqqa and al-Qaim were governed from the provincial capital of Aleppo. Baghdad Province extended northward to Tikrit on the Tigris and Ana on the Euphrates. Deir Ezzour was a stand-alone district (*sanjak*) reporting directly to Istanbul. Mosul was elevated to the capital of its own province (*wilayet*) that extended southward to the confluence of the Tigris and Lesser Zab Rivers. Cf. Eliezer Tauber, "The Struggle for Dayr al-Zur: The Determination of Borders between Syria and Iraq," *International Journal of Middle East Studies* 23.3 (1991): 363; Kevin Mazur, "Local Communities and Outside Authorities in the Syrian Uprising: A View from Deir Al-Zor," unpublished manuscript, 10; Winter, "The Province of Raqqa under Ottoman Rule, 1535–1800," 253–254.

30. Stephen H. Longrigg, *Iraq, 1900 to 1950: A Political, Social, and Economic History* (New York: Oxford University Press, 1956), 59; William I. Shorrock, "The Origin of the French Mandate in Syria and Lebanon: The Railroad Question, 1901–1914," *International Journal of Middle East Studies* 1.2 (1970): 133–153.

31. Camille Lyans Cole, "Precarious Empires: A Social and Environmental History of Steam Navigation on the Tigris," *Journal of Social History* 50.1 (2016): 74–101.

32. H. Charles Woods, "The Baghdad Railway and Its Tributaries," *Geographical Journal* 50.1 (1917): 34.

33. Cited in James Denselow, "Mosul, the Jazira Region and the Syrian-Iraqi Borderlands," in *An Iraq of Its Regions: Cornerstones of a Federal Democracy?* ed. Reidar Visser and Gareth Stansfield (New York: Columbia University Press, 2008), 109.

34. Daniel Neep, *Occupying Syria under the French Mandate: Insurgency, Space and State Formation* (New York: Cambridge University Press, 2012), 186.

35. Fletcher, "The ʿAmārāt, their Sheikh, and the Colonial State," 165.

36. Tauber, "Struggle for Dayr al-Zur," 379.

37. Johann Büssow, "Negotiating the Future of a Bedouin Polity in Mandatory Syria: Political Dynamics of the Sbaʾa-ʾAbada during the 1930s," *Nomadic Peoples* 15:1 (2011): 78.

38. Longrigg, *Iraq, 1900 to 1950*, 160.

39. David Cuthell, "A Kemalist Gambit," in *The Creation of Iraq, 1914–1921*, ed. Reeva S. Simon and Eleanor Harvey Tejirian (New York: Columbia University Press, 2004), 80–95.

40. Tauber, "Struggle for Dayr al-Zur," 267–272.

41. Sarah Shields, "Mosul, the Ottoman Legacy and the League of Nations," *International Journal of Contemporary Iraqi Studies* 3.2 (2009): 217–230. On the Yezidis, see Nelida Fuccaro, "Ethnicity, State Formation, and Conscription in Postcolonial Iraq: The Case of the Yazidi Kurds of Jabal Sinjar," *International Journal of Middle East Studies* 29.4 (1997): 559–580.

42. Hassan Mneimneh, "From Communitarianism to Sectarianism: The Trajectory of Factionalism in the Arab Middle East," *Muslim World* 106.1 (2016): 67–70.

43. Malik Mufti, *Sovereign Creations: Pan-Arabism and Political Order in Syria and Iraq* (Ithaca, NY: Cornell University Press, 1996); Adeed Dawisha, *Arab Nationalism in the Twentieth Century: From Triumph to Despair* (Princeton, NJ: Princeton University Press, 2016).

44. Charles Tripp, *A History of Iraq* (New York: Cambridge University Press, 2002), 45; Abbas Kadhim, *Reclaiming Iraq: The 1920 Revolution and the Founding of the Modern State* (Austin: University of Texas Press, 2012), 148–150. For a broader discussion of the fate of the ex-Ottoman elite, see Michael Provence, *The Last Ottoman Generation and the Making of the Modern Middle East* (New York: Cambridge University Press, 2017).

45. Cited in Kadhim, *Reclaiming Iraq*, 151.

46. Fanar Haddad, *Sectarianism in Iraq: Antagonistic Visions of Unity* (New York: Oxford University Press, 2011), 42.

47. See Yitzhak Nakash, *Reaching for Power: The Shi'a in the Modern Arab World* (Princeton, NJ: Princeton University Press, 2006), chapter 3; Eric Davis, *Memories of State: Politics, History, and Collective Identity in Modern Iraq* (Berkeley: University of California Press, 2005).

48. Kadhim, *Reclaiming Iraq*, 148–150; Johann Büssow, "Negotiating the Future of a Bedouin Polity in Mandatory Syria: Internal and External Political Dynamics of the Sba'a-'Abada during the 1930s," *Nomadic Peoples* 15.1 (2011): 78; Nur Masalha, "Faisal's Pan-Arabism, 1921–33," *Middle Eastern Studies* 27.4 (1991): 679–693.

49. David Pool, "From Elite to Class: The Transformation of Iraqi Leadership, 1920–1939," *International Journal of Middle East Studies* 12.3 (1980): 331–350.

50. Hanna Batatu, *The Old Social Classes and the Revolutionary Movements of Iraq* (Princeton, NJ: Princeton University Press, 1978), 44. For discussion of Mosul's treatment under the monarchy, see Thanoon al-Taee, *Al-Awda al-idariyah fi al-mawsil khilal al-'ahd al-Maliki, 1921–1958* [Administrative circumstances in Mosul curing the monarchical era, 1921–1958] (Mosul: Mosul University, 2008).

51. Government of Iraq, Principal Bureau of Statistics, *Statistical Abstract* (Baghdad: Dā'irah al-Ra'isīyah lil-Iḥṣā', 1963–65).

52. Harith Al-Qarawee, *Imagining the Nation: Nationalism, Sectarianism and Socio-Political Conflict in Iraq* (Lulu.com, 2016), 239.

53. On the Mosul uprising, and its antecedents and aftermath, see K. Sorby, "Iraq: The Mosul Uprising of 1959," *Asian and African Studies* 2.15 (2006): 133–151; Batatu, *Old Social Classes*, 869–871.

54. Amatzia Baram, "Mesopotamian Identity in Ba'thi Iraq," *Middle Eastern Studies* 19.4 (1983): 426–455; Davis, *Memories of State*, chapters 5 and 6.

55. Majid Khadduri, *Socialist Iraq: A Study in Iraqi Politics since 1968* (Washington, DC: Middle East Institute, 1978). For a more critical reading, see Joseph Sassoon, *Saddam Hussein's Ba'th Party: Inside an Authoritarian Regime* (New York: Cambridge University Press, 2011); Dina Rizk Khoury, *Iraq in Wartime: Soldiering, Martyrdom, and Remembrance* (New York: Cambridge University Press, 2013); Martin Bunton, "From Developmental Nationalism to the End of Nation-State in Iraq?" *Third World Quarterly* 29.3 (2008): 631–646.

56. Amazia Baram, "The Ruling Political Elite in Ba'thi Iraq, 1968–1986: The Changing Features of a Collective Profile," *International Journal of Middle East Studies* 21.4 (1989): 447–493; Amatzia Baram, "Saddam's Power Structure: The Tikritis before, during and after the War," *Adelphi Series* 43.354 (2003): 99–97; Sassoon, *Saddam Hussein's Ba'th Party*, 105–106. For a larger discussion of Iraq's tribal confederacies, tribes, and sub-tribes, see Abd al-'Awn Radwan, *Mawsū'at 'ashā'ir al-'Irāq* (Amman: al-Ahliyya, 2003).

57. M. Anis Al-Layla and S. M. Al-Rawi, "Impact of Mosul Textile Factory Effluents on Tigris River Water Quality," *Journal of Environmental Science & Health Part A* 23.6 (1988):

559–568; Nasrat Adamo and Nadhir Al-Ansari, "Mosul Dam[,] the Full Story: Engineering Problems," *Journal of Earth Sciences and Geotechnical Engineering* 6.3 (2016): 213–244.

58. Robert Springborg, "Infitah, Agrarian Transformation, and Elite Consolidation in Contemporary Iraq," *Middle East Journal* (1986): 45; Amal Rassam, "Al-Tabaiyya: Power, Patronage and Marginal Groups in Northern Iraq," in *Patrons and Clients in Mediterranean Societies*, ed. Ernest Gellner and John Waterbury (London: Duckworth, 1977), 157–167; Isam Al-Khafaji, "State Incubation of Iraqi Capitalism," *Middle East Report* 142 (1986): 4–12.

59. Amatzia Baram, "Neo-Tribalism in Iraq: Saddam Hussein's Tribal Policies, 1991–96," *International Journal of Middle East Studies* 29.1 (1997): 1–31; Adeed Dawisha, " 'Identity' and Political Survival in Saddam's Iraq," *Middle East Journal* 53.4 (1999): 553–567; Faleh A. Jabar, "Shaykhs and Ideologues: Detribalization and Retribalization in Iraq, 1968–1998," *Middle East Report* 215 (2000): 28–48; Ronen Zeidel, "Tribes in Iraq," in *Tribes and States in a Changing Middle East*, ed. Uzi Rabi (New York: Oxford University Press, 2016).

60. Zainab Saleh, "On Iraqi Nationality: Law, Citizenship, and Exclusion," *Arab Studies Journal* 21.1 (2013): 48–78.

61. Amatzia Baram, *Saddam Husayn and Islam, 1968–2003: Ba'thi Iraq from Secularism to Faith* (Washington, DC: Woodrow Wilson Center Press, 2014), 259; Aaron M. Faust, *The Ba'thification of Iraq: Saddam Hussein's Totalitarianism* (Austin: University of Texas Press, 2015), 133–134, 140–141.

62. Benjamin White, "The Nation-State Form and the Emergence of 'Minorities' in Syria," *Studies in Ethnicity and Nationalism* 7.1 (2007): 64–85.

63. Hanna Batatu, *Syria's Peasantry, the Descendants of its Lesser Rural Notables, and Their Politics* (Princeton, NJ: Princeton University Press, 1999), 158.

64. Philip Shukry Khoury, *Syria and the French Mandate: The Politics of Arab Nationalism, 1920–1945* (Princeton, NJ: Princeton University Press, 2014); Elizabeth Thompson, *Colonial Citizens: Republican Rights, Paternal Privilege, and Gender in French Syria and Lebanon* (New York: Columbia University Press, 2000).

65. Dawn Chatty, "The Bedouin in Contemporary Syria: The Persistence of Tribal Authority and Control," *Middle East Journal* 64.1 (2010): 32–35; Haian Dukhan, "Tribes and Tribalism in the Syrian Uprising," *Syria Studies* 6.2 (2014): 4.

66. Michael H. Van Dusen, "Political Integration and Regionalism in Syria," *Middle East Journal* 26.2 (1972): 124–126.

67. Batatu, *Syria's Peasantry*, 77, 85, 120; Philip S. Khoury, "The Tribal Shaykh, French Tribal Policy, and the Nationalist Movement in Syria between Two World Wars," *Middle Eastern Studies* 18.2 (1982): 180–193; Springborg, "Infitah, Agrarian Transformation, and Elite Consolidation," 45.

68. Nikolaos van Dam, "Sectarian and Regional Factionalism in the Syrian Political Elite," *Middle East Journal* 32.2 (1978): 201–210. See also Mahmud A. Faksh, "The Alawi Community of Syria: A New Dominant Political Force," *Middle Eastern Studies* 20.2 (1984): 133–153.

69. For the history of the Alawis, see Stefan Winter, *A History of the 'Alawis: From Medieval Aleppo to the Turkish Republic* (Princeton, NJ: Princeton University Press, 2016); Matti Moosa, *Extremist Shiites: The Ghulat Sects* (Syracuse, NY: Syracuse University Press, 1987), 254–398.

70. Kais M. Firro, "The Alawis in Modern Syria: From Nusayriya to Islam via Alawiya," *Der Islam* 82.1 (2005): 1–32; )Mordechai Kedar, "In Search of Legitimacy: Asad's Islamic Image in the Syrian Official Press," in *Modern Syria: From Ottoman Rule to Pivotal Role in the Middle East*, ed. Moshe Ma'oz, Joseph Ginat, and Onn Winckler (Brighton: Sussex Academic Press, 2005).

71. On the construction of this capitalism, see Steven Heydemann, *Authoritarianism in Syria: Institutions and Social Conflict, 1946–1970* (Ithaca, NY: Cornell University Press, 1999); Bassam Haddad, "The Syrian Regime's Business Backbone," *Middle East Report* 262 (2012): 26–27.

72. Hanna Batatu, "Syria's Muslim Brethren," *Middle East Reports* 110 (1982): 13. For a broader discussion, see Raphaël Lefèvre, *Ashes of Hama: The Muslim Brotherhood in Syria* (New York: Oxford University Press, 2013).

73. Raymond A. Hinnebusch, *Peasant and Bureaucracy in Ba'thist Syria: The Political Economy of Rural Development* (Boulder, CO: Westview, 1989), 214–215, 237.
74. Chatty, "The Bedouin," 46.
75. Kevin Mazur, "The Islamic State Identity and Legacies of Baath Rule in Syria's Northeast," in *Islamism in the IS Age*, POMEPS Studies 12, March 2015, 34, https://pomeps.org/wp-content/uploads/2015/03/POMEPS_Studies_12_ISAge_Web.pdf (accessed March 3, 2018); Batatu, *Syria's Peasantry*, 186.
76. Chatty, "The Bedouin," 44; Dukhan, "Tribes and Tribalism," 4–5.
77. Nicholas Heras, Bassam Barabandi, and Nidal Betare, "Deir Azzour Tribal Mapping Project," Center for New American Security, October 2, 2017, 4, https://www.cnas.org/publications/reports/deir-azzour-tribal-mapping-project (accessed February 9, 2018). The conversion of tribes to Shi'ism is not exceptional. Many of the tribes in southern Iraq converted to Shi'ism in the nineteenth century, and some tribes, like the Shammar, include Sunni and Shi'i branches. See Yitzhak Nakash, "The Conversion of Iraq's Tribes to Shi'ism," *International Journal of Middle East Studies* 26.3 (1994): 443–463.
78. Hinnebusch, *Peasant and Bureaucracy*, 242; Myriam Ababsa, "Raqqa, capitale de la révolution pui de l'état islamique," *Confluences Méditerranée* 101.2 (2017): 54.
79. Alasdair Drysdale, "The Regional Equalization of Health Care and Education in Syria since the Ba'thi Revolution," *International Journal of Middle East Studies* 13.1 (1981): 93–111.
80. Batatu, *Syria's Peasantry*, 68.
81. Syrian Central Bureau of Statistics, "The Medical Professions by Mohafazat, 2003–2008," http://www.cbssyr.sy/yearbook/2009/Data-Chapter12/TAB-2-12-2009.htm (accessed February 4, 2018).
82. Oren Barak, "Dilemmas of Security in Iraq," *Security Dialogue* 38.4 (2007): 455–475.
83. Ahmed S. Hashim, *Iraq's Sunni Insurgency* (New York: Routledge, 2013); Amatzia Baram, "Who Are the Insurgents? Sunni Arab Rebels in Iraq," US Institute of Peace Special Report 134, April 2005, http://www.usip.org/files/resources/sr134.pdf (accessed December 3, 2009).
84. Ronen Zeidel, "A Harsh Readjusment: The Sunnis and the Political Process in Contemporary Iraq," *Middle East Review of International Affairs* 12.1 (2008): 40–50, http://www.rubincenter.org/meria/2008/03/Zeidel.pdf (accessed March 2, 2018); Gerges, *ISIS*, 219, 223.
85. Joseph Felter and Brian Fishman, "Al-Qa'ida's Foreign Fighters in Iraq: A First Look at the Sinjar Records," Combating Terrorism Center at West Point, 2007, https://ctc.usma.edu/al-qaidas-foreign-fighters-in-iraq-a-first-look-at-the-sinjar-records/ (accessed March 2, 2018); Gary Gambil, "How Significant Is Syria's Role in Iraq?" *Jamestown Foundation Terrorism Monitor* 2.19 (2004), https://jamestown.org/program/how-significant-is-syrias-role-in-iraq-2/ (accessed March 2, 2018).
86. Cole Bunzel, "From Paper State to Caliphate: The Ideology of the Islamic State," Brookings Project on U.S. Relations with the Islamic World, Analysis Paper 19, March 2015, 18, https://www.brookings.edu/wp-content/uploads/2016/06/The-ideology-of-the-Islamic-State.pdf (accessed March 2, 2018).
87. Zarqawi Letter," February 2004, US Department of State Archive, https://2001-2009.state.gov/p/nea/rls/31694.htm (accessed June 12, 2018).
88. Bunzel, "From Paper State to Caliphate," 15.
89. Taha Abdulrazaq and Gareth Stansfield, "The Enemy Within: ISIS and the Conquest of Mosul," *Middle East Journal* 70.4 (2016): 531.
90. Joby Warrick, *Black Flags: The Rise of ISIS* (New York: Doubleday, 2015), 206; Charles R. Lister, *The Syrian Jihad* (New York: Oxford University Press, 2011), 313; Norman Cigar, *Al-Qaida, the Tribes, and the Government: Lessons and Prospects for Iraq's Unstable Triangle* (Quantico, VA: Marine Corps University Press, 2011), 21.
91. Bunzel, "From Paper State to Caliphate," 17.
92. Gerges, *ISIS*, 102–103.
93. Quoted in Bunzel, "From Paper State to Caliphate," 18.
94. Bunzel, "From Paper State to Caliphate," 18.
95. McCants, *The ISIS Apocalypse*, 19–20; Bunzel, "From Paper State to Caliphate," 19–21.

96. David Romano, "Iraq's Descent into Civil War: A Constitutional Explanation," *Middle East Journal* 68.4 (2014): 549; Scott Johnson, "The Sunni Question," *Newsweek*, September 4, 2005, http://www.newsweek.com/sunni-question-118181; Dawisha, *Iraq*, 249.

97. Al-Qarawee, *Imagining the Nation*, 165.

98. Abdulrazaq and Stansfield, "The Enemy Within," 531.

99. Carter Malkasian, *Illusions of Victory: The Anbar Awakening and the Rise of the Islamic State* (New York: Oxford University Press, 2017), 72–75.

100. McCants, *The ISIS Apocalypse*, 35–38; Cigar, *Al-Qaida, the Tribes, and the Government*, chapters 2 and 3.

101. Hashim, *Iraq's Sunni Insurgency*, 303, 306; Human Rights Watch, "No One is Safe: Abuse of Women in Iraq's Criminal Justice System," February 2014, 1–5, http://www.hrw.org/sites/default/files/reports/iraq0214webwcover.pdf (accessed October 7, 2014); Amnesty International, "Iraq: A Decade of Abuse," March 2013, http://www.amnesty.org/en/library/asset/MDE14/001/2013/en/bbd876ee-aa83-4a63-bff3-7e7c6ee130eb/mde140012013en.pdf (accessed November 6, 2014).

102. Michael Gordon, "The Former-Insurgent Counterinsurgency," *New York Times*, September 2, 2007, https://www.nytimes.com/2007/09/02/magazine/02iraq-t.html; William McCallister, "Sons of Iraq: A Study in Irregular Warfare," *Small Wars Journal*, September 8, 2008. For a larger discussion, see Marc Lynch, "Explaining the Awakening: Engagement, Publicity, and the Transformation of Iraqi Sunni Political Attitudes," *Security Studies* 20.1 (2011): 36–72.

103. Gerges, *ISIS*, 107.

104. Malkasian, *Illusions of Victory*, 161–164.

105. Alisa Rubin and Stephen Farrell, "Awakening Councils by Region," *New York Times*, December 22, 2007, https://www.nytimes.com/2007/12/22/world/middleeast/23awake-graphic.html.

106. Cited in Gerges, *ISIS*, 101–102.

107. Anthony H. Cordesman and Emma R. Davies, *Iraq's Insurgency and the Road to Civil Conflict* (Westport, CT: Praeger, 2008), 284–285, 514–516; David Kilcullen, *The Accidental Guerrilla: Fighting Small Wars in the Midst of a Big One* (New York: Oxford University Press, 2011) 163–165.

108. Malkasian, *Illusions of Victory*, 72; Ned Parker, "The Iraq We Left Behind: Welcome to the World's Next Failed State," *Foreign Affairs* (2012): 94–110.

109. Malkasian, *Illusions of Victory*, 166; Cigar, *Al-Qaida, the Tribes, and the Government*, chapter 10.

110. Adeed Dawisha, *Iraq: A Political History from Independence to Occupation* (Princeton, NJ: Princeton University Press, 2009), 272.

111. Jawad Kathim, "Baghdad tu'akid at-tizameha difa' murtabat as-sahwa," *Al-Hayat*, April 15, 2009; Hadi Jasim, "Baghdad: 'Ansar Sahwa al-fadhil yu'bashiroon 'amalahum ma' al-jaysh," *Asharq al-Awsat*, April 1, 2009.

112. See the interview Vice President Tariq al-Hashemi gave to *al-Hayat* in March 2010, Iraqi Vice President Al-Hashimi Warns of Possible 'Coup d'Etat'—Paper," BBC Monitoring, *Al-Hayat* website on March 4, 2010, Document 12E4EF5BB93AAO.

113. Romano, "Iraq's Descent into Civil War," 560–561; International Crisis Group, "Iraq's Federalism Quandary," February 23, 2012, https://www.crisisgroup.org/middle-east-north-africa/gulf-and-arabian-peninsula/iraq/iraq-s-federalism-quandary (accessed March 7, 2018); Katherine Blue Carroll, "Not Your Parents' Political Party: Young Sunnis and the New Iraqi Democracy," *Middle East Policy* 18.3 (2011): 101–121.

114. Gerges, *ISIS*, 134–141.

115. Lister, *The Islamic State*, 35; Truls H. Tønnessen, "Heirs of Zarqawi or Saddam? The Relationship between al-Qaida in Iraq and the Islamic State," *Perspectives on Terrorism* 9.4 (2015); Craig Whiteside, "A Pedigree of Terror: The Myth of the Ba'athist Influence in the Islamic State Movement," *Perspectives on Terrorism* 11.3 (2017).

116. David Siddhartha Patel, "ISIS in Iraq: What We Got Wrong and Why 2015 Is Not 2007 Redux," Brandeis University Crown Center for Middle East Studies, Middle East Brief 87, 2015, 3, http://www.brandeis.edu/crown/publications/meb/MEB87.pdf (accessed

February 2, 2018); Ronen Zeidel, "The Dawa'ish: A Collective Profile of IS Commanders," *Perspectives on Terrorism* 11.4 (2017), 25; Michael Weiss and Hassan Hassan, *ISIS: Inside the Army of Terror* (New York: Simon & Schuster, 2016). 122–126; Faust, *Ba'thification*, 12.

117. Abdulrazaq and Stansfield, "The Enemy Within," 536; Cigar, *Al-Qaida, the Tribes, and the Government*, 103–120.

118. Raymond Hinnebusch, "Defying the Hegemon: Syria and the Iraq War," *International Journal of Contemporary Iraqi Studies* 2.3 (2009): 375–389.

119. Denselow, "Mosul, the Jazira Region and the Syrian-Iraqi Borderlands," 20.

120. Gambil, "How Significant Is Syria's Role in Iraq?" .

121. Francesca de Châtel, "The Role of Drought and Climate Change in the Syrian Uprising: Untangling the Triggers of the Revolution," *Middle Eastern Studies* 50.4 (2014): 524–527; Myriam Ababsa, "Privatisation in Syria: State Farms and the case of the Euphrates Project," European University Institute, RSCAS Working Paper 2005/02 (2005), http://cadmus. eui.eu/bitstream/handle/1814/2789/05_02.pdf (accessed March 2, 2018); Jessica Barnes, "Managing the Waters of Bath Country: The Politics Of Water Scarcity in Syria," *Geopolitics* 14.3 (2009): 510–530.

122. Mazur, "Local Communities and Outside Authorities," 4.

123. Ashraf al-Khalidi, Sophia Hoffmann, and Victor Tanner, "Iraqi Refugees in the Syrian Arab Republic: A Field-Based Snapshot," Brookings Institution–University of Bern Project on Internal Displacement, Occasional Paper, June 2007,https://www.brookings.edu/wp-content/uploads/2016/06/0611humanrights_alkhalidi.pdf (accessed March 2, 2018); Géraldine Chatelard and Mohamed Kamel Doraï, "La présence irakienne en Syrie et en Jordanie: dynamiques sociales et spatiales, et modes de gestion par les pays d'accueil," 2008, https://hal.archives-ouvertes.fr/hal-00338403v1 (accessed March 3, 2018).

124. Sophia Hoffmann, *Iraqi Migrants in Syria: The Crisis before the Storm* (Syracuse, NY: Syracuse University Press, 2016), 41–50. On prostitution, see Deborah Amos, *Eclipse of the Sunnis: Power, Exile, and Upheaval in the Middle East* (New York: Perseus Books, 2010), 108–111.

125. Anonymous, "Smuggling, Syria, and Spending," in *Bombers, Bank Accounts, and Bleedout: al-Qa'ida's Road in and out of Iraq*, ed. Brian Fishman, Combating Terrorism Center at West Point, 2008, 85–87, https://scholar.princeton.edu/sites/default/files/jns/files/sinjar_2_july_23.pdf (accessed March 3, 2018); Pete Moore and Christopher Parker, "The War Economy of Iraq," *Middle East Report* 243 (2007): 6–15.

126. Anonymous, "Smuggling, Syria, and Spending," 83.

127. Ghaith Abdul-Ahad, "Outside Iraq but Deep in the Fight," *Washington Post*, June 8, 2005, http://www.washingtonpost.com/wp-dyn/content/article/2005/06/07/AR2005060702026.html (accessed March 3, 2018).

128. Felter and Fishman, "Al-Qa'ida's Foreign Fighters in Iraq."

129. Gerges, *ISIS*, 199.

130. Mazur, "The Islamic State Identity and Legacies of Baath Rule in Syria's Northeast," 36.

131. Malkasian, *Illusions of Victory*, 168–169; Abdulrazaq and Stansfield, "The Enemy Within," 537–538 .

132. Gerges, *ISIS*, 126.

133. Gerges, *ISIS*, 122.

134. Weiss and Hassan, *ISIS: Inside the Army of Terror*, 135–137.

135. Quoted in Mazur, "The Islamic State Identity and Legacies of Baath Rule in Syria's Northeast," 30. See also Dukhan, "Tribes and Tribalism," 7–8, 12; Ababsa, "Raqqa, capitale de la révolution," 57; Mazur, "Local Communities and Outside Authorities," 18–19.

136. Dukhan, "Tribes and Tribalism," 13–14, 20.

137. Dukhan, "Tribes and Tribalism," 10–11; Heras, Barabandi, and Betare, "Deir Azzour Tribal Mapping Project," 4; Lister, *The Syrian Jihad*, 123; Mazur, "Local Communities and Outside Authorities," 18–21.

138. See Lister, *The Syrian Jihad*, 76–79.

139. Syria's al-Nusra Front Leader Interviewed on Conflict, Political Vision," BBC Monitoring, al-Jazeera TV, Doha, on December 19, 2013, Document 14ADB8A989888570.

140. Lister, *The Syrian Jihad*, 81, 87, 124–128; Gerges, *ISIS*, 174–175, 182–188; Weiss and Hassan, *ISIS: Inside the Army of Terror*, 161.
141. Lister, *The Syrian Jihad*, 123; Mazur, "Local Communities and Outside Authorities," 21, 25; Ababsa, "Raqqa, capitale de la révolution," 58.
142. Lister, *The Syrian Jihad*, 139–140; Dukhan, "Tribes and Tribalism," 18–19; Warrick, *Black Flags*, 286.
143. Warrick, *Black Flags*, 260.
144. Lister, *The Syrian Jihad*, 168; Barak Mendelsohn, *The al-Qaeda Franchise: The Expansion of al-Qaeda and Its Consequences* (New York: Oxford University Press, 2015), 175–178.
145. Lister, *The Syrian Jihad*, 184.
146. Malkasian, *Illusions of Victory*, 176–177.
147. Warrick, *Black Flags*, 298.
148. Gerges, *ISIS*, 124.
149. Malkasian, *Illusions of Victory*, 187; Erika Solomon, "Sunni Tribes in Bitter Rift over Isis's Iraq Gains," *Financial Times*, May 27, 2015, https://www.ft.com/content/a39fb628-044d-11e5-a5c3-00144feabdc0.
150. Malkasian, *Illusions of Victory*, 178–182; Warrick, *Black Flags*, 290.
151. Cited in Gerges, *ISIS*, 195.
152. Zaydan al-Jibouri, quoted in David Ignatius, "Iraq and the U.S. Are Losing Ground to the Islamic State," *Washington Post*, October 23, 2014, https://www.washingtonpost.com/opinions/david-ignatius-iraq-and-the-us-are-losing-ground-to-the-islamic-state/2014/10/23/201a56e0-5adf-11e4-bd61-346aee66ba29_story.html?utm_term=.258ce4509a76.
153. Warrick, *Black Flags*, 302–304; Gerges, *ISIS*, 127.
154. Gerges, *ISIS*, 127, 167.
155. Malkasian, *Illusions of Victory*, 187.
156. Liveleak.com, http://www.liveleak.com/view?i=d43_1404046312.
157. Hamza Mustafa, "There Is a 'Tribal Revolution' in Iraq: Anbar Tribal Chief," *Asharq al-Awsat* English Archive, June 17, 2014, https://eng-archive.aawsat.com/hamzamustafa/news-middle-east/there-is-a-tribal-revolution-in-iraq-anbar-tribal-chief (accessed May 18, 2018). See also Daveed Gartenstein-Ross and Sterling Jensen, "The Role of Iraqi Tribes after the Islamic State's Ascendance," *Military Review* 95.4 (2015): 102–110.
158. Hadi H. Jaafar and Eckart Woertz, "Agriculture as a Funding Source of ISIS: A GIS and Remote Sensing Analysis," *Food Policy* 64 (2016): 23.
159. McCants, *The ISIS Apocalypse*, 123.
160. Bunzel, "From Paper State to Caliphate," 25–27, 34; Lister, *The Syrian Jihad*, 263.
161. Syria's al-Nusra Front Leader Interviewed on Conflict, Political Vision," BBC Monitoring.
162. Lister, *The Syrian Jihad*, 280.
163. McCants, *The ISIS Apocalypse*, 27, 124.
164. The Soufan Group, "Foreign Fighters: An Updated Assessment of the Flow of Foreign Fighters into Syria and Iraq," December 2015, http://soufangroup.com/wp-content/uploads/2015/12/TSG_ForeignFightersUpdate_FINAL3.pdf (accessed March 11, 2018); Arie Perliger and Daniel Milton, "From Cradle to Grave: The Lifecycle of Foreign Fighters in Iraq and Syria," Combating Terrorism Center at West Point, November 11, 2016, https://ctc.usma.edu/from-cradle-to-grave-the-lifecycle-of-foreign-fighters-in-iraq-and-syria/ (accessed March 12, 2018).
165. Bunzel, "From Paper State to Caliphate," 32.
166. Bunzel, "From Paper State to Caliphate," 32.
167. Aaron Zelin, "The Islamic State's Model," in *Islamism in the IS Age*, POMEPS Studies 12, March 2015, 25, https://pomeps.org/wp-content/uploads/2015/03/POMEPS_Studies_12_ISAge_Web.pdf (accessed March 3, 2018).
168. Lister, *The Islamic State*, 48–49.
169. Warrick, *Black Flags*, 289.
170. Weiss and Hassan, *ISIS: Inside the Army of Terror*, 230.
171. Malkasian, *Illusions of Victory*, 187; Patel, "ISIS in Iraq," 5; Roxanne L. Euben, "Spectacles of Sovereignty in Digital Time: ISIS Executions, Visual Rhetoric and Sovereign Power," *Perspectives on Politics* 15.4 (2017): 1007–1033.

172. Ariel I. Ahram, "Sexual Violence and the Making of ISIS," *Survival* 57.3 (2015): 57–78; Peter Nicolaus and Serkan Yuce, "Sex-Slavery: One Aspect of the Yezidi Genocide," *Iran and the Caucasus* 21.2 (2017): 196–229; Younus Y. Mirza, " 'The Slave Girl Gives Birth to Her Master': Female Slavery from the Mamlūk Era (1250–1517) to the Islamic State (2014–)," *Journal of the American Academy of Religion* 85.3 (2017): 577–599.

173. Mara Revkin and Ariel I. Ahram, "Exit, Voice, and Loyalty under the Islamic State," in *Adaptation Strategies of Islamist Movements*, POMEPS Studies 26, April 2017, 26–31, https://pomeps.org/wp-content/uploads/2017/04/POMEPS_Studies_26_Adaptation_Draft2.pdf (accessed March 3, 2018).

174. Mara Revkin, "The Legal Foundations of the Islamic State," Brookings Project on U.S. Relations with the Islamic World, Analysis Paper 23, July 2016, https://www.brookings.edu/wp-content/uploads/2016/07/Brookings-Analysis-Paper_Mara-Revkin_Web.pdf (accessed March 2, 2018).

175. David J. Wasserstein, *Black Banners of ISIS: The Roots of the New Caliphate* (New Haven, CT: Yale University Press, 2017), 104.

176. Mazur, "Local Communities and Outside Authorities," 29–30; Weiss and Hassan, *ISIS: Inside the Army of Terror*, 204–205.

177. Gerges, *ISIS*, 178.

178. Jaafar and Woertz, "Agriculture as a Funding Source of ISIS."

179. Mazur, "Local Communities and Outside Authorities," 5; Erika Solomon and Sam Jones, "Isis Inc: Loot and Taxes Keep Jihadi Economy Churning," *Financial Times*, December 14, 2015, https://www.ft.com/content/aee89a00-9ff1-11e5-beba-5e33e2b79e46.

180. ISIS Gold Coins Revealed on Social Media," al-Arabiyya, June 24, 2015, http://english.alarabiya.net/en/variety/2015/06/24/ISIS-gold-coins-revealed-on-social-media.html (accessed March 3, 2018).

181. Cited in Mazur, "Local Communities and Outside Authorities," 6.

182. Gerges, *ISIS*, 150.

183. Zeidel, "The Dawa'ish," 22; Malkasian, *Illusions of Victory*, 175.

184. Zeidel, "The Dawa'ish," 22.

185. Weiss and Hassan, *ISIS: Inside the Army of Terror*, 206–209; Zeidel, "The Dawa'ish," 25.

186. Abdel Bari Atwan, *Islamic State: The Digital Caliphate* (Berkeley: University of California Press, 2015), 111–113.

187. Lister, *The Syrian Jihad*, 155.

188. Rey, "L'état islamique, terre de frontières?"

189. Lister, *The Syrian Jihad*, 404; Sharif Nashashibi, "The Ramifications of the Nusra's Split from al-Qaeda," al-Jazeera, August 7, 2016, https://www.aljazeera.com/indepth/opinion/2016/08/ramifications-nusra-split-al-qaeda-160807080125157.html (accessed March 1, 2018).

190. Renad Mansour and Faleh A. Jabar, "The Popular Mobilization Forces and Iraq's Future," Carnegie Middle East Center, April 2017, http://carnegie-mec.org/2017/04/28/popular-mobilization-forces-and-iraq-s-future-pub-68810 (accessed March 3, 2018).

191. Jones and Solomon, "Isis Inc."

192. "Turkey Closes Off Euphrates River Flow to Syria, Cuts Off Power to Thousands of Civilians," *American Herald Tribune*, February 26, 2017, https://ahtribune.com/world/north-africa-south-west-asia/syria-crisis/1525-turkey-euphrates-river.html (accessed March 3, 2018).

193. Jaafar and Woertz, "Agriculture as a Funding Source of ISIS" ; Maggie Fick, "Special Report: For Islamic State, Wheat Season Sows Seeds of Discontent," Reuters, January 20, 2015, https://www.reuters.com/article/us-mideast-crisis-planting-specialreport/special-report-for-islamic-state-wheat-season-sows-seeds-of-discontent-idUSKBN0KT0W420150120 (accessed May 18, 2018); Maggie Fick, "Special Report: Islamic State Uses Grain to Tighten Grip in Iraq," Reuters, September 30, 2014. https://www.reuters.com/article/us-mideast-crisis-wheat/special-report-islamic-state-uses-grain-to-tighten-grip-in-iraq-idUSKCN0HP12J20140930 (accessed March 12, 2018).

194. Cf. Human Rights Watch, "Iraq: Militia Abuses Mar Fight against ISIS," September 20, 2015, https://www.hrw.org/news/2015/09/20/iraq-militia-abuses-mar-fight-against-isis (accessed March 2, 2018).

195. Martin Chulov and Kareem Shaheen, "Destroying Great Mosque of al-Nuri 'Is Isis Declaring Defeat,'" *Guardian*, June 22, 2017, https://www.theguardian.com/world/2017/jun/21/mosuls-grand-al-nouri-mosque-blown-up-by-isis-fighters.
196. Robin Wright, "After the Islamic State," *New Yorker*, December 12, 2016, https://www.newyorker.com/magazine/2016/12/12/after-the-islamic-state.
197. Text of Audio Statement by Islamic State Leader al-Baghdadi," BBC Monitoring, telegram messaging service in Arabic, on September 28, 2017, Document 16739B8A6EB6B998.
198. The last sentences are allusions to Surat at-Tauba 9:52.
199. Shelly Kittelson, "Local Iraqi Forces Keep Eye on Border as Life Resumes," Al-Monitor, February 27, 2018, https://www.al-monitor.com/pulse/originals/2018/02/iraq-qaim-syria-isis-security.html (accessed March 3, 2018).
200. Ayman Husayn, "Wahidat Kurdiyya fi'l raqa" [The Kurdish units in Raqqa], al-Jazeera, December 24, 2015, http://www.aljazeera.net/news/arabic/2015/12/24/%D9%88%D8%AD%D8%AF%D8%A7%D8%AA-%D9%83%D8%B1%D8%AF%D9%8A%D8%A9-%D8%A8%D8%A7%D9%84%D8%B1%D9%82%D8%A9-%D8%AC%D9%8A%D8%B4-%D8%A7%D9%84%D8%B9%D8%B4%D8%A7%D8%A6%D8%B1-%D8%AA%D9%86%D8%B8%D9%8A%D9%85-%D8%A5%D8%B1%D9%87%D8%A7%D8%A8%D9%8A (accessed March 3, 2018); "Arab Tribes to Form Army against PYD/PKK, Daesh in Syria," *Daily Sabah*, March 14, 2017, https://www.dailysabah.com/syrian-crisis/2017/03/14/arab-tribes-to-form-army-against-pydpkk-daesh-in-syria (accessed March 12, 2018); Daniel Wilkofsky and Khalid Fatah, "North Syria's Anti-Islamic State Coalition Has an Arab Problem," *War on the Rocks* blog, September 18, 2017, https://warontherocks.com/2017/09/northern-syrias-anti-islamic-state-coalition-has-an-arab-problem/ .
201. Mara Revkin, "After the Islamic State: Reintegration and Transitional Justice in Iraq," unpublished paper; Fick, "Special Report: For Islamic State, Wheat Season Sows Seeds of Discontent,"; "Anbar Residents Warn of New Unrest if ISIS Relatives Return," *Asharq al-Awsat*, February 13, 2018, https://aawsat.com/english/home/article/1173797/anbar-residents-warn-new-unrest-if-isis-relatives-return; (accessed March 12, 2018); Human Rights Watch, "Flawed Justice: Accountability for ISIS Crimes in Iraq," December 5, 2017, https://www.hrw.org/report/2017/12/05/flawed-justice/accountability-isis-crimes-iraq (accessed March 12, 2018).
202. As Gerges states: "There is no credible evidence to show that ISIS's ideology of Sunni pan-Islamism is the adopted identity in Sunni areas in Iraq and Syria." Gerges, *ISIS*, 168.

## Conclusion

1. Larry Wolff, "Woodrow Wilson's Name Has Come and Gone Before," *Washington Post*, December 3, 2015, https://www.washingtonpost.com/posteverything/wp/2015/12/03/woodrow-wilsons-name-has-come-and-gone-before/?noredirect=on&utm_term=.3afea84221db.
2. Rabab El-Mahdi, "The Failure of the Regime or the Demise of the State?" *International Journal of Middle East Studies* 50.2 (2018): 328–332.
3. Ana Arjona, "Wartime Institutions: A Research Agenda," *Journal of Conflict Resolution* 58.8 (2014): 1360–1381. For a critique, see Zachariah Cherian Mampilly, *Rebel Rulers: Insurgent Governance and Civilian Life during War* (Ithaca, NY: Cornell University Press, 2011); Bart Klem and Sidharthan Maunaguru, "Insurgent Rule as Sovereign Mimicry and Mutation: Governance, Kingship, and Violence in Civil Wars," *Comparative Studies in Society and History* 59.3 (2017), 629–656.
4. Benjamin Smith, "Separatist Conflict in the Former Soviet Union and Beyond: How Different Was Communism?" *World Politics* 65.2 (2013): 350–381; David S. Siroky and John Cuffe, "Lost Autonomy, Nationalism and Separatism," *Comparative Political Studies* 48.1 (2015): 3–34; Lars-Erik Cederman et al., "Territorial Autonomy in the Shadow of Conflict: Too Little, Too Late?" *American Political Science Review* 109.2 (2015): 354–370; Adrian Florea, "De Facto States: Survival and Disappearance (1945–2011)," *International Studies Quarterly* 61.1 (2017): 337–351.

5. Allan Hoben and Robert Hefner, "The Integrative Revolution Revisited," *World Development* 19.1 (1991): 18.

6. Frederic Wehrey, "Bahrain's Decade of Discontent," *Journal of Democracy* 24.3 (2013): 116–126; Kristin Smith Diwan, "Royal Factions, Ruling Strategies, and Sectarianism in Bahrain," in *Sectarian Politics in the Persian Gulf*, ed. Lawrence G. Potter (New York: Oxford University Press, 2014), 143–179.

7. On the Berber, see Bruce Maddy-Weitzman, *The Berber Identity Movement and the Challenge to North African States* (Austin: University of Texas Press, 2011).

8. Hisham Aidi, "Is Morocco Headed toward Insurrection?" *Nation*, July 13, 2017, https://www.thenation.com/article/is-morocco-headed-toward-insurrection/; Hans van Amersfoort and Anja van Heelsum, "Moroccan Berber Immigrants in the Netherlands, Their Associations and Transnational Ties: A Quest for Identity and Recognition," *Immigrants & Minorities* 25.3 (2007): 234–262.

9. Stephen D. Krasner, *Sovereignty: Organized Hypocrisy* (Princeton, NJ: Princeton University Press, 1999).

10. Andrew Phillips, "The Islamic State's Challenge to International Order," *Australian Journal of International Affairs* 68.5 (2014): 495–498; Richard Nielsen, "Does the Islamic State Believe in Sovereignty?" in *Islamism in the IS Age*, POMEPS Studies 12 (2015), 28–30, https://pomeps.org/wp-content/uploads/2015/03/POMEPS_Studies_12_ISAge_Web.pdf (accessed August 23, 2018).

11. Han Liu, "Two Faces of Self-determination in Political Divorce," *ICL Journal* 10.4 (2016): 355–385.

12. Geraint Alun Hughes, "Syria and the Perils of Proxy Warfare," *Small Wars & Insurgencies* 25.3 (2014): 522–538; Andreas Krieg, "Externalizing the Burden of War: The Obama Doctrine and US Foreign Policy in the Middle East," *International Affairs* 92.1 (2016): 97–113; Daniel Byman, "Why Engage in Proxy War? A State's Perspective," Brookings *Order from Chaos* blog, May 21, 2018, https://www.brookings.edu/blog/order-from-chaos/2018/05/21/why-engage-in-proxy-war-a-states-perspective/ (accessed August 24, 2018).

13. Amitav Acharya, "State Sovereignty after 9/11: Disorganised Hypocrisy," *Political Studies* 55.2 (2007): 274–296.

14. For some of these arguments, see Liam Anderson, "Ethnofederalism: The Worst Form of Institutional Arrangement . . . ?" *International Security* 39.1 (2014): 165–204; Chaim Kaufmann, "Possible and Impossible Solutions to Ethnic Civil Wars," *International Security* 20.4 (1996): 136–175; Jaroslav Tir, "Dividing Countries to Promote Peace: Prospects for Long-Term Success of Partitions," *Journal of Peace Research* 42.5 (2005): 545–562; Monica Duffy Toft, "Self-determination, Secession, and Civil War," *Terrorism and Political Violence* 24.4 (2012): 581–600; Eiki Berg, "Examining Power-Sharing in Persistent Conflicts: De Facto Pseudo-Statehood versus De Jure Quasi-Federalism," *Global Society* 21.2 (2007): 199–217.

15. David A. Lake, "Authority, Coercion, and Power in International Relations," in *Back to Basics: State Power in a Contemporary World*, ed. Martha Finnemore and Judith Goldstein (New York: Oxford University Press, 2013), 55–78.

16. Sari Nusseibeh, *What Is a Palestinian State Worth?* (Cambridge, MA: Harvard University Press, 2011), 17.

17. As Nusseibeh points out, "The so-called Palestinian Authority Territory, consisting of Gaza and the West Bank, is a curious geopolitical creature, almost like a make-believe princedom closed up in a keeper's cellar, but it is certainly not a state." Nusseibeh, *What Is a Palestinian State Worth?* 63. For an alternative argument, see John Quigley, "Palestine Is a State: A Horse with Black and White Stripes Is a Zebra," *Michigan Journal of International Law* 32 (2010): 749–765. On the process of Palestinian state building, see Yezid Sayigh, *Armed Struggle and the Search for State: The Palestinian National Movement, 1949–1993* (New York: Oxford University Press, 1997); Glenn E. Robinson, *Building a Palestinian State: The Incomplete Revolution* (Bloomington: Indiana University Press, 1997); Mehran Kamrava, *The Impossibility of Palestine: History, Geography, and the Road Ahead* (New Haven, CT: Yale University Press, 2016).

18. Rosa Ehrenreich Brooks, "Failed States, or the State as Failure?" *University of Chicago Law Review* (2005): 1159–1196; Martin van Creveld, *The Rise and Decline of the State* (New York: Cambridge University Press, 1999).

19. Philip G. Roeder, *Where Nation-States Come From: Institutional Change in the Age of Nationalism* (Princeton, NJ: Princeton University Press, 2007), 351; Tanisha M. Fazal and Ryan D. Griffiths, "Membership Has Its Privileges: The Changing Benefits of Statehood," *International Studies Review* 16.1 (2014): 79–106.

20. Ellen Lust, "Layered Authority and Social Institutions: Reconsidering State-centric Theory and Development Policy," *International Journal of Middle East Studies* 50.2 (2018): 333–336. See also Lisa Anderson, "The State and Its Competitors," *International Journal of Middle East Studies* 50.2 (2018): 317–322.

21. Susan Woodward, "State-Building for Peace-Building: What Theory and Whose Role?" in *Securing Peace: State-Building and Economic Development in Post-Conflict Countries*, ed. Richard Kozul-Wright and Piergiuseppe Fortunato (New York: Bloomsbury, 2011), 93; Merilee S. Grindle, "Good Enough Governance Revisited," *Development Policy Review* 25.5 (2007): 533–574; Ariel I. Ahram, "Learning to Live with Militias: Toward a Critical Policy on State Frailty," *Journal of Intervention and Statebuilding* 5.2 (2011): 175–192.

# INDEX

Abadi, Haidar, 156, 194–195
Abd al-Jalil, Mustafa Muhammad, 48–51, 54–55
Abkhazia, 41–42
Abu Salim Martyrs Brigade, 82–84, 91
Abyan, 103, 106, 108–112, 114, 117–118
Aden, 63–64, 95–97, 99–120
Adnani, Abu Mohammed, 194–195
African Union, 40, 50
Afrin-Kurd Dagh, 130, 136, 151, 154, 159
Ahrar ash-Sham, 186–187
Akrama Agreement, 75
Al-Assad, Bashar, 3, 175–176
    and Islamic State, 175–183, 192–194
    and Syrian uprising, 57–62
Al-Assad, Hafez, 56–57, 136, 162–163, 175
Alawis, 3–4, 12, 24–25, 56–57, 59, 130,
    174–176, 190–191
Al-Baghdadi, Abu Bakr (Ibrahim Awad Ibrahim
    al-Badri), 161–163
Al-Baghdadi, Abu Umar (Hamid Dawud
    Mohammed Khalil al-Zawi), 179,
    182–191, 193, 196–197
Al-Baraasi, Abd ar-Rabbo, 87
Al-Barassi, Faraj, 92
Al-Beidh, Ali, 106–109, 112
Albu Kamal, 167–168, 184–185, 194–195
Al-Douri, Izzat Ibrahim, 173–174, 180, 188–189
Aleppo, 21–22, 24–25, 130–131, 151, 154, 156,
    161–162, 164–165, 167, 174–176, 184,
    186–187, 190, 193
Al-Fadhli, Tariq, 108, 112
Algiers Accord, 140
Al-Joulani, Abu Muhammad (Ahmed Hussein
    al-Shar'a), 186–187, 189–190, 193–194
Al-Keib, Abd al-Rahman, 110
Al-Khatib, Muaz, 61
Al-Khattabi, Mohammed (Muhend) ibn Abd
    al-Karim, 26

Al-Maliki, Nuri, 155–156, 179, 182–189,
    191, 198
Al-Masri, Abu Ayyub (Abu Hamza al-Hijri),
    177–180
Al-Mukhtar, Omar, 69–71, 75–76, 80–81,
    84–85
Al-Qaeda in Mesopotamia, 41, 166, 177–183,
    186–187, 198
Al-Qaeda in the Arabian Peninsula, 62, 95–96,
    112–118
Al-Qaeda, 40, 43–44, 58, 62, 82–83, 188–190,
    193–194, 203–204
    in Iraq, 178–181, 186–187
Al-Qaim, 167–168, 181, 183–184, 187–189, 193,
    196–197
Al-Senussi, Ahmed Zubayr, 84–85, 112
Al-Sewehli, Ramadan, 75
Al-Yawer, Ahmed Ajil, 171–172
Al-Yawer, Ajil, 168–169, 171–172
Al-Yawer, Ghazi, 176–177
Al-Zawahiri, Ayman, 49, 57, 187, 193–194
Al-Zarqawi, Abu Musab, 177–179, 182–183,
    186–187, 189–190, 197
Anbar Awakening, 180–188, 198
Anfal campaign, 142–143
Arab Belt, 136, 175–176
Arab League, 32–33, 50–52
    and Libya, 52–54
    and Syria, 58–60
    and Yemen, 106
Arafat, Yasser, 32
Ararat rebellion, 129–130
Asir, 27, 100–101, 202–203
Assyrian Christians, 27, 56–57, 128, 138–139,
    141, 158, 169
Atlantic Charter, 28–29
Authoritarian bargains, 31, 33–34, 45–46,
    134–142

Ba'th Party, 30–31, 134
    Iraqi branch, 135–136, 138–141, 172–174,
        180, 183, 185–186, 188–189
    Syrian branch, 121–149, 175–177,
        180–183, 187
Baghdad, 2–3, 25, 35, 126, 128–129, 166–170,
        179, 185
    threatened by Islamic State, 188–189, 194
    under U.S. occupation, 41, 146–147, 181
Bahrain, 12, 15, 202
Balfour Declaration, 21
Baoum, Hassan, 112–114, 118
Barzani, Massoud, 19–20, 121–124, 140, 159
    formation of KRG, 144–147
    president of the KRG, 147–159
Barzani, Mullah Mustafa, 121–122, 131–140
Barzani, Nechirvan, 156
Barzinji, Mahmud, 127–128
Basra, 34–35, 167–169
Bayda, 74, 78–79, 82, 85–87
Benghazi
    2011 protests in, 48–49, 51–54
    in Libyan independence, 69–72
    Islamist militias in, 91
    status of Tripolitians in, 78, 89
    under colonialism, 76
    under Qaddafi, 105–106
Berbers, 26–27, 74, 88–89, 98–99, 202–203
Bin Brik, Hani, 116–119
Bin Laden, Osama, 3, 40, 43–44, 49
    and Iraqi insurgency, 177–178, 180
    and Yemen insurgency, 107–108
Borders, 1–4, 8, 64, 89–90, 104, 142–143, 145, 157
    between Iraq and Kurdish Region of Iraq, 140,
        148–149
    Islamic State, 1–2, 164–166, 186–189,
        192–195
    Syrian-Iraqi-Turkish 150–152, 154, 164, 166,
        175–176, 178–179, 183–185
    Yemeni, 104, 106, 112
Bosnia, 37, 41–42
Bouteflika, Abdelaziz, 40
Buera, Abu Bakr, 82, 87–92
Bush, George H.W., 34–36, 38–39, 143, 146
Bush, George W., 40


Central banks, 52–55, 64, 90–91, 116–118, 156
Chalabi, Ahmed, 38–41
China, 20, 41–42, 47, 52–53, 58, 94, 105–106
Clinton, Bill, 38–39
Clinton, Hillary, 43–45, 58, 61
Comparative historical analysis, 13–14
Crane, Charles, 19–23, 100–101. See also King-
        Crane Commission
Cyrenaica Political Bureau, 87
Cyrenaica Transitional Council, 84–86

Cyrenaica, 2, 202
    during 2014 Libyan civil war, 88–94
    emergence of separatism, 81–88
    Emirate of, 12, 69–72, 75–76
    under Italian and British rule, 75–77
    under Libyan monarchy, 77–79
    under Ottoman rule, 73–74
    under Qaddafi, 79–81
Czechoslovakia, 47


Da'wa Party, 38–39, 146–147
Damascus Declaration, 149–150
Damascus, 2011 uprising, 56–57, 61–62
Damascus, 21–22, 24–25, 75–76, 128, 130–131,
        136, 151, 168, 174–176, 183–184
Dams and irrigation
    in Iraq and Syria, 141, 148, 154–155, 157,
        172–173, 175, 189, 192, 194
    in Libya, 79–80
    in Yemen, 99
Deir Ezzour
    connection to the Jazira, 165–166, 174, 184–185
    growth of, 136, 149, 167, 175–176
    initial protests in, 56, 175–176, 183–184
    integration into Syria and connection to Iraq,
        167–169, 184
    under the Islamic State, 186–187, 193–195
Democratic Federation of Northern Syria
        (DFNS), 152–153. See also Rojava
Deraa, 185–186
Dersim rebellion, 129–130
Dhofar War, 31


Egypt, 3, 13, 28–29, 31, 49, 140, 170–171, 179,
        190–191, 202
    decolonization, 20–26
    influence on Libya, 49, 51, 69, 73–77, 79–81,
        89–90, 94, 106
    involvement in Yemeni, 31, 103, 113
    role in Arab uprising, 50
Erbil, 121–123, 128–129, 133, 143–145,
        155–156, 158–159
Erdogan, Recip Tayyib, 152, 154


Faisal bin Hussein al-Hashemi, 3, 43,
        123, 165–166
    as king of Iraq, 29, 128, 171
    claim to self-determination in Syria, 20–25,
        167–170
Fallujah, 154–155, 172–173, 178–179, 181, 183,
        185, 188–189, 193–195
Federalism, 9, 11, 204–205
    in Iraq, 148–149, 182
    in Libya, 72, 79, 82, 84–89, 92, 156, 180,
        201–202

in Syria, 151
in Yemen, 108, 113–120
Federation of South Arabia, 102, 119
Fezzan, 73–74, 77–78, 85–87, 89, 93
Free Syrian Army, 57–62, 150–152, 159,
    186–188
Friends of Syria, 60
Friends of Yemen, 44–45, 62–63

General National Congress, 83–86, 88–91
Ghalioun, Burhan, 56–57, 59–60
Gorran Party, 155, 157–158
Government of National Accord, 91–92
Graziani, Rodolfo, 69–70, 75–76

Hadi, Abdu Rabbu Mansour, 62–64, 95–98,
    108–110, 113–118
Hadramawt, 13, 63–64, 99–106, 110, 114–116,
    118–119, 201–202
Haftar, Khalifa, 88–94, 204
Halabja, 142, 149, 158, 201–202
Hama, 56–57, 175, 187, 193
Harik, Ilya, 11–12
Hasakah, 12, 56, 130–131, 135, 151–152, 154,
    165–166, 174–176, 183–186, 194
Hejaz, 20–22, 28, 74, 126, 165–166, 202–203
House of Representatives, 86–92
Houthis, 15, 44–45, 63–64, 95–96, 110–111,
    114–116
Hudson, Michael, 11–12
Humanitarian intervention, 38, 40, 46–47,
    51–54, 64–65, 203–204
in Iraq, 117–143
in Libya, 52–53, 81–82
in Yemen, 109, 117
Humanitarianism, 8, 34–35, 91, 95–96, 152, 187
Hussein, Saddam, 3, 38–41, 188–189
and invasion of Kuwait, 32–33
and the Kurds, 139–147
assumption of power, 34–35, 172–173

Iran, 5, 34–35, 38–39, 59, 166–167, 173–174,
    178, 183, 204
and Kurds, 121–128, 131–133, 137–140, 145,
    148, 150, 153–155
involvement in Yemen, 110–113, 115
and Islamic State, 188, 194–195
Iraq, 19–20, 204–205
and authoritarian government, 30–31
and Islamic State, 161–198
and Kurds, 121–160
colonial origins, 25–29
test of sovereignty during the 1990s, 32–35,
    38–41

Iraqi National Congress, 38–41, 144–147
Islamic State
    caliphate, 1, 15–16, 161–163, 178–180,
        185–198
    conquest of the Jazira, 1–4, 185–198
    emergence and relationship to al-Qaeda,
        176–185
Ismail, Abdul Fattah, 106, 112
Israel, 31, 33–34, 60, 110, 139–140, 156–157,
    187, 205
Italy, 19–20, 25–26, 69–72, 74–76, 100–101

Jabhat al-Nusra (JAN), 57–58, 186–190, 192–194
Jadhran, Ibrahim, 86–92
Jaysh Rijal Tariqat Naqshbandi (Army of the
    Men of the Naqshbandi Order, JRTN),
    180–181, 185, 188–189
Jazira (region), 12, 29, 131, 164–198, 202, 205
Jeladat Badr Khan, 149
Jibril, Mahmoud, 50–52, 54–55

Kerry, John, 62
Khoybun, 130–131, 149
King, Henry Churchill, 19–23
King-Crane Commission, 19–23, 162–163,
    167–168
Kingdom of Kurdistan, 12–13, 128, 159
Kirkuk, 122–123, 125–127, 137, 141
    and Islamic State, 179, 193–194
    disputed between KRG and Baghdad, 147–148,
        155–159
    ethnic tensions, 137–140, 142–144
    oil fields, 128–129, 140
Kobani, 130, 151–152, 154
Kufra, 73–75, 79, 84, 88–89, 93
Kurdish Democratic Party, 121–123
    formation of, 132–134
    in Iraq, 136–149, 155, 158–159
    in Syria, 135, 149–150, 152
Kurdish Futures Movement, 149–151
Kurdish National Council, 150–152, 155
Kurdish Regional Government (KRG), 121–124,
    143–147, 151–152, 155–160, 192, 194,
    201–202
Kurdistan Workers' Party see PKK

Lansing, Robert, 19–20, 24, 27–28
Latakia, 24–25, 56, 175
Lausanne, Treaty of, 129, 157, 169
League of Nations, 2–3, 20–29, 32, 123, 129,
    136, 146, 167, 169, 197–198
Lebanon, 2–3, 21–25, 28–29, 31, 44, 174
    civil war, 31–34, 64–65
    Kurdish activism in, 130, 136

Lenin, Vladimir, 20, 120, 127, 131–132, 136
Libya, 2, 204
    2011 uprising, 48–56, 81–88
    2014 civil war and separatism, 88–94
    under Ottoman and European imperialism,
        69–77
    unification, independence and revolutionary
        period, 77–81
Libya Contact Group, 53–56
Libya Dawn, 88–92
Libyan Islamic Fighting Groups, 105, 107–109,
        111–112
Libyan National Army, 48–49, 88–92
Local Coordinating Committees, 57, 61

Mahabad, Kurdish Republic of, 121–123,
        131–134, 201–202
Maronites, 2–3, 21, 31–32
Matar, Hisham, 92
Mayadin, 167–168, 185–187, 194–195
McCain, John, 52–53
Misrata, 20, 48–49, 51–55, 73–74, 81–83, 93, 105
Mohammed Idris bin Mohammed al-Mahdi
        es-Senussi, 69–71, 75–79
Mohammed, Ali Nasir, 106, 112
Mohammed, Qazi, 131–134
Morocco, 13, 20, 25–26, 28–29, 202–203
Morsi, Mohammed, 113
Mosul, 1, 103–105, 126, 136–139, 154, 156–157,
        164–173, 176–196
    under the Islamic State, 161–163, 183–185
Mubarak, Hosni, 12
Mukalla, 99, 102, 105, 109–110, 117–119

Nagorno-Karabakh, 36, 158
Muslim, Salih, 151, 153
National Coalition for Syrian Revolution and
        Opposition Forces, 56, 61
National Coordinating Council, 57
National Dialogue Council, 63–64, 114–116
National Forces Alliance, 87, 90–91
National oil companies
    in Iraq, 156–157
    in Libya, 53–54, 79, 88, 90–91
Nationalism and national identity, 6–7, 30–31,
        35–36, 45–46
    Kurdish, 121–123, 126–128, 133–135, 141,
        148–150
    Yemeni, 101–102, 120
    Syrian and Iraqi, 170–175, 178, 198–202
NATO, 53, 81–82
No fly zones, 51–53, 143–144, 159–160
Nur al-Din bin Imad al-Din al-Zangi, 161–162,
        186–187
Nusseibeh, Sari, 205

Obama, Barack, 44, 50, 52–53
Ocalan, Abdullah, 136, 149, 152, 159
Oil and gas, 1, 7–8, 11–12, 15, 23, 39–40, 43,
        200, 203–204
    in Libya, 45–46, 49–54, 72–73, 78–82, 85–88
    in Syria, 60–61, 135–136, 149–151, 166, 175,
        187, 192
    in Yemen, 102–103, 106, 110, 114, 116–118, 120
    in Iraq, 123, 128–129, 138–139, 145–146, 148,
        155–157, 166–169, 172–173, 182, 194–195
Ottoman empire, 162–163, 166–167
    breakdown of, 1, 3, 19–23, 25–26, 35
    in Kurdistan, 125–126, 159, 166–167
    in Libya, 73–76
    in Yemen, 99–101
    legacy in Syria and Iraq, 170–171, 174,
        199–200

Palestine and Palestinians, 21, 24–25, 32–33, 205
Panetta, Leon, 60
Patriotic Union of Kurdistan
    after 2003, 147, 155
    and the Islamic State, 157–159
    as opposition alliance, 144–146
    during Iran-Iraq war, 140–143
    formation 138
PKK, 57, 122–123, 136, 143–145, 149,
        151–155, 158
Proxy war, 5, 204
PYD (Democratic Union Party), 57, 62, 124,
        159–160, 201–202. See also Rojava
    and YPG, 151–153, 159
    conflict with Islamic State, 152–154
    conflict with Turkey, 158–159
    formation of, 149
    relationship with Syrian regime and opposition,
        151–152

Qaddafi, Muammar, 12, 15, 49–56, 72,
        79–89, 92
Qaddafi, Saif al-Islam, 49
Qamishli, 122–123, 151, 175
    1930s autonomy movement in, 27, 131,
        174–175
    Kurdish revival in, 148–151
Qatar, 3, 43–45
    involvement in Libya, 50–56, 89–90
    involvement in Syria, 53–54, 56–61

Ramadi, 171–172, 178–179, 181, 183, 185,
        188, 193–195
Raqqa
    government control of, 185–187
    modernization in, 136, 175–176

under Ottoman and colonial rule, 166–167
under the Islamic State, 154, 188–192, 194–195
Rebel diplomacy, 8, 20–21, 26–28, 47–48, 64–65
in Iraqi Kurdistan, 140, 156–157
in Libya, 48–56
in Syria, 56–62
in Yemen, 62–64, 118–119
Recognition, 5, 8, 10–11, 20, 29, 32, 36–37, 129, 199, 203–204, figure 1.1
of Iraq, 28, 129
of Libyan rebels, 51, 81–82, 88, 94
of Syrian rebels, 59, 61
of Yemen rebels, 100–101, 109, 116, 118–119
Responsibility to protect (R2P), see humanitarian intervention
Rif, Republic. 13, 26–27, 202–203
Rojava, 15, 122–124, 151–154, 159–160, 199–202
Roosevelt, Franklin, 28
Russia/Soviet Union, 1–2, 8–10, 24, 31, 33, 36–37, 41–42, 47, 123–124, 126, 131–132
involvement in Libya, 52–55, 77, 87–89, 92, 204
involvement in Syria, 61–62, 150–151, 154, 194
imperial breakdown, 9–10
involvement in Yemen, 105
involvement with the Kurds, 131–134

Sahrawis, 20
Salahudin Declaration, 38–39, 62
Salafis and Salafism, 84, 92–93, 110–111, 116, 161–162, 174, 177, 182–185
Saleh, Ali Abdullah, 12, 44–45, 98
collapse of regime, 62–64, 113
in Yemeni civil war, 115–116
presidency of, 106–113, 120
San Remo Conference, 24, 197–198
Sanctions, 39
on Iraq, 1990s, 35, 39–40, 144–145, 180, 182–184
on Libya, 2010s, 50–51, 53–54, 57–58
on Syria, 2010s, 58–59
on Yemen, 44–45
Sarkozy, Nicholas, 28
Saudi Arabia, 3, 5, 28–31, 41–42, 44–45, 202–204
and League of Nations, 28
and Syrian opposition, 58–59
involvement in Libya, 89–90
involvement in Yemen, 62–64, 95–97, 102–104, 106, 109–113, 115–119
rivalry with Qatar, 55
Self-determination, 2–5, 8–16, 199–200, 205
and Libya, 69–70, 72–73, 76, 93
and the Arab uprising, 45–65
and the Kurds, 123–125, 127, 131–134, 139–140, 142, 146, 150–151, 156, 158–160, 162–163, 165–166, 169, 174, 197–198

and Wilson, 19–23
and Yemen, 100–102, 115, 118–119
in the Middle East and North Africa, 23–29
Sennusi dynasty, 69–79. See also Mohammed Idris bin Mohammed al-Mahdi
Separatism
"conquered state syndrome", 4–5, 9–10
and ethnicity, 201–202
definition, 4
in the Middle East and North Africa, 11–13
origins, 6–11
Serbia, 21–22, 44, 46
Sèvres, Treaty of, 123, 127, 133–134, 136, 143, 201–202
Sherif Pasha, 123, 127
Sinjar, 138–139, 143–144, 152, 157
Sisi, Abd al-Fateh, 89–90, 94
Sistani, Ali, 146–147, 194
Socotra, 103, 114, 118–119
South Ossetia, 8, 41–42
Southern Movement, 15, 63, 95–99
and Yemeni civil war, 116–120
role in 2011 uprising, 113–116
origins of, 111–113
as successor to South Yemen, 115, 199–200
Southern Transitional Council, 118–119
Sovereignty, 4–5
and separatism. 6–11
consensus and dissensus about, 47, 199
extraverted notion, 28, 46–47, 81–82
Iraqi, 35, 39–40, 144–145, 179–180, 182–184
Libyan, 47–56
Syrian, 56–62, 164
Yemeni, 47–48, 62–64
State failure, 1, 15, 33–34, 177
State formation, theories of, 2–3, 7–11, 197, 202–203
Statehood, 2–3, 5, 7
alternatives to, 33–34, 37, 151, 153, 203–206
and "dead states", 4–5, 9–10
and revolution, 45–48
de facto, 33–34, 37, 41–42, figure 1.1
nation-state crisis, 34–42, 64–65, 124, 142, 199, 204
Sulaymaniya, 125–128, 137, 143–145, 155, 158
Sykes-Picot agreement, 1–8, 43, 59–60, 121–122, 157, 160, 164–165, 168–169, 178, 189
Syria, 1, 3–4, 204–205
2011 uprising, 56–62
and Islamic State, 183–198
formation and development of statehood, 166–176
Kurds in, 130–131, 134–136, 149–155, 159
Syrian Democratic Forces, 152–154
Syrian Islamic Front, 187
Syrian National Council, 56–61, 185–187
relationship with Kurds, 150–151

*Index*

Taiz, 63–64, 99–100, 105, 113, 115
Talabani, Jalal, 138–141, 145–147, 155, 159
Tammo, Mishal, 150–151
Territorial integrity, 4, 11–12, 19, 32–35, 38–42,
    52–53, 60–62, 64–65, 104, 108–109,
    119–120, 139, 142, 144, 151, 154, 158–159,
    186–187, 199, 204
Thinni, Abdullah, 90–91
Tillerson, Rex, 158
Tilly, Charles, 8–9, 31
Tobruk, 48–49, 78, 83, 87–92
Transitional National Council
    and Libyan sovereignty, 81–82
    comparison to Syrian National Council, 57
    involvement in 2011 uprising and revolution,
        47–56, 81–82
    relationship with federalist movement,
        82–93
Tripoli, 20, 48–49, 51, 54–55, 69, 79, 81–83, 85,
    87, 89–92
Tripolitanian Republic, 20, 75–76
Tuareg, 93
Tunisia, 25–29
    2011 uprising, 13, 44–45, 49–50, 81,
        109–110, 202–203
Turkey, 34–35, 58, 166–167, 169, 189–190, 192,
    194–195, 200, 204
    and the Kurds, 123–131, 136, 140,
        148–159
    involvement in Libya, 53, 89–90
    involvement in Syria, 56–57

Ukraine, 35–36, 41–42, 44, 46
United Arab Emirates, 53
    Intervention in Libya, 53–59, 89–90, 204
    Intervention in Yemen, 64, 95–97, 115–119
United Nations, 28–29, 32
United Nations Security Council, 33–35, 50–53,
    62–63, 88, 109, 115, 123, 143, 145
United States
    and Iraq, 33–36, 38–42, 123, 139–140,
        142–143, 145–148, 150, 156, 158–159,
        176–178, 180–183, 194, 198, 204

and Libya, 49, 52–54, 77–78, 81–82,
    87–90, 92, 94
and Qatar, 43–44
and self-determination, 8–9, 20, 25–26, 28–29,
    36–37, 130, 133
and Syria, 22, 58, 60, 151–154, 183–185
and Yemen, 31, 44–45, 64, 95–96, 102–103,
    109, 112–113, 115–118
Intervention in MENA, 5, 47, 200
Uti posseditis, 32–33, 36–37

Versailles, Peace of, 21, 75, 165–166, 197–198

Wilson, Woodrow, 2–3, 19–23, 199
Wilsonianism, 4–5, 13–16, 19–29, 32–33, 35–37,
    108, 119–122, 131, 134–135, 143, 159–160,
    162–163, 165–166, 169, 197–200, 204–206

Yale, William, 23, 29
Yemen
    2011 uprising, 62–65, 113
    under Ottoman and British empires, 99–104
    independence of north and south, 100–109
    southern separatism movement in, 109–119
    civil war, 115–119
Yemen Socialist Party, 105–106, 115–116
    and 1994 Civil war, 108–109
    and National Dialogue Conference, 114–115
    and Southern Movement, 112–114
    and Yemeni unification, 106–108
    Declaration of Principles and Accord,
        108–112, 119
Yezidis, 125, 138–139, 152, 158, 161–162, 170,
    190–192
Younis, Abdul Fateh, 48–49, 53–55, 83, 88–89

Zaghlul, Sa'd, 20, 25
Zaydis, 99–100, 104, 110–111, 120
Zeidan, Ali, 88
Zubaidi, Aidarous, 95–97, 116–119